Management Policies 2006

U.S. Department of the Interior | National Park Service

U.S. GOVERNMENT OFFICIAL EDITION NOTICE

Use of ISBN Prefix. This is the Official U.S. Government edition of this publication and is herein identified to certify its authenticity. Use of the 0-16-076874-8 ISBN is for U.S. Government Printing Office Official Editions only. The Superintendent of Documents of the U.S. Government Printing Office requests that any reprinted edition clearly be labeled as a copy of the authentic work with a new ISBN.

Legal Status and Use of Seals and Logos. The Arrowhead symbol of the National Park Service authenticates *Management Policies 2006* as the National Park Service's official guide to managing national parks. The National Park Service symbol is protected under 18 USC 701, 15 USC 1051 et seq, and regulations published in 36 CFR Part II. The use of the National Park Service Arrowhead symbol on any republication of this material without the express, written permission of the Director of the National Park Service is prohibited. Any person using the National Park Service symbol in a manner inconsistent with the provisions of 36 CFR Part II is subject to the penalties specified in 18 USC 701.

For sale by the Superintendent of Documents, U.S. Government Printing Office
Internet: bookstore.gpo.gov   Phone: toll free (866) 512-1800; DC area (202) 512-1800
Fax: (202) 512-2104   Mail: Stop IDCC, Washington, DC 20402-0001

ISBN 0-16-076874-8

Table of Contents

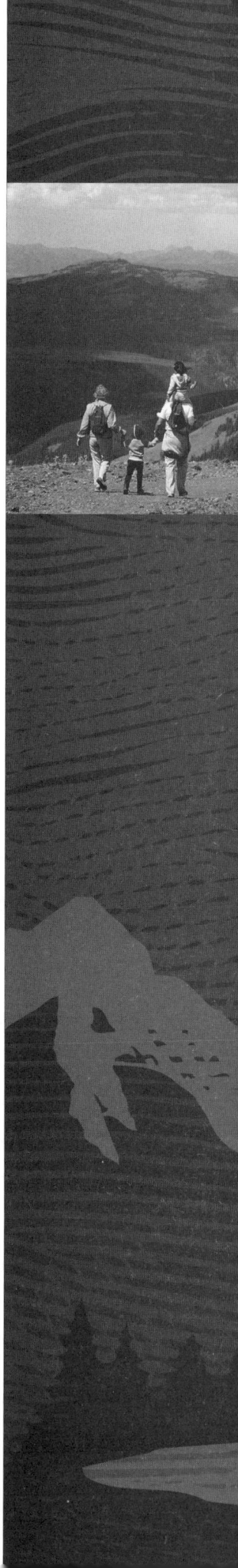

Management Policies		1
The Guide to Managing the National Park System		1
Underlying Principles		2
Introduction		3
Law, Policy, and Other Guidance		3
Hierarchy of Authorities		4
Policy Development		4
Compliance, Accountability, and Enforceability		4
The Directives System		4
Other Sources of Guidance		5
NPS Program Policies		5

1 The Foundation — 7

1.1	The National Park Idea	8
1.2	The National Park System	8
1.3	Criteria for Inclusion	8
1.3.1	National Significance	8
1.3.2	Suitability	9
1.3.3	Feasibility	9
1.3.4	Direct NPS Management	9
1.4	Park Management	10
1.4.1	The Laws Generally Governing Park Management	10
1.4.2	"Impairment" and "Derogation": One Standard	10
1.4.3	The NPS Obligation to Conserve and Provide for Enjoyment of Park Resources and Values	10
1.4.3.1	Park Purposes and Legislatively Authorized Uses	11
1.4.4	The Prohibition on Impairment of Park Resources and Values	11
1.4.5	What Constitutes Impairment of Park Resources and Values	11
1.4.6	What Constitutes Park Resources and Values	11
1.4.7	Decision-making Requirements to Identify and Avoid Impairments	12
1.4.7.1	Unacceptable Impacts	12
1.4.7.2	Improving Resource Conditions within the Parks	12
1.5	Appropriate Use of the Parks	13
1.6	Cooperative Conservation Beyond Park Boundaries	13
1.7	Civic Engagement	14
1.8	Environmental Leadership	14
1.9	Management Excellence	14
1.9.1	Human Resources	15
1.9.1.1	Career Development, Training, and Management	15
1.9.1.2	Succession Planning	15
1.9.1.3	Workforce Planning	15
1.9.1.4	Employee Safety and Health	15
1.9.1.5	Workforce Diversity	15
1.9.1.6	Volunteers in the Parks	15
1.9.2	Managing Information	16
1.9.2.1	Information Sharing	16
1.9.2.2	Proprietary Information	16
1.9.2.3	Information Confidentiality	16
1.9.3	Accessibility for Persons with Disabilities	17
1.9.4	Public Information and Media Relations	17
1.9.5	Management Accountability	17
1.9.5.1	Financial Sustainability	17
1.9.5.2	Facilities	18
1.9.5.3	Budget Performance and Accountability Programs	18
1.10	Partnerships	18
1.11	Relationship with American Indian Tribes	19
1.11.1	Government-to-Government Relationship	19
1.11.2	Consultation	19
1.11.3	Trust Resources	19
1.12	Native Hawaiians, Pacific Islanders, and Caribbean Islanders	20
1.13	An Enduring Message	20

2 Park System Planning — 21

2.1	General Principles	22
2.1.1	Decision-making	22
2.1.2	Scientific, Technical, and Scholarly Analysis	22
2.1.3	Public Participation	22
2.1.4	Goal Orientation	22
2.2	Major Elements of Park Planning and Decision-making	22
2.3	Levels of Park Planning	23
2.3.1	General Management Planning	23
2.3.1.1	Statutory Requirements	24
2.3.1.2	Management Zoning	24
2.3.1.3	Planning Team	24
2.3.1.4	Science and Scholarship	24
2.3.1.5	Public Involvement	24
2.3.1.6	Alternative Futures	25
2.3.1.7	Environmental Analysis	25
2.3.1.8	Cooperative Planning	25
2.3.1.9	Wild and Scenic Rivers	25
2.3.1.10	Wilderness	25
2.3.1.11	Alaska Park Units	26
2.3.1.12	Periodic Review of General Management Plans	26
2.3.2	Program Management Planning	26
2.3.3	Strategic Planning	26
2.3.3.1	Relationship between the Strategic Plan and the General Management Plan	27
2.3.4	Implementation Planning	27
2.3.4.1	Environmental Analysis	27
2.3.5	Park Annual Performance Planning and Reporting	27

3 Land Protection — 29

3.1	General	30
3.2	Land Protection Methods	30
3.3	Land Protection Plans	30

3.4	Cooperative Conservation	31
3.5	Boundary Adjustments	31
3.6	Land Acquisition Authority	32
3.7	Land Acquisition Funding	32
3.8	Condemnation	33

4 Natural Resource Management 35

Introduction 36

4.1 General Management Concepts 36

4.1.1	Planning for Natural Resource Management	37
4.1.2	Natural Resource Information	38
4.1.3	Evaluating Impacts on Natural Resources	38
4.1.4	Partnerships	38
4.1.5	Restoration of Natural Systems	39
4.1.6	Compensation for Injuries to Natural Resources	39

4.2 Studies and Collections 39

4.2.1	NPS-conducted or -sponsored Inventory, Monitoring, and Research Studies	40
4.2.2	Independent Studies	40
4.2.3	Natural Resource Collections	41
4.2.4	Collection Associated with the Development of Commercial Products	41

4.3 Special Designations 41

4.3.1	Research Natural Areas	41
4.3.2	Experimental Research Areas	41
4.3.3	Wilderness Areas	41
4.3.4	National Wild and Scenic Rivers System	41
4.3.5	National Natural Landmarks	42
4.3.6	Biosphere Reserves	42
4.3.7	World Heritage List	42

4.4 Biological Resource Management 42

4.4.1	General Principles for Managing Biological Resources	42
4.4.1.1	Plant and Animal Population Management Principles	43
4.4.1.2	Genetic Resource Management Principles	43
4.4.1.3	Definition of Native and Exotic Species	43
4.4.2	Management of Native Plants and Animals	44
4.4.2.1	NPS Actions That Remove Native Plants and Animals	44
4.4.2.2	Restoration of Native Plant and Animal Species	45
4.4.2.3	Management of Threatened or Endangered Plants and Animals	45
4.4.2.4	Management of Natural Landscapes	46
4.4.2.5	Maintenance of Altered Plant Communities	46
4.4.3	Harvest of Plants and Animals by the Public	46
4.4.4	Management of Exotic Species	47
4.4.4.1	Introduction or Maintenance of Exotic Species	47
4.4.4.2	Removal of Exotic Species Already Present	48
4.4.5	Pest Management	48
4.4.5.1	Pests	48
4.4.5.2	Integrated Pest Management Program	48
4.4.5.3	Pesticide Use	49
4.4.5.4	Biological Control Agents and Bioengineered Products	49
4.4.5.5	Pesticide Purchase and Storage	49

4.5 Fire Management 49

4.6 Water Resource Management 50

4.6.1	Protection of Surface Waters and Groundwaters	50
4.6.2	Water Rights	50
4.6.3	Water Quality	51
4.6.4	Floodplains	51
4.6.5	Wetlands	51
4.6.6	Watershed and Stream Processes	52

4.7 Air Resource Management 52

4.7.1	Air Quality	52
4.7.2	Weather and Climate	53

4.8 Geologic Resource Management 53

4.8.1	Protection of Geologic Processes	53
4.8.1.1	Shorelines and Barrier Islands	54
4.8.1.2	Karst	54
4.8.1.3	Geologic Hazards	54
4.8.2	Management of Geologic Features	54
4.8.2.1	Paleontological Resources and Their Contexts	54
4.8.2.2	Caves	55
4.8.2.3	Geothermal and Hydrothermal Resources	55
4.8.2.4	Soil Resource Management	56

4.9 Soundscape Management 56

4.10 Lightscape Management 57

4.11 Chemical Information and Odors 57

5 Cultural Resource Management 59

Introduction 60

5.1 Research 60

5.1.1	NPS Research	60
5.1.2	Independent Research	61
5.1.3	Identification and Evaluation of Resources	61
5.1.3.1	Inventories	61
5.1.3.2	Evaluation and Categorization	62
5.1.3.2.1	National Register Nomination	62
5.1.3.2.2	National Historic Landmark Designation	62
5.1.3.2.3	Nominations for World Heritage List Designation	62

5.2 Planning 63

5.2.1	Consultation	63
5.2.2	Agreements	64
5.2.3	Confidentiality	64

5.3 Stewardship 65

5.3.1	Protection and Preservation of Cultural Resources	65
5.3.1.1	Emergency Management	65
5.3.1.2	Fire Detection, Suppression, and Post-fire Rehabilitation and Protection	65
5.3.1.3	Compensation for Injuries to Cultural Resources	65
5.3.1.4	Environmental Monitoring and Control	66
5.3.1.5	Pest Management	66
5.3.1.6	Visitor Carrying Capacity	66
5.3.1.7	Cultural Soundscape Management	66
5.3.2	Physical Access for Persons with Disabilities	66
5.3.3	Historic Property Leases and Cooperative Agreements	66
5.3.4	Stewardship of Human Remains and Burials	67
5.3.5	Treatment of Cultural Resources	67
5.3.5.1	Archeological Resources	68
5.3.5.1.1	Preservation	68
5.3.5.1.2	Stabilization	68
5.3.5.1.3	Rehabilitation, Restoration, and Reconstruction	68
5.3.5.1.4	Protection	68
5.3.5.1.5	Archeological Data Recovery	68
5.3.5.1.6	Earthworks	68
5.3.5.1.7	Submerged Cultural Resources	69
5.3.5.2	Cultural Landscapes	69
5.3.5.2.1	Preservation	69
5.3.5.2.2	Rehabilitation	69
5.3.5.2.3	Restoration	69
5.3.5.2.4	Reconstruction of Obliterated Landscapes	69
5.3.5.2.5	Biotic Cultural Resources	69
5.3.5.2.6	Land Use and Ethnographic Value	70
5.3.5.2.7	New Construction	70
5.3.5.3	Ethnographic Resources	70
5.3.5.3.1	Resource Access and Use	71

5.3.5.3.2	Sacred Sites	71
5.3.5.3.3	Research	72
5.3.5.4	Historic and Prehistoric Structures	72
5.3.5.4.1	Preservation	72
5.3.5.4.2	Rehabilitation	72
5.3.5.4.3	Restoration	72
5.3.5.4.4	Reconstruction of Missing Structures	72
5.3.5.4.5	Movement of Historic Structures	72
5.3.5.4.6	New Construction	73
5.3.5.4.7	Use of Historic Structures	73
5.3.5.4.8	Park Structures Owned or Managed by Others	73
5.3.5.4.9	Damaged or Destroyed Historic Structures	73
5.3.5.4.10	Historic and Prehistoric Ruins	73
5.3.5.5	Museum Collections	74
5.3.5.5.1	Preservation	74
5.3.5.5.2	Restoration	74
5.3.5.5.3	Reproduction	74
5.3.5.5.4	Acquisition, Management, Disposition, and Use	74
5.3.5.5.5	Historic Furnishings	75
5.3.5.5.6	Archives and Manuscripts	75

6 Wilderness Preservation and Management — 77

6.1	General Statement	78
6.2	Identification and Designation of the Wilderness Resource	78
6.2.1	Assessment of Wilderness Eligibility or Ineligibility	78
6.2.1.1	Primary Eligibility Criteria	78
6.2.1.2	Additional Considerations in Determining Eligibility	78
6.2.1.3	The Assessment Process	79
6.2.2	Wilderness Studies	79
6.2.2.1	Potential Wilderness	79
6.2.2.2	Proposed Wilderness	79
6.2.3	Recommended Wilderness	79
6.2.4	Designated Wilderness	80
6.3	Wilderness Resource Management	80
6.3.1	General Policy	80
6.3.2	Responsibility	80
6.3.3	Consistency	81
6.3.4	Wilderness-related Planning and Environmental Compliance	81
6.3.4.1	Zoning for Wilderness	81
6.3.4.2	Wilderness Management Planning	81
6.3.4.3	Environmental Compliance	81
6.3.5	Minimum Requirement	81
6.3.6	Scientific Activities in Wilderness	82
6.3.6.1	General Policy	82
6.3.6.2	Monitoring Wilderness Resources	83
6.3.7	Natural Resources Management	83
6.3.8	Cultural Resources	83
6.3.9	Fire Management	84
6.3.10	Management Facilities	84
6.3.10.1	Administrative Facilities	84
6.3.10.2	Trails in Wilderness	84
6.3.10.3	Shelters and Campsites	85
6.3.10.4	Signs	85
6.3.11	Wilderness Boundaries	85
6.3.11.1	Legal Descriptions and Boundary Maps	85
6.3.11.2	Caves	85
6.3.11.3	Waters in Wilderness	85
6.3.12	American Indian Access and Associated Sites	85
6.4	Wilderness Use Management	86
6.4.1	General Policy	86
6.4.2	Wilderness Interpretation and Education	86
6.4.3	Recreational Use Management in Wilderness	86
6.4.3.1	Recreation Use Evaluation	86
6.4.3.2	Outdoor Skills and Ethics	87
6.4.3.3	Use of Motorized Equipment	87
6.4.4	Commercial Services	87
6.4.5	Special Events	87
6.4.6	Existing Private Rights	87
6.4.7	Grazing and Livestock Driveways	87
6.4.8	Rights-of-Way	88
6.4.9	Mineral Development	88
6.4.10	Accessibility for Persons with Disabilities	88

7 Interpretation and Education — 89

	Introduction	90
7.1	Interpretive and Educational Programs	90
7.2	Interpretive Planning	91
7.3	Personal and Nonpersonal Services	91
7.3.1	Personal Services	91
7.3.1.1	Curriculum-based Education Programs	91
7.3.2	Nonpersonal Services	91
7.3.2.1	Park Brochures	92
7.3.3	Technology and Interpretation	92
7.3.4	Interpretive and Educational Services Beyond Park Boundaries	92
7.4	Interpretive Competencies and Skills	92
7.5	Requirements for All Interpretive and Educational Services	93
7.5.1	Interpretation and 21st Century Relevancy	93
7.5.2	Access to Interpretive and Educational Opportunities	93
7.5.3	Resource Issue Interpretation and Education	93
7.5.4	Research and Scholarship	93
7.5.5	Evaluation of Interpretation and Education Effectiveness	93
7.5.6	Consultation	94
7.5.7	Cultural Demonstrators	94
7.5.8	Historic Weapons	94
7.5.9	Reenactments	94
7.6	Interpretive and Educational Partnerships	95
7.6.1	Volunteers in Parks (VIPs)	95
7.6.2	Cooperating Associations	95

8 Use of the Parks — 97

8.1	General	98
8.1.1	Appropriate Use	98
8.1.2	Process for Determining Appropriate Uses	98
8.2	Visitor Use	99
8.2.1	Visitor Carrying Capacity	100
8.2.2	Recreational Activities	101
8.2.2.1	Management of Recreational Use	101
8.2.2.2	Commercial Visitor Services	102
8.2.2.3	River Use	102
8.2.2.4	Backcountry Use	102
8.2.2.5	Fishing	102
8.2.2.6	Hunting and Trapping	103
8.2.2.7	Parachuting	103
8.2.2.8	Recreational Pack and Saddle Stock Use	103
8.2.3	Use of Motorized Equipment	103
8.2.3.1	Motorized Off-road Vehicle Use	104
8.2.3.2	Snowmobiles	104
8.2.3.3	Personal Watercraft Use	104
8.2.4	Accessibility for Persons with Disabilities	104
8.2.5	Visitor Safety and Emergency Response	105
8.2.5.1	Visitor Safety	105
8.2.5.2	Emergency Preparedness and Emergency Operations	105
8.2.5.3	Search and Rescue	106
8.2.5.4	Dive Operations	106
8.2.5.5	Public Health Program	106
8.2.5.6	Emergency Medical Services	106
8.2.6	Recreation Fees and Reservations	106

8.2.6.1	Recreation Fees	107
8.2.6.2	National Recreation Reservation Service	107
8.2.7	Tourism	107

8.3 Law Enforcement Program — 108

8.3.1	General	108
8.3.2	The Context for Law Enforcement	108
8.3.3	Shared Responsibilities	108
8.3.4	Enforcement Authority	108
8.3.5	Jurisdiction	109
8.3.6	Use of Force	109
8.3.7	Law Enforcement Public Information and Media Relations	109
8.3.8	Homeland Security	109
8.4	Overflights and Aviation Uses	109
8.4.1	Alaska and Remote Areas	110
8.4.2	Education	110
8.4.3	General Aviation	110
8.4.4	Administrative Use	110
8.4.5	Military Aviation	110
8.4.6	Commercial Air Tour Management	110
8.4.7	Permitted Overflights	110
8.4.8	Airports and Landing Sites	110
8.5	Use by American Indians and Other Traditionally Associated Groups	111

8.6 Special Park Uses — 112

8.6.1	General	112
8.6.1.1	Requests for Permits	112
8.6.1.2	Fees	112
8.6.2	Special Events	112
8.6.2.1	General	112
8.6.2.2	Helium-filled Balloons	113
8.6.2.3	Fireworks Displays	113
8.6.2.4	Sale of Food or Merchandise	113
8.6.3	First Amendment Activities	113
8.6.4	Rights-of-Way for Utilities and Roads	113
8.6.4.1	General	113
8.6.4.2	Utilities	114
8.6.4.3	Telecommunication Sites	114
8.6.4.4	Roads and Highways and Petroleum-based Pipelines	115
8.6.5	Access to Private Property	115
8.6.6	Filming and Photography	115
8.6.6.1	General	115
8.6.6.2	Permits and Fees	115
8.6.6.3	NPS Participation	115
8.6.7	Agricultural Uses	116
8.6.8	Domestic and Feral Livestock	116
8.6.8.1	General	116
8.6.8.2	Managing Agricultural Grazing	116
8.6.8.2.1	Permitting Agricultural Grazing	117
8.6.8.2.2	Structures for Agricultural Grazing	117
8.6.8.3	Trespass and Feral Livestock	117
8.6.9	Military Operations	117
8.6.10	Cemeteries and Burials	117
8.6.10.1	National Cemeteries	117
8.6.10.2	Family Cemeteries	117
8.6.10.3	Other Burials and the Scattering of Ashes	117
8.6.11	Other Special Park Uses	118

8.7 Mineral Exploration and Development — 118

8.7.1	Mining Claims	118
8.7.2	Federal Mineral Leases	118
8.7.3	Nonfederally Owned Minerals	119

8.8 Collecting Natural Products — 119

8.9 Consumptive Uses — 119

8.10 Natural and Cultural Studies, Research, and Collection Activities — 120

8.11 Social Science Studies — 120

8.11.1	General	120
8.11.2	NPS-supported Studies	120
8.11.3	Independent and Commercial Studies	121
8.11.4	Management and Conduct of Studies	121

8.12 Leases — 121

8.12.1	Additional Criteria	122
8.12.2	Prior Approval	122
8.12.3	Noncompetitive Awards	122
8.12.4	Historic Properties	122

9 Park Facilities — 123

9.1 General — 124

9.1.1	Facility Planning and Design	124
9.1.1.1	Life-cycle Costs	124
9.1.1.2	Integration of Facilities into the Park Environment	125
9.1.1.3	Protection of Cultural Values	125
9.1.1.4	Adaptive Use	125
9.1.1.5	Siting Facilities to Avoid Natural Hazards	126
9.1.1.6	Sustainable Energy Design	126
9.1.2	Accessibility for Persons with Disabilities	126
9.1.3	Construction	127
9.1.3.1	Construction Sites	127
9.1.3.2	Revegetation and Landscaping	127
9.1.3.3	Borrow Pits and Spoil Areas	127
9.1.4	Maintenance	128
9.1.4.1	General	128
9.1.4.2	Acquisition of Environmentally Preferable and Energy-Efficient Products	128
9.1.5	Utilities	128
9.1.5.1	Water Supply Systems	129
9.1.5.2	Wastewater Treatment Systems	129
9.1.5.3	Utility Lines	129
9.1.5.4	Historic Utilities	129
9.1.6	Waste Management and Contaminant Issues	129
9.1.6.1	Waste Management	129
9.1.6.2	NPS Response to Contaminants	130
9.1.7	Energy Management	131
9.1.8	Structural Fire Protection and Suppression	131

9.2 Transportation Systems and Alternative Transportation — 131

9.2.1	Road Systems	132
9.2.1.1	Park Roads	132
9.2.1.2	Non-NPS Roads	132
9.2.1.2.1	Existing Commercial and Other Through-Traffic	133
9.2.1.2.2	Construction and Expansion Proposals	133
9.2.2	Trails and Walks	133
9.2.2.1	Cooperative Trail Planning	133
9.2.2.2	Hiking Trails	134
9.2.2.3	Equestrian Trails	134
9.2.2.4	Bicycle Trails	134
9.2.2.5	Water Trails	134
9.2.2.6	Interpretive Trails	134
9.2.2.7	National Trails	134
9.2.2.8	Trailheads	134
9.2.2.9	Trail Bridges	134
9.2.3	Traffic Signs and Markings	135
9.2.4	Parking Areas	135
9.2.5	Navigation Aids	135

9.3 Visitor Facilities — 135

9.3.1	Informational and Interpretive Facilities	135
9.3.1.1	Signs	135
9.3.1.2	Entrance Stations	135
9.3.1.3	Visitor Centers	136
9.3.1.4	Amphitheaters	136
9.3.1.5	Wayside Exhibits	136
9.3.1.6	Viewing Devices	136
9.3.1.7	Facilities for Arts and Culture	136
9.3.2	Overnight Accommodations and Food Services	136
9.3.2.1	Campgrounds	136
9.3.2.2	Backcountry Campsites	137

9.3.2.3	Hostels and Shelters	137
9.3.3	Comfort Stations	137
9.3.4	Other Visitor Facilities	137
9.3.4.1	Picnic and Other Day Use Areas	137
9.3.4.2	Facilities for Water Recreation	138
9.3.4.3	Skiing Facilities	138
9.3.5	Advertising	138
9.4	**Management Facilities**	**138**
9.4.1	Administrative Offices	138
9.4.2	Museum Collections Management Facilities	139
9.4.3	Employee Housing	139
9.4.3.1	Housing Management Plan	139
9.4.3.2	Eligible Residents	139
9.4.3.3	Historic Structures	139
9.4.3.4	Design and Construction	139
9.4.4	Maintenance Structures	139
9.4.5	Miscellaneous Management Facilities	139
9.5	**Dams and Reservoirs**	**140**
9.6	**Commemorative Works and Plaques**	**140**
9.6.1	General	140
9.6.2	Interpretive Works That Commemorate	140
9.6.3	Approval of Commemorative Works	141
9.6.4	Preexisting Commemorative Works	141
9.6.5	Donated Commemorative Works	141
9.6.6	Commemorative Works in National Cemeteries	141

10 Commercial Visitor Services — 143

10.1	**General**	**144**
10.1.1	Leasing	144
10.2	**Concessions**	**144**
10.2.1	Concession Policies	144
10.2.2	Commercial Visitor Services Planning	144
10.2.3	Concession Contracting	144
10.2.3.1	Terms and Conditions of Contracts	144
10.2.3.2	Modifications/Amendments	144
10.2.3.3	Extension	144
10.2.3.4	Competition	144
10.2.3.5	Third-party Agreements and Subconcessions	145
10.2.3.6	Multipark Contracts	145
10.2.3.7	Termination	145
10.2.4	Concession Operations	145
10.2.4.1	Operating Plans	145
10.2.4.2	Service Type and Quality	145
10.2.4.3	Evaluation of Concession Operations	145
10.2.4.4	Interpretation by Concessioners	145
10.2.4.5	Merchandise	145
10.2.4.6	Artifacts and Specimens	146
10.2.4.7	Rates	146
10.2.4.8	Risk Management Program	146
10.2.4.9	Natural and Cultural Resource Management Requirements	146
10.2.4.10	Environmental Program Requirements	146
10.2.4.11	Insurance	147
10.2.4.12	Food Service Sanitation Inspections	147
10.2.4.13	Smoking	147
10.2.4.14	Wireless Local Area Networks	147
10.2.5	Concessions Financial Management	147
10.2.5.1	Franchise Fees	147
10.2.5.2	Franchise Fee Special Account	147
10.2.5.3	Record-keeping System	147
10.2.5.4	Annual Financial Reports	147
10.2.5.5	Donations to the National Park Service	148
10.2.6	Concession Facilities	148
10.2.6.1	Design	148
10.2.6.2	Accessibility of Commercial Services	148
10.2.6.3	Maintenance	148
10.2.6.4	Utilities and Services	148
10.2.6.5	Closure of Commercial Operations during Government Shutdown	148
10.2.7	Concessioner Employees and Employment Conditions	149
10.2.7.1	Nondiscrimination	149
10.2.7.2	Substance Abuse	149
10.2.8	NPS Employees	149
10.2.8.1	Accepting Gifts and Reduced Rates from Concessioners	149
10.2.8.2	Employment of NPS Personnel or Family Members by Concessioners	149
10.2.8.3	NPS Employee Ownership or Investment in Concession Businesses	149
10.2.8.4	Concession Management Personnel Qualifications	149
10.3	**Commercial Use Authorizations**	**149**
10.3.1	General	150
10.3.2	Requirements	150
10.3.3	Limitations	150
10.3.4	Construction Prohibition	150
10.3.5	Duration	150
10.3.6	Other Contracts	150

Appendix A		**151**
	Laws Cited in Text	151
Appendix B		**155**
	Executive Orders and Memoranda Cited in Text	155
Appendix C		**157**
	Director's Orders	157
Glossary		**161**
Index		**167**

Management Policies

The Guide to Managing the National Park System

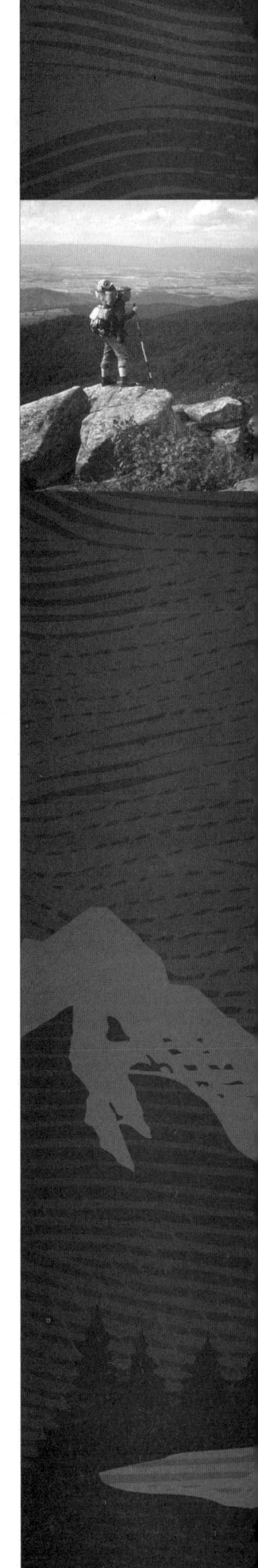

The national park system was created to conserve unimpaired many of the world's most magnificent landscapes, places that enshrine our nation's enduring principles, and places that remind us of the tremendous sacrifices Americans have made on behalf of those principles. They are the most remarkable collection of places in America for recreation and learning. Visitors can immerse themselves in places where events actually happened and enjoy some of the most significant natural and historic places in America. These are places that offer renewal for the body, the spirit and the mind. As required by the 1916 Organic Act, these special places must be managed in a special way—a way that allows them to be enjoyed not just by those who are here today, but also by generations that follow. Enjoyment by present and future generations can be assured only if these special places are passed on to them in an unimpaired condition. And that is the challenge that faces all the employees of the National Park Service. It is a challenge eagerly embraced, but employees must have the tools required to perform the job successfully. The policies contained in these pages represent one of the most important tools available. Through their judicious and consistent application, these policies will set a firm foundation for stewardship that will continue to earn the trust and confidence of the American people.

Underlying Principles

The National Park Service adhered to a number of principles in preparing this 2006 edition of *Management Policies*. The key principles were that the policies must:

◆ comply with current laws, regulations and executive orders;

◆ prevent impairment of park resources and values;

◆ ensure that conservation will be predominant when there is a conflict between the protection of resources and their use;

◆ maintain NPS responsibility for making decisions and for exercising key authorities;

◆ emphasize consultation and cooperation with local/state/tribal/federal entities;

◆ support pursuit of the best contemporary business practices and sustainability;

◆ encourage consistency across the system —"one national park system";

◆ reflect NPS goals and a commitment to cooperative conservation and civic engagement;

◆ employ a tone that leaves no room for misunderstanding the National Park Service's commitment to the public's appropriate use and enjoyment, including education and interpretation, of park resources, while preventing unacceptable impacts;

◆ pass on to future generations natural, cultural, and physical resources that meet desired conditions better than they do today, along with improved opportunities for enjoyment.

Introduction

Law, Policy, and Other Guidance

This volume is the basic Service-wide policy document of the National Park Service. Adherence to policy is mandatory unless specifically waived or modified by the Secretary, the Assistant Secretary, or the Director.

In carrying out their responsibilities under the 1916 National Park Service[1] Organic Act and other pertinent statutes, all NPS officials and employees must be knowledgeable about the laws, regulations, and policies that pertain to their work. The property clause of the U.S. Constitution, which is the supreme law of the United States, gives Congress the authority to develop laws governing the management of the national park system. The property clause specifically directs that "The Congress will have the Power to dispose of and make all needful Rules and Regulations respecting the Territory or other Property belonging to the United States" (article IV, section 3). Once laws are enacted, authority for interpreting and implementing them is delegated to appropriate levels of government. In carrying out this function, the National Park Service, like other federal agencies, develops policy to interpret the ambiguities of the law and to fill in the details left unaddressed by Congress in the statutes.

Hierarchy of Authorities

The management of the national park system and NPS programs is guided by the Constitution, public laws, treaties, proclamations, executive orders, regulations, and directives of the Secretary of the Interior and the Assistant Secretary for Fish and Wildlife and Parks. NPS policy must be consistent with these higher authorities and with appropriate delegations of authority. Many of the public laws and other guidance affecting the various facets of NPS administration and management are cited for reference purposes throughout these *Management Policies*. Other laws, regulations, and policies related to the administration of federal programs, although not cited, may also apply. For example, many, but not all, of the legislative requirements of the Alaska National Interest Lands Conservation Act (ANILCA) are cited at different places throughout these *Management Policies*. The additional legislative requirements of ANILCA, although not cited, must also be considered in the interpretation and application of these policies, as must all other applicable legislative requirements. It is especially important that superintendents and other park staff review their park's enabling legislation to determine whether it contains explicit guidance that would prevail over Service-wide policy.

Policy Development

Policy sets the framework and provides direction for all management decisions. This direction may be general or specific; it may prescribe the process through which decisions are made, how an action is to be accomplished, or the results to be achieved. Policy initiatives may originate as a sudden, urgent response to an unanticipated problem or issue, or through a slow, evolutionary process as the Park Service gains increased experience or insight regarding a problem or issue. Sometimes the initiative does not originate within the Park Service, but rather with persons or organizations outside the Park Service who have a strong interest in how the Service manages the parks. However, NPS policy is usually developed through a concerted workgroup and consensus-building team effort involving extensive field review, consultation with NPS senior managers, and review and comment by affected parties and the general public.

All policy must be articulated in writing and must be approved by an NPS official who has been delegated authority to issue the policy. Policy must be published or otherwise made available to the public—particularly those whom it affects—and those who must implement it in the Washington office, regional offices, and parks. Unwritten or informal "policy," and various understandings of NPS traditional practices, will not be recognized as official policy.

Compliance, Accountability, and Enforceability

Service-wide policy is articulated by the Director of the National Park Service. NPS employees must follow these policies unless specifically waived or modified in writing by the Secretary, the Assistant Secretary, or the Director. Waivers and modifications will be considered on a case-by-case basis, and previous waivers or modifications will not necessarily be regarded as precedents for future waivers or modifications. A request for a waiver or modification of policy must include a written justification and be submitted to the Director through the Office of Policy, which will coordinate with appropriate program offices.

The policies contained within this document are intended only to improve the internal management of the National Park Service; they are not intended to, and do not, create any right or benefit, substantive or procedural, enforceable at law or equity by a party against the United States, its departments, agencies, instrumentalities or entities, its officers or employees, or any other person. Park superintendents will be held accountable for their and their staff's, adherence to Service-wide policy.

The Directives System

This volume of NPS *Management Policies* is the basic Service-wide policy document of the National Park Service, superseding the 2001 edition. It is the highest of three levels of guidance documents in the NPS Directives System. The Directives System is designed to provide NPS management and staff with clear and continuously updated information on NPS policy and required and/or recommended actions, as well as any other information that will help them manage parks and programs effectively.

The *Management Policies* will be revised at appropriate intervals to consolidate Service-wide policy decisions, or to respond to new laws and technologies, new understandings of park resources and the factors that affect them, or changes in American society. Interim updates or amendments may be accomplished through director's orders (the second level of the Directives System), which also serve as a vehicle to clarify or supplement the

---

[1] The terms "National Park Service," "Park Service," "Service," and "NPS" are used interchangeably in this document.

Management Policies to meet the needs of NPS managers. Any previously dated statement of policy not consistent with these *Management Policies*, or with a director's order that updates, amends, or clarifies policy, is to be disregarded.

Under the Directives System, the most detailed and comprehensive guidance on implementing Service-wide policy is found in "level 3" documents, which are usually in the form of handbooks or reference manuals issued by associate directors. These documents provide NPS field employees with compilations of legal references, operating policies, standards, procedures, general information, recommendations, and examples to assist them in carrying out *Management Policies* and director's orders. Level 3 documents may not impose any new Service-wide requirements unless the Director has specifically authorized them to do so, but they may reiterate or compile requirements (for example, laws, regulations, and policies) that have been imposed by higher authorities.

This document is intended to be read in its entirety. While certain chapters or sections provide important guidance by themselves, that guidance must be supplemented by the overriding principles listed below, which provide insight into the reading of this document. In addition there is an interrelationship among the chapters that provides for clarity and continuity for the management of the national park system. Also, the glossary contains important terms that apply throughout the document and should be incorporated into the reading of the document.

Whenever *Management Policies* are revised in the future they should

- comply with current laws, regulations, and executive orders;
- prevent impairment of park resources and values;
- ensure that conservation will be predominant when there is a conflict between the protection of resources and their use;
- maintain NPS responsibility for making decisions and for exercising key authorities;
- emphasize consultation and cooperation with local/state/tribal/federal entities;
- support pursuit of the best contemporary business practices and sustainability;
- encourage consistency across the system — "one national park system";
- reflect NPS goals and a commitment to cooperative conservation and civic engagement;
- employ a tone that leaves no room for misunderstanding the Park Service's commitment to the public's appropriate use and enjoyment, including education and interpretation, of park resources, while preventing unacceptable impacts;
- pass on to future generations natural, cultural and physical resources that meet desired conditions better than they do today, along with improved opportunities for enjoyment.

Other Sources of Guidance

Instructions, guidance, and directives of regional or otherwise-limited application supplementary to and in conformance with Service-wide policies may be issued by regional directors or associate directors within formal delegations of authority. Superintendents may issue, within formal delegations of authority, park-specific instructions, procedures, directives, and other supplementary guidance (such as hours of operation or dates for seasonal openings), provided that the guidance does not conflict with Service-wide policy.

NPS Program Policies

This volume addresses only those policies applicable to management of the national park system. It does not address policies applicable to NPS-administered programs that serve the conservation and recreation needs of the nation, but are not directly related to the national park system. Examples include the National Register of Historic Places; the National Historic Landmarks Program; the National Natural Landmarks Program; the Land and Water Conservation Fund Grants Program; the Historic American Buildings Survey; the Historic American Engineering Record; the Historic American Landscapes Survey; the American Battlefield Protection Program; the National Maritime Heritage Grants Program; the Rivers, Trails and Conservation Assistance Program; the Tribal Heritage Preservation Grants Program; the Preserve America Grants Program; and the National Heritage Areas Program.

The Foundation

1

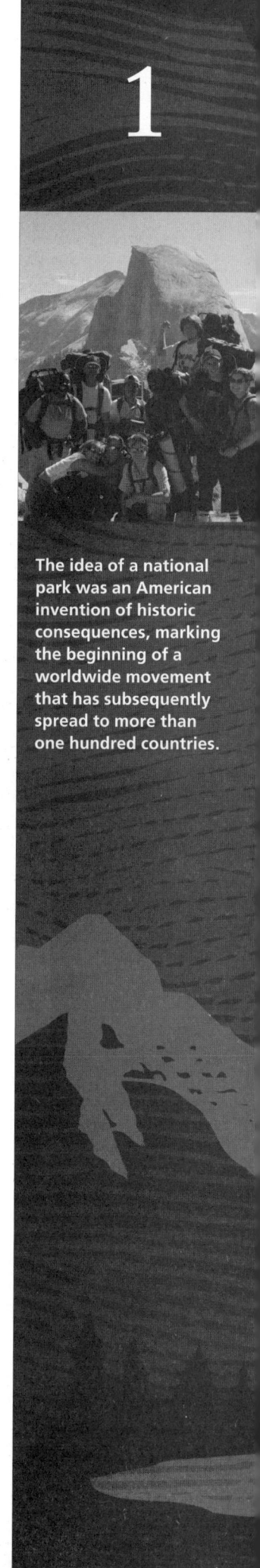

The idea of a national park was an American invention of historic consequences, marking the beginning of a worldwide movement that has subsequently spread to more than one hundred countries.

Beginning with Yellowstone, the idea of a national park was an American invention of historic consequences. The areas that now make up the national park system, and those that will be added in years to come, are cumulative expressions of a single national heritage. The National Park Service must manage park resources and values in such manner and by such means as will leave them unimpaired for the enjoyment of future generations.

1.1 The National Park Idea

The world's first national park—Yellowstone—was created in 1872, at which time Congress set aside more than one million acres as "a public park or pleasuring ground for the benefit and enjoyment of the people." The legislation assigned control of the new park to the Secretary of the Interior, who would be responsible for issuing regulations to provide for the "preservation, from injury or spoliation, of all timber, mineral deposits, natural curiosities, or wonders, within the park, and their retention in their natural condition." Other park management functions were to include the development of visitor accommodations, the construction of roads and bridle trails, the removal of trespassers, and protection "against the wanton destruction of the fish and game found within the park" (16 United States Code 21-22).

This idea of a national park was an American invention of historic consequences, marking the beginning of a worldwide movement that has subsequently spread to more than 100 countries. However, when Yellowstone National Park was created, no concept or plan existed upon which to build a system of such parks. The concept now described as the national park system, which embraces, nationwide, a wide variety of natural and cultural resources, evolved slowly over the years—often through the consolidation of federal land management responsibilities.

As interest grew in preserving the great scenic wonders of the West, efforts were also underway to protect the sites and structures associated with early Native American culture, particularly in the Southwest. The Antiquities Act of 1906 authorized the President "to declare by public proclamation [as national monuments] historic landmarks, historic and prehistoric structures, and other objects of historic or scientific interest that are situated upon the lands owned or controlled" by the U.S. government (16 USC 431).

In 1916 Congress created the National Park Service in the Department of the Interior to promote and regulate the use of the federal areas known as national parks, monuments, and reservations (16 USC 1). (As noted in the Introduction, the terms "National Park Service," "Park Service," "Service," and "NPS" are used interchangeably in this document.)

1.2 The National Park System

The number and diversity of parks within the national park system grew as a result of a government reorganization in 1933, another following World War II, and yet another during the 1960s. Today there are nearly 400 units in the national park system. These units are variously designated as national parks, monuments, preserves, lakeshores, seashores, wild and scenic rivers, trails, historic sites, military parks, battlefields, historical parks, recreation areas, memorials, and parkways. Regardless of the many names and official designations of the park units that make up the national park system, all represent some nationally significant aspect of our natural or cultural heritage. They are the physical remnants of our past—great scenic and natural places that continue to evolve, repositories of outstanding recreational opportunities, classrooms of our heritage, and the legacy we leave to future generations—and they warrant the highest standard of protection.

It should be noted that, in accordance with provisions of the Wild and Scenic Rivers Act, any component of the National Wild and Scenic Rivers System that is administered by the Park Service is automatically a part of the national park system. Although there is no analogous provision in the National Trails System Act, several national trails managed by the Service have been included in the national park system. These national rivers and trails that are part of the national park system are subject to the policies contained herein, as well as to any other requirements specified in the Wild and Scenic Rivers Act or the National Trails System Act.

1.3 Criteria for Inclusion

Congress declared in the National Park System General Authorities Act of 1970 that areas comprising the national park system are cumulative expressions of a single national heritage. Potential additions to the national park system should therefore contribute in their own special way to a system that fully represents the broad spectrum of natural and cultural resources that characterize our nation. The National Park Service is responsible for conducting professional studies of potential additions to the national park system when specifically authorized by an act of Congress, and for making recommendations to the Secretary of the Interior, the President, and Congress. Several laws outline criteria for units of the national park system and for additions to the National Wild and Scenic Rivers System and the National Trails System.

To receive a favorable recommendation from the Service, a proposed addition to the national park system must (1) possess nationally significant natural or cultural resources, (2) be a suitable addition to the system, (3) be a feasible addition to the system, and (4) require direct NPS management instead of protection by other public agencies or the private sector. These criteria are designed to ensure that the national park system includes only the most outstanding examples of the nation's natural and cultural resources. These criteria also recognize that there are other management alternatives for preserving the nation's outstanding resources.

1.3.1 National Significance

NPS professionals, in consultation with subject-matter experts, scholars, and scientists, will determine whether a resource is nationally significant. An area will be considered nationally significant if it meets all of the following criteria:

◆ It is an outstanding example of a particular type of resource.

◆ It possesses exceptional value or quality in illustrating or interpreting the natural or cultural themes of our nation's heritage.

- It offers superlative opportunities for public enjoyment or for scientific study.
- It retains a high degree of integrity as a true, accurate, and relatively unspoiled example of a resource.

National significance for cultural resources will be evaluated by applying the National Historic Landmarks criteria contained in 36 CFR Part 65 (*Code of Federal Regulations*).

1.3.2 Suitability

An area is considered suitable for addition to the national park system if it represents a natural or cultural resource type that is not already adequately represented in the national park system, or is not comparably represented and protected for public enjoyment by other federal agencies; tribal, state, or local governments; or the private sector.

Adequacy of representation is determined on a case-by-case basis by comparing the potential addition to other comparably managed areas representing the same resource type, while considering differences or similarities in the character, quality, quantity, or combination of resource values. The comparative analysis also addresses rarity of the resources, interpretive and educational potential, and similar resources already protected in the national park system or in other public or private ownership. The comparison results in a determination of whether the proposed new area would expand, enhance, or duplicate resource protection or visitor use opportunities found in other comparably managed areas.

1.3.3 Feasibility

To be feasible as a new unit of the national park system, an area must be (1) of sufficient size and appropriate configuration to ensure sustainable resource protection and visitor enjoyment (taking into account current and potential impacts from sources beyond proposed park boundaries), and (2) capable of efficient administration by the Service at a reasonable cost.

In evaluating feasibility, the Service considers a variety of factors for a study area, such as the following:

- size
- boundary configurations
- current and potential uses of the study area and surrounding lands
- landownership patterns
- public enjoyment potential
- costs associated with acquisition, development, restoration, and operation
- access
- current and potential threats to the resources
- existing degradation of resources
- staffing requirements
- local planning and zoning
- the level of local and general public support (including landowners)
- the economic/socioeconomic impacts of designation as a unit of the national park system

The feasibility evaluation also considers the ability of the National Park Service to undertake new management responsibilities in light of current and projected availability of funding and personnel.

An overall evaluation of feasibility will be made after taking into account all of the above factors. However, evaluations may sometimes identify concerns or conditions, rather than simply reach a yes or no conclusion. For example, some new areas may be feasible additions to the national park system only if landowners are willing to sell, or the boundary encompasses specific areas necessary for visitor access, or state or local governments will provide appropriate assurances that adjacent land uses will remain compatible with the study area's resources and values.

1.3.4 Direct NPS Management

There are many excellent examples of the successful management of important natural and cultural resources by other public agencies, private conservation organizations, and individuals. The National Park Service applauds these accomplishments and actively encourages the expansion of conservation activities by state, local, and private entities and by other federal agencies. Unless direct NPS management of a studied area is identified as the clearly superior alternative, the Service will recommend that one or more of these other entities assume a lead management role, and that the area not receive national park system status.

Studies will evaluate an appropriate range of management alternatives and will identify which alternative or combination of alternatives would, in the professional judgment of the Director, be most effective and efficient in protecting significant resources and providing opportunities for appropriate public enjoyment. Alternatives for NPS management will not be developed for study areas that fail to meet any one of the four criteria for inclusion listed in section 1.3.

In cases where a study area's resources meet criteria for national significance but do not meet other criteria for inclusion in the national park system, the Service may instead recommend an alternative status, such as "affiliated area." To be eligible for affiliated area status, the area's resources must (1) meet the same standards for significance and suitability that apply to units of the national park system; (2) require some special recognition or technical assistance beyond what is available through existing NPS programs; (3) be managed in accordance with the policies and standards that apply to units of the national park system; and (4) be assured of sustained resource protection, as documented in a formal agreement between the Service and the nonfederal management entity. Designation as a "heritage area" is another option that may be recommended. Heritage areas have a nationally important, distinctive assemblage of resources that is best managed for conservation, recreation, education, and continued use through partnerships among public and private entities at the local or regional level. Either of these two alternatives (and others as well) would recognize an area's importance to the nation without requiring or implying management by the National Park Service.

(See National Significance 1.3.1; Suitability 1.3.2)

1.4 Park Management

1.4.1 The Laws Generally Governing Park Management

The most important statutory directive for the National Park Service is provided by interrelated provisions of the NPS Organic Act of 1916 and the NPS General Authorities Act of 1970, including amendments to the latter law enacted in 1978.

The key management-related provision of the Organic Act is as follows:

> [The National Park Service] shall promote and regulate the use of the Federal areas known as national parks, monuments, and reservations hereinafter specified... by such means and measures as conform to the fundamental purpose of the said parks, monuments, and reservations, which purpose is to conserve the scenery and the natural and historic objects and the wild life therein and to provide for the enjoyment of the same in such manner and by such means as will leave them unimpaired for the enjoyment of future generations. (16 USC 1)

Congress supplemented and clarified these provisions through enactment of the General Authorities Act in 1970, and again through enactment of a 1978 amendment to that act (the "Redwood amendment," contained in a bill expanding Redwood National Park), which added the last two sentences in the following provision. The key part of that act, as amended, is as follows:

> Congress declares that the national park system, which began with establishment of Yellowstone National Park in 1872, has since grown to include superlative natural, historic, and recreation areas in every major region of the United States, its territories and island possessions; that these areas, though distinct in character, are united through their inter-related purposes and resources into one national park system as cumulative expressions of a single national heritage; that, individually and collectively, these areas derive increased national dignity and recognition of their superlative environmental quality through their inclusion jointly with each other in one national park system preserved and managed for the benefit and inspiration of all the people of the United States; and that it is the purpose of this Act to include all such areas in the System and to clarify the authorities applicable to the system. Congress further reaffirms, declares, and directs that the promotion and regulation of the various areas of the National Park System, as defined in section 1c of this title, shall be consistent with and founded in the purpose established by section 1 of this title [the Organic Act provision quoted above], to the common benefit of all the people of the United States. The authorization of activities shall be construed and the protection, management, and administration of these areas shall be conducted in light of the high public value and integrity of the National Park System and shall not be exercised in derogation of the values and purposes for which these various areas have been established, except as may have been or shall be directly and specifically provided by Congress. (16 USC 1a-1)

This section 1.4 of *Management Policies* represents the agency's interpretation of these key statutory provisions.

1.4.2 "Impairment" and "Derogation": One Standard

Congress intended the language of the Redwood amendment to the General Authorities Act to reiterate the provisions of the Organic Act, not create a substantively different management standard. The House committee report described the Redwood amendment as a "declaration by Congress" that the promotion and regulation of the national park system is to be consistent with the Organic Act. The Senate committee report stated that under the Redwood amendment, "The Secretary has an absolute duty, which is not to be compromised, to fulfill the mandate of the 1916 Act to take whatever actions and seek whatever relief as will safeguard the units of the national park system." So, although the Organic Act and the General Authorities Act, as amended by the Redwood amendment, use different wording ("unimpaired" and "derogation") to describe what the National Park Service must avoid, they define a single standard for the management of the national park system—not two different standards. For simplicity, *Management Policies* uses "impairment" (or a variation thereof), not both statutory phrases, to refer to that single standard.

1.4.3 The NPS Obligation to Conserve and Provide for Enjoyment of Park Resources and Values

The fundamental purpose of the national park system, established by the Organic Act and reaffirmed by the General Authorities Act, as amended, begins with a mandate to conserve park resources and values. This mandate is independent of the separate prohibition on impairment and applies all the time with respect to all park resources and values, even when there is no risk that any park resources or values may be impaired. NPS managers must always seek ways to avoid, or to minimize to the greatest extent practicable, adverse impacts on park resources and values. However, the laws do give the Service the management discretion to allow impacts to park resources and values when necessary and appropriate to fulfill the purposes of a park, so long as the impact does not constitute impairment of the affected resources and values.

The fundamental purpose of all parks also includes providing for the enjoyment of park resources and values by the people of the United States. The enjoyment that is contemplated by the statute is broad; it is the enjoyment of all the people of the United States and includes enjoyment both by people who visit parks and by those who appreciate them from afar. It also includes deriving benefit (including scientific knowledge) and inspiration from parks, as well as other forms of enjoyment and inspiration. Congress, recognizing that the enjoyment by future generations of the national parks can be ensured only if the superb quality of park resources and values is left unimpaired, has provided that when there is a conflict between conserving resources and values and providing for enjoyment of them, conservation is to be predominant. This is how courts have consistently interpreted the Organic Act.

1.4.3.1 Park Purposes and Legislatively Authorized Uses

Park purposes are found in the general laws pertaining to the national park system, as well as the enabling legislation or proclamation establishing each unit. In addition to park purposes, in many cases the enabling legislation or proclamation for a park unit may also identify uses that are either mandated or authorized. In the administration of mandated uses, park managers must allow the use; however, they do have the authority to and must manage and regulate the use to ensure, to the extent possible, that impacts on park resources from that use are acceptable. In the administration of authorized uses, park managers have the discretionary authority to allow and manage the use, provided that the use will not cause impairment or unacceptable impacts. In determining whether or how to allow the use, park managers must consider the congressional or presidential interest, as expressed in the enabling legislation or proclamation, that the use or uses continue. Where there is strong public interest in a particular use, opportunities for civic engagement and cooperative conservation should be factored into the decision-making process.

(See Unacceptable Impacts 1.4.7.1; Civic Engagement 1.7; Major Elements of NPS Park Planning and Decision-making 2.2; General 8.1)

1.4.4 The Prohibition on Impairment of Park Resources and Values

While Congress has given the Service the management discretion to allow impacts within parks, that discretion is limited by the statutory requirement (generally enforceable by the federal courts) that the Park Service must leave park resources and values unimpaired unless a particular law directly and specifically provides otherwise. This, the cornerstone of the Organic Act, establishes the primary responsibility of the National Park Service. It ensures that park resources and values will continue to exist in a condition that will allow the American people to have present and future opportunities for enjoyment of them.

The impairment of park resources and values may not be allowed by the Service unless directly and specifically provided for by legislation or by the proclamation establishing the park. The relevant legislation or proclamation must provide explicitly (not by implication or inference) for the activity, in terms that keep the Service from having the authority to manage the activity so as to avoid the impairment.

1.4.5 What Constitutes Impairment of Park Resources and Values

The impairment that is prohibited by the Organic Act and the General Authorities Act is an impact that, in the professional judgment of the responsible NPS manager, would harm the integrity of park resources or values, including the opportunities that otherwise would be present for the enjoyment of those resources or values. Whether an impact meets this definition depends on the particular resources and values that would be affected; the severity, duration, and timing of the impact; the direct and indirect effects of the impact; and the cumulative effects of the impact in question and other impacts.

An impact to any park resource or value may, but does not necessarily, constitute an impairment. An impact would be more likely to constitute impairment to the extent that it affects a resource or value whose conservation is

- ◆ necessary to fulfill specific purposes identified in the establishing legislation or proclamation of the park, or
- ◆ key to the natural or cultural integrity of the park or to opportunities for enjoyment of the park, or
- ◆ identified in the park's general management plan or other relevant NPS planning documents as being of significance.

An impact would be less likely to constitute an impairment if it is an unavoidable result of an action necessary to preserve or restore the integrity of park resources or values and it cannot be further mitigated.

An impact that may, but would not necessarily, lead to impairment may result from visitor activities; NPS administrative activities; or activities undertaken by concessioners, contractors, and others operating in the park. Impairment may also result from sources or activities outside the park. This will be addressed consistent with sections 1.6 and 1.7 on Cooperative Conservation and Civic Engagement.

(See Unacceptable Impacts 1.4.7.1)

1.4.6 What Constitutes Park Resources and Values

The "park resources and values" that are subject to the no-impairment standard include

- ◆ the park's scenery, natural and historic objects, and wildlife, and the processes and conditions that sustain them, including, to the extent present in the park: the ecological, biological, and physical processes that created the park and continue to act upon it; scenic features; natural visibility, both in daytime and at night; natural landscapes; natural soundscapes and smells; water and air resources; soils; geological resources; paleontological resources; archeological resources; cultural landscapes; ethnographic resources; historic and prehistoric sites, structures, and objects; museum collections; and native plants and animals;

- ◆ appropriate opportunities to experience enjoyment of the above resources, to the extent that can be done without impairing them;

- the park's role in contributing to the national dignity, the high public value and integrity, and the superlative environmental quality of the national park system, and the benefit and inspiration provided to the American people by the national park system; and
- any additional attributes encompassed by the specific values and purposes for which the park was established.

(See introduction to chapter 4)

1.4.7 Decision-making Requirements to Identify and Avoid Impairments

Before approving a proposed action that could lead to an impairment of park resources and values, an NPS decision-maker must consider the impacts of the proposed action and determine, in writing, that the activity will not lead to an impairment of park resources and values. If there would be an impairment, the action must not be approved.

In making a determination of whether there would be an impairment, an NPS decision-maker must use his or her professional judgment. This means that the decision-maker must consider any environmental assessments or environmental impact statements required by the National Environmental Policy Act of 1969 (NEPA); consultations required under section 106 of the National Historic Preservation Act (NHPA), relevant scientific and scholarly studies; advice or insights offered by subject matter experts and others who have relevant knowledge or experience; and the results of civic engagement and public involvement activities relating to the decision. The same application of professional judgment applies when reaching conclusions about "unacceptable impacts."

When an NPS decision-maker becomes aware that an ongoing activity might have led or might be leading to an impairment of park resources or values, he or she must investigate and determine if there is or will be an impairment. This investigation and determination may be made independent of, or as part of, a park planning process undertaken for other purposes. If it is determined that there is, or will be, an impairment, the decision-maker must take appropriate action, to the extent possible within the Service's authorities and available resources, to eliminate the impairment. The action must eliminate the impairment as soon as reasonably possible, taking into consideration the nature, duration, magnitude, and other characteristics of the impacts on park resources and values, as well as the requirements of the National Environmental Policy Act, National Historic Preservation Act, the Administrative Procedure Act, and other applicable laws.

(See Levels of Park Planning 2.3; Evaluating Impacts on Natural Resources 4.1.3; Planning 5.2; General 8.1; Visitor Use 8.2; General 9.1; Glossary definition of Professional Judgment. Also see Director's Order #12: Conservation Planning, Environmental Impact Analysis, and Decision-making)

1.4.7.1 Unacceptable Impacts

The impact threshold at which impairment occurs is not always readily apparent. Therefore, the Service will apply a standard that offers greater assurance that impairment will not occur. The Service will do this by avoiding impacts that it determines to be unacceptable. These are impacts that fall short of impairment, but are still not acceptable within a particular park's environment. Park managers must not allow uses that would cause unacceptable impacts; they must evaluate existing or proposed uses and determine whether the associated impacts on park resources and values are acceptable.

Virtually every form of human activity that takes place within a park has some degree of effect on park resources or values, but that does not mean the impact is unacceptable or that a particular use must be disallowed. Therefore, for the purposes of these policies, unacceptable impacts are impacts that, individually or cumulatively, would

- be inconsistent with a park's purposes or values, or
- impede the attainment of a park's desired future conditions for natural and cultural resources as identified through the park's planning process, or
- create an unsafe or unhealthful environment for visitors or employees, or
- diminish opportunities for current or future generations to enjoy, learn about, or be inspired by park resources or values, or
- unreasonably interfere with
  - park programs or activities, or
  - an appropriate use, or
  - the atmosphere of peace and tranquility, or the natural soundscape maintained in wilderness and natural, historic, or commemorative locations within the park.
  - NPS concessioner or contractor operations or services.

The following graphic illustrates the relationship between appropriate use, unacceptable impacts and impairment.

Managing for Resource Conservation

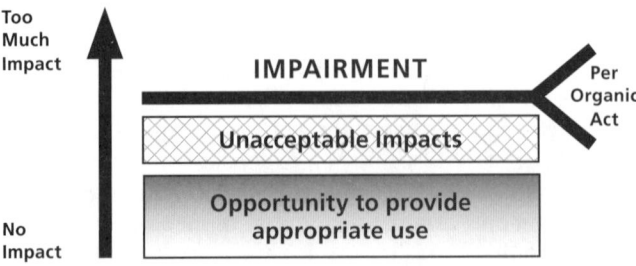

(See Appropriate Use of the Parks 1.5; General 8.1)

1.4.7.2 Improving Resource Conditions within the Parks

The Service will also strive to ensure that park resources and values are passed on to future generations in a condition that is as good as, or better than, the conditions that exist today. In particular, the Service will strive to restore the integrity of park resources that have been damaged or compromised in the past. Restoration activities will be guided by the natural and cultural resource-specific policies identified in chapters 4 and 5 of these *Management Policies*.

(See Planning for Natural Resource Management 4.1.1; Restoration of Natural Systems 4.1.5; Compensation for Injuries to Natural Resources 4.1.6; Restoration of Native Plant and Animal Species 4.4.2.2; Restoration (of Cultural Landscapes) 5.3.5.2.3; Restoration (of Historic and Prehistoric Structures) 5.3.5.4.3; Restoration (of Museum Collections) 5.3.5.5.2. Also see Director's Order #12 and Handbook.)

1.5 Appropriate Use of the Parks

The National Park Service embraces appropriate use of the parks because these uses are key to the enjoyment of the parks and the appreciation and inspiration derived from the resources. Park resources have profound effects on those who experience them through appropriate park uses. An "appropriate use" is a use that is suitable, proper, or fitting for a particular park, or to a particular location within a park. Not all uses are appropriate or allowable in units of the national park system, and what is appropriate may vary from one park to another and from one location to another within a park.

In its role as steward of park resources, the National Park Service must ensure that park uses that are allowed would not cause impairment of, or unacceptable impacts on, park resources and values. When proposed park uses and the protection of park resources and values come into conflict, the protection of resources and values must be predominant. A new form of park use may be allowed within a park only after a determination has been made in the professional judgment of the superintendent that it will not result in unacceptable impacts. The National Park Service will always consider allowing activities that are appropriate to the parks, although conditions may preclude certain activities or require that limitations be placed on them. Park superintendents must continually monitor all park uses to prevent unanticipated and unacceptable impacts. If unanticipated and unacceptable impacts emerge, the superintendent must engage in a thoughtful, deliberate process to further manage or constrain the use, or discontinue it.

Appropriate visitor enjoyment is often associated with the inspirational qualities of the parks. As a general matter, preferred forms of enjoyment are those that are uniquely suited to the superlative natural and cultural resources found in the parks and that (1) foster an understanding of and appreciation for park resources and values, or (2) promote enjoyment through a direct association with, interaction with, or relation to park resources.

These preferred forms of use contribute to the personal growth and well-being of visitors by taking advantage of the inherent educational value of parks. Equally important, many appropriate uses also contribute to the health and personal fitness of park visitors. These are the types of uses that the Service will actively promote, in accordance with the Organic Act. Other forms of park uses may be allowed within a park in accordance with the policies found in chapter 8.

(See Park Purposes and Legislatively Authorized Uses 1.4.3.1; Chapter 2, Park System Planning; Process for Determining New Appropriate Uses 8.1.2. Also see Director's Order #17: National Park Service Tourism; 36 CFR 1.5)

1.6 Cooperative Conservation Beyond Park Boundaries

Cooperative conservation beyond park boundaries is necessary as the National Park Service strives to fulfill its mandate to preserve the natural and cultural resources of parks unimpaired for future generations. Ecological processes cross park boundaries, and park boundaries may not incorporate all of the natural resources, cultural sites, and scenic vistas that relate to park resources or the quality of the visitor experience. Therefore, activities proposed for adjacent lands may significantly affect park programs, resources, and values. Conversely, NPS activities may have impacts outside park boundaries. Recognizing that parks are integral parts of larger regional environments, and to support its primary concern of protecting park resources and values, the Service will work cooperatively with others to

- ◆ anticipate, avoid, and resolve potential conflicts;
- ◆ protect park resources and values;
- ◆ provide for visitor enjoyment; and
- ◆ address mutual interests in the quality of life of community residents, including matters such as compatible economic development and resource and environmental protection.

Such local and regional cooperation may involve other federal agencies; tribal, state, and local governments; neighboring landowners; nongovernmental and private sector organizations; and all other concerned parties. The Service will do these things because cooperative conservation activities are a vital element in establishing relationships that will benefit the parks and in fostering decisions that are sustainable.

The Service will use all available tools to protect park resources and values from unacceptable impacts. The Service will also seek to advance opportunities for conservation partnerships. Superintendents will monitor land use proposals, changes to adjacent lands, and external activities for their potential impacts on park resources and values. It is appropriate for superintendents to engage constructively with the broader community in the same way that any good neighbor would. Superintendents will encourage compatible adjacent land uses and seek to avoid and mitigate potential adverse impacts on park resources and values by actively participating in the planning and regulatory processes of other federal agencies and tribal, state, and local governments having jurisdiction over property affecting, or affected by, the park. If a decision is made or is imminent that will result in unacceptable impacts on park resources, superintendents must take appropriate action, to the extent possible within the Service's authorities and available resources, to manage or constrain the use to minimize impacts. When engaged in these activities, superintendents should fully apply the principles of civic engagement to promote better understanding and communication by (1) documenting the park's concerns and sharing them with all who are interested, and (2) listening to the concerns of those who are affected by the park's actions.

The Service will also cooperate with federal, state, local, and tribal governments, as well as individuals and organizations, to advance the goal of creating seamless networks of parks. These partnership activities are intended to establish corridors that link together, both physically and with a common sense of purpose, open spaces such as those found in parks, other protected areas, and compatibly managed private lands. The Service's goals in participating in a park network will be to increase protection and enhancement of biodiversity and to create a greater array of educational and appropriate recreational opportunities. When participating in a park network, the Service will not relinquish any of its authority to manage areas under its jurisdiction, nor will it expect other partners to relinquish theirs.

(See Civic Engagement 1.7; Cooperative Planning 2.3.1.8; Cooperative Conservation 3.4; Chapter 4, Natural Resource Management. Also see Director's Order #17: National Park Service Tourism; Director's Order #75A: Civic Engagement and Public Involvement)

1.7 Civic Engagement

The Service will embrace civic engagement as a fundamental discipline and practice. The Service's commitment to civic engagement is founded on the central principle that preservation of the nation's heritage resources relies on continued collaborative relationships between the Service and American society. Civic engagement will be viewed as a commitment to building and sustaining relationships with neighbors and other communities of interest—both near and far. This will require that the Service communicate by both talking and listening. Through its practice of civic engagement, the Service will actively encourage a two-way, continuous, and dynamic conversation with the public.

Civic engagement will take place on many levels to strengthen understanding of the full meaning and contemporary relevance of park resources and values. The goal of civic engagement will be to reinforce the Service's and the public's commitment to the preservation and stewardship of cultural and natural heritage resources.

The Service will welcome people to enjoy their parks in appropriate, sustainable ways. This practice will promote civic responsibility by building long-term, collaborative relationships with a broad range of communities, which in turn will foster a widespread investment in stewardship of the nation's resources. Park and program managers will seek opportunities to work in partnership with all interested parties to jointly sponsor, develop, and promote public involvement activities and thereby improve mutual understanding, decisions, and work products. Through these efforts the Service will also learn from the communities it serves, including gateway communities.

A better understanding of the changing demographics of our nation is critical to the future of the National Park Service. The Park Service must actively seek to understand the values and connections our changing population has or does not have for natural and cultural heritage if it is to remain responsive and relevant to public needs and desires. This includes understanding why people do or do not visit—or care—about national parks. It is vital that the Service help those who do not visit to understand and support their national park system.

(See Relationship with American Indian Tribes 1.11. Also see Director's Order #75A: Civic Engagement and Public Involvement)

1.8 Environmental Leadership

Given the scope of its responsibility for the resources and values entrusted to its care, the Service has an obligation to demonstrate and work with others to promote leadership in environmental stewardship. The Park Service must set an example not only for visitors, other governmental agencies, the private sector, and the public at large, but also for a worldwide audience. Touching so many lives, the Service's management of the parks presents a unique opportunity to awaken the potential of each individual to play a proactive role in protecting the environment.

Environmental leadership will be demonstrated in all aspects of NPS activities, including policy development; park planning; all aspects of park operations; land protection; natural and cultural resource management; wilderness management; interpretation and education; facilities design, construction, and management; and commercial visitor services. In demonstrating environmental leadership, the Service will (1) fully comply with the letter and the spirit of the National Environmental Policy Act and the National Historic Preservation Act, and (2) continually assess the impact its operations have on natural and cultural resources so that it may identify areas for improvement. The Service will institute a Service-wide environmental auditing program that will evaluate a broad array of NPS activities to ensure that they meet the highest standards for environmental protection and compliance. The program will also screen for opportunities to implement sustainable practices and tangibly demonstrate the highest levels of environmental ethic.

(See Facility Planning and Design 9.1.1)

1.9 Management Excellence

Successful and sustained accomplishment of the Service's mission requires sound professional judgment and attentive employment of the most effective and efficient business principles and practices. Opportunities to protect resources and provide opportunities for public enjoyment will be severely limited unless park managers can demonstrate their responsibility to and accountability for concepts ranging from competent management of information technology and finances to the successful management and development of human resources.

(See Introduction—Compliance, Accountability and Enforceability)

1.9.1 Human Resources

The Service will pursue a human resources program that is comprehensive, that is based on competency, and that encompasses the entire workforce, including employees, volunteers, contractors, concession employees, interns, and partners.

1.9.1.1 Career Development, Training, and Management

Employee development helps organizations achieve greater success. The goals of the Park Service's employee development activities are to help employees strengthen their skills, knowledge, and experiences, as well as to promote broader employee engagement in the NPS mission. Employee development planning and strategies will be directly linked to core competencies and ensure the highest return on investment for the organization. Employees will also have opportunities to broaden their experiences and to progress in their careers through continuing education, undergraduate and graduate level courses, seminars, training, teaching, attendance at professional workshops and conferences, and other programs sponsored by scholarly institutions. In accordance with section 102 of the National Parks Omnibus Management Act of 1998 (16 USC 5912), the Park Service will implement a comprehensive training program for employees in all professional careers and a goal of ensuring that the workforce has the best, up-to-date knowledge, skills, and abilities with which to manage, interpret, and protect the resources of the national park system.

1.9.1.2 Succession Planning

The Service will develop the capacity to supply future leadership through a strategic and conscious effort to develop a diverse workforce with the potential to take on leadership positions. This process will include a collaborative effort among all possible interests (including pre-employment/educational institutions) to prepare employees to meet the needs for leadership talent over time. The Service will cultivate talent for the short term and the long term to ensure the availability of a sufficient number of people who reflect the diversity of America.

In accordance with section 103 of the National Parks Omnibus Management Act of 1998 (16 USC 5913), the Service will implement a management training and development plan whereby career, professional NPS employees from any appropriate academic field may obtain sufficient training, experience, and advancement opportunity to enable those qualified to move into park management positions, including the position of park superintendent. Similar efforts will be made for central office positions.

1.9.1.3 Workforce Planning

The Service will implement a process to

- evaluate the workforce;
- identify the competencies needed by the workforce in each of the career fields;
- evaluate present and future trends;
- develop strategies to address competency gaps;
- benchmark best practices; and
- develop a plan that will allow the Service to meet mission and strategic goals.

In concert with employee development and succession planning, workforce planning will ensure that all elements of the workforce are provided the orientation and training necessary to support the NPS mission.

1.9.1.4 Employee Safety and Health

The safety and health of employees, contractors, volunteers, and the public are core Service values. In making decisions on matters concerning employee safety and health, NPS managers must exercise good judgment and discretion and, above all, keep in mind that the safeguarding of human life must not be compromised. The Service must ensure that all employees are trained and informed on how to do their jobs safely, and that they have the necessary clothing, materials, and equipment to perform their duties with minimal personal risk.

(See Visitor Safety and Emergency Response 8.2.5)

1.9.1.5 Workforce Diversity

The Park Service will continue to seek ways to achieve its workforce diversity goals and to recognize workforce diversity as a sound business practice. Success in achieving workforce diversity will also enhance the Service's ability to more successfully connect with park visitors who represent America's diverse population. Continuing efforts will be made to increase public awareness of employment opportunities and to develop partnerships with diverse populations and organizations for the purpose of improving workforce diversity.

1.9.1.6 Volunteers in the Parks

Increasingly, American citizens who are not employed by the Service make important contributions by supplementing the efforts of the NPS workforce. The Service welcomes their efforts and will continue to use its authority under the Volunteers in the Parks Act of 1969 to

- protect park resources and values;
- improve its service to the public;
- foster stronger ties with the pubic; and
- provide opportunities for the public to learn about and experience the parks.

Pursuant to this statute, volunteers may be recruited without regard to civil service regulations; are covered for tort liability and work-injury compensation; and may be reimbursed for out-of-pocket expenses while participating in the program. However, volunteers cannot be used for law enforcement work or in policymaking processes, or to displace NPS employees. Volunteers may perform hazardous duties only if they possess the necessary skills to perform the duties assigned to them. Volunteers will be accepted without regard to race, creed, religion, age, sex, color, national origin, disability, or sexual orientation. NPS housing may be used for volunteers.

(See Volunteers in Parks 7.6.1. Also see Director's Order #7: Volunteers in Parks, and associated Reference Manual 7)

1.9.2 Managing Information

The future of individual parks and of the Service as an accountable organization depends heavily on (1) the availability, management, and dissemination of comprehensive information, and (2) the Service's success in the long-term preservation of, management of, and access to that information. NPS information resources exist in a variety of different media, including paper records, electronic documents, maps, databases, photographs, videos, and audio recordings. The Service will implement professional quality programs to preserve, manage, and integrate these resources and make them accessible. The Service will also use tools and technologies that will enhance

- information capture in permanent and durable forms;
- information management that is required by NPS policy and by legal and professional standards, including information security;
- management of electronic, textual, and audiovisual information resources, including still images, for continuous accessibility by NPS staff and the public;
- Internet and World Wide Web capabilities, while maintaining information security;
- geographic information systems (GIS);
- the understanding and management of the nation's natural and cultural resources; and
- the accessibility and availability of information to persons with disabilities.

1.9.2.1 Information Sharing

The Service is committed to the widest possible availability and sharing of knowledge and to fostering discussion about the national park system, America's natural and cultural heritage that is found in national parks, and the national experiences and values they represent. Most information shared with the public is presumed to be in the public domain, and therefore available to anyone who is interested. The only exceptions to information sharing are where disclosure could jeopardize specific park resources or donor agreements or violate legal or confidentiality requirements.

1.9.2.2 Proprietary Information

When producing or acquiring new works (such as images, graphic designs, logos, writing, Web sites, or other proprietary information) through acquisition by donation, contracting, partnerships, or other means, the Service will acquire the appropriate copyrights and any necessary releases whenever there is a current or anticipated need for unrestricted access to those works. The Service will respect the rights of owners of copyrights to control how their works are used and comply with fair use standards when information or works are not licensed for dissemination.

(Also see Director's Order #67: Copyright and Trademarks)

1.9.2.3 Information Confidentiality

Although it is the general NPS policy to share information widely, the Service also realizes that providing information about the location of park resources may sometimes place those resources at risk of harm, theft, or destruction. This can occur, for example, with regard to caves, archeological sites, tribal information, and rare plant and animal species. Some types of personnel, financial, and law enforcement matters are other examples of information that may be inappropriate for release to the public. Therefore, information will be withheld when the Service foresees that disclosure would be harmful to an interest protected by an exemption under the Freedom of Information Act (FOIA).

Information will also be withheld when the Park Service has entered into a written agreement (e.g., deed of gift, interview release, or similar written contract) to withhold data for a fixed period of time at the time of acquisition of the information. Such information will not be provided unless required by the Freedom of Information Act or other applicable law, a subpoena, a court order, or a federal audit.

NPS managers will use these exemptions sparingly, and only to the extent allowed by law. In general, if information is withheld from one requesting party, it must be withheld from anyone else who requests it, and if information is provided to one requesting party, it must be provided to anyone else who requests it. Procedures contained in Director's Order #66: FOIA and Protected Resource Information will be followed to document any decisions to release information or to withhold information from the public. Director's Order #66 also provides more detailed information regarding the four specific statutes and an executive order that exempt park resource information from FOIA disclosure.

(See Natural Resource Information 4.1.2; Studies and Collections 4.2; Caves 4.8.2.2; Research 5.1; Confidentiality 5.2.3; Access to Interpretive and Educational Opportunities 7.5.2. Also see Director's Orders #5: Paper and Electronic Communications; #19: Records Management; #84: Library Management; and #11C: Web Publishing. Also see Reference Manual 53, chapter 5)

1.9.3 Accessibility for Persons with Disabilities

All practicable efforts will be made to make NPS facilities, programs, services, employment, and meaningful work opportunities accessible and usable by all people, including those with disabilities. This policy reflects the commitment to provide access to the widest cross section of the public and ensure compliance with the Architectural Barriers Act of 1968, the Rehabilitation Act of 1973, the Equal Employment Opportunity Act of 1972, and the Americans with Disabilities Act of 1990. Specific guidance for implementing these laws is found in the Secretary of the Interior's regulations regarding enforcement of nondiscrimination on the basis of disability in Department of the Interior programs (43 CFR Part 17, Subpart E), and the General Services Administration's regulations adopting accessibility standards for the Architectural Barriers Act (41 CFR Part 102-76, Subpart C).

A primary principle of accessibility is that, to the highest degree practicable, people with disabilities should be able to participate in the same programs, activities, and employment opportunities available to everyone else. In choosing among methods of providing accessibility, higher priority will be given to methods that offer programs and activities in the most integrated setting appropriate. Special, separate, or alternative facilities, programs, or services will be provided only when existing ones cannot reasonably be made accessible. The determination of what is practicable will be made only after careful consultation with persons with disabilities or their representatives. Any decision that would result in less than equal opportunity is subject to the filing of an official disability rights complaint under the departmental regulations cited above.

(See Physical Access for Persons with Disabilities 5.3.2; Accessibility for Persons with Disabilities 8.2.4; Accessibility of Commercial Services 10.2.6.2. Also see Americans with Disabilities Act and Architectural Barriers Act Accessibility Standards)

1.9.4 Public Information and Media Relations

The Park Service will provide timely and accurate information to the public and news media in accordance with applicable laws, departmental policy, and director's orders. Park managers should identify appropriate opportunities to inform and educate the public about park resources and values and ways to enjoy them. Every effort should be made to provide early notification of changes in park management practices and conduct active civic engagement pursuant to Directors Order #75A. Park managers should keep the public informed of ongoing events in parks, especially as they may affect visitors and gateway communities. In some instances, certain information about individuals or events may need to be withheld for privacy, security, or other reasons, consistent with the Freedom of Information Act and the Privacy Act of 1974.

(Also see Director's Order #66: FOIA and Protected Resource Information)

1.9.5 Management Accountability

Managers are responsible for the quality and timeliness of program performance, increasing productivity, controlling costs, mitigating the adverse aspects of agency operations, and ensuring that programs are managed with integrity and in compliance with applicable law. Management accountability systems will be designed and implemented to add value and contribute to the efficiency and effectiveness of NPS programs.

The National Park Service will comply with OMB (Office of Management and Budget) Circular A-123, the Federal Managers' Financial Integrity Act of 1982 (31 USC 3512), and the Government Performance and Results Act of 1993 (31 USC 1115), which require that all federal agencies and individual managers take systematic and proactive measures to (1) develop and implement appropriate, cost-effective management controls for results-oriented management, (2) assess the adequacy of management controls in federal programs and operations, (3) identify needed improvements, (4) take corresponding corrective action, and (5) report annually on management controls.

The concept of management accountability will be applied to all strategies, plans, guidance, and procedures that govern programs and operations throughout the Park Service, including those at the park level, the program center level, and the Service-wide level. The Service will, through its organization, policies, and procedures, implement systems of controls to reasonably ensure that

- programs achieve their intended results;
- resources are used consistently with the NPS mission;
- programs and resources are managed to prevent waste, fraud, abuse, and mismanagement;
- laws and regulations are followed; and
- reliable and timely information is obtained, maintained, reported, and used for decision making.

(See Strategic Planning 2.3.3, and Director's Order #54: Management Accountability)

1.9.5.1 Financial Sustainability

The Park Service will strive to be an effective and efficient steward of appropriated and nonappropriated funds and services. These include revenues from recreation, concessions, and other fees, as well as financial and in-kind support from cooperating associations, friends' groups, other partnership entities, and volunteers. The Park Service will attempt to meet management goals consistently through strategic planning that anticipates budget requirements, changing conditions, and reasonably foreseeable trends and events.

The Service will continually implement best management practices to achieve financial sustainability, including

- analyzing and revising work processes to achieve greater efficiency;

- making full use of information technology;
- anticipating and addressing funding availability through accepted business practices;
- ensuring that the out-year budget implications of decision-making are carefully considered in planning and other processes;
- ensuring that both short- and long-term costs of facility development and operation are factored into the project formulation and selection process;
- using value-based decision-making processes such as value analysis, capital asset planning, benefit-cost analysis, life-cycle cost estimating, risk analysis, and total cost of ownership analysis;
- linking performance management elements to achieving and maintaining financial sustainability;
- embracing preventative maintenance and management that prevents the degradation of park resources and facilities, thereby avoiding costly restoration or rehabilitation efforts; and
- using best financial management practices to ensure transparent information and public accountability consistent with proven financial accounting standards.

The Service will continually seek improvement and innovation in the areas covered by the following subsections.

1.9.5.2 Facilities

The National Park Service will provide visitor and administrative facilities that are necessary, appropriate, and consistent with the conservation of park resources and values. Facilities will be harmonious with park resources, compatible with natural processes, esthetically pleasing, functional, energy- and water-efficient, cost-effective, universally designed, and as welcoming as possible to all segments of the population. Park facilities and operations of all sizes will demonstrate environmental leadership by incorporating sustainable practices to the maximum extent practicable in planning, design, siting, construction, and maintenance.

1.9.5.3 Budget Performance and Accountability Programs

The Park Service will also continue to improve the budget formulation and accounting and financial reporting processes, particularly related to park specifics and assets, including heritage assets, by making them more transparent. The goal of these efforts will be to ensure that

- funds are spent in support of a park's purpose or NPS mission;
- funds are spent in an efficient, transparent, and effective manner;
- a park's request for funding is credible; and
- there are adequate funds and staff to conserve and protect the resources for which parks are responsible and provide for the enjoyment of the same.

1.10 Partnerships

The Service recognizes the benefits of cooperative conservation (in accordance with Executive Order 13352, Facilitation of Cooperative Conservation), as well as the significant role partners play in achieving conservation goals and funding conservation initiatives on behalf of the national park system. The Service has had many successful partnerships with individuals; organizations; tribal, state, and local governments; and other federal agencies that have helped fulfill the NPS mission. Through these partnerships, the Service has received valuable assistance in the form of educational programs, visitor services, living history demonstrations, search-and-rescue operations, fund-raising campaigns, habitat restoration, scientific and scholarly research, ecosystem management, and a host of other activities. These partnerships, both formal and informal, have produced countless benefits for the Service and for the national park system.

Benefits often extend into the future, because many people who participate as partners connect more strongly with the parks and commit themselves to long-term stewardship. The Service will continue to welcome and actively seek partnership activities with individuals, organizations, and others who share the Service's commitment to protecting park resources and values and providing for their enjoyment. The Service will embrace partnership opportunities that will help accomplish the NPS mission provided that personnel and funding requirements do not make it impractical for the Service to participate and that the partnership activity would not (1) violate legal or ethical standards, (2) otherwise reflect adversely on the NPS mission and image, or (3) imply or indicate an unwillingness by the Service to perform an inherently governmental function.

In the spirit of partnership, the Service will also seek opportunities for cooperative management agreements with state or local agencies that will allow for more effective and efficient management of the parks, as authorized by section 802(a) of the National Parks Omnibus Management Act of 1998 (16 USC 1a-2(l)).

Whenever groups are created, controlled, or managed for the purpose of providing advice or recommendations to the Service, the Service will first consult with the Office of the Solicitor to determine whether the Federal Advisory Committee Act requires the chartering of an advisory committee. Consultation with the Office of the Solicitor will not be necessary when the Service meets with individuals, groups, or organizations simply to exchange views and information or to solicit individual advice on proposed actions. This act does not apply to intergovernmental meetings held exclusively between federal officials and elected officers of state, local and tribal governments (or their designated employees with authority to act on their behalf) acting in their official capacities, when (1) the meetings relate to intergovernmental responsibilities or administration, and (2) the purpose of the committee is solely to exchange views, information, or advice relating to the management or implementation of federal programs established pursuant to statute that explicitly or inherently share intergovernmental responsibilities or administration.

(See Public Involvement 2.3.1.5; Partnerships 4.1.4; Studies and Collections 4.2; Independent Research 5.1.2; Agreements 5.2.2; Interpretive and Educational Partnerships 7.6; Volunteers in Parks 7.6.1; Cooperating Associations 7.6.2; Enforcement Authority 8.3.4; Commercial Visitor Services Chapter 10. Also see Director's Orders #7: Volunteers in Parks;#17: National Park Service Tourism; #20: Agreements, #21: Donations and Fundraising; #27: Challenge Cost-share Program; #32: Cooperating Associations; #75A: Civic Engagement and Public Involvement; NPS Guide to the Federal Advisory Committee Act; Executive Order 13352 (Facilitation of Cooperative Conservation)

1.11 Relationship with American Indian Tribes

The National Park Service has a unique relationship with American Indian tribes, which is founded in law and strengthened by a shared commitment to stewardship of the land and resources. The Service will honor its legal responsibilities to American Indian tribes as required by the Constitution of the United States, treaties, statutes, and court decisions. For the purposes of these policies, "American Indian tribe" means any band, nation, or other organized group or community of Indians, including any Alaska Native Village, which is recognized as eligible for the special programs and services provided by the United States to Indians because of their status as Indians.

The formal legal rationale for the relationship between the National Park Service and tribes is augmented by the historical, cultural, and spiritual relationships that American Indian tribes have with park lands and resources. As the ancestral homelands of many American Indian tribes, parks protect resources, sites, and vistas that are highly significant for the tribes. Therefore, the Service will pursue an open, collaborative relationship with American Indian tribes to help tribes maintain their cultural and spiritual practices and enhance the Park Service's understanding of the history and significance of sites and resources in the parks. Within the constraints of legal authority and its duty to protect park resources, the Service will work with tribal governments to provide access to park resources and places that are essential for the continuation of traditional American Indian cultural or religious practices.

1.11.1 Government-to-Government Relationship

In accordance with the Presidential Memorandum of April 29, 1994, and Executive Order 13175 (Consultation and Coordination with Indian Tribal Governments), the Service will maintain a government-to-government relationship with federally recognized tribal governments. This means that NPS officials will work directly with appropriate tribal government officials whenever plans or activities may directly or indirectly affect tribal interests, practices, and/or traditional use areas such as sacred sites.

1.11.2 Consultation

Consultations, whether initiated by a tribe or the Park Service, will be respectful of tribal sovereignty. The Federal Advisory Committee Act does not apply to consultation meetings held exclusively between federal officials and elected officers of tribal governments or their designees.

Tribal needs for privacy and confidentiality of certain kinds of information will be respected. Such information will be deemed confidential when authorized by law, regulation, or policy. Before beginning government-to-government consultations, park managers will consider what information is necessary to record. Culturally sensitive information will be collected and recorded only to the extent necessary to support sound management decisions and only in consultation with tribal representatives.

Mutually acceptable consultation protocols to guide government-to-government relationships will be developed at the park and program levels with assistance from regional and support offices as needed. The protocols will be developed with an understanding of special circumstances present at individual parks. These protocols and the actual consultation itself will be informed by national, regional, and park-based subject matter experts.

NPS managers will be open and candid with tribal governments during consultations so that the affected tribes may fully evaluate the potential impact of the proposal and the Service may fully consider tribal views in its decision-making processes. This means that government-to-government consultation should begin at the earliest possible stages of planning.

(See Consultation 5.2.1; Ethnographic Resources 5.3.5.3. Also see Director's Order #66: FOIA and Protected Resource Information)

1.11.3 Trust Resources

Activities carried out on park lands may sometimes affect tribal trust resources. Trust resources are those natural resources reserved by or for Indian tribes through treaties, statutes, judicial decisions, and executive orders, which are protected by a fiduciary obligation on the part of the United States. In accordance with the government-to-government relationship and mutually established protocols, the Service will interact directly with tribal governments regarding the potential impacts of proposed NPS activities on Indian tribes and trust resources.

In considering a proposed program, project, or action, the Service will ensure that effects on trust resources are explicitly identified and evaluated in consultation with potentially concerned tribes and that they are addressed in planning, decision, and operational documents. With regard to activities that may impact Indian trust resources or tribal health and safety, the Service will consult with the Bureau of Indian Affairs, the Office of the Solicitor, and other offices and agencies, as appropriate.

(Also see Secretarial Order 3206, June 5, 1997)

1.12 Native Hawaiians, Pacific Islanders, and Caribbean Islanders

The National Park Service administers parks in Hawaii, Guam, the Commonwealth of the Northern Mariana Islands, American Samoa, Puerto Rico, and the Virgin Islands. The Service will maintain open, collaborative relationships with native peoples for whom these islands are their ancestral homes. The Service will also meet any responsibilities that may have been defined in the enabling legislation of these island parks and to Native Hawaiians in the administration of the Native American Graves Protection and Repatriation Act and the National Historic Preservation Act.

1.13 An Enduring Message

The need for *Management Policies* in the National Park Service was first articulated by Secretary of the Interior Franklin K. Lane in a letter to the first Director of the National Park Service, Stephen T. Mather, on May 13, 1918.

Secretary Lane stated that administrative policy should adhere to three broad principles based on the 1916 Organic Act:

> First, that the national parks must be maintained in absolutely unimpaired form for the use of future generations as well as those of our own time; second, that they are set apart for the use, observation, health, and pleasure of the people; and third, that the national interest must dictate all decisions affecting public or private enterprise in the parks.

Today's national parks have become important to our nation in more ways than Secretary Lane could possibly have imagined. Parks are a true reflection of our nation's collective history, heritage, and ideals. They can be models of healthy, natural, sustainable ecosystems. To remain relevant now and into the future, parks must be welcoming in order that visitors may understand and appreciate these special places that have been set aside for their enjoyment. As America's story continues to evolve, new park units will be added in the future, and they will carry equally compelling reasons for their inclusion in the national park system.

Secretary Lane's guiding principles remain fundamentally valid, and they serve as a useful reminder of the need for a sustained commitment to park resource protection so that they are left unimpaired for the enjoyment of future generations. The Service's commitment to protecting the national parks and ensuring public enjoyment for present and future generations is embodied in this 2006 edition of *Management Policies*.

Park System Planning

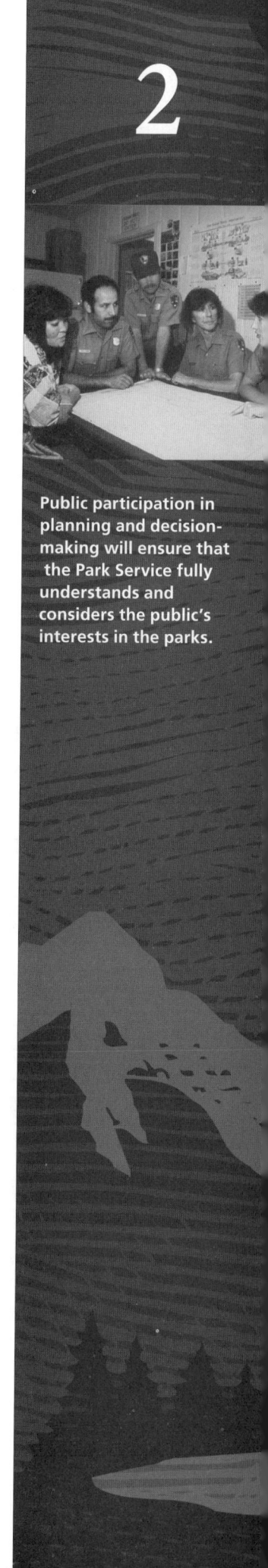

Public participation in planning and decision-making will ensure that the Park Service fully understands and considers the public's interests in the parks.

Park planning helps define the set of resource conditions, visitor experiences, and management actions that, taken as a whole, will best achieve the mandate to preserve resources unimpaired for the enjoyment of present and future generations. NPS planning processes will flow from broad-scale general management planning through progressively more specific strategic planning, implementation planning, and annual performance planning and reporting, all of which will be grounded in foundation statements.

2.1 General Principles

2.1.1 Decision-making

The National Park Service will use planning to bring logic, analysis, public involvement, and accountability into the decision-making process. Park planning and decision-making will be conducted as a continuous, dynamic cycle, from broad visions shared with the public to individual, annual work assignments and evaluations. Each park will be able to demonstrate to decision-makers, staff, and the public how decisions relate to one another in terms of a comprehensive, logical, and trackable rationale.

2.1.2 Scientific, Technical, and Scholarly Analysis

Decision-makers and planners will use the best available scientific and technical information and scholarly analysis to identify appropriate management actions for protection and use of park resources. Analysis will be interdisciplinary and tiered. Tiering is a staged approach to environmental analysis that addresses broad programs and issues in initial or systems-level analyses. Site-specific proposals and impacts are analyzed in subsequent studies. The tiered process supports decision-making on issues that are ripe for decision and provides a means to sustain those decisions. The focus of analysis starts with the park as a whole (including its global, national, and regional contexts) and then moves to site-specific details. At key points of planning and decision-making, the Park Service will identify reasonable alternatives and analyze and compare their differences with respect to

- consistency with the park's purpose,
- the quality of visitor experiences,
- the impacts on park resources,
- short- and long-term costs, and
- environmental consequences that may extend beyond park boundaries.

2.1.3 Public Participation

Public participation in planning and decision-making will ensure that the Service fully understands and considers the public's interests in the parks, which are part of the public's national heritage, cultural traditions, and community surroundings. The Service will actively seek out and consult with existing and potential visitors, neighbors, American Indians, other people with traditional cultural ties to park lands, scientists and scholars, concessioners, cooperating associations, gateway communities, other partners, and government agencies. The Service will work cooperatively with others to improve the condition of parks; to enhance public service; and to integrate parks into sustainable ecological, cultural, and socioeconomic systems.

(See Cooperative Conservation Beyond Park Boundaries 1.6; Civic Engagement 1.7; Public Involvement 2.3.1.5; Consultation 5.2.1. Also see Director's Order #75A: Civic Engagement and Public Involvement)

2.1.4 Goal Orientation

Managers will be held accountable for identifying and accomplishing measurable long-term goals and annual goals that are incremental steps to carrying out the park mission. Such planning is a critical and essential part of the NPS performance management system that is designed to improve the Park Service's performance and results. Park staff will monitor resource conditions and visitor experiences and plan, track, and report performance. If goals are not being met, managers will seek to understand why and take appropriate action. The goals will be periodically reassessed, taking into account new knowledge or previously unforeseen circumstances, and then the planning cycle will be reinitiated at the appropriate point.

(See Park Management 1.4)

2.2 Major Elements of Park Planning and Decision-making

A documented, comprehensive, logical, trackable rationale for decisions will be created through several levels of planning that are complementary and become increasingly detailed. The process begins with determining why the park was established and what resource conditions and visitor experiences should exist there; the process will become increasingly focused on how resource conditions and visitor experiences should be achieved.

The following planning elements are part of an interrelated framework that will inform NPS decision-making:

- **Foundation Statement** — The planning process begins with the development of a foundation statement that is based on the park's enabling legislation or presidential proclamation and that documents the park purpose, significance, fundamental resources and values and primary interpretive themes. It also includes any relevant laws and executive orders that apply to the national park system or to the individual park unit. The foundation statement is generally developed (or reviewed and expanded or revised, if appropriate) early as part of the public and agency scoping and data collection for the general management plan (GMP). Once a park has developed a complete foundation statement, it should remain relatively stable from one GMP cycle to the next, although new scientific and scholarly information may require expansion and revision to reflect the most current knowledge about what is most important about the park. General management planning is the most appropriate context for developing or reviewing a foundation statement because of the comprehensive public involvement and NEPA analysis that occurs during general management planning. The foundation statement may be vetted within the agency and with the public, then formally adopted as part of the final general management plan, or may be produced as a stand-alone foundation document for the park unit.

- **General Management Plan** — This is a broad umbrella document that sets the long-term goals for the park based on the foundation statement. The general management plan (1) clearly defines the desired natural and cultural resource conditions to be achieved and maintained over time; (2) clearly defines the necessary conditions for visitors to understand, enjoy, and appreciate the park's significant resources, and (3) identifies the kinds and levels of management activities, visitor use, and development that are appropriate for maintaining the desired conditions; and (4) identifies indicators and standards for maintaining the desired conditions. For wild and scenic rivers and national trails, the analogous documents are a comprehensive river management plan and comprehensive management plan, respectively. Each of these plans has requirements very similar to a general management plan, so units usually refer to these plans as GMPs. Additional requirements for river and trail studies are covered in the Wild and Scenic Rivers Act and the National Trails System Act.

- **Program Management Plans** — These more detailed documents follow the general management plan and provide program-specific information on strategies to achieve and maintain the desired resource conditions and visitor experiences, including identification of appropriate visitor use where applicable (for example, resource stewardship strategy and comprehensive interpretation plan).

- **Strategic Plans** — These plans provide 1- to 5-year direction and objective, measurable, long-term goals. The long-term goals will define the resource conditions and visitor experiences to be achieved in the near future, for which the superintendent will be held accountable. Results on progress towards these goals will be reported annually. These goals are based on the park's foundation statement; an assessment of the park's natural and cultural resources; park visitors' experiences; and the park's performance capability given available personnel, funding, and external factors.

- **Implementation Plans** — These plans provide project-specific details needed to implement an action in an area of a park and explain how the action(s) helps achieve long-term goals.

- **Annual Performance Plans** —Annual goals and an annual work plan that will guide park efforts for a fiscal year are in annual performance plans.

- **Annual Performance Reports** — These reports contain an accounting of annual results in relation to annual goals.

Park managers and regional directors are responsible for ensuring that planning is properly conducted within this planning framework and making management decisions that are supported by public involvement, the best available information, and analysis. However, many parks may initially lack one or more of these planning elements. In the interim, management will be guided by the park's foundation statement, strategic plan, and other current approved plans. No major new development or other major commitment of park land or natural or cultural resources will be authorized without an approved general management plan.

(See Visitor Use 8.2)

2.3 Levels of Park Planning

The order of plan development will generally flow from broad general management plans to progressively more specific implementation plans.

When determining a plan's scope, it will be important to distinguish which issues can most appropriately be addressed by general management planning, and which can be most appropriately addressed by more detailed strategic or implementation planning. Each level of planning has a distinct function, and all levels are designed to interrelate with a minimum of duplication and confusion. At each level, plans will be written to make the links and relationships among the planning levels apparent to readers.

Environmental analysis of alternatives and public involvement required under section 102(2)(C) of the National Environmental Policy Act (NEPA) (42 USC 4332(2)(C)) will be conducted at any level of planning in which the decisions to be made constitute a major federal action significantly affecting the quality of the human environment. Normally, NEPA analysis and public participation will be done at the general management planning level, when the overall direction for the park's future is decided, and again at the implementation planning level before funding and resources are committed to carry out specific actions (see 2.3.1 and 2.3.4, below). In keeping with the Council on Environmental Quality guidelines for NEPA compliance, environmental analysis for more specific programs or actions will follow, or flow from, earlier NEPA documents for the broader general management plan.

(See Civic Engagement 1.7. Also see Director's Orders #2: Park Planning, and #12: Conservation Planning, Environmental Impact Analysis, and Decision-making)

2.3.1 General Management Planning

The Park Service will maintain a general management plan for each unit of the national park system. The purpose of each general management plan, which will begin with the development of a foundation statement for the park unit, will be to ensure that the park has a clearly defined direction for resource preservation and visitor use. This basic foundation for decision-making will be developed by an interdisciplinary team, in consultation with relevant NPS offices, other federal and state agencies, local and tribal governments, other interested parties, and the general public. The management plans will be based on full and proper use of scientific and scholarly information related to existing and potential resource conditions, visitor experiences, environmental impacts, and relative costs of alternative courses of action.

The approved plan will create a realistic vision for the future, setting a direction for the park that takes into consideration the environmental and financial impact of proposed facilities and programs and ensures that the final plan is achievable and sustainable. The plan will take the long view, which may project many years into the future, when dealing with the time frames of natural and cultural processes. The first phase of general management planning will be the development of the foundation statement. The plan will consider the park in its full ecological, scenic, and cultural contexts as a unit of the national park system and as part of a surrounding region. The general management plan will also establish a common management direction for all park divisions and districts. This integration will help avoid inadvertently creating new problems in one area while attempting to solve problems in another.

(See Decision-making Requirements to Identify and Avoid Impairments 1.4.7; Visitor Use 8.2)

2.3.1.1 Statutory Requirements

General management plans will meet all statutory requirements contained in 16 USC 1a-7(b) and will include

- the types of management actions required for the preservation of park resources;
- the types and general intensities of development (including visitor circulation and transportation patterns, systems, and modes) associated with public enjoyment and use of the area, including general locations, timing of implementation, and anticipated costs;
- visitor carrying capacities and implementation commitments for all areas of the park; and
- potential modifications to the external boundaries of the park—if any—and the reasons for the proposed changes.

For NPS-administered components of the National Wild and Scenic Rivers System and the National Trails System, comprehensive management plans will meet all the statutory requirements of 16 USC 1271-1287 or 16 USC 1244.

(See Visitor Carrying Capacity 8.2.1)

2.3.1.2 Management Zoning

Each park's approved general management plan will include a map that delineates management zones or districts that correspond to a description of the desired resource and visitor experience conditions for each area of the park. Management zoning will outline the criteria for (or describe the kind of) appropriate uses and facilities necessary to support these desired conditions. For example, highly sensitive natural areas might tolerate little, if any, visitor use, while other areas might accommodate much higher levels of use. Even in historic structures, one floor might be most appropriate for exhibits, while another could accommodate offices or administrative uses. Some desired conditions may apply parkwide, but the delineation of management zones will illustrate where there are differences in intended resource conditions, visitor experiences, and management activities.

2.3.1.3 Planning Team

Interdisciplinary teams, including park managers and technical experts, will prepare general management plans. Planning teams will work with the park superintendent and regional directors and consult with other park staff, NPS leadership, other agencies with jurisdiction by virtue of law or expertise, other knowledgeable persons, and the public concerning future management of park resources. The superintendent will be involved with all phases of the plan's development. The superintendent and regional director have ultimate responsibility for the contents of the plan, ensuring that there is consistency in direction and decisions between parks with similar resources and values. The regional director is the official responsible for approving general management plans.

2.3.1.4 Science and Scholarship

Decisions documented in general management plans and other planning products, including environmental analyses and documentation, will be based on current scientific and scholarly understanding of park ecosystems and cultural contexts and the socioeconomic environment both internal and external to the park. The collection and analysis of information about park resources will be a continuous process that will help ensure that decisions are consistent with park purposes.

(See Decision-making Requirements to Avoid Impairments 1.4.7; Planning for Natural Resource Management 4.1.1; Planning 5.2)

2.3.1.5 Public Involvement

Members of the public—including existing and potential visitors, park neighbors, American Indians, other people with traditional cultural ties to lands within the park, concessioners, cooperating associations, other partners, scientists and scholars, and other government agencies—will be encouraged to participate during the preparation of a general management plan and the associated environmental analysis. Public involvement strategies, practices, and activities will be developed and conducted within the framework of civic engagement. (Whereas civic engagement is the philosophy of welcoming people into the parks and building relationships around a shared stewardship mission, public involvement—also called public participation—is the specific, active involvement of the public in NPS planning and other decision-making processes.) Public involvement will meet NEPA and other federal requirements for

- identifying the scope of issues,
- developing the range of alternatives considered in planning,
- reviewing the analysis of potential impacts, and
- disclosing the rationale for decisions about the park's future.

The Park Service will use the public involvement process to

- share information about legal and policy mandates, the planning process, issues, and proposed management directions,
- learn about the values placed by other people and groups on the same resources and visitor experiences, and

- build support for implementing the plan among local interests, visitors, Congress, and others at the regional and national levels.

Whenever groups are created, controlled, or managed for the purpose of providing advice or recommendations to the Service, the Service will first consult with the Office of the Solicitor to determine whether the Federal Advisory Committee Act requires the chartering of an advisory committee. Consultation with the Office of the Solicitor will not be necessary when the Service meets with individuals, groups, or organizations simply to exchange views and information, or to solicit individual advice on proposed actions. This act does not apply to intergovernmental meetings held exclusively between federal officials and elected officers of state, local and tribal governments (or their designated employees with authority to act on their behalf) acting in their official capacities, when the meetings relate to intergovernmental responsibilities or administration.

(See Civic Engagement 1.7; Consultation 5.2.1. Also see NPS Guide to the Federal Advisory Committee Act. Also see Director's Order #75A: Civic Engagement and Public Involvement)

2.3.1.6 Alternative Futures

Alternative futures for the park will be explored and assessed during general management planning and environmental analysis. Within the broad parameters of the park mission and mission goals, various approaches to park resource preservation, use, and development may be possible, some of which may represent competing demands for the same resource base. The general management plan will be the principal tool for resolving such issues. The range of alternatives will examine different combinations of management zoning, within the limits of laws, regulations, and policies governing national parks.

2.3.1.7 Environmental Analysis

The analysis of alternatives will meet the program standards for NPS implementation of the National Environmental Policy Act and related legislation, including the National Historic Preservation Act. In most cases, an environmental impact statement (EIS) will be prepared for general management plans. In a few cases, the regional director, in consultation with the NPS Environmental Quality Division, through the Associate Director for Natural Resource Stewardship and Science, may approve an exception to this general rule if

- completion of scoping demonstrates that there is no public controversy concerning potential environmental effects, and
- the initial analysis of alternatives clearly indicates there is no potential for significant impact by any alternative.

Where the National Environmental Policy Act and sections 106 and 110 of the National Historic Preservation Act (16 USC 470f and 470h-2, respectively) both apply, NEPA procedures will be used to inform the public about undertakings having the potential to affect properties listed on, or eligible for listing on, the National Register of Historic Places, consistent with the Advisory Council on Historic Preservation's regulatory provisions governing coordination with the National Environmental Policy Act and the NPS nationwide programmatic agreement on section 106 compliance (36 CFR Part 800). The tiered approach to environmental analysis will be used as often as possible, in accordance with 40 CFR 1502.20.

(See Evaluating Environmental Impacts 4.1.3; Planning 5.2. Also see Director's Order #12: Conservation Planning, Environmental Impact Analysis, and Decision-making)

2.3.1.8 Cooperative Planning

General management planning will be conducted as part of cooperative regional planning and ecosystem planning whenever possible. NPS participation in cooperative regional planning will be undertaken with the hope of better coordinating and focusing the independent efforts of multiple parties. NPS participation in such planning efforts will acknowledge the rights and interests of other landowners. While being consistent with NPS *Management Policies* and park goals, plans will identify and consider potential effects outside and inside park boundaries, and plans will identify ways to enhance beneficial effects and mitigate adverse effects.

2.3.1.9 Wild and Scenic Rivers

Potential national wild and scenic rivers will be considered in planning for the use and development of a park's water and related land resources. The Park Service will compile a complete listing of all rivers and river segments in the national park system that it considers eligible for the National Wild and Scenic Rivers System. General management plans and other plans potentially affecting river resources will propose no actions that could adversely affect the values that qualify a river for the National Wild and Scenic Rivers System. After a determination of eligibility is made, a decision concerning whether or not to seek legislation to designate a river or river segment may be made only through a general management plan, an amendment to a general management plan, or the legislative review process.

2.3.1.10 Wilderness

The Wilderness Act directs agencies responsible for managing wilderness to study wilderness resources and values. The Park Service will develop wilderness studies and plans as part of the comprehensive planning framework for each park. Managers are encouraged to incorporate these studies and plans within general management plans when possible. To preserve Congress's prerogative to designate wilderness, general management plans and other plans potentially affecting eligible wilderness resources will propose no actions that could adversely affect the wilderness characteristics and values that make them eligible for consideration for inclusion in the National Wilderness Preservation System.

Lands and waters found to possess the characteristics and values of wilderness, as defined in the Wilderness Act, can be studied to develop a recommendation to Congress for wilderness designation in a general management plan/wilderness study. Where designated wilderness exists, park mangers have a responsibility to develop and maintain a wilderness management plan or equivalent planning document to guide the preservation, management, and use of these resources. A comprehensive management plan for wilderness is appropriately done in tandem with a general management plan, and wilderness should be taken into consideration in subsequent program management and implementation plans.

When wilderness eligibility and suitability are evaluated as a part of the GMP process, a determination of eligibility or suitability will not necessarily mean that the Service will seek designation. After the determination is made, a decision concerning whether to seek legislation to designate wilderness may be made only through a general management plan, an amendment to a general management plan, or the legislative review process.

(See Wilderness Review Process 6.2)

2.3.1.11 Alaska Park Units

General management plans for park system units in Alaska that were established or expanded by the Alaska National Interest Lands Conservation Act will address the provisions for conservation and management planning specified in section 1301 of that act (16 USC 3191).

2.3.1.12 Periodic Review of General Management Plans

As necessary, general management plans will be reviewed and amended or revised, or a new plan will be prepared, to keep them current. GMP reviews may be needed every 10 to 15 years, but may be needed sooner if conditions change significantly. If conditions remain substantially unchanged, a longer period between reviews would be acceptable. Even in parks with strong traditions and established patterns of use and development, managers will be responsible for assessing whether resources are threatened with impairment, the visitor experience has been degraded, or the park's built environment is difficult to sustain. Periodically reassessing the general management plan will give everyone with a major stake in the park an opportunity to revalidate the park's role in the nation and in the region and reevaluate whether the kinds of resource conditions and visitor experiences being pursued are the best possible mix for the future. An approved management plan may be amended or revised, rather than a new plan prepared, if conditions and management prescriptions governing most of the area covered by the plan remain essentially unchanged from those present when the plan was originally approved. Amendments or revisions to a general management plan will be accompanied by a supplemental environmental impact statement or other suitable NEPA analysis and public involvement.

(See Chapter 1: The Foundation; Chapter 3: Land Protection; Chapter 4: Natural Resource Management; Chapter 5: Cultural Resource Management; Chapter 6: Wilderness Preservation and Management; Chapter 8: Use of the Parks; Chapter 9: Park Facilities; Chapter 10: Commercial Visitor Services. Also see Director's Orders #2: Park Planning; and #12: Conservation Planning, Environmental Impact Analysis, and Decision-making)

2.3.2 Program Management Planning

Program management planning for a park provides a bridge between the broad direction provided in the general management plan and specific actions taken to achieve goals. These plans provide a comprehensive approach for a single park program area across most or all of the park. Program management planning may include special emphasis plans, such as a park resource stewardship strategy, a comprehensive interpretive plan, a land protection plan, a visitor use plan, a fire management plan, an asset management plan, or a management stewardship plan. Integrated, interdisciplinary approaches to program planning are encouraged. Program management plans will provide comprehensive recommendations about specific actions needed to achieve and maintain the desired resource conditions and visitor experiences.

2.3.3 Strategic Planning

The Service is committed to performance management and accountability. Managers are responsible for the quality and timeliness of program performance, increasing productivity, controlling costs, mitigating the adverse aspects of agency operations, and ensuring that programs are managed with integrity and in compliance with applicable laws. Strategic planning will be conducted for the National Park Service as a whole, and every park, program, and central office will be covered by a strategic plan. Strategic plans will address both Service-wide and local outcomes. Park-related strategic plans will be recommended by the superintendent, approved by the regional director, and consistent with the department's overall strategic plan. Strategic plans will contain

- mission statement and purpose from the foundation document
- long-term performance goals (with performance targets)
- a short description of the strategies chosen to accomplish the goals
- a description of how the annual goals will relate to the long-term goals
- a description of the analysis used to establish or revise goals
- a section that identifies the civic engagement strategy used to involve stakeholders and communities in the development of the strategic plan
- an identification of the key external factors that could significantly affect achievement of the goals
- a list of those who developed the plan

Information in park strategic plans is used to compile Service-wide achievements; therefore, these plans must contain similar information.

(See Management Accountability 1.9.5)

2.3.3.1 Relationship between the Strategic Plan and the General Management Plan

The park's strategic plan will be consistent with the Department of the Interior's strategic plan and the park's general management plan, and it will build from the foundation statement. Parks that lack a current general management plan will work from their existing plans or an updated foundation document. A strategic plan will focus on a shorter time frame than a general management plan, target measurable results; and not require the comprehensive resource analysis, consultation, and compliance required for a general management plan.

Should a park decide, through its strategic planning process, that a major shift in direction or emphasis is needed, the strategic plan will identify the need for a new general management plan or a GMP amendment. Strategic plans may also identify the need for more detailed program management or implementation plans.

2.3.4 Implementation Planning

Implementation planning will focus on how to implement activities and projects needed to achieve the desired conditions identified in the general management plan, strategic plan, and program management planning documents. Implementation plans may deal with complex, technical, and sometimes controversial issues that often require a level of detail and thorough analysis beyond that appropriate for other planning documents.

Implementation plans may concentrate on individual projects or components of the general management plan, and they may specify the techniques, disciplines, equipment, infrastructure, schedule, and funding necessary to accomplish outcomes.

Implementation plan details may vary widely and may direct a finite project (such as reintroducing an extirpated species or developing a trail) or a continuous activity (such as maintaining a historic structure). Examples of implementation plan details include management plans for specific species and habitats, site designs, off-road-vehicle management plans, and interpretive media plans. Details will generally be deferred until the activity or project under consideration has attained sufficient priority to indicate that action will be taken within the next two to five years and will be included in an annual work plan. This will help ensure that decisions about how to best achieve a certain goal are relevant, timely, and based on current data. As a means for providing flexibility in the face of changing natural conditions, park managers are encouraged to use an adaptive management approach when appropriate (see glossary for definition of adaptive management).

Technical specialty teams under the direction of the program leader in the park (usually a division chief) or in the regional office will develop implementation plans, and the plans will be approved by the superintendent (or at a higher level when appropriate).

Development of an implementation plan may overlap other planning efforts if this is appropriate for the purposes of planning efficiency or public involvement. However, the decisions made for the general management plan will precede—and direct—more detailed decisions regarding projects and activities. Major new development or rehabilitation and major actions or commitments aimed at changing resource conditions or visitor use in a park must be consistent with an approved general management plan.

2.3.4.1 Environmental Analysis

Many actions taken by the National Park Service, unless categorically excluded from further NEPA analysis, require public involvement and analysis of alternatives. They also require compliance with the National Historic Preservation Act and related legislation. Although general management planning addresses key environmental quality and cultural resource issues at the programmatic level over the long term, resolution of resource issues must continue during implementation planning. This will generally be accomplished through the appropriate NEPA and NHPA section 106 compliance processes and the application of the tiered approach to environmental analysis.

(See Park Management 1.4; Chapter 3: Land Protection; Chapter 4: Natural Resource Management; Chapter 5: Cultural Resource Management; Chapter 6: Wilderness Preservation and Management; Chapter 8: Use of the Parks; Chapter 9: Park Facilities; Chapter 10: Commercial Visitor Services. Also see Director's Orders #2: Park Planning; Director's Order #12: Conservation Planning, Environmental Impact Analysis, and Decision-making (and the related Environmental Screening Form); Executive Order 12898 (Federal Actions to Address Environmental Justice in Minority Populations and Low Income Populations))

2.3.5 Park Annual Performance Planning and Reporting

Each park will prepare annual performance plans (articulating annual goals for each fiscal year) and annual performance reports (describing the progress made in meeting the annual goals). The development of the annual performance plan and report will be synchronized with NPS budget development.

Land Protection

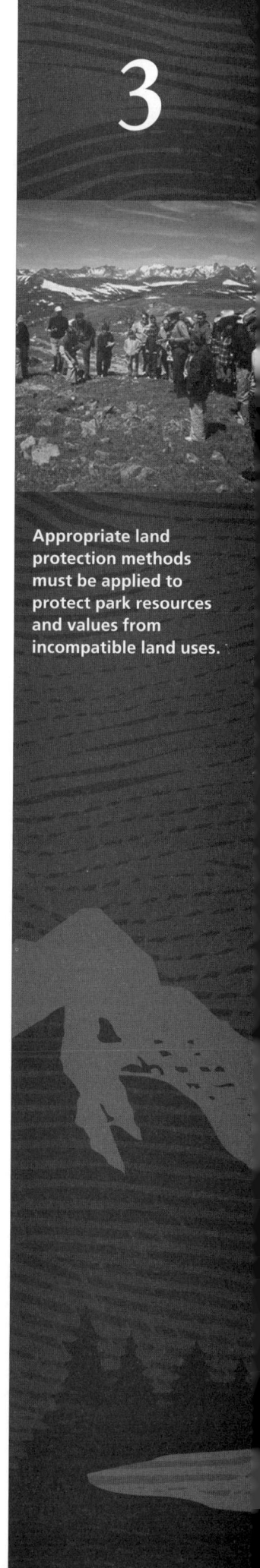

The National Park Service will use all available authorities to protect lands and resources within units of the national park system, and the Park Service will seek to acquire nonfederal lands and interests in land that have been identified for acquisition as promptly as possible. For lands not in federal ownership, both those that have been identified for acquisition and other nonfederally owned lands within a park unit's authorized boundaries, the Service will cooperate with federal agencies; tribal, state, and local governments; nonprofit organizations; and property owners to provide appropriate protection measures. Cooperation with these entities will also be pursued, and other available land protection tools will be employed when threats to resources originate outside boundaries.

Appropriate land protection methods must be applied to protect park resources and values from incompatible land uses.

3.1 General

The National Park Service is required by the 1916 Organic Act to protect and preserve unimpaired the resources and values of the national park system while providing for public use and enjoyment. A number of park units have nonfederally owned lands within their authorized boundaries. When nonfederal lands exist within park boundaries, acquisition of those lands and/or interests in those lands may be the best way to protect and manage natural and cultural resources or provide for visitor enjoyment. When acquisition is necessary and appropriate, the Park Service will acquire those lands and/or interests as promptly as possible, consistent with departmental land transaction and appraisal policies. Practical, cost-effective alternatives will be considered and pursued by the Service to advance protection and management goals.

The boundaries of most park units are not based strictly on ecological processes or other resource protection principles, and park units are increasingly subject to impacts from external sources. Examples include air pollution, water pollution, and the loss of scenic vistas, natural quiet, and wildlife habitat. To fulfill NPS protection responsibilities, strategies and actions beyond park boundaries may be employed. External threats may be addressed by using available tools—such as gateway community planning and partnership arrangements; NPS educational programs; and participation in the planning processes of federal agencies and tribal, state, and local governments. Strong fulfillment of Service responsibilities is required by the National Environmental Policy Act, the National Historic Preservation Act, and other applicable laws to minimize impacts on park resources and values.

3.2 Land Protection Methods

The Park Service may employ a variety of different methods, as appropriate, for protecting park resources. These methods will be considered in the land protection planning process for each unit. Examples include

- acquisition of fee-simple real property interest, possibly with arrangements for some rights to be reserved;
- acquisition of less-than-fee real property interests, such as easements or rights-of-way; and
- cooperative approaches, such as cooperative agreements, participation in regional consortiums, local planning and zoning processes, or other measures that do not involve federal acquisition of any interest in real property.

Federal fee-simple ownership (all of the rights associated with real property) provides the Service with the greatest ability to protect and manage resources and provide for public use and enjoyment. Less-than-fee interests (some of the rights associated with real property) require a federal commitment to monitor and enforce the Service's interest in the affected property. Acquisition of less-than-fee interests may be appropriate in instances in which the Service needs only a specific interest in land, or in which it needs to modify uses of the land to protect resources or values but full fee ownership is not required or possible.

Acquisition of fee-simple interests is a critically important and effective land protection method for lands within park unit boundaries. The Service may employ, as appropriate, a broad strategy to protect land and resources, including innovative techniques; partnerships; participation in the planning and decision-making processes of other federal agencies; and vigilance at the regional and local levels of government where nonfederal land use decisions are generally made.

Some park units created by Congress have been specifically authorized to continue historical or traditional activities such as farming, ranching, or low-density residential uses. Congress may also restrict the method of acquisition or prohibit acquisition without owner consent. In all cases, the Park Service will acquire the lands and/or interests in land only by the method or methods authorized.

When nonfederal land is identified for acquisition, the Service will make every reasonable effort to reach an agreement with the owner on the purchase price, in accordance with the uniform appraisal standards for departmental land transaction policies. If an agreement cannot be reached, the Service will take further steps in accordance with authorities and congressional directions that apply to the unit in question. NPS policy is to acquire lands and interests in lands from willing sellers, and condemnation is generally considered only as a last resort. However, acquisition by condemnation is sometimes necessary to establish just compensation, to clear a title, or to prevent imminent damage or unacceptable threats to park resources and values.

(See Condemnation 3.8)

3.3 Land Protection Plans

Planning for the protection of park lands will be integrated into the planning process for park management. Land protection plans (LPPs) should be prepared to determine and publicly document what lands or interests in land need to be in public ownership and what means of protection are available to achieve the purposes for which the unit was created. These plans will be prepared for each unit of the national park system containing nonfederal land or interests in land within its authorized boundary. A thorough review of a park's authorizing statutes and complete legislative history will be conducted as part of the land protection planning process.

Land acquisition priorities will be guided by a park unit's land protection plan. Superintendents will ensure that land protection plans are developed, and periodically reviewed and updated to identify what land or interests in land would facilitate achieving park purposes. These purposes and the desired conditions for resources and visitor experiences are normally defined in the park's general management plan. Strategic plans define what results can be accomplished in the foreseeable future—usually a five-year period. Land protection plans will be coordinated with general management plans, strategic plans, and other plans for resource management and visitor use. Decisions about acquisition within park boundaries will consider the relationship between the park and its adjacent lands. Superintendents have the responsibility to be aware of uses or activities that are planned for lands around the park that may have impacts on park resources and opportunities for visitor enjoyment.

A land protection plan should be simple and concise and document (1) what lands or interests in land would advance park purposes through public ownership, (2) what means of protection are available to achieve park purposes as established by Congress, (3) the protection methods and funds that will be sought or applied to protect resources and to provide for visitor use and park facility development, and (4) acquisition priorities. Historic structures and objects on the land under consideration within the land protection plan will be evaluated for their relevance to the park mission and the scope of the park museum collection. The land protection plan will specify those structures and objects that benefit the public through public ownership and identify the appropriate source of funding. Personal property not identified for acquisition should be removed by the property owner. For acquisition of water rights, see chapter 4, section 4.6.2.

When appropriate, the land protection plan may serve as a vehicle for addressing land protection issues external to a park's boundaries. When external impacts or opportunities are addressed, plans will clearly distinguish between the authorities related to land acquisition and the authorities for the Service to cooperate with other entities beyond the park boundary.

3.4 Cooperative Conservation

Superintendents will be aware of and monitor state government programs for managing state-owned submerged lands and resources within NPS units. When there is potential for such programs to adversely impact park resources or values, superintendents will make their concerns known to appropriate state government officials and encourage compatible land uses that avoid or mitigate potential adverse impacts. When federal acquisition of state-owned submerged lands and resources within NPS units is not feasible, the Park Service will seek to enter into cooperative agreements with state governments to ensure the adequate protection of park resources and values.

External threats may originate with proposed uses outside a park that may adversely impact park resources or values. Superintendents will therefore be aware of and monitor land use proposals and changes to adjacent lands and their potential impacts. They will also seek to encourage compatible adjacent land uses to avoid or to mitigate potential adverse effects. Superintendents will make their concerns known and, when appropriate, actively participate in the planning and regulatory processes of neighboring jurisdictions, including other federal agencies and tribal, state, and local governments.

In working cooperatively with surrounding landowners and managers a superintendent might, for example, comment on potential zoning changes for proposed development projects, or brief the public and officials about park resources and related studies that are relevant to proposed zoning or other changes. Superintendents should, whenever possible, work cooperatively and communicate their concerns as early as possible in the process to minimize potential conflict. Superintendents should seek advice from the appropriate NPS program managers and the Solicitor's Office when dealing with complicated external land protection issues and threats, especially those with potential for Service-wide controversy or consequences.

In some cases—such as air or water pollution—the source of a significant threat may be far removed from the park's boundaries. In such cases the Park Service will coordinate at the regional or national level in making its concerns known and in seeking a remedy to the problem. Threats to parks from external sources should be identified and addressed in the general management plan or in other planning documents. The result will be enhanced public awareness of the far-reaching impacts of these threats and an increased likelihood of remedial actions by those who are responsible.

(See Cooperative Conservation Beyond Park Boundaries 1.6; Evaluating Impacts on Natural Resources 4.1.3; Partnerships 4.1.4; Biological Resource Management 4.4; Removal of Exotic Species Already Present 4.4.4.2; Water Resource Management 4.6; Air Resource Management 4.7; Geologic Resource Management 4.8; Soundscape Management 4.9; Lightscape Management 4.10; Stewardship 5.3. Also see Director's Order #25: Land Protection, and Reference Manual 25); Director's Order #75A: Civic Engagement and Public Involvement)

3.5 Boundary Adjustments

The boundary of a national park may be modified only as authorized by law. For many parks, such statutory authority is included in the enabling legislation or subsequent legislation that specifically authorizes a boundary revision. Where park-specific authority is not available, the Land and Water Conservation Fund Act of 1965, as amended, provides an additional but limited authority to adjust boundaries.

The act provides for boundary adjustments that essentially fall into three distinct categories: (1) technical revisions; (2) minor revisions based upon statutorily defined criteria; and (3) revisions to include adjacent real property acquired by donation, purchased with donated funds, transferred from any other federal agency, or obtained by exchange. Adjacent real property is considered to be land located contiguous to but outside the boundary of a national park system unit.

As part of the planning process, the Park Service will identify and evaluate boundary adjustments that may be necessary or desirable for carrying out the purposes of the park unit. Boundary adjustments may be recommended to

- protect significant resources and values, or to enhance opportunities for public enjoyment related to park purposes;
- address operational and management issues, such as the need for access or the need for boundaries to correspond to logical boundary delineations such as topographic or other natural features or roads; or
- otherwise protect park resources that are critical to fulfilling park purposes.

If the acquisition will be made using appropriated funds, and it is not merely a technical boundary revision, the criteria set forth by Congress at 16 USC 460l-9(c) (2) must be met. All recommendations for boundary changes must meet the following two criteria:

- The added lands will be feasible to administer considering their size, configuration, and ownership; costs; the views of and impacts on local communities and surrounding jurisdictions; and other factors such as the presence of hazardous substances or exotic species.
- Other alternatives for management and resource protection are not adequate.

These criteria apply conversely to recommendations for the deletion of lands from the authorized boundaries of a park unit. For example, before recommending the deletion of land from a park boundary, a finding would have to be made that the land did not include a significant resource, value, or opportunity for public enjoyment related to the purposes of the park. Full consideration should be given to current and future park needs before a recommendation is made to delete lands from the authorized boundaries of a park unit. Actions consisting solely of deletions of land from existing park boundaries would require an act of Congress.

3.6 Land Acquisition Authority

The National Park Service acquires lands or interests in land within parks when authorized to do so by an act of Congress or by presidential proclamation. Although acquisition outside authorized boundaries is generally prohibited, certain statutes provide limited systemwide authority for minor boundary changes and the acceptance of donated lands adjacent to a park's boundaries. There is no single statute authorizing land acquisition. There are, however, several laws that provide limited acquisition authority that is applicable systemwide. For most parks, acquisition authority is provided by statutes specific to the park. The Park Service land acquisition process and land protection planning process will comply with all applicable legislation, congressional guidelines, executive orders, and Department of the Interior policies. For delegations of authority for land acquisition, see Director's Order #25: Land Protection.

3.7 Land Acquisition Funding

When the acquisition of lands and/or interests in land within a park boundary is necessary, the Park Service will consider acquisition by

- purchase with appropriated or donated funds;
- exchange;
- donation;
- bargain sale;
- transfer or withdrawal from public domain; or
- condemnation, as a last resort.

Funding for land acquisition within the national park system is derived primarily from the Land and Water Conservation Fund. LWCF monies are restricted to uses associated with the acquisition of land and/or interests in land within the authorized boundaries of NPS units. As outlined in Department of the Interior policy, the federal portion of the fund will be used to acquire the lands, waters, and interests therein necessary to achieve the Service's natural, cultural, wildlife, and recreation management objectives. To implement this policy, the fund will be used in accordance with management objectives for each park unit based on the NPS mission and congressional mandates and in accordance with an analysis of long-range goals for resource protection, safe public access, and park management. As further required by departmental policy, the Service will, to the extent consistent with statutory authorities,

- prioritize acquisition of lands or interests in land within unit boundaries to achieve park purposes consistent with management objectives;
- use to the maximum extent practical, cost-effective alternatives to the direct federal purchase of privately owned lands, and, when acquisition is necessary, acquire or retain only the minimum interests determined by park officials to be necessary to meet management objectives;
- cooperate with landowners; other federal agencies; tribal, state, and local governments; and the private sector to manage land for public use or protect it for resource conservation; and
- formulate, or revise as necessary, plans for land acquisition and resource use or protection to ensure that sociocultural impacts are considered and that the most outstanding areas are adequately managed.

3.8 Condemnation

As a general policy and in accordance with congressional direction, condemnation is the acquisition method of last resort for the Park Service when acquiring lands or interests in lands.

It is the Service's goal to acquire lands or interests in lands through a cooperative negotiation process with a willing seller. Under certain circumstances, however, condemnation may be necessary. Friendly condemnations with willing sellers may be appropriate to ensure that the United States acquires clear title to the property in question, or to enable a court to determine the fair market value to be paid for the property. If there is no willing seller, the Service may pursue condemnation proceedings if

- it is first determined that other acquisition means will not be successful;
- the acquisition would be consistent with any restrictions applicable to that park unit; and
- approval has been obtained from the Director and any other required sources (e.g., by the Department of the Interior or Congress).

In Alaska, consideration of a land exchange is required before acquisition through condemnation.

Natural Resource Management

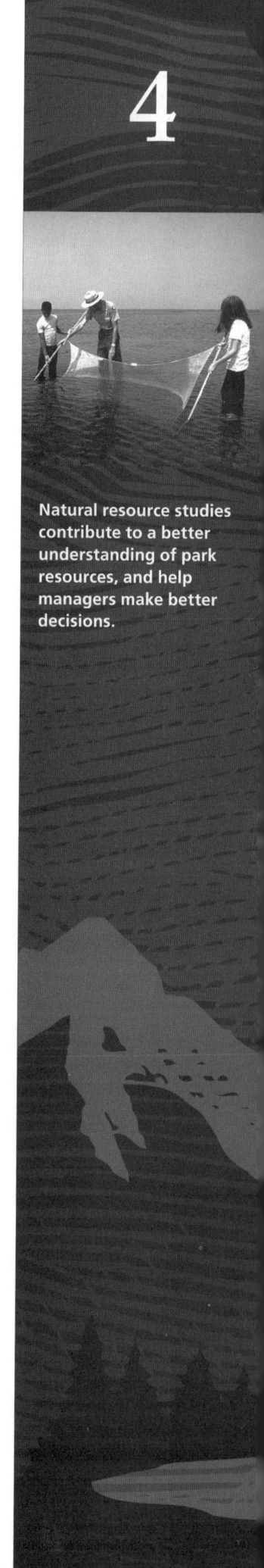

Natural resource studies contribute to a better understanding of park resources, and help managers make better decisions.

The National Park Service will preserve and protect the natural resources, processes, systems, and values of units of the national park system in an unimpaired condition to perpetuate their inherent integrity and to provide present and future generations with the opportunity to enjoy them.

Introduction

The National Park Service will strive to understand, maintain, restore, and protect the inherent integrity of the natural resources, processes, systems, and values of the parks while providing meaningful and appropriate opportunities to enjoy them. The Service recognizes that natural processes and species are evolving, and the Service will allow this evolution to continue—minimally influenced by human actions. The natural resources, processes, systems, and values that the Service preserves are described generally in the 1916 NPS Organic Act and in the enabling legislation or presidential proclamation establishing each park. They are described in greater detail in management plans specific to each park. Natural resources, processes, systems, and values found in parks include

- physical resources such as water, air, soils, topographic features, geologic features, paleontological resources, and natural soundscapes and clear skies, both during the day and at night
- physical processes such as weather, erosion, cave formation, and wildland fire
- biological resources such as native plants, animals, and communities
- biological processes such as photosynthesis, succession, and evolution
- ecosystems
- highly valued associated characteristics such as scenic views

In this chapter, natural resources, processes, systems, and values are all included in the term "natural resources." The term "natural condition" is used here to describe the condition of resources that would occur in the absence of human dominance over the landscape.

The Service manages the natural resources of parks to maintain them in an unimpaired condition for present and future generations in accordance with NPS-specific statutes, including the NPS Organic Act and the National Parks Omnibus Management Act of 1998; general environmental laws such as the Clean Air Act, the Clean Water Act, the Endangered Species Act of 1973, the National Environmental Policy Act, and the Wilderness Act; executive orders; and applicable regulations.

Activities that take place outside park boundaries and that are not managed by the Service can profoundly affect the Service's ability to protect natural resources inside the parks. The Service will act to protect natural resources from impacts caused by external activities by working cooperatively with federal, state, and local agencies; tribal authorities; user groups; adjacent landowners; and others to identify and achieve broad natural resource goals. By working cooperatively through both formal and informal lines of communication and consultation, the Service will better achieve park management objectives and the protection of parks' natural resources.

(See Park Management 1.4; Cooperative Conservation Beyond Park Boundaries 1.6; Partnerships 4.1.4)

4.1 General Management Concepts

As explained in chapter 1 of these *Management Policies*, preserving park resources and values unimpaired is the core or primary responsibility of NPS managers. The Service cannot conduct or allow activities in parks that would impact park resources and values to a level that would constitute impairment. To comply with this mandate, park managers must determine in writing whether proposed activities in parks would impair natural resources. Park managers must also take action to ensure that ongoing NPS activities do not cause the impairment of park natural resources. In cases of uncertainty as to the impacts of activities on park natural resources, the protection of natural resources will predominate. The Service will reduce such uncertainty by facilitating and building a science-based understanding of park resources and the nature and extent of the impacts involved.

Natural resources will be managed to preserve fundamental physical and biological processes, as well as individual species, features, and plant and animal communities. The Service will not attempt to solely preserve individual species (except threatened or endangered species) or individual natural processes; rather, it will try to maintain all the components and processes of naturally evolving park ecosystems, including the natural abundance, diversity, and genetic and ecological integrity of the plant and animal species native to those ecosystems. Just as all components of a natural system will be recognized as important, natural change will also be recognized as an integral part of the functioning of natural systems. By preserving these components and processes in their natural condition, the Service will prevent resource degradation and therefore avoid any subsequent need for resource restoration. In managing parks to preserve naturally evolving ecosystems, and in accordance with requirements of the National Parks Omnibus Management Act of 1998, the Service will use the findings of science and the analyses of scientifically trained resource specialists in decision-making.

Park units with significant natural resources range in size from just a few acres to millions of acres and from urban to remote and wilderness settings. As integral parts of a national park system, these park units individually and cumulatively contribute to America's natural heritage and provide the places where that heritage can be better understood and enjoyed.

Science has demonstrated that few if any park units can fully realize or maintain their physical and biological integrity if managed as biogeographic islands. Instead, park units must be managed in the context of their larger ecosystems. The ecosystem context for some species and processes may be relatively small, while for others this context is vast. In any case, superintendents face the challenge of placing each of the resources they protect in their appropriate ecosystem context and then working with all involved and affected parties to advance their shared conservation goals and avoid adverse impacts on these resources.

Superintendents must be mindful of the setting in which they undertake the protection of park resources. The practicability of achieving a natural soundscape may be quite reasonable at a park unit in a remote setting, but the same may not be true at a popular roadside viewpoint in the same park unit, or at a park unit in a more urban locale. Similarly, the restoration and maintenance of natural fire regimes can advance more rapidly and on a larger landscape scale in wilderness areas where considerations for public safety and the protection of private property and physical developments can usually be readily addressed. However, the restoration and maintenance of natural fire regimes in more developed and highly visited locations with the same considerations can be extremely complicated. The goal of protecting natural resources and values while providing for their enjoyment remains the same in all cases except to the extent that Congress has directly and specifically provided otherwise. The degree to which a park can adequately restore and maintain its natural resources to a desired condition will depend on a variety of factors—such as size, past management events, surrounding land uses, and the availability of resources. Through its planning processes, the Park Service will determine the desired future conditions for each park unit and identify a strategy to achieve them. This strategy should include working cooperatively with adjacent land and resource managers, as appropriate.

The Service will not intervene in natural biological or physical processes, except

- when directed by Congress;
- in emergencies in which human life and property are at stake;
- to restore natural ecosystem functioning that has been disrupted by past or ongoing human activities; or
- when a park plan has identified the intervention as necessary to protect other park resources, human health and safety, or facilities.

Any such intervention will be kept to the minimum necessary to achieve the stated management objectives.

Natural systems in the national park system, and the human influences upon them, will be monitored to detect change. The Service will evaluate possible causes and effects of changes that might cause impacts on park resources and values. The Service will use the results of monitoring and research to understand the detected change and to develop appropriate management actions.

Biological or physical processes altered in the past by human activities may need to be actively managed to restore them to a natural condition or to maintain the closest approximation of the natural condition when a truly natural system is no longer attainable. Prescribed burning and the control of ungulates when predators have been extirpated are two examples. Decisions about the extent and degree of management actions taken to protect or restore park ecosystems or their components will be based on clearly articulated, well-supported management objectives and the best scientific information available.

There may be situations in which an area may be closed to visitor use to protect the natural resources (for example, during an animal breeding season) or for reasons of public safety (for example, during a wildland fire). Such closures may be accomplished under the superintendent's discretionary authority and will comply with applicable regulations (36 CFR 1.5 and 1.7).

(See The Prohibition on Impairment of Park Resources and Values 1.4.4; Environmental Leadership 1.8; General Management Planning 2.3.1; Facility Planning and Design 9.1.1. Also see Director's Order #11B: Ensuring Quality of Information Disseminated by the NPS; Director's Order #75A: Civic Engagement and Public Involvement)

4.1.1 Planning for Natural Resource Management

Each park with a significant natural resource base (as exemplified by participation in the Vital Signs component of the Natural Resource Challenge) will prepare and periodically update a long-range (looking at least one to two decades ahead) comprehensive strategy for natural resource management. This long-range strategy will describe the comprehensive program of activities needed to achieve the desired future conditions for the park's natural resources. It will integrate the best available science and prescribe activities such as inventories, research, monitoring, restoration, mitigation, protection, education, and management of resource uses. The strategy will also describe the natural-resource-related activities needed to achieve desired future conditions for cultural resources (such as historic landscapes) and visitor enjoyment.

Similarly, planning for park operations, development, and management activities that might affect natural resources will be guided by high-quality, scientifically acceptable information, data, and impact assessment. Where existing information is inadequate, the collection of new information and data may be required before decision-making. Long-term research or monitoring may also be necessary to correctly understand the effects of management actions on natural resources whose function and significance are not clearly understood.

(See Decision-making Requirements to Identify and Avoid Impairments 1.4.7; General Management Planning 2.3.1; Land Protection Plans 3.3; NPS-conducted or -sponsored Inventory, Monitoring, and Research Studies 4.2.1; Cultural Landscapes 5.3.5.2; Chapter 8: Use of the Parks; Chapter 9: Park Facilities. Also see 516 DM 4.16—Adaptive Management)

4.1.2 Natural Resource Information

Information about natural resources that is collected and developed will be maintained for as long as it is possible to do so. All forms of information collected through inventorying, monitoring, research, assessment, traditional knowledge, and management actions will be managed to professional NPS archival and library standards.

Most information about park natural resources will be made broadly available to park employees, the scientific community, and the public. Pursuant to provisions of the National Parks Omnibus Management Act, the Service will withhold information about the nature and specific location of sensitive park natural resources—specifically caves and mineral, paleontological, endangered, threatened, rare, or commercially valuable resources— unless the Service determines, in writing, that disclosure of the information would further the purposes of the park; would not create an unreasonable risk of harm, theft, or destruction of resources; and would be consistent with other applicable laws.

Under the Freedom of Information Act, the Park Service may be able to withhold sensitive natural resource data and information that is used in ongoing law enforcement investigations or subject to national security clearance classification. The Service may be able to withhold data provided through interim project reporting, pending the completion of relevant projects and the receipt of final project reports, as specified in approved scientific research and collecting permits and associated research proposals if the release of information will cause foreseeable harm to the NPS interests. Information that is made available to the public (that is, not withheld under the Freedom of Information Act or other laws) will remain searchable and accessible under the professional and NPS archival and library standards.

(See Information Confidentiality 1.9.2.3; Confidentiality 5.2.3; Interpretive and Educational Programs 7.1. Also see Director's Order #66: FOIA and Protected Resource Information; Museum Handbook 24-Part II)

4.1.3 Evaluating Impacts on Natural Resources

Planning, environmental evaluation, and civic engagement regarding management actions that may affect the natural resources of the national park system are essential for carrying out the Service's responsibilities to present and future generations. The Service will ensure that the environmental costs and benefits of proposed operations, development, and resource management are fully and openly evaluated before taking actions that may impact the natural resources of parks. This evaluation must include appropriate participation by the public; the application of scholarly, scientific, and technical information in the planning, evaluation, and decision-making processes; the use of NPS knowledge and expertise through interdisciplinary teams and processes; and the full incorporation of mitigation measures, pollution prevention techniques, and other principles of sustainable park management.

Every environmental assessment and environmental impact statement produced by the Service will include an analysis of whether the impacts of a proposed activity constitute impairment of park natural resources and values. Every finding of no significant impact, record of decision, and National Historic Preservation Act Section 106 memorandum of agreement signed by the Park Service will contain a discrete certification that the impacts of the proposed activity will not impair park natural resources and values.

(See Park Management 1.4; Implementation Planning 2.3.4; NPS-conducted or -sponsored Inventory, Monitoring, and Research Studies 4.2.1. Also see Director's Order #12: Conservation Planning, Environmental Impact Analysis, and Decision-making)

4.1.4 Partnerships

The Service will pursue opportunities to improve natural resource management within parks and across administrative boundaries by pursuing cooperative conservation with public agencies, appropriate representatives of American Indian tribes and other traditionally associated peoples, and private landowners in accordance with Executive Order 13352 (Facilitation of Cooperative Conservation). The Service recognizes that cooperation with other land and resource managers can accomplish ecosystem stability and other resource management objectives when the best efforts of a single manager might fail. Therefore, the Service will develop agreements with federal, tribal, state, and local governments and organizations; foreign governments and organizations; and private landowners, when appropriate, to coordinate plant, animal, water, and other natural resource management activities in ways that maintain and protect park resources and values. Such cooperation may include park restoration activities, research on park natural resources, and the management of species harvested in parks. Cooperation also may involve coordinating management activities in two or more separate areas, integrating management practices to reduce conflicts, coordinating research, sharing data and expertise, exchanging native biological resources for species management or ecosystem restoration purposes, establishing native wildlife corridors, and providing essential habitats adjacent to or across park boundaries.

In addition, the Service will seek the cooperation of others in minimizing the impacts of influences originating outside parks by controlling noise and artificial lighting, maintaining water quality and quantity, eliminating toxic substances, preserving scenic views, improving air quality, preserving wetlands, protecting threatened or endangered species, eliminating exotic species, managing the use of pesticides, protecting shoreline processes, managing fires, managing boundary influences, and using other means of preserving and protecting natural resources.

(See Cooperative Conservation Beyond Park Boundaries 1.6; Partnerships 1.10; Cooperative Conservation 3.4; Agreements 5.2.2)

4.1.5 Restoration of Natural Systems

The Service will reestablish natural functions and processes in parks unless otherwise directed by Congress. Landscapes disturbed by natural phenomena, such as landslides, earthquakes, floods, hurricanes, tornadoes, and fires, will be allowed to recover naturally unless manipulation is necessary to protect other park resources, developments, or employee and public safety. Impacts on natural systems resulting from human disturbances include the introduction of exotic species; the contamination of air, water, and soil; changes to hydrologic patterns and sediment transport; the acceleration of erosion and sedimentation; and the disruption of natural processes. The Service will seek to return such disturbed areas to the natural conditions and processes characteristic of the ecological zone in which the damaged resources are situated. The Service will use the best available technology, within available resources, to restore the biological and physical components of these systems, accelerating both their recovery and the recovery of landscape and biological community structure and function. Efforts may include, for example

- removal of exotic species
- removal of contaminants and nonhistoric structures or facilities
- restoration of abandoned mineral lands, abandoned or unauthorized roads, areas overgrazed by domestic animals, or disrupted natural waterways and/or shoreline processes
- restoration of areas disturbed by NPS administrative, management, or development activities (such as hazard tree removal, construction, or sand and gravel extraction) or by public use
- restoration of natural soundscapes
- restoration of native plants and animals
- restoration of natural visibility

When park development/facilities are damaged or destroyed and replacement is necessary, the development will be replaced or relocated to promote the restoration of natural resources and processes.

(See Decision-making Requirements to Identify and Avoid Impairments 1.4.7; Restoration of Native Plant and Animal Species 4.4.2.2; Management of Natural Landscapes 4.4.2.4; Siting Facilities to Avoid Natural Hazards 9.1.1.5. Also see Director's Order #18: Wildland Fire Management)

4.1.6 Compensation for Injuries to Natural Resources

The Service will use all legal authorities that are available to protect and restore natural resources and the environmental benefits they provide when actions of another party cause the destruction or loss of, or injury to, park resources or values. As a first step, damage assessments provide the basis for determining the restoration and compensation needs that address the public's loss and are a key milestone toward the ultimate goal, which is restoration, replacement, and/or reclamation of resources for the American public.

Pursuant to applicable provisions of the Comprehensive Environmental Response, Compensation and Liability Act of 1980; the Oil Pollution Act of 1990; the Federal Water Pollution Control Act (as amended by the Clean Water Act of 1977); and the National Park System Resource Protection Act, the Service will

- determine the injury caused to natural resources, assess all appropriate damages, and monitor damages;
- seek to recover all appropriate costs associated with responses to such actions and the costs of assessing resource damages, including the direct and indirect costs of response, restoration, and monitoring activities; and
- use all sums recovered in compensation for resource injuries to restore, replace, or acquire the equivalent of the resources that were the subject of the action.

(See Compensation for Injuries to Cultural Resources 5.3.1.3. Also see Director's Order #14: Resource Damage Assessment and Restoration)

4.2 Studies and Collections

The Service will encourage appropriately reviewed natural resource studies whenever such studies are consistent with applicable laws and policies. These studies support the NPS mission by providing the Service, the scientific community, and the public with an understanding of park resources, processes, values, and uses that will be cumulative and constantly refined. This approach will provide a scientific and scholarly basis for park planning, development, operations, management, education, and interpretive activities.

As used here, the term studies means short- or long-term scientific or scholarly investigations or educational activities that may involve natural resource surveys, inventories, monitoring, and research, including data and specimen collection. Studies include projects conducted by researchers and scholars in universities, foundations and other institutions; tribal colleges and organizations; other federal, tribal, and state agencies; and NPS staff. The data and information acquired through studies conducted in parks will be made publicly available, consistent with section 4.1.2, and will be obtained and disseminated in accordance with the standards found in Director's Order #11B: Ensuring Quality of Information Disseminated by the NPS.

The Service will promote cooperative relationships with educational and scientific institutions and qualified individuals when that relationship can assist the Service in obtaining information and when the opportunity for research and study in the parks offers the cooperators a significant benefit to their programs. NPS facilities and assistance may be made available to qualified cooperators who are conducting NPS-authorized studies.

Studies in parks will be preceded by (1) an approved scope of work, proposal, or other detailed written description of the work to be performed; and (2) a written statement of environmental and cultural resource compliance appropriate to the proposed methodology and study site. All studies in parks will employ nondestructive methods to the maximum extent feasible with respect to resource protection, research methodology, and the scientific and management value of the information and collections to be obtained. Although studies involving physical impacts to park resources or the removal of objects or specimens may be permitted, studies and collecting activities that will lead to the impairment of park resources and values are prohibited.

Scientific natural resource collecting activities are governed by 36 CFR 2.5. A very limited number of other types of natural resource collecting are governed by 36 CFR 2.1. In most cases, only small quantities may be collected. The repeated collection of materials to ensure a continuing source of supply for research or propagation is prohibited unless the proposed activity clearly requires repeated collection, as might be the case with a monitoring or park restoration program.

(See Decision-making Requirements to Identify and Avoid Impairments 1.4.7; Managing Information 1.9.2; Research 5.1; Resource Access and Use 5.3.5.3.1; Collecting Natural Products 8.8; Consumptive Uses 8.9; Social Science Studies 8.11. Also see Director's Order #28B: Ethnography Program; Director's Order #74: Studies and Collecting; Director's Order #78: Social Science)

4.2.1 NPS-conducted or -sponsored Inventory, Monitoring, and Research Studies

The Service will

- identify, acquire, and interpret needed inventory, monitoring, and research, including applicable traditional knowledge, to obtain information and data that will help park managers accomplish park management objectives provided for in law and planning documents;
- define, assemble, and synthesize comprehensive baseline inventory data describing the natural resources under NPS stewardship, and identify the processes that influence those resources;
- use qualitative and quantitative techniques to monitor key aspects of resources and processes at regular intervals;
- analyze the resulting information to detect or predict changes (including interrelationships with visitor carrying capacities) that may require management intervention and provide reference points for comparison with other environments and time frames; and
- use the resulting information to maintain—and where necessary restore—the integrity of natural systems.

The Service may support studies to (among other things)

- ensure a systematic, current, and fully adequate park information base;
- provide a sound basis for policy, guidelines, and management actions;
- develop effective strategies, methods, and technologies to (1) restore disturbed resources, and (2) predict, avoid, or minimize adverse impacts on natural and cultural resources and on visitors and related activities;
- ensure that plans and actions reflect contemporary knowledge about the natural and cultural context of special natural areas, cultural landscapes, and natural resources having traditional cultural meaning and value to associated human groups;
- determine the causes of natural resource management problems and identify alternative strategies for potentially resolving them;
- understand the ceremonial and traditional resource management practices of Native Americans, subsistence uses by rural Alaska residents, and traditional uses by groups with demonstrated ties to particular natural resources of parks;
- further understand park ecosystems and related human social systems, including visitors and gateway communities, and document their components, condition, and significance; and
- ensure that the interpretation of the parks' natural resources and issues reflects current standards of scholarship relating to the history, science, and condition of the resources.

Superintendents may authorize NPS staff to carry out routine inventory, monitoring, study, and related duties without requiring an NPS scientific research and collecting permit. With or without an NPS permit, staff will comply appropriately with professional standards and with general and park-specific research and collecting permit conditions. All research and data and specimen collection conducted by NPS employees will be appropriately documented and carried out in accordance with all laws, regulations, policies, and professional standards pertaining to survey, inventory, monitoring, and research. NPS staff will be expected to make their findings available to the public, such as by publication in professional journals or presentation in interpretive programs.

Park inventory, monitoring, and research needs and specific research objectives will be identified in the appropriate management plans for each park, or in park, regional, or Service-wide program plans.

(See Decision-making Requirements to Identify and Avoid Impairments 1.4.7; Natural Resource Information 4.1.2; Restoration of Natural Systems 4.1.5; Weather and Climate 4.7.2; Miscellaneous Management Facilities 9.4.5)

4.2.2 Independent Studies

Non-NPS studies conducted in parks are not required to address specifically identified NPS management issues or information needs. However, these studies, including data and specimen collection, require an NPS scientific research and collecting permit. The studies must conform to NPS policies and guidelines regarding the collection and publication of data, the conduct of studies, wilderness restrictions, and park-specific requirements identified in the terms and conditions of the permit. Projects will be administered and conducted only by fully qualified personnel and conform to current standards of scholarship. NPS scientific research and collecting permits may include requirements that permittees provide for parks, within agreed-upon time frames, copies of appropriate field notes, cataloging, and other data; information about the data; progress reports; interim and final reports; and publications derived from the permitted activities.

(See Independent Research 5.1.2)

4.2.3 Natural Resource Collections

Natural resource collections include non-living and living specimens. Guidance for collecting and managing specimens and associated field records can be found in the Code of Federal Regulations (36 CFR 2.5) and NPS guidance documents, including the museum handbook. Nonliving specimens and their associated field records are managed as museum collections. Living collections will be managed in accordance with the provisions of a park's general management plan, the Animal Welfare Act, and other appropriate requirements.

Field data, objects, specimens, and features obtained for preservation during inventory, monitoring, research, and study projects, together with associated records and reports, will be managed over the long term within the museum collection. Specimens that are not authorized for consumptive analysis remain federal property and will be labeled and cataloged into the NPS cataloging system (ANCS+, or its successor) in accordance with applicable regulations (36 CFR 2.5).

(See Paleontological Resources and Their Contexts 4.8.2.1; Collecting Natural Products 8.8; Consumptive Uses 8.9; Natural and Cultural Studies, Research, and Collection Activities 8.10; Social Science Studies 8.11. Also see Director's Order #24: NPS Museum Collections Management)

4.2.4 Collection Associated with the Development of Commercial Products

Extractive use of park resources for commercial purposes is prohibited except when specifically authorized by law or in the exercise of valid existing rights.

The results of research conducted on any material originating as a research specimen collected under an NPS scientific research and collecting permit (including progeny, replicates, or derivatives) may be used only for scientific purposes and not for commercial purposes without supplemental written authorization from the Park Service. The sale of collected research specimens from the permitted collector to third parties is prohibited; these research specimens remain federal property. Specimens and any material originating as a specimen may be loaned for scientific purposes related to commercial use in accordance with the terms of applicable written authorization from the Park Service.

Similarly, the results of other research conducted under an NPS scientific research and collecting permit that does not involve the collection of specimens may be used for scientific purposes only and may not be used for commercial purposes without supplemental written authorization.

(Also see Director's Order #74: Studies and Collecting)

4.3 Special Designations

The Park Service recognizes that special designations apply to parts or all of some parks to highlight the additional management considerations that those designated areas warrant. These designations include research natural area, experimental research area, wilderness area, national wild and scenic river, national natural landmark, biosphere reserve, and world heritage listing. These designations do not reduce the Service's authority for managing the parks, although in some cases they may create additional management requirements or considerations.

4.3.1 Research Natural Areas

Research natural areas contain prime examples of natural resources and processes, including significant genetic resources that have value for long-term observational studies or as control areas for manipulative research taking place outside the parks. Superintendents recommend areas of parks to their regional director, who is authorized to designate them as research natural areas. Superintendents cooperate with other federal land managers in identifying park sites for designation and planning research and educational activities for this interagency program.

Activities in research natural areas generally will be restricted to nonmanipulative research, education, and other activities that will not detract from an area's research values.

4.3.2 Experimental Research Areas

Experimental research areas are specific tracts that are set aside and managed for approved manipulative research. Manipulative research is defined as research in which conscious alteration of existing conditions is part of the experiment. The limited situations that may warrant establishment of experimental research areas are identified in *Natural Resources Reference Manual 77*. Superintendents may recommend areas of the park to their regional director, who is authorized to designate them as experimental research areas.

4.3.3 Wilderness Areas

See chapter 6.

4.3.4 National Wild and Scenic Rivers System

Parks containing one or more river segments listed in the NPS National Rivers Inventory, or that have characteristics that might make them eligible for the National Wild and Scenic Rivers System, will comply with section 5(d)(1) of the Wild and Scenic Rivers Act (16 USC 1276(d)(1)), which instructs each federal agency to assess whether those rivers are suitable for inclusion in the system. The assessments, and any resulting management requirements, may be incorporated into a park's general management plan or other management plan. No management actions may be taken that could adversely affect the values that qualify a river for inclusion in the National Wild and Scenic Rivers System.

(See Wild and Scenic Rivers 2.3.1.9. Also see Director's Order #46A: Wild and Scenic Rivers within the National Park System; Wild and Scenic Rivers Act)

4.3.5   National Natural Landmarks

Park sites that are among the best examples of a type of biotic community or geological feature in a park's physiographic province may be nominated to the Secretary of the Interior for inclusion in the National Registry of Natural Landmarks. As the agency responsible for maintaining the registry, the Park Service has developed criteria for eligibility (36 CFR Part 62).

4.3.6   Biosphere Reserves

Biosphere reserves are sites that are part of a worldwide network of natural reserves recognized for their roles in conserving genetic resources; facilitating long-term research and monitoring; and encouraging education, training, and the demonstration of sustainable resource use. A biosphere reserve is usually representative of a biogeographic province.

With the approval of the NPS Director, parks may be nominated for recognition as biosphere reserves, or as constituents of biosphere reserves. Specific guidance for recognition is provided by the United States Man and Biosphere (MAB) Programme based on the general guidance of the United Nations Education, Scientific, and Cultural Organization (UNESCO). Working within the Man and Biosphere Programme, the Park Service may assist in determining the suitability and feasibility of including parks in U.S. biosphere reserves, may participate in research and educational activities, and may furnish information on its biosphere reserves for inclusion in domestic and international information systems.

The designation of park lands as biosphere reserves or constituents of biosphere reserves does not alter the purposes for which the parks were established, change the management requirements, or reduce NPS jurisdiction over parks. To the extent practicable, superintendents of parks that are recognized as biosphere reserves will incorporate biosphere reserve objectives into general management plans, implementation plans, action plans, and park interpretive programs. Superintendents will pursue opportunities to use the biosphere reserve designation as a framework for local, regional, and international cooperation.

4.3.7   World Heritage List

Park properties containing natural features believed to possess outstanding universal value to humanity may qualify for placement on the World Heritage List under criteria described in the *World Heritage Committee Operational Guidelines* and in accordance with the World Heritage Convention. Before they can be nominated, all such properties must be assessed according to World Heritage criteria, and before the United States can submit a nomination to the World Heritage Committee, the property must first be included on the U.S. Tentative List of Potential Future World Heritage Nominations.

Any park superintendent who believes that part or all of the park they manage should be considered for inscription on the World Heritage List must consult with the NPS Office of International Affairs, the NPS Director, and the Department of the Interior before proceeding. U.S. recommendations are approved by an interagency panel chaired by the Assistant Secretary for Fish and Wildlife and Parks based on criteria promulgated by the World Heritage Committee. These criteria and the rules for U.S. participation in the Convention Concerning the Protection of the World Cultural and Natural Heritage are published in 36 CFR Part 73.

Once a property is placed on the World Heritage List, the Park Service will recognize the designation in public information and interpretive programs. Where appropriate, superintendents should use the park's world heritage status to promote sustainable tourism (tourism that does not adversely impact park resources and values) and the preservation of the world's natural and cultural heritage. Placement on the World Heritage List will not alter the purposes for which a park was established, or its management requirements, or reduce NPS jurisdiction over the park.

(See Nominations for World Heritage List Designation 5.1.3.2.3)

4.4   Biological Resource Management

4.4.1   General Principles for Managing Biological Resources

The National Park Service will maintain as parts of the natural ecosystems of parks all plants and animals native to park ecosystems. The term "plants and animals" refers to all five of the commonly recognized kingdoms of living things and includes such groups as flowering plants, ferns, mosses, lichens, algae, fungi, bacteria, mammals, birds, reptiles, amphibians, fishes, insects, worms, crustaceans, and microscopic plants or animals. The Service will successfully maintain native plants and animals by

- preserving and restoring the natural abundances, diversities, dynamics, distributions, habitats, and behaviors of native plant and animal populations and the communities and ecosystems in which they occur;

- restoring native plant and animal populations in parks when they have been extirpated by past human-caused actions; and

- minimizing human impacts on native plants, animals, populations, communities, and ecosystems, and the processes that sustain them.

4.4.1.1 Plant and Animal Population Management Principles

The individual plants and animals found in parks are genetically parts of species populations that may extend across both park and nonpark lands. As local populations within a group of populations naturally fluctuate in size, they become vulnerable to extirpation during periods when their numbers are low. The periodic disappearance of local populations is common in some species, and the regional persistence of these species depends upon the natural recolonization of suitable habitat by individuals from the remaining local populations. Thus, providing for the persistence of a species in a park may require maintaining a number of local populations, often both within and outside the park.

In addition, some populations of vertebrate and invertebrate animals, such as bats, caribou, warblers, marine turtles, frogs, salmon, whales, and butterflies, migrate at regular intervals into and out of parks. For these migratory populations, the parks provide only one of the several major habitats they need, and survival of the species in parks also depends on the existence and quality of habitats outside the parks, including in many cases outside the United States. The Service will adopt park resource preservation, development, and use management strategies that are intended to maintain the natural population fluctuations and processes that influence the dynamics of individual plant and animal populations, groups of plant and animal populations, and migratory animal populations in parks.

In addition to maintaining all native plant and animal species and their habitats inside parks, the Service will work with other land managers to encourage the conservation of the populations and habitats of these species outside parks whenever possible. To meet its commitments for maintaining native species in parks, the Service will cooperate with states, tribal governments, the U.S. Fish and Wildlife Service, NOAA Fisheries, and other countries, as appropriate, to

- participate in local and regional scientific and planning efforts, identify ranges of populations of native plants and animals, and develop cooperative strategies for maintaining or restoring these populations in the parks;

- suggest mutually beneficial harvest regulations for lands and waters outside the parks for populations that extend across park boundaries, such as resident deer or fishes; for short-distance seasonal migrant populations, such as elk or fishes; or for long-distance migrant populations, such as salmon;

- develop data, through monitoring, for use in plant and animal management programs (such as local land management decision-making for assessing resident plant and animal population trends and in international management negotiations for such far-ranging seasonal migrants as geese, whales, and marine turtles);

- present information about species life cycles, ranges, and population dynamics in park interpretive programs for use in increasing public awareness of management needs for all species, both resident and migrant, that occur in parks; and

- prevent the introduction of exotic species into units of the national park system, and remove, when possible, or otherwise contain individuals or populations of these species that have already become established in parks.

(See Civic Engagement 1.7; Cooperative Conservation Beyond Park Boundaries 1.6)

4.4.1.2 Genetic Resource Management Principles

The Service will strive to protect the full range of genetic types (genotypes) of native plant and animal populations in the parks by perpetuating natural evolutionary processes and minimizing human interference with evolving genetic diversity.

The restoration of native plants and animals will be accomplished using organisms taken from populations as closely related genetically and ecologically as possible to park populations, preferably from similar habitats in adjacent or local areas. Deviations from this general policy may be made where the management goal is to increase the variability of the park gene pool to mitigate past, human-induced loss of genetic variability. Actions to transplant organisms for purposes of restoring genetic variability through gene flow between native breeding populations will be preceded by an assessment of the genetic compatibility of the populations.

The need to maintain appropriate levels of genetic diversity will guide decisions on what actions to take to manage isolated populations of species or to enhance the recovery of populations of rare, threatened, or endangered species. All resource management actions involving planting or relocating species, subspecies, or varieties will be guided by detailed knowledge of site ecological histories and knowledge of local adaptations, ranges, and habitat requirements.

When native plants or animals are removed for any reason—such as hunting, fishing, pest management, or culling to reduce unnatural population conditions resulting from human activities—the Service will maintain the appropriate levels of natural genetic diversity.

(See Restoration of Natural Systems 4.1.5; Restoration of Native Plant and Animal Species 4.4.2.2)

4.4.1.3 Definition of Native and Exotic Species

Native species are defined as all species that have occurred, now occur, or may occur as a result of natural processes on lands designated as units of the national park system. Native species in a place are evolving in concert with each other. Exotic species are those species that occupy or could occupy park lands directly or indirectly as the result of deliberate or accidental human activities. Exotic species are also commonly referred to as nonnative, alien, or invasive species. Because an exotic species did not evolve in concert with the species native to the place, the exotic species is not a natural component of the natural ecosystem at that place. Genetically modified organisms exist solely due to human activities and therefore are managed as exotic species in parks.

4.4.2 Management of Native Plants and Animals

Whenever possible, natural processes will be relied upon to maintain native plant and animal species and influence natural fluctuations in populations of these species. The Service may intervene to manage individuals or populations of native species only when such intervention will not cause unacceptable impacts to the populations of the species or to other components and processes of the ecosystems that support them. The second is that at least one of the following conditions exists:

- Management is necessary
  - because a population occurs in an unnaturally high or low concentration as a result of human influences (such as loss of seasonal habitat, the extirpation of predators, the creation of highly productive habitat through agriculture or urban landscapes) and it is not possible to mitigate the effects of the human influences;
  - to protect specific cultural resources of parks;
  - to accommodate intensive development in portions of parks appropriate for and dedicated to such development;
  - to protect rare, threatened, or endangered species;
  - to protect human health as advised by the U.S. Public Health Service (which includes the Centers for Disease Control and the NPS public health program);
  - to protect property when it is not possible to change the pattern of human activities; or
  - to maintain human safety when it is not possible to change the pattern of human activities.

Or,

- Removal of individuals or parts thereof
  - is part of an NPS research project described in an approved management plan, or is part of research being conducted by others who have been issued a scientific research and collecting permit;
  - is done to provide plants or animals for restoring native populations in parks or cooperating areas without diminishing the viability of the park populations from which the individuals are taken; or
  - meets specific park management objectives.

In planning and implementing plant and animal population management actions, the Service will follow established planning procedures, including provisions for public review and comment. The Service will consult, as appropriate, with other federal land-management agencies, the U.S. Fish and Wildlife Service, the NOAA Fisheries, state wildlife management agencies, other appropriate state agencies, tribal governments, and others. Such consultation will address (1) the management of selected animal populations, (2) research involving the taking of animal species of interest to these agencies, and (3) cooperative studies and plans dealing with the public hunting and fishing of animal populations that occur across park boundaries.

The Service's cooperative conservation efforts concerning fish and wildlife management will be consistent with departmental policy articulated at 43 CFR Part 24. This departmental policy recognizes the broad authorities and responsibilities of federal and state agencies with regard to the management of the nation's fish and wildlife resources; this policy also promotes cooperative management relationships among these agencies. In particular, the policy calls on the Service to consult with state agencies on certain fish and wildlife management actions and encourages the execution of memoranda of understanding as appropriate to ensure the conduct of programs that meet mutual objectives as long as they do not conflict with federal law or regulation.

The Service will assess the results of managing plant and animal populations by conducting follow-up monitoring or other studies to determine the impacts of the management methods on nontargeted and targeted components of the ecosystem.

4.4.2.1 NPS Actions That Remove Native Plants and Animals

Whenever the Service removes native plants or animals, manages plant or animal populations to reduce their sizes, or allows others to remove plants or animals for an authorized purpose, the Service will seek to ensure that such removals will not cause unacceptable impacts on native resources, natural processes, or other park resources. Whenever the Service identifies a possible need for reducing the size of a park plant or animal population, the Service will use scientifically valid resource information obtained through consultation with technical experts, literature review, inventory, monitoring, or research to evaluate the identified need for population management; the Service will document it in the appropriate park management plan.

In addition, the Service will manage such removals to prevent them from interfering broadly with

- natural habitats, natural abundances, and natural distributions of native species and natural processes
- rare, threatened, and endangered plant or animal species or their critical habitats
- scientific study, interpretation, environmental education, appreciation of wildlife, or other public benefits
- opportunities to restore depressed populations of native species
- breeding or spawning grounds of native species

Where the need to reduce animal populations may be due to persistent human/animal conflicts, the Service will determine whether or not it can eliminate or mitigate the conflicts by modifying or curtailing the conflicting visitor use or other human activities. Where visitor use or other human activities cannot be modified or curtailed, the Service may directly reduce the animal population by using several animal population management techniques, either separately or together. These techniques include relocation, public hunting on lands outside a park or where legislatively authorized within a park, habitat management, predator restoration, reproductive

intervention, and destruction of animals by NPS personnel or their authorized agents. Where animal populations are reduced, destroyed animals may be left in natural areas of the park to decompose unless there are human safety concerns regarding attraction of potentially harmful scavengers to populated sites or trails or other human health and sanitary concerns associated with decomposition. Live animals or carcasses may be removed from parks according to the provisions of applicable laws, agreements, and regulations, including the granting of preference to Native Americans.

(See Pest Management 4.4.5. Also see Director's Order #18: Wildland Fire Management)

4.4.2.2 Restoration of Native Plant and Animal Species

The Service will strive to restore extirpated native plant and animal species to parks whenever all of the following criteria are met:

- Adequate habitat to support the species either exists or can reasonably be restored in the park and if necessary also on adjacent public lands and waters; once a natural population level is achieved, the population can be self-perpetuating.

- The species does not, based on an effective management plan, pose a serious threat to the safety of people in parks, park resources, or persons or property within or outside park boundaries.

- The genetic type used in restoration most nearly approximates the extirpated genetic type.

- The species disappeared or was substantially diminished as a direct or indirect result of human-induced change to the species population or to the ecosystem.

- Potential impacts upon park management and use have been carefully considered.

Programs to restore animal species may include confining animals in small field enclosures during restoration efforts, but only until the animals have become accustomed to the new area or they have become sufficiently established to minimize threats from predators, poaching, disease, or other factors. Programs to restore animal species may also include confining animals in cages for captive breeding to increase the number of offspring for release to the wild or to manage the population's gene pool. Programs to restore plant species may include propagating plants in greenhouses, gardens, or other confined areas to develop propagation materials (propagules) for restoration efforts or to manage a population's gene pool.

(See Restoration of Natural Systems 4.1.5)

4.4.2.3 Management of Threatened or Endangered Plants and Animals

The Service will survey for, protect, and strive to recover all species native to national park system units that are listed under the Endangered Species Act. The Service will fully meet its obligations under the NPS Organic Act and the Endangered Species Act to both proactively conserve listed species and prevent detrimental effects on these species. To meet these obligations, the Service will

- cooperate with both the U.S. Fish and Wildlife Service and the NOAA Fisheries to ensure that NPS actions comply with both the written requirements and the spirit of the Endangered Species Act. This cooperation should include the full range of activities associated with the Endangered Species Act, including consultation, conferencing, informal discussions, and securing all necessary scientific and/or recovery permits;

- undertake active management programs to inventory, monitor, restore, and maintain listed species' habitats; control detrimental nonnative species; manage detrimental visitor access; and reestablish extirpated populations as necessary to maintain the species and the habitats upon which they depend;

- manage designated critical habitat, essential habitat, and recovery areas to maintain and enhance their value for the recovery of threatened and endangered species;

- cooperate with other agencies to ensure that the delineation of critical habitat, essential habitat, and/or recovery areas on park-managed lands provides needed conservation benefits to the total recovery efforts being conducted by all the participating agencies;

- participate in the recovery planning process, including the provision of members on recovery teams and recovery implementation teams where appropriate;

- cooperate with other agencies, states, and private entities to promote candidate conservation agreements aimed at precluding the need to list species; and

- conduct actions and allocate funding to address endangered, threatened, proposed, and candidate species.

The National Park Service will inventory, monitor, and manage state and locally listed species in a manner similar to its treatment of federally listed species to the greatest extent possible. In addition, the Service will inventory other native species that are of special management concern to parks (such as rare, declining, sensitive, or unique species and their habitats) and will manage them to maintain their natural distribution and abundance.

The Service will determine all management actions for the protection and perpetuation of federally, state, or locally listed species through the park management planning process, and will include consultation with lead federal and state agencies as appropriate.

(See Cooperative Conservation Beyond Park Boundaries 1.6; Partnerships 1.10 and 4.1.4; Cooperative Planning 2.3.1.8; Visitor Use 8.2)

4.4.2.4 Management of Natural Landscapes

Natural landscapes disturbed by natural phenomena, such as landslides, earthquakes, floods, hurricanes, tornadoes, and fires, will be allowed to recover naturally unless manipulation is necessary to (1) mitigate for excessive disturbance caused by past human effects, (2) preserve cultural and historic resources as appropriate based on park planning documents, or (3) protect park developments or the safety of people. Landscape and vegetation conditions altered by human activity may be manipulated where the park management plan provides for restoring the lands to a natural condition. Management activities to restore human-altered landscapes may include, but are not restricted to

- removing constructed features, restoring natural topographic gradients, and revegetating with native park species on acquired inholdings and on sites from which previous development is being removed;
- restoring natural processes and conditions to areas disturbed by human activities such as fire suppression;
- rehabilitating areas disturbed by visitor use or by the removal of hazard trees; and
- maintaining open areas and meadows in situations in which they were formerly maintained by natural processes that now are altered by human activities.

Landscape revegetation efforts will use seeds, cuttings, or transplants representing species and gene pools native to the ecological portion of the park in which the restoration project is occurring. Where a natural area has become so degraded that restoration with gene pools native to the park has proven unsuccessful, improved varieties or closely related native species may be used.

Landscape restoration efforts will use geological materials and soils obtained in accordance with geological and soil resource *Management Policies*. Landscape restoration efforts may use, on a temporary basis, appropriate soil fertilizers or other soil amendments so long as that use does not unacceptably alter the physical, chemical, or biological characteristics of the soil and biological community and does not degrade surface or groundwaters.

(See Restoration of Natural Systems 4.1.5; Cultural Landscapes 5.3.5.2)

4.4.2.5 Maintenance of Altered Plant Communities

In altered plant communities managed for a specified purpose, plantings will consist of species that are native to the park or that are historically appropriate for the period or event commemorated. Communities altered to maintain habitat for threatened or endangered species may only use native plants, and the manipulation of existing plants will be carried out to enhance the recovery of the threatened or endangered species or the recovery of the natural functioning of the plant and animal community that endangered species are a part of. Use of exotic plants must conform to exotic species policy. Use of nonnatural plantings in altered communities may be permitted under any of the following conditions:

- In localized, specific areas, screen plantings may be used to protect against the undesirable impacts of adjacent land uses provided that the plantings do not result in the invasion of exotic species.

- Where necessary to preserve and protect the desired condition of specific cultural resources and landscapes, plants and plant communities generally will be managed to reflect the character of the landscape that prevailed during the historic period. Efforts may be made to extend the lives of specimen trees dating from the historic period being commemorated. An individual tree or shrub known to be of historic value that is diseased beyond recovery and has become hazardous will be removed and may be replaced. While specimen trees or shrubs that need to be perpetuated are still healthy, their own progeny will be propagated from seeds or through vegetative reproduction, such as cuttings.

- Where cultivated crop plants may be needed for livestock or agricultural uses that are allowed as part of the cultural landscape, authorized by federal law, or retained as a property right, with rigorous review given to any proposal to introduce a genetically modified organism.

- Where needed for intensive development areas. Such plantings will use noninvasive native or nonnative historic species and materials to the maximum extent possible. Certain native species may be fostered for esthetic, interpretive, or educational purposes.

Exotic species may not be used to vegetate vista clearings in otherwise natural vegetation.

Limited, recurring use of soil fertilizers or other soil amendments may be allowed only as needed to maintain the desired condition of the altered plant community, and only where such use does not unacceptably alter the physical, chemical, or biological characteristics of the soil and biological community or degrade surface or groundwaters.

(See Management of Exotic Species 4.4.4; Cultural Landscapes 5.3.5.2)

4.4.3 Harvest of Plants and Animals by the Public

Public harvesting of designated species of plants and animals, or their components, may be allowed in park units when

- hunting, trapping, subsistence use, or other harvesting is specifically authorized by statute or regulation and not subsequently prohibited by regulation;

- harvest of certain plant parts or unoccupied seashells for personal consumption or use is specifically authorized by the superintendent in accordance with 36 CFR 2.1(c)(1);
- recreational fishing is not specifically prohibited; or
- commercial fishing is specifically authorized by statute or regulation.

Where harvesting is allowed and subject to NPS control, the Service will allow harvesting only when (1) the monitoring requirement contained in section 4.4.2 and the criteria in section 4.4.2.1 above have been met, and (2) the Service has determined that the harvesting will not unacceptably impact park resources or natural processes, including the natural distributions, densities, age-class distributions, and behavior of

- harvested species
- native species that the harvested species use for any purpose, or
- native species that use the harvested species for any purpose

In consultation and cooperation, as appropriate, with individual state or tribal governments, the Service will manage harvesting programs and any associated habitat management programs intended to restore and maintain habitats supporting harvested plant or animal populations to conform with applicable federal and state regulations.

Habitat manipulation for harvested species may include the restoration of a disturbed area to its natural condition so it can become self-perpetuating, but this will not include the artificial manipulation of habitat to increase the numbers of a harvested species above its natural range in population levels.

The Service may encourage the intensive harvesting of exotic species in certain situations when needed to meet park management objectives.

The Service does not engage in activities to reduce the numbers of native species for the purpose of increasing the numbers of harvested species (i.e., predator control), nor does the Service permit others to do so on lands managed by the National Park Service.

The Service manages harvest to allow for self-sustaining populations of harvested species and does not engage in the stocking of plants or animals to increase harvest. In some special situations, the Service may stock native or exotic animals for recreational harvesting purposes, but only when such stocking will not unacceptably impact park natural resources or processes and when

- the stocking is of fish into constructed large reservoirs or other significantly altered large water bodies and the purpose is to provide for recreational fishing; or
- the intent for stocking is a treaty right or expressed in statute, other applicable law, or a House or Senate report accompanying a statute.

The Service will not stock waters that are naturally barren of harvested aquatic species.

4.4.4 Management of Exotic Species

Exotic species will not be allowed to displace native species if displacement can be prevented.

4.4.4.1 Introduction or Maintenance of Exotic Species

In general, new exotic species will not be introduced into parks. In rare situations, an exotic species may be introduced or maintained to meet specific, identified management needs when all feasible and prudent measures to minimize the risk of harm have been taken and it is

- a closely related race, subspecies, or hybrid of an extirpated native species; or
- an improved variety of a native species in situations in which the natural variety cannot survive current, human-altered environmental conditions; or
- used to control another, already established exotic species; or
- needed to meet the desired condition of a historic resource, but only where it is noninvasive and is prevented from being invasive by such means as cultivating (for plants), or tethering, herding, or pasturing (for animals). In such cases, the exotic species used must be known to be historically significant, to have existed in the park during the park's period of historical significance, to be a contributing element to a cultural landscape, or to have been commonly used in the local area at that time; or
- an agricultural crop used to maintain the character of a cultural landscape, with rigorous review given to any proposal to introduce a genetically modified organism; or
- necessary to provide for intensive visitor use in developed areas and both of the following conditions exist:
  ◇ Available native species will not meet park management objectives.
  ◇ The exotic species is managed so it will not spread or become a pest on park or adjacent lands.
- a sterile, noninvasive plant that is used temporarily for erosion control; or
- directed by law or expressed legislative intent.

Domestic livestock such as cattle, sheep, goats, horses, mules, burros, reindeer, and llamas are exotic species that are maintained in some parks for commercial herding, pasturing, grazing, or trailing; for recreational use; or for administrative use for maintaining the cultural scene or supporting park operations. The policies applicable to the grazing of commercial domestic livestock are discussed in chapter 8, section 8.6.8. The Service will phase out the commercial grazing of livestock whenever possible and manage recreational and administrative uses of livestock to prevent those uses from unacceptably impacting park resources.

4.4.4.2 Removal of Exotic Species Already Present

All exotic plant and animal species that are not maintained to meet an identified park purpose will be managed—up to and including eradication—if (1) control is prudent and feasible, and (2) the exotic species

- interferes with natural processes and the perpetuation of natural features, native species or natural habitats, or
- disrupts the genetic integrity of native species, or
- disrupts the accurate presentation of a cultural landscape, or
- damages cultural resources, or
- significantly hampers the management of park or adjacent lands, or
- poses a public health hazard as advised by the U.S. Public Health Service (which includes the Centers for Disease Control and the NPS public health program), or
- creates a hazard to public safety.

High priority will be given to managing exotic species that have, or potentially could have, a substantial impact on park resources, and that can reasonably be expected to be successfully controlled. Lower priority will be given to exotic species that have almost no impact on park resources or that probably cannot be successfully controlled. Where an exotic species cannot be successfully eliminated, managers will seek to contain the exotic species to prevent further spread or resource damage.

The decision to initiate management should be based on a determination that the species is exotic. For species determined to be exotic and where management appears to be feasible and effective, superintendents should (1) evaluate the species' current or potential impact on park resources; (2) develop and implement exotic species management plans according to established planning procedures; (3) consult, as appropriate, with federal, tribal, local, and state agencies as well as other interested groups; and (4) invite public review and comment, where appropriate. Programs to manage exotic species will be designed to avoid causing significant damage to native species, natural ecological communities, natural ecological processes, cultural resources, and human health and safety. Considerations and techniques regarding removal of exotic species are similar to those used for native species (see 4.4.2.1 NPS Actions That Remove Native Plants and Animals).

(Also see Executive Order 13112 (Invasive Species))

4.4.5 Pest Management

All park employees, concessioners, contractors, permittees, licensees, and visitors on all lands managed or regulated by the National Park Service will comply with NPS pest *Management Policies*.

4.4.5.1 Pests

Pests are living organisms that interfere with the purposes or management objectives of a specific site within a park or that jeopardize human health or safety. Decisions concerning whether or not to manage a pest or pest population will be influenced by whether the pest is an exotic or a native species. Exotic pests will be managed according to both the policies in this section (4.4.5) and the exotic species policies in section 4.4.4. Native pests will be allowed to function unimpeded, except as noted below. Many fungi, insects, rodents, disease organisms, and other organisms that may be perceived as pests are, in fact, native organisms existing under natural conditions and are natural elements of the ecosystem. Also, native pests that were evident in pesticide-free times are traditional elements in park cultural settings.

The Service may control native pests to

- conserve threatened, rare, or endangered species, or unique specimens or communities;
- preserve, maintain, or restore the historical integrity of cultural resources;
- conserve and protect plants, animals, and facilities in developed areas;
- prevent outbreaks of a pest from invading uninfested areas outside the park;
- manage a human health hazard when advised to do so by the U.S. Public Health Service (which includes the Centers for Disease Control and the NPS public health program); or
- to otherwise protect against a significant threat to human safety.

4.4.5.2 Integrated Pest Management Program

The Service conducts an integrated pest management (IPM) program to reduce risks to the public, park resources, and the environment from pests and pest-related management strategies. Integrated pest management is a decision-making process that coordinates knowledge of pest biology, the environment, and available technology to prevent unacceptable levels of pest damage by cost-effective means while posing the least possible risk to people, resources, and the environment.

The Service and each park unit will use an IPM approach to address pest issues. Proposed pest management activities must be conducted according to the IPM process prescribed in Director's Order #77-7: Integrated Pest Management. Pest issues will be reviewed on a case-by-case basis. Controversial issues, or those that have potential to negatively impact the environment, must be addressed through established planning procedures and be included in an approved park management or IPM plan. IPM procedures will be used to determine when to implement pest management actions and which combination of strategies will be most effective for each pest situation.

Under the Service's IPM program, all pesticide use on lands managed or regulated by the Service, whether that use was authorized or unauthorized, must be reported annually.

4.4.5.3 Pesticide Use

A pesticide, as defined by the Federal Insecticide, Fungicide and Rodenticide Act, is any substance or mixture that is used in any manner to destroy, repel, or control the growth of any viral, microbial, plant, or animal pest. Except as identified in the next paragraph, all prospective users of pesticides in parks must submit pesticide use requests, which will be reviewed on a case-by-case basis, taking into account environmental effects, cost and staffing, and other relevant considerations. The decision to incorporate a chemical, biological, or bioengineered pesticide into a management strategy will be based on a determination by a designated IPM specialist that it is necessary and other available options are either not acceptable or not feasible. Pesticide applications will only be performed by or under the supervision of certified or registered applicators licensed under the procedures of a federal or state certification system.

Insect repellents, bear deterrent sprays, and insecticides applied to persons or to livestock must conform to NPS policies and approval procedures, except that pesticides used under the following conditions do not require approval:

- cleansers and disinfectants used in restrooms and restaurants
- personal insect repellents, insecticides, and bear deterrent sprays that employees or park visitors personally obtain and use to meet personal needs
- insect repellents and insecticides applied to personally owned pets and pack and saddle stock

4.4.5.4 Biological Control Agents and Bioengineered Products

The application or release of any bio-control agent or bioengineered product relating to pest management activities must be reviewed by designated IPM specialists in accordance with Director's Order #77-7 and conform to the exotic species policies in section 4.4.4.

4.4.5.5 Pesticide Purchase and Storage

Pesticides must not be stockpiled. No pesticides may be purchased unless they are authorized and expected to be used within one year from the date of purchase. Pesticide storage, transport, and disposal will comply with procedures established by (1) the Environmental Protection Agency; (2) the individual states in which parks are located; and (3) Director's Order #30A: Hazardous and Solid Waste Management, Director's Order #77-1: Wetland Protection, and Director's Order 77-7: Integrated Pest Management.

(See Planning for Natural Resource Management 4.1.1; Genetic Resource Management Principles 4.4.1.2; Management of Exotic Species 4.4.4; Maintenance 9.1.4)

4.5 Fire Management

Naturally ignited fire, including the smoke it produces, is part of many of the natural systems that are being sustained in parks. Such natural systems contain plant and animal communities that are characterized as fire-adapted or fire-dependent. They require periodic episodes of fire to retain their ecological integrity and, in the human-caused absence of fire, they can experience undesirable impacts that diminish their integrity—such as unnatural successional trends, loss of habitat for fire-adapted plant and animal species, or vulnerability to unnaturally intense wildland fire. Other park natural systems are characterized by a natural absence or very low frequency of fire. These systems are at risk of losing their ecological integrity when the natural fire regime is subjected to human interference.

Fires that burn natural or landscaped vegetation in parks are called wildland fires. Wildland fires occur from both natural and human sources of ignition. Wildland fires may contribute to or hinder the achievement of park management objectives, and management response to each wildland fire is determined by whether or not the fire occurs within prescription as identified in the park's fire management plan. Wildland fire use is the application of an appropriate management response to naturally ignited wildland fires to accomplish specific resource management objectives in predefined areas outlined in fire management plans. Prescribed fires are the deliberate ignition of fires under prescribed circumstances to accomplish resource management objectives in predefined areas outlined in approved fire management plans.

Fire management consists of a program of activities designed to meet management objectives for protection of resource values, life, and property and, where appropriate, for using naturally ignited and human-ignited wildland fires as management tools. Park fire management programs designed specifically to meet park resource management objectives—including allowing fire to perform its natural role as much as practicable—will ensure that firefighter and public safety are not compromised.

Parks with vegetation capable of burning will prepare a fire management plan that is consistent with federal law and departmental fire *Management Policies*, and that includes addressing the need for adequate funding and staffing to support the planned fire management program. The plan will be designed to guide a program that

- responds to the park's natural and cultural resource objectives;
- provides for safety considerations for park visitors, employees, and developed facilities;
- addresses potential impacts on public and private neighbors and their property adjacent to the park; and
- protects public health and safety.

The fire management plan will also include guidance on determining in which situations natural regeneration of a burned ecosystem is appropriate and when management actions are needed to restore, stabilize, or rehabilitate an area following wildland fire.

Environmental and cultural resource compliance documentation developed in support of the plan will consider the effects of fire on air quality, water quality, and human health and safety. It will also discuss the influence of fire, fire management, and the potential consequences and effects of fire exclusion on the ability of the park to meet its natural and cultural resource management objectives. Preparation of the plan and supporting documents will include collaboration with appropriate NPS natural and cultural resource offices, adjacent communities, interest groups, state and federal agencies, and tribal governments, with cooperating agency status granted when requested by eligible adjacent communities, state and federal agencies, and tribal governments.

All wildland fires will be effectively managed through application of the appropriate strategic and tactical management options as guided by the park's fire management plan. These options will be selected after comprehensive consideration of the resource values to be protected, firefighter and public safety, costs, availability of firefighting resources, weather, and fuel conditions. Naturally ignited and human-ignited fires managed to achieve resource management and fuel treatment objectives, and the smoke they produce, will both be managed to comply with applicable local, state, and federal air quality regulations. Such fires will also include monitoring programs that record fire behavior, smoke behavior, fire decisions, and fire effects to provide information on whether specific objectives are met and to improve future fire management strategies. All parks will use a systematic decision-making process identified in their fire management plans or other documents to determine the most appropriate management strategies for all unplanned ignitions and for any naturally or management-ignited fires that are no longer meeting resource management objectives.

Parks lacking an approved fire management plan may not use resource benefits as a consideration influencing the selection of a suppression strategy; they must consider the resource impacts of suppression alternatives in their decisions. Until a plan is approved, parks must immediately suppress all wildland fires, taking into consideration park resources and values to be protected, firefighter and public safety, costs, availability of firefighting resources, weather, and fuel conditions. Parks will use methods to suppress wildland fires that minimize the impacts of the suppression action and the fire and are commensurate with effective control, firefighter and public safety, and resource values to be protected.

Burnable vegetation in many parks includes areas that are hazardous to specific park resources or human safety and property because of the presence of fuels that could carry wildland fire into special resource protection zones, developed areas, or outside park boundaries. The fire management plan will address strategies for preventing the accumulation of hazardous fuels in specific areas and for eliminating hazardous conditions that may have developed over time due to past fire suppression programs or ongoing development activities. These strategies will entail strategic planning, interdisciplinary coordination, and interorganizational collaboration as needed to provide appropriate treatment using adaptive management practices that range from site specific to landscape level. Although prescribed fire remains the preferred and most widely used NPS tool for managing the accumulation of hazardous fuels, the strategies will incorporate other activities, such as manual, mechanical, biological and, rarely, chemical treatments (applying integrated pest management principles), that may be appropriate in specific instances, as guided by NPS and DOI policies and legal requirements.

More details on wildland fire management, including interagency and Department of the Interior policies and requirements, are contained in Director's Order #18: Wildland Fire Management.

Fire management or suppression activities conducted within wilderness, including the categories of designated, recommended, potential, proposed, and eligible areas, will be consistent with the "minimum requirement" concept identified in chapter 6 and Director's Order #41: Wilderness Preservation and Management.

(See General Management Concepts 4.1; Partnerships 4.1.4; Restoration of Natural Systems 4.1.5; Air Resource Management 4.7; Fire Detection, Suppression, and Post-fire Rehabilitation and Protection 5.3.1.2; Fire Management 6.3.9; Visitor Safety 8.2.5.1; Structural Fire Protection and Suppression 9.1.8)

4.6 Water Resource Management

4.6.1 Protection of Surface Waters and Groundwaters

The Service will perpetuate surface waters and groundwaters as integral components of park aquatic and terrestrial ecosystems.

4.6.2 Water Rights

Water for the preservation and management of the national park system will be obtained and used in accordance with legal authorities. The Park Service will consider all available authorities on a case-by-case basis and will pursue those that are the most appropriate to protect water-related resources in parks. While preserving its legal remedies, the Service will work with state water administrators to protect park resources and participate in negotiations to seek the resolution of conflicts among multiple water claimants. Water essential for NPS needs will be purchased if it is not otherwise available. NPS consumptive use of water will be efficient and frugal, especially in water-scarce areas.

All rights to the use of water diverted from or used on federal lands within the national park system by the United

States or its concessioners, lessors, or permittees will be perfected in the name of the United States.

Park surface waters or groundwater will be withdrawn for consumptive use only when such withdrawal is absolutely necessary for the use and management of the park. All park water withdrawn for domestic or administrative uses will be returned to the park watershed system once it has been treated to a degree that ensures that there will be no impairment of park resources.

The Service may enter into contracts for the sale or lease of water to persons, states, or their political subdivisions that provide public accommodations or services for park visitors outside and near the park that have no reasonable alternative sources of water. The Service will authorize such contracts only if

- the transfer does not jeopardize or unduly interfere with the natural or cultural resources of the park, and
- the government's costs are fully recovered, and
- the contract is for a short term, true emergency.

The Service will follow the requirements and procedures of Director's Orders #35A and #35B when considering the sale or lease of park water.

(See Decision-making Requirements to Identify and Avoid Impairments 1.4.7; Cooperative Conservation Beyond Park Boundaries 1.6)

4.6.3 Water Quality

The pollution of surface waters and groundwaters by both point and nonpoint sources can impair the natural functioning of aquatic and terrestrial ecosystems and diminish the utility of park waters for visitor use and enjoyment. The Service will determine the quality of park surface and groundwater resources and avoid, whenever possible, the pollution of park waters by human activities occurring within and outside the parks. The Service will

- work with appropriate governmental bodies to obtain the highest possible standards available under the Clean Water Act for the protection for park waters;
- take all necessary actions to maintain or restore the quality of surface waters and groundwaters within the parks consistent with the Clean Water Act and all other applicable federal, state, and local laws and regulations; and
- enter into agreements with other agencies and governing bodies, as appropriate, to secure their cooperation in maintaining or restoring the quality of park water resources.

(See Pest Management 4.4.5; Soil Resource Management 4.8.2.4; Backcountry Use 8.2.2.4; Domestic and Feral Livestock 8.6.8; Mineral Exploration and Development 8.7; Water Supply Systems 9.1.5.1; Wastewater Treatment Systems 9.1.5.2; Waste Management and Contaminant Issues 9.1.6; Facilities for Water Recreation 9.3.4.2. Also see Director's Order #83: Public Health)

4.6.4 Floodplains

In managing floodplains on park lands, the National Park Service will (1) manage for the preservation of floodplain values; (2) minimize potentially hazardous conditions associated with flooding; and (3) comply with the NPS Organic Act and all other federal laws and executive orders related to the management of activities in flood-prone areas, including Executive Order 11988 (Floodplain Management), the National Environmental Policy Act, applicable provisions of the Clean Water Act, and the Rivers and Harbors Appropriation Act of 1899. Specifically, the Service will

- protect, preserve, and restore the natural resources and functions of floodplains;
- avoid the long- and short-term environmental effects associated with the occupancy and modification of floodplains; and
- avoid direct and indirect support of floodplain development and actions that could adversely affect the natural resources and functions of floodplains or increase flood risks.

When it is not practicable to locate or relocate development or inappropriate human activities to a site outside and not affecting the floodplain, the Service will

- prepare and approve a statement of findings, in accordance with procedures described in Director's Order 77-2 (Floodplain Management);
- use nonstructural measures as much as practicable to reduce hazards to human life and property while minimizing the impact to the natural resources of floodplains;
- ensure that structures and facilities are designed to be consistent with the intent of the standards and criteria of the National Flood Insurance Program (44 CFR Part 60).

(See Siting Facilities to Avoid Natural Hazards 9.1.1.5)

4.6.5 Wetlands

The Service will manage wetlands in compliance with NPS mandates and the requirements of Executive Order 11990 (Protection of Wetlands), the Clean Water Act, the Rivers and Harbors Appropriation Act of 1899, and the procedures described in Director's Order 77-1 (Wetland Protection). The Service will (1) provide leadership and take action to prevent the destruction, loss, or degradation of wetlands; (2) preserve and enhance the natural and beneficial values of wetlands; and (3) avoid direct and indirect support of new construction in wetlands unless there are no practicable alternatives and the proposed action includes all practicable measures to minimize harm to wetlands.

The Service will implement a "no net loss of wetlands" policy. In addition, the Service will strive to achieve a longer-term goal of net gain of wetlands across the national park system through restoration of previously degraded or destroyed wetlands.

When natural wetland characteristics or functions have been degraded or lost due to previous or ongoing human actions, the Service will, to the extent practicable, restore them to predisturbance conditions.

The Service will conduct or obtain parkwide wetland inventories to help ensure proper planning with respect to the management and protection of wetland resources. Additional, more detailed wetland inventories will be conducted in areas that are proposed for development or are otherwise susceptible to degradation or loss due to human activities.

When practicable, the Service will not simply protect but will seek to enhance natural wetland values by using them for educational, recreational, scientific, and similar purposes that do not disrupt natural wetland functions.

For proposed new development or other new activities, plans, or programs that are either located in or otherwise could have adverse impacts on wetlands, the Service will employ the following sequence:

◆ Avoid adverse wetland impacts to the extent practicable.

◆ Minimize impacts that cannot be avoided.

◆ Compensate for remaining unavoidable adverse wetland impacts by restoring wetlands that have been previously destroyed or degraded.

Compensation for wetland impacts or losses will require that at least 1 acre of wetlands be restored for each acre destroyed or degraded.

Actions proposed by the Park Service that have the potential to cause adverse impacts on wetlands must be addressed in an environmental assessment or an environmental impact statement. If the preferred alternative will result in adverse impacts on wetlands, a statement of findings must be prepared and approved in accordance with Director's Order #77-1: Wetland Protection.

(See Decision-making Requirements to Identify and Avoid Impairments 1.4.7; Siting Facilities to Avoid Natural Hazards 9.1.1.5)

4.6.6 Watershed and Stream Processes

The Service will manage watersheds as complete hydrologic systems and minimize human- caused disturbance to the natural upland processes that deliver water, sediment, and woody debris to streams. These processes include runoff, erosion, and disturbance to vegetation and soil caused by fire, insects, meteorological events, and mass movements. The Service will manage streams to protect stream processes that create habitat features such as floodplains, riparian systems, woody debris accumulations, terraces, gravel bars, riffles, and pools. Stream processes include flooding, stream migration, and associated erosion and deposition.

The Service will protect watershed and stream features primarily by avoiding impacts on watershed and riparian vegetation and by allowing natural fluvial processes to proceed unimpeded. When conflicts between infrastructure (such as bridges and pipeline crossings) and stream processes are unavoidable, NPS managers will first consider relocating or redesigning facilities rather than manipulating streams. Where stream manipulation is unavoidable, managers will use techniques that are visually nonobtrusive and that protect natural processes to the greatest extent practicable.

(See Floodplains 4.6.4; Shorelines and Barrier Islands; 4.8.1.1; Facility Planning and Design 9.1.1. Also see "Unified Federal Policy for a Watershed Approach to Federal Land and Resource Management," 65 FR 62566, October 18, 2000)

4.7 Air Resource Management

4.7.1 Air Quality

The National Park Service has a responsibility to protect air quality under both the 1916 Organic Act and the Clean Air Act (CAA). Accordingly, the Service will seek to perpetuate the best possible air quality in parks to (1) preserve natural resources and systems; (2) preserve cultural resources; and (3) sustain visitor enjoyment, human health, and scenic vistas. Vegetation, visibility, water quality, wildlife, historic and prehistoric structures and objects, cultural landscapes, and most other elements of a park environment are sensitive to air pollution and are referred to as "air quality-related values." The Service will actively promote and pursue measures to protect these values from the adverse impacts of air pollution. In cases of doubt as to the impacts of existing or potential air pollution on park resources, the Service will err on the side of protecting air quality and related values for future generations.

Superintendents will take actions consistent with their affirmative responsibilities under the Clean Air Act to protect air quality-related values in Class I areas. Class I areas are national parks over 6, 000 acres and national wilderness areas over 5,000 acres that were in existence on August 7, 1977. The act establishes a national goal of preventing any future and remedying any existing human-made visibility impairment in Class I areas. The Service supports that goal and will take advantage of opportunities created by the act to help achieve it. The federal land manager shares the responsibility to protect air quality-related values in Class I areas. As the federal land manager for the department, the Secretary of the Interior has delegated this responsibility to the Assistant Secretary for Fish and Wildlife and Parks.

The Clean Air Act also recognizes the importance of integral vistas, which are those views perceived from within Class I areas of a specific landmark or panorama located outside the boundary of the Class I area. Integral vistas have been identified by the Service and are listed in Natural Resources Reference Manual 77. There are no regulations requiring special protection of these integral vistas, but the

Service will strive to protect these park-related resources through cooperative means.

Although the Clean Air Act gives the highest level of air quality protection to Class I areas, it provides many opportunities for the Service to participate in the development of pollution control programs to preserve, protect, and enhance the air quality of all units of the national park system. Regardless of Class I designation, the Service will take advantage of these opportunities.

Air resource management requirements will be integrated into NPS operations and planning, and all air pollution sources within parks—including prescribed fire management and visitor use activities—will comply with all federal, state, and local air quality regulations and permitting requirements. Superintendents will make reasonable efforts to notify visitors and employees when air pollution concentrations within an area exceed the national or state air quality standards established to protect public health. Furthermore, because the current and future quality of park air resources depends heavily on the actions of others, the Service will acquire the information needed to effectively participate in decision-making that affects park air quality. The Service will

- inventory the air quality-related values associated with each park;
- monitor and document the condition of air quality and related values;
- evaluate air pollution impacts and identify causes;
- minimize air quality pollution emissions associated with park operations, including the use of prescribed fire and visitor use activities; and
- ensure healthful indoor air quality in NPS facilities.

External programs needed to remedy existing and prevent future impacts on park resources and values from human-caused air pollution will be aggressively pursued by NPS participation in the development of federal, state, and local air pollution control plans and regulations. Permit applications for major new air pollution sources will be reviewed, and potential impacts will be assessed. If it is determined that any such new source might cause or contribute to an adverse impact on air quality-related values, the Park Service will recommend to the permitting authority that the construction permit be denied or modified to eliminate adverse impacts.

The public's understanding of park air quality issues and the positive role and efforts of the Service toward improving the air quality in parks will be promoted through educational and interpretive programs.

(See Cooperative Conservation Beyond Park Boundaries 1.6; Fire Management 4.5; Environmental Monitoring and Control 5.3.1.4; Resource Issue Interpretation and Education 7.5.3; Visitor Safety and Emergency Response 8.2.5; Energy Management 9.1.7)

4.7.2 Weather and Climate

Earth's climate has changed throughout history. Although national parks are intended to be naturally evolving places that conserve our natural and cultural heritage for generations to come, accelerated climate change may significantly alter park ecosystems. Thus, parks containing significant natural resources will gather and maintain baseline climatological data for reference.

Because any human attempt to modify weather has the potential to alter the natural conditions in parks, the Service will not conduct weather-modification activities, the Service will seek to prevent weather modification activities conducted by others from affecting a park's weather, climate, and resources.

(See NPS-conducted or -sponsored Inventory, Monitoring, and Research Studies 4.2.1; Miscellaneous Management Facilities 9.4.5)

4.8 Geologic Resource Management

The Park Service will preserve and protect geologic resources as integral components of park natural systems. As used here, the term "geologic resources" includes both geologic features and geologic processes. The Service will (1) assess the impacts of natural processes and human activities on geologic resources; (2) maintain and restore the integrity of existing geologic resources; (3) integrate geologic resource management into Service operations and planning; and (4) interpret geologic resources for park visitors.

4.8.1 Protection of Geologic Processes

The Service will, except as identified below, allow natural geologic processes to proceed unimpeded. Geologic processes are the natural physical and chemical forces that act within natural systems and on human developments across a broad spectrum of space and time. Such processes include, but are not limited to, exfoliation, erosion and sedimentation, glaciation, karst processes, shoreline processes, and seismic and volcanic activity. Geologic processes will be addressed during planning and other management activities in an effort to reduce hazards that can threaten the safety of park visitors and staff and the long-term viability of the park infrastructure.

Intervention in natural geologic processes will be permitted only when

- directed by Congress;
- necessary in emergencies that threaten human life and property;
- there is no other feasible way to protect natural resources, park facilities, or historic properties;
- intervention is necessary to restore impacted conditions and processes, such as restoring habitat for threatened or endangered species.

4.8.1.1 Shorelines and Barrier Islands

Natural shoreline processes (such as erosion, deposition, dune formation, overwash, inlet formation, and shoreline migration) will be allowed to continue without interference.

Where human activities or structures have altered the nature or rate of natural shoreline processes, the Service will, in consultation with appropriate state and federal agencies, investigate alternatives for mitigating the effects of such activities or structures and for restoring natural conditions. The Service will comply with the provisions of Executive Order 11988 (Floodplain Management) and state coastal zone management plans prepared under the Coastal Zone Management Act of 1972.

Any shoreline manipulation measures proposed to protect cultural resources may be approved only after an analysis of the degree to which such measures would impact natural resources and processes, so that an informed decision can be made through an assessment of alternatives.

Where erosion control is required by law, or where present developments must be protected in the short run to achieve park management objectives, including high-density visitor use, the Service will use the most effective method feasible to achieve the natural resource management objectives while minimizing impacts outside the target area.

New developments will not be placed in areas subject to wave erosion or active shoreline processes unless (1) the development is required by law; or (2) the development is essential to meet the park's purposes, as defined by its establishing act or proclamation, and

- no practicable alternative locations are available;
- the development will be reasonably assured of surviving during its planned life span without the need for shoreline control measures; and
- steps will be taken to minimize safety hazards and harm to property and natural resources.

(See Floodplains 4.6.4; Cultural Resources Chapter 5; Siting Facilities to Avoid Natural Hazards 9.1.1.5. Also see Director's Order #77-2: Floodplain Management)

4.8.1.2 Karst

The Service will manage karst terrain to maintain the inherent integrity of its water quality, spring flow, drainage patterns, and caves. Karst processes (the processes by which water dissolves soluble rock such as limestone) create areas typified by sinkholes, underground streams, caves, and springs.

Local and regional hydrological systems resulting from karst processes can be directly influenced by surface land use practices. If existing or proposed developments do or will significantly alter or adversely impact karst processes, these impacts will be mitigated. Where practicable, these developments will be placed where they will not have an effect on the karst system.

4.8.1.3 Geologic Hazards

Naturally occurring geologic processes, which the Park Service is charged to preserve unimpaired, can be hazardous to humans and park infrastructure. These include earthquakes, volcanic eruptions, mudflows, landslides, floods, shoreline processes, tsunamis, and avalanches. The Service will work closely with specialists at the U.S. Geological Survey and elsewhere, and with local, state, tribal, and federal disaster management officials, to devise effective geologic hazard identification and management strategies. Although the magnitude and timing of future geologic hazards are difficult to forecast, park managers will strive to understand future hazards and, once the hazards are understood, minimize their potential impact on visitors, staff, and developed areas. Before interfering with natural processes that are potentially hazardous, superintendents will consider other alternatives.

The Service will try to avoid placing new visitor and other facilities in geologically hazardous areas. Superintendents will examine the feasibility of phasing out, relocating, or providing alternative facilities for park developments subject to hazardous processes, consistent with other sections of these *Management Policies*.

(See Siting Facilities to Avoid Natural Hazards 9.1.1.5)

4.8.2 Management of Geologic Features

The Service will protect geologic features from the unacceptable impacts of human activity while allowing natural processes to continue. The term "geologic features" describes the products and physical components of geologic processes. Examples of geologic features in parks include rocks, soils, and minerals; geysers and hot springs in geothermal systems; cave and karst systems; canyons and arches in erosional landscapes; sand dunes, moraines, and terraces in depositional landscapes; dramatic or unusual rock outcrops and formations; and paleontological and paleoecological resources such as fossilized plants or animals or their traces.

4.8.2.1 Paleontological Resources and Their Contexts

Paleontological resources, including both organic and mineralized remains in body or trace form, will be protected, preserved, and managed for public education, interpretation, and scientific research. The Service will study and manage paleontological resources in their paleoecological context (that is, in terms of the geologic data associated with a particular fossil that provides information about the ancient environment).

Superintendents will establish programs to inventory paleontological resources and systematically monitor for newly exposed fossils, especially in areas of rapid erosion. Scientifically significant resources will be protected by collection or by on-site protection and stabilization. The Service will encourage and help the academic community to conduct paleontological field research in accordance with the terms of a scientific research and collecting permit. Fossil localities and associated geologic data will be adequately documented when specimens are collected. Paleontological resources found in an archeological context are also subject to the policies for archeological resources. Paleontological specimens that are to be retained permanently are subject to the policies for museum objects.

The Service will take appropriate action to prevent damage to and unauthorized collection of fossils. To protect paleontological resources from harm, theft, or destruction, the Service will ensure, where necessary, that information about the nature and specific location of these resources remains confidential, in accordance with the National Parks Omnibus Management Act of 1998.

Parks will exchange fossil specimens only with other museums and public institutions that are dedicated to the preservation and interpretation of natural heritage and qualified to manage museum collections. Fossils to be deaccessioned in an exchange must fall outside the park's scope of collection statement. Systematically collected fossils in an NPS museum collection in compliance with 36 CFR 2.5 cannot be outside the scope of collection statement. Exchanges must follow deaccession procedures in the Museum Handbook, Part II, chapter 6.

The sale of original paleontological specimens is prohibited in parks.

The Service generally will avoid purchasing fossil specimens. Casts or replicas should be acquired instead. A park may purchase fossil specimens for the park museum collection only after making a written determination that

- the specimens are scientifically significant and accompanied by detailed locality data and pertinent contextual data;
- the specimens were legally removed from their site of origin, and all transfers of ownership have been legal;
- the preparation of the specimens meets professional standards;
- the alternatives for making these specimens available to science and the public are unlikely; and
- acquisition is consistent with the park's enabling legislation and scope of collection statement, and acquisition will ensure the specimens' availability in perpetuity for public education and scientific research.

All NPS construction projects in areas with potential paleontological resources must be preceded by a preconstruction surface assessment prior to disturbance. For any occurrences noted, or when the site may yield paleontological resources, the site will be avoided or the resources will, if necessary, be collected and properly cared for before construction begins. Areas with potential paleontological resources must also be monitored during construction projects.

(See Natural Resource Information 4.1.2; Studies and Collections 4.2; Independent Research 5.1.2; Artifacts and Specimens 10.2.4.6. Also see 36 CFR 2.5)

4.8.2.2 Caves

As used here, the term "caves" includes karst (such as limestone and gypsum caves) and nonkarst caves (such as lava tubes, littoral caves, and talus caves). The Service will manage caves in accordance with approved cave management plans to perpetuate the natural systems associated with the caves, such as karst and other drainage patterns, air flows, mineral deposition, and plant and animal communities. Wilderness and cultural resources and values will also be protected.

Many caves or portions of caves contain fragile nonrenewable resources and have no natural restorative processes. In these cases, most impacts are cumulative and essentially permanent. As a result, no developments or uses, including those that allow for general public entry (such as pathways, lighting, and elevator shafts), will be allowed in, above, or adjacent to caves until it can be demonstrated that they will not unacceptably impact natural cave resources and conditions, including subsurface water movements, and that access will not result in unacceptable risks to public safety. Developments already in place above caves will be removed if they are impairing or threatening to impair natural conditions or resources.

Parks will manage the use of caves when such actions are required for the protection of cave resources or for human safety. Some caves or portions of caves may be managed exclusively for research, with access limited to permitted research personnel. In accordance with the Federal Cave Resources Protection Act of 1988, recreational use of undeveloped caves will be governed by a permit system, and cave use will be regulated or restricted if necessary to protect and preserve cave resources. Under 43 CFR Part 37 regulations for the act, all caves in the national park system are deemed to be significant. As further established by this act, specific locations of significant cave entrances may be kept confidential and exempted from FOIA requests.

(See Decision-making Requirements to Identify and Avoid Impairments 1.4.7; Information Confidentiality 1.9.2.3; Caves 6.3.11.2)

4.8.2.3 Geothermal and Hydrothermal Resources

Thermal resources, also known as geothermal or hydrothermal systems, comprise a subsurface heat source, heat conduit rock formations, and air and/or water that circulates through the formations and may discharge at the surface. Such resources create features such as geysers, hot springs, mudpots, fumaroles, unique/rare mineral precipitates and formations, and hydrophilic biotic communities. Thermal resources in park units will be protected, preserved, and managed as a critical component of the units' natural resource systems, and for public education, interpretation, and scientific research.

Superintendents will strive to maintain the natural integrity of thermal systems, including the movement of air and/or water through the heated rock, cold water recharge, the proximity of the hot and warm water to the heat source, and the hydrostatic pressure and elevated temperature.

Superintendents will work to prevent unacceptable impacts on thermal resources caused by development. Such impacts include the loss of surface thermal features; land subsidence; an increase in seismic activity; the release of noxious gases; noise and surface disturbance from drilling or power plant construction; and the release of polluted water or brines. Because thermal systems may extend well beyond park boundaries, the Service will work closely with tribes and federal, state, local agencies to delineate the full extent of thermal resources and protect those that occur in parks. In protecting park thermal resources, superintendents should consider authorities available under the Geothermal Steam Act of 1970, as amended; state water rights; and mineral leasing laws.

As required by the Geothermal Steam Act, the Service will maintain a list of significant thermal features in park units. The criteria and procedures for designating significant thermal resources in parks are specified in the Geothermal Steam Act Amendments of 1988. In cooperation with the U.S. Geological Survey, the Service will conduct a monitoring program for the designated significant thermal features.

4.8.2.4 Soil Resource Management

The Service will actively seek to understand and preserve the soil resources of parks, and to prevent, to the extent possible, the unnatural erosion, physical removal, or contamination of the soil or its contamination of other resources. Parks will obtain adequate soil surveys for the management of park resources. All soil surveys will follow National Cooperative Soil Survey Standards. Products will include soil maps, determinations of the physical and chemical characteristics of soils, and the interpretations needed to guide resource management and development decisions.

Management action will be taken by superintendents to prevent or at least minimize adverse, potentially irreversible impacts on soils. Soil conservation and soil amendment practices may be implemented to reduce impacts. Importation of off-site soil or soil amendments may be used to restore damaged sites. Off-site soil normally will be salvaged soil, not soil removed from pristine sites, unless the use of pristine site soil can be achieved without causing any overall ecosystem impairment. Before using any off-site materials, parks must develop a prescription and select the materials that will be needed to restore the physical, chemical, and biological characteristics of original native soils without introducing any exotic species.

When soil excavation is an unavoidable part of an approved facility development project, the Service will minimize soil excavation, erosion, and off-site soil migration during and after the development activity.

When use of a soil fertilizer or other soil amendment is an unavoidable part of restoring a natural landscape or maintaining an altered plant community, the use will be guided by a written prescription. The prescription will be designed to ensure that such use of soil fertilizer or soil amendment does not unacceptably alter the physical, chemical, or biological characteristics of the soil, biological community, or surface or groundwaters.

(See Evaluating Impacts on Natural Resources 4.1.3; Natural Resource Collections 4.2.3; Floodplains 4.6.4; Wetlands 4.6.5; Facility Planning and Design 9.1.1)

4.9 Soundscape Management

Park natural soundscape resources encompass all the natural sounds that occur in parks, including the physical capacity for transmitting those natural sounds and the interrelationships among park natural sounds of different frequencies and volumes. Natural sounds occur within and beyond the range of sounds that humans can perceive, and they can be transmitted through air, water, or solid materials. The National Park Service will preserve, to the greatest extent possible, the natural soundscapes of parks.

Some natural sounds in the natural soundscape are also part of the biological or other physical resource components of the park. Examples of such natural sounds include

- sounds produced by birds, frogs, or katydids to define territories or aid in attracting mates
- sounds produced by bats or porpoises to locate prey or navigate
- sounds received by mice or deer to detect and avoid predators or other danger
- sounds produced by physical processes, such as wind in the trees, claps of thunder, or falling water.

The Service will restore to the natural condition wherever possible those park soundscapes that have become degraded by unnatural sounds (noise), and will protect natural soundscapes from unacceptable impacts.

Using appropriate management planning, superintendents will identify what levels and types of unnatural sound constitute acceptable impacts on park natural soundscapes. The frequencies, magnitudes, and durations of acceptable levels of unnatural sound will vary throughout a park, being generally greater in developed areas. In and adjacent to parks, the Service will monitor human activities that generate noise that adversely affects park soundscapes, including noise caused by mechanical or electronic devices. The Service will take action to prevent or minimize all noise that through frequency, magnitude, or duration adversely affects the natural soundscape or other park resources or values, or that exceeds levels that have been identified through monitoring as being acceptable to or appropriate for visitor uses at the sites being monitored.

(See General 4.1; Cultural Soundscape Management 5.3.1.7; Recreational Activities 8.2.2; Use of Motorized Equipment 8.2.3; Overflights and Aviation Uses 8.4. Also see 36 CFR 2.12: Audio Disturbances)

4.10 Lightscape Management

The Service will preserve, to the greatest extent possible, the natural lightscapes of parks, which are natural resources and values that exist in the absence of human-caused light. The absence of light in areas such as caves and at the bottom of deep bodies of water influences biological processes and the evolution of species, such as the blind cave fish. The phosphorescence of waves on dark nights helps hatchling sea turtles orient to the ocean. The stars, planets, and earth's moon that are visible during clear nights influence humans and many other species of animals, such as birds that navigate by the stars or prey animals that reduce their activities during moonlit nights.

Improper outdoor lighting can impede the view and visitor enjoyment of a natural dark night sky. Recognizing the roles that light and dark periods and darkness play in natural resource processes and the evolution of species, the Service will protect natural darkness and other components of the natural lightscape in parks. To prevent the loss of dark conditions and of natural night skies, the Service will minimize light that emanates from park facilities, and also seek the cooperation of park visitors, neighbors, and local government agencies to prevent or minimize the intrusion of artificial light into the night scene of the ecosystems of parks. The Service will not use artificial lighting in areas such as sea turtle nesting locations where the presence of the artificial lighting will disrupt a park's dark-dependent natural resource components.

The Service will

◆ restrict the use of artificial lighting in parks to those areas where security, basic human safety, and specific cultural resource requirements must be met;

◆ use minimal-impact lighting techniques;

◆ shield the use of artificial lighting where necessary to prevent the disruption of the night sky, natural cave processes, physiological processes of living organisms, and similar natural processes.

The decision about whether or not to install artificial lighting in particular circumstances is left to the discretion of the superintendent and is made through the planning process.

(See Cooperative Conservation Beyond Park Boundaries 1.6; Visitor Safety and Emergency Response 8.2.5, Facility Planning and Design 9.1.1; Integration of Facilities into the Park Environment 9.1.1.2; Energy Management 9.1.7)

4.11 Chemical Information and Odors

Natural chemicals and odors transmit information that is received by living organisms. Natural chemicals involved in the transmission of information are released by animals, plants, and geologic materials. Once released, these chemicals can be transmitted through air and water. Many animals can perceive these natural chemicals and modify their behaviors, such as mating, migration, feeding, predator avoidance, prey selection, and the establishment of social structures, as a response. Specific examples of relationships that involve natural chemical information and odors include, among others,

◆ scent posts where one animal deposits one or more chemicals by rubbing, urination, defecation, or other means, and where other animals can detect the passage of the first animal because of the odor produced by a deposited chemical;

◆ flowers that produce odors that attract insects, birds, and other animals, with resulting cross-pollination of the flowers and reproduction of the species as the outcome;

◆ female insects that release chemicals (pheromones) that attract males, with fertilization of the female's eggs and reproduction of the species as the outcome;

◆ stressed trees that emit chemicals that some types of beetles use to find weakened trees, which they then successfully can colonize and use as habitat for reproducing themselves; and

◆ geologic materials (soils or bedrock) that emit characteristic chemicals that fish can sense and use as guides to find the places in streams where they hatched and where they subsequently return to breed and deposit fertilized eggs, with reproduction of the species as the outcome.

The Service will preserve, to the greatest extent possible, the natural flow of natural chemical information and odors by preventing (1) the release of human-generated chemicals that can block the release, deposition, or perception of natural chemicals; and (2) human actions that disrupt or commingle the pathways through which natural chemicals are dispersed.

The Service acknowledges that some of its management activities may necessarily alter the natural flow of natural chemical information and odors. The Service may, for example,

◆ introduce pesticides or pheromones into parks as part of an integrated pest management program;

◆ construct and operate intensive development areas that eliminate animal scent stations and introduce unnatural chemicals;

◆ change the vegetation and thereby change the kinds of natural plant chemicals released to the air;

◆ move water from one drainage to another through water and sewer systems; or

◆ provide for the use of exhaust-emitting motors in the air, on land, and on water.

Whenever the Service engages in activities that disrupt the natural flow of natural chemical information or odors, it will comply with all applicable laws, regulations, and policies and seek to minimize harm to the environment. In no case will the Service engage in an activity if it will impair park resources or values.

Cultural Resource Management

The National Park Service will protect, preserve, and foster appreciation of the cultural resources in its custody and demonstrate its respect for the peoples traditionally associated with those resources through appropriate programs of research, planning, and stewardship.

The National Park Service is steward of many of America's most important cultural resources, including the home of President Franklin D. Roosevelt in Hyde Park, NY.

Introduction

The National Park Service is the steward of many of America's most important cultural resources. These resources are categorized as archeological resources, cultural landscapes, ethnographic resources, historic and prehistoric structures, and museum collections. The Service's cultural resource management program involves

- research to identify, evaluate, document, register, and establish basic information about cultural resources and traditionally associated peoples;

- planning to ensure that management processes for making decisions and setting priorities integrate information about cultural resources and provide for consultation and collaboration with outside entities; and

- stewardship to ensure that cultural resources are preserved and protected, receive appropriate treatments (including maintenance) to achieve desired conditions, and are made available for public understanding and enjoyment.

The cultural resource *Management Policies* of the National Park Service are derived from a suite of historic preservation, environmental, and other laws, proclamations, executive orders, and regulations. A comprehensive list can be found in the Cultural Resource Management Handbook issued pursuant to Director's Order #28. Taken collectively, this guidance provides the Service with the authority and responsibility for managing cultural resources in every unit of the national park system so that those resources may be preserved unimpaired for future generations. Cultural resource management will be carried out in a manner that is consistent with these legislative and regulatory provisions and with implementing policies and procedures such as the Secretary of the Interior's *Standards and Guidelines for Archeology and Historic Preservation (48 Federal Register (FR) 44716-740)*, and *Standards and Guidelines for Federal Agency Historic Preservation Programs Pursuant to the National Historic Preservation Act (63 FR 20497-508)*.

Superintendents and qualified cultural resource professionals will work together to carry out the Park Service's cultural resource management program. Other NPS staff and volunteers participating in cultural resource research, planning, and stewardship activities will be supervised by full-performance-level cultural resource professionals of the appropriate disciplines. Law enforcement professionals will consult with full-performance-level cultural resource professionals of the appropriate disciplines when investigating cultural resource crimes.

Superintendents and cultural resource professionals will ensure that research about and stewardship of cultural resources are carried out only after adequate planning and consultation with interested or affected individuals, groups, and other outside entities.

(See Decision-making Requirements to Identify and Avoid Impairments 1.4.7. Also see NHPA [16 USC 470h-4]; Secretary of the Interior's Professional Qualification Standards [48 FR 44738-44739]; Employee Training and Development Planning and Tracking Kit [1996])

5.1 Research

5.1.1 NPS Research

The National Park Service will conduct a vigorous interdisciplinary program of research into the cultural resources of each park. The principal goals of such research will be to

- ensure a systematic, adequate, and current information base representing park cultural resources and traditionally associated peoples in support of planning, management, and operations;

- ensure appropriate protection, preservation, treatment, and interpretation of cultural resources, employing the best current scholarship;

- develop approaches for managing park cultural and natural resources that ensure consideration of the views held by traditionally associated peoples and others by emphasizing cooperative conservation and civic engagement;

- collect data on subsistence and other consumptive uses of park resources in order to reach informed decisions; and

- develop appropriate technologies and methods for monitoring, protecting, preserving, and treating cultural resources.

Adequate research to support informed planning and compliance with legal requirements will precede any final decisions about the treatment of cultural resources, or about park operations, development, and natural resource management activities that might affect cultural resources. Research will be periodically updated to reflect changing issues, sources, and methods. Research needs will be identified and justified in a park's approved resource stewardship strategy.

A written scope of work, research design, project agreement, proposal, or other description of work to be performed will be prepared and approved before any research is conducted. All archeological research, whether for inventory, data recovery, or other purposes, must comply with the Archaeological Resources Protection Act of 1979 (ARPA), the Antiquities Act, and the Native American Graves Protection and Repatriation Act (NAGPRA), as applicable. The National Park Service will not take or allow any action that reduces the research potential of cultural resources without first performing an appropriate level of research, consultation, and documentation. Because research involving physical intervention into cultural resources or the removal of objects or specimens is a destructive process entailing an irretrievable commitment of the resources and often affecting traditional practices associated with the resources, research in parks will employ nondestructive methods to the maximum extent feasible.

The features of sites, landscapes, and structures will be left in place unless impracticable. Field data, objects, specimens, and features of sites and structures retrieved for preservation during cultural resource research and treatment projects, together with associated records and reports, will be managed within the park museum collection, stored in NPS or non-NPS repositories, as appropriate, including repositories maintained by partners. All collections of archeological material remains and associated records will be maintained in repositories in accordance with applicable regulations.

Research conducted by NPS personnel, contractors, and cooperative researchers will be subjected to peer review both inside and outside the Service to ensure that it meets professional standards, reflects current scholarship, and adheres to the principles of conduct for the appropriate discipline. The data and knowledge acquired through research will be recorded on permanent and durable (long-lived) media, documented in the appropriate Service-wide databases, and placed permanently in park museum and library collections and park files. This information will be made widely available and be incorporated, as appropriate, into park planning documents, exhibits, and interpretive programs. As appropriate, information will be shared with proper state and tribal historic preservation offices, other tribal offices, and certified local governments.

Certain research data may be withheld from public disclosure to protect sensitive or confidential information about archeological, historic, or other NPS resources when doing so would be consistent with the Freedom of Information Act, section 304 of the National Historic Preservation Act, or section 9 of the Archaeological Resources Protection Act. In some circumstances, the Service may withhold information about ethnographic resources. The Solicitor's Office should be consulted when there is any question about the legal authority to withhold information.

(See Levels of Park Planning 2.3; Studies and Collections 4.2; Confidentiality 5.2.3; Research and Scholarship 7.5.4; Use by American Indians and Other Traditionally Associated Groups 8.5. Also see 36 CFR 79; 36 CFR Part 800; 43 CFR Parts 3, 7, and 10; NHPA; Secretary of the Interior's Standards and Guidelines for Preservation Planning [48 FR 44716-720]; Secretary of the Interior's Standards and Guidelines for Historical Documentation [48 FR 44728-730]; Director's Order #28: Cultural Resource Management; Cultural Resource Management Handbook; Director's Order #66: FOIA and Protected Resource Information)

5.1.2   Independent Research

The National Park Service will promote relationships with individuals and organizations qualified to perform research, and encourage them to direct their research toward park management objectives and the broader contexts within which park resources exist. The Park Service will encourage independent researchers to follow the Secretary of the Interior's standards and guidelines and NPS guidelines to the fullest extent possible; the Service will also require that the views of traditionally associated peoples be fully considered. Research done in cooperation with tribal governments, tribal colleges, and tribal organizations should include mutually agreed upon conditions concerning the dissemination of data as well as consideration of the confidentiality of culturally sensitive information.

Research that includes taking plants, fish, wildlife, rocks, or minerals must comply with the permit requirements of 36 CFR 2.5. Permits that would allow cultural resources to be physically disturbed or allow objects or specimens to be collected will be issued only when there is compelling evidence that the proposed research is essential to significant research concerns, and when that the purpose of the research can be reasonably achieved only by using park resources. Permits must require provision for the long-term preservation and management of any recovered objects and specimens and for their cataloging, together with any associated records, in the NPS museum cataloging system. Independent researchers will be authorized to conduct archeological research on park lands only through the issuance of an ARPA or Antiquities Act permit by the appropriate regional director. This permitting authority cannot be further delegated. As appropriate, parks will also issue other necessary permits, such as a special use permit. Archeological research conducted by independent researchers must comply with the Native American Graves Protection and Repatriation Act when applicable.

NPS facilities, collections, and assistance will be made available to qualified scholars conducting NPS-authorized research as long as park operations are not substantially impeded or park resources are not adversely impacted.

(See Independent Studies 4.2.2; Consultation 5.2.1; Natural and Cultural Studies, Research, and Collection Activities 8.10. Also see 43 CFR Parts 3, 7, and 10)

5.1.3   Identification and Evaluation of Resources

The National Park Service will conduct surveys to identify and evaluate the cultural resources of each park, assessing resources within their larger cultural, chronological, and geographic contexts. The resulting inventories will provide the substantive data required for (1) nominating resources to the National Register of Historic Places; (2) general park planning and specific proposals for preserving, protecting, and treating cultural resources to achieve desired conditions; (3) land acquisition, development, and maintenance activities; (4) interpretation, education, and natural and cultural resource management activities; and (5) compliance with legal requirements.

5.1.3.1   Inventories

The Park Service will (1) maintain and expand the following inventories (or their successors) about cultural resources in units of the national park system, (2) enter information into appropriate related databases, and (3) develop an integrated information system—

◆ Archeological sites inventory for historic and prehistoric archeological resources and the related

Archeological Sites Management Information System (ASMIS) database

- Cultural Landscapes Inventory (CLI) of historic designed landscapes, historic vernacular landscapes, ethnographic landscapes, and historic sites
- List of Classified Structures (LCS), encompassing historic and prehistoric structures
- National Catalog of Museum Objects, encompassing all cultural objects, archival and manuscript materials, and natural history specimens in NPS collections and the related automated version, the Automated National Catalog System (ANCS+)

(See Levels of Park Planning 2.3; Confidentiality 5.2.3. Also see Secretary of the Interior's Standards and Guidelines for Identification [48 FR 44720-723]; Director's Order #28: Cultural Resource Management; Cultural Resource Management Handbook)

5.1.3.2 Evaluation and Categorization

Cultural resources will be professionally evaluated and categorized to assist in management decisions about their treatment and use. Cultural resources will be evaluated for significance using the National Register Criteria for Evaluation (36 CFR 60.4), and those meeting the criteria will be nominated for listing. Museum collections are inappropriate for listing and will not be evaluated using these criteria. Some collections in their original structures can be included as contributing elements to a listed structure. As appropriate, cultural resources will be categorized using other management categories established by the National Park Service and listed in the *Cultural Resource Management Handbook*.

Cultural resource professionals will evaluate cultural resources in consultation with the appropriate state and tribal historic preservation officers. Ethnographically meaningful cultural and natural resources, including traditional cultural properties, will be identified and evaluated in consultation with peoples having traditional associations to park resources. Examples of traditionally associated peoples include Acadians, African Americans, Hispanic Americans, and Native Americans. Some ethnographically meaningful resources do not meet the National Register Criteria for Evaluation, but will be inventoried in consultation with traditionally associated peoples and considered in management decisions about treatment and use.

(See Consultation 5.2.1. Also see Secretary of the Interior's Standards and Guidelines for Evaluation [48 FR 44723-726])

5.1.3.2.1 National Register Nomination

Park resources that appear to meet the criteria for the National Register of Historic Places will be nominated—either individually, as components of historic districts, or within multiple property nominations—for listing by the Keeper of the National Register. National historic sites, national historical parks, and other parks that are significant primarily for their cultural resources are entered automatically in the National Register upon establishment. However, nomination forms will be prepared and submitted to document the qualifying and contributing features of such parks and other National Register-eligible resources within them.

(Also see 36 CFR Parts 60 and 63; Secretary of the Interior's Standards and Guidelines for Registration [48 FR 44726-728]; National Register Bulletins 16A and 16B [Guidelines for Completing National Register of Historic Places Forms])

5.1.3.2.2 National Historic Landmark Designation

Historic and cultural units of the national park system are nationally significant by virtue of their authorizing legislation or presidential proclamation. National historic landmark designations are appropriate for park cultural resources that meet national historic landmark criteria if the national significance of those resources is not adequately recognized in the park's authorizing legislation or presidential proclamation. Cultural parks may warrant landmark designation as parts of larger areas encompassing resources associated with their primary themes. Modified National Register forms will be prepared and submitted to nominate such resources for landmark designation by the Secretary of the Interior.

(Also see 36 CFR Part 65)

5.1.3.2.3 Nominations for World Heritage List Designation

Park properties containing cultural features believed to possess outstanding universal value to humanity may qualify for placement on the World Heritage List under criteria described in the World Heritage Committee Operational Guidelines and in accordance with the World Heritage Convention. Before they can be nominated, all such properties must be assessed according to World Heritage criteria, and before the United States can submit a nomination to the World Heritage Committee the property must first be included on the U.S. Tentative List of Potential Future World Heritage Nominations.

Any park superintendent who believes that part or all of the park they manage should be considered for inscription on the World Heritage List must consult with the NPS Office of International Affairs, the NPS Director, and the Department of the Interior before proceeding. U.S. recommendations are approved by an interagency panel chaired by the Assistant Secretary for Fish and Wildlife and Parks, based on criteria promulgated by the World Heritage Committee. These criteria and the rules for U.S. participation in the Convention Concerning the Protection of World Cultural and Natural Heritage are published in 36 CFR Part 73.

Once a property is placed on the World Heritage List, the Park Service will recognize the designation in public information and interpretive programs. Where appropriate, superintendents should use a park's world heritage status to promote the park and encourage sustainable tourism (tourism that does not adversely impact park resources and values) and the preservation of the world's natural and cultural heritage. Placement on the World Heritage List will not alter the purposes for which a park was established, change management requirements, or reduce NPS jurisdiction over a park.

(See World Heritage Sites 4.3.7. Also see 36 CFR Part 73)

5.2 Planning

Effective park stewardship requires informed decision-making about a park's cultural resources. This is best accomplished through a comprehensive planning process. Effective planning is based on an understanding of what a park's cultural resources are and why those resources are significant. To gain this understanding, the Service must obtain baseline data on the nature and types of cultural resources, and their (1) distribution; (2) condition; (3) significance; and (4) local, regional, and national contexts. Cultural resource planning, and the resource evaluation process that is part of it, will include consultation with cultural resource professionals and scholars having relevant expertise; traditionally associated peoples; and other groups and individuals. Current scholarship and needs for research are considered in this process, along with the park's legislative history and other relevant information.

Each park's resource stewardship strategy will provide comprehensive recommendations about specific actions needed to achieve and maintain the desired resource conditions and visitor experiences for the park's cultural resources. This will include activities necessary to identify, evaluate, manage, monitor, protect, preserve, and treat the park's cultural resources, and to provide for enjoyment and understanding of the resources by the public.

Superintendents will ensure full consideration of the park's cultural resources and values in all proposals for operations, development, and natural resource programs, including the management of wilderness areas. When proposed undertakings may adversely affect national historic sites, national battlefields, and other predominantly cultural units of the national park system that were established in recognition of their national historical significance, superintendents will provide opportunities for the same level of review and consideration by the Advisory Council on Historic Preservation and the Secretary of the Interior that the Advisory Council's regulations require for undertakings that may adversely affect national historic landmarks (36 CFR 800.10).

(See Decision-making Requirements to Identify and Avoid Impairments 1.4.7; Strategic Planning 2.3.3; Implementation Planning 2.3.4. Also see Executive Order 13007 (Indian Sacred Sites); Secretary of the Interior's Standards and Guidelines for Federal Agency Historic Preservation Programs Pursuant to the National Historic Preservation Act [63 FR 20496-508]; Secretary of the Interior's Standards and Guidelines for Preservation Planning [48 FR 44716-720]; Secretary of the Interior's Standards for the Treatment of Historic Properties)

5.2.1 Consultation

The National Park Service is committed to the open and meaningful exchange of knowledge and ideas to enhance (1) the public's understanding of park resources and values and the policies and plans that affect them; and (2) the Service's ability to plan and manage the parks by learning from others. Open exchange requires that the Service seek and employ ways to reach out to and consult with all those who have an interest in the parks.

Each superintendent will consult with outside parties having an interest in the park's cultural resources or in proposed NPS actions that might affect those resources, and provide them with opportunities to learn about and comment on those resources and planned actions. Consultation may be formal, as when it is required pursuant to the Native American Graves Protection and Repatriation Act or section 106 of the National Historic Preservation Act, or it may be informal, when there is not a specific statutory requirement. Consultation will be initiated, as appropriate, with tribal, state, and local governments; state and tribal historic preservation officers; the Advisory Council on Historic Preservation; other interested federal agencies; traditionally associated peoples; present-day park neighbors; and other interested groups.

Consultations on proposed NPS actions will take place as soon as practical and in an appropriate forum that ensures, to the maximum extent possible, effective communication and the identification of mutually acceptable alternatives. The Service will establish and maintain continuing relationships with outside parties to facilitate future collaboration, formal consultations, and the ongoing informal exchange of views and information on cultural resource matters.

Because national parks embody resources and values of interest to a national audience, efforts to reach out and consult must be national in scope. However, the Service will be especially mindful of consulting with traditionally associated peoples—those whose cultural systems or ways of life have an association with park resources and values that predates establishment of the park. Traditionally associated peoples may include park neighbors, traditional residents, and former residents who remain attached to the park area despite having relocated. Examples of traditionally associated peoples include both federally designated and nondesignated American Indian tribes in the contiguous 48 states, Alaska Natives, Native Hawaiians, African Americans at Jean Lafitte, Asian Americans at Manzanar, Hispanic Americans at Tumacacori, and others.

In particular, traditionally associated peoples should be consulted about

- proposed research on and stewardship of cultural and natural resources with ethnographic meaning for the groups;
- development of park planning and interpretive documents that may affect resources traditionally associated with the groups;

- proposed research that entails collaborative study of the groups;
- identification, treatment, use, and determination of affiliation of objects subject to the Native American Graves Protection and Repatriation Act;
- repatriation of Native American cultural items or human remains based on requests by affiliated groups in accordance with the Native American Graves Protection and Repatriation Act;
- planned excavations and proposed responses to inadvertent discoveries of cultural resources that may be culturally affiliated with the groups;
- other proposed NPS actions that may affect the treatment of, use of, and access to cultural and natural resources with known or potential cultural meaning for the groups; and
- designation of National Register, National Historic Landmark, and World Heritage Sites with known or potential cultural meaning for the groups.

Consultation with federally recognized American Indian tribes will be on a government-to-government basis. The Service will notify appropriate tribal authorities (such as tribal historic preservation officers) about proposed actions when first conceived, and by subsequently consulting their appointed representatives whenever proposed actions may affect tribal interests, practices, and traditional resources (such as places of religious value).

There are other groups and individuals with strong connections to the land through experiencing a significant life event within or near a park unit. Through its civic engagement activities, the Service will be sensitive to and carefully consider the views of those who have these associations.

Whenever groups are created, controlled, or managed for the purpose of providing advice or recommendations to the Service, the Service will first consult with the Office of the Solicitor to determine whether the Federal Advisory Committee Act requires the chartering of an advisory committee. Consultation with the Office of the Solicitor will not be necessary when the Service meets with individuals, groups, or organizations simply to exchange views and information or to solicit individual advice on proposed actions. The act does not apply to intergovernmental meetings held exclusively between federal officials and elected officers of state, local, and tribal governments (or their designated employees with authority to act on their behalf) acting in their official capacities, when (1) the meetings relate to intergovernmental responsibilities or administration, and (2) the purpose of the committee is solely to exchange views, information, or advice relating to the management or implementation of federal programs established pursuant to statute that explicitly or inherently share intergovernmental responsibilities or administration.

(See Civic Engagement 1.7; Relationship with American Indian Tribes 1.11; Ethnographic Resources 5.3.5.3. Also see ARPA; NAGPRA; NEPA; NHPA [16 USC 470f]; 36 CFR Part 800; 40 CFR Parts 1500-1508; 41 CFR Part 101;, 43 CFR Parts 7 and 10; Executive Memorandum on Government-to-Government Relations with Native American Tribal Governments; Executive Order 13007 (Indian Sacred Sites); Executive Order 13175 (Consultation and Coordination with Indian Tribal Governments); 512 Department of the Interior Manual [DM] 2; Director's Order #71: Government-to-government Relationships with Tribal Governments; NPS Guide to the Federal Advisory Committee Act)

5.2.2 Agreements

The National Park Service will seek to establish mutually beneficial agreements with interested groups to facilitate collaborative research, consultation, park planning, training, and cooperative management approaches with respect to park cultural resources and culturally important natural resources. The NPS goal is to allow traditionally associated peoples to exercise traditional cultural practices in parks to the extent allowable by law and consistent with the criteria listed in section 8.2. To the extent this goal can be legally reached through agreements, park superintendents should do so.

Whenever parks have cultural resources that are owned or managed by others, agreements will clarify how the resources are to be managed. Agreements will provide ways for periodically reviewing their effectiveness, making mutually agreed-upon modifications, and avoiding and resolving disagreements and disputes. All agreements will conform to the requirements of Director's Order #20: Agreements.

(See Decision-making Requirements to Identify and Avoid Impairments 1.4.7; Partnerships 1.10; Partnerships 4.1.4; Park Structures Owned or Managed by Others 5.3.5.4.8; Submerged Cultural Resources 5.3.5.1.6; Use by American Indians and Other Traditionally Associated Groups 8.5; Consumptive Uses 8.9. Also see Executive Order 13007 (Indian Sacred Sites); 36 CFR 2.1)

5.2.3 Confidentiality

Sensitive or confidential information is sometimes acquired during consultations and during other research, planning, and stewardship activities. Under certain circumstances and to the extent permitted by law, information about the specific location, character, nature, ownership, or acquisition of cultural resources on park lands will be withheld from public disclosure. If a question arises about withholding information, and disclosure could result in a significant invasion of privacy or a risk of harm to a cultural resource, the Park Service will consult the provisions of the Archaeological Resources Protection Act (16 USC 470hh); the National Parks Omnibus Management Act (16 USC 5937); and the National Historic Preservation Act (16 USC 470w-3) before making a decision. Under some conditions, the Service may be required by law to disclose confidential information acquired during consultations, public meetings, and other research, planning, and stewardship activities, or in association with the acquisition of resources, including museum collections. Before these activities occur, NPS staff and authorized researchers will make every effort to inform affected parties that, while the information they provide will not be shared voluntarily, confidentiality cannot be guaranteed.

To the extent permitted by law, the Service will withhold from public disclosure (1) information provided by individuals who wish the information to remain confidential, and (2) the identities of individuals who wish to remain anonymous and who are protected from release by exemption under the Freedom of Information Act. In each instance the Service will document its decision to disseminate or withhold sensitive or confidential information from public disclosure.

More detailed guidance on sensitive and confidential information can be found in Director's Order #66: FOIA and Protected Resource Information and the Museum Handbook, Part III.

(See Information Confidentiality 1.9.2.3; Natural Resource Information 4.1.2. Also see 43 CFR Part 2; 43 CFR 7.18; Privacy Act)

5.3 Stewardship

5.3.1 Protection and Preservation of Cultural Resources

The National Park Service will employ the most effective concepts, techniques, and equipment to protect cultural resources against theft, fire, vandalism, overuse, deterioration, environmental impacts, and other threats without compromising the integrity of the resources.

5.3.1.1 Emergency Management

Measures to protect or rescue cultural resources in the event of an emergency, disaster, or fire will be developed as part of a park's emergency operations and fire management planning processes. Designated personnel will be trained to respond to all emergencies in a manner that maximizes visitor and employee safety and the protection of resources and property.

(See Emergency Preparedness and Emergency Operations 8.2.5.2. Also see 36 CFR Part 78)

5.3.1.2 Fire Detection, Suppression, and Post-fire Rehabilitation and Protection

The Park Service will take action to prevent or minimize the impact of wildland, prescribed, and structural fires on cultural resources, including the impact of suppression and rehabilitation activities.

In the preservation of historic structures and museum and library collections, every attempt will be made to comply with national building and fire codes. When these cannot be met without significantly impairing a structure's integrity and character, management and use of the structure will be modified to minimize potential hazards rather than modifying the structure itself.

Subject to the previous paragraph, when warranted by the significance of a historic structure or a museum or library collection, adequate and appropriate fire detection, warning, and suppression systems will be installed. Pre-fire plans will be developed for historic structures and buildings housing museum or library collections; these plans will be designed to identify the floor plan, utilities, hazards, and areas and objects requiring special protection. This information will be kept current and made available to local and park fire personnel.

Park and local fire personnel will be advised of the locations and characteristics of cultural resources threatened by fire and of any priorities for protecting them during any planned or unplanned fire incident. At parks with cultural resources, park fire personnel will receive cultural resource protection training. At parks that have wildland or structural fire risks and programs, cultural resource management specialists will receive fire prevention and emergency response training. Cultural resource management specialists who assist with wildland fire programs will be certified for incident management positions commensurate with their individual responsibilities.

Smoking will not be permitted in spaces housing museum or library collections or in historic structures (except those used as residences in which smoking is permitted by the park superintendent).

(See Fire Management 4.5; Fire Management 6.3.9; Structural Fire Protection and Suppression 9.1.8. Also see Director's Order #18: Wildland Fire Management; Director's Order #58: Structural Fire Management and Reference Manual 58)

5.3.1.3 Compensation for Injuries to Cultural Resources

The Service will use all legal authorities that are available to protect and restore cultural resources and the benefits they provide when actions of another party cause the destruction or loss of or injury to park resources or values. As a first step, damage assessments provide the basis for determining the restoration and compensation needs that address the public's loss and are a key milestone toward the ultimate goal, which is restoration of resources for the American public. In accordance with the National Park System Resource Protection Act, the Park Service will take all necessary and appropriate steps to recover costs and damages from any person who destroys, causes the loss of, or injures any resource of the national park system. When such incidents involve cultural resources, the Service will

- prevent or minimize the destruction or loss of or injury to the cultural resource, or abate or minimize the imminent risk of such destruction, loss, or injury;

- assess and monitor damage to the cultural resource;

- recover any and all costs associated with the restoration or replacement of the cultural resource or costs associated with the acquisition of an equivalent resource;

♦ recover the value of any significant loss of use of the cultural resource pending its restoration or replacement or the acquisition of an equivalent, or the value of the cultural resource in the event it cannot be restored or replaced; and

♦ recover any and all costs incurred in responding to, assessing, and/or monitoring damage to the cultural resource.

(See Compensation for Injuries to Natural Resources 4.1.6. Also see Director's Order #14: Resource Damage Assessment and Restoration)

5.3.1.4 Environmental Monitoring and Control

When necessary to preserve a historic structure or a museum collection, appropriate measures will be taken to control relative humidity, temperature, light, and air quality. When museum collections are housed in a historic structure, the needs of both the collection and the structure will be identified and evaluated, weighing relative rarity and significance, before environmental control measures are introduced. The environmental conditions of all areas housing museum collections will be regularly monitored, according to a schedule specific to each condition, to determine whether appropriate levels of relative humidity, temperature, and light are being maintained.

(See Air Quality 4.7.1. Also see Director's Order #24: NPS Museum Collections Management)

5.3.1.5 Pest Management

The Park Service will follow an integrated pest management approach in addressing pest problems (including invasive vegetation) related to cultural resources. Pest occurrences will be dealt with on a case-by-case basis according to the principles identified in section 4.4.5 and Director's Order #77: Natural Resource Protection to ensure the most effective and lowest risk management strategy.

(See Pest Management 4.4.5)

5.3.1.6 Visitor Carrying Capacity

Superintendents will set, enforce, and monitor carrying capacities to limit public visitation to or use of cultural resources that would be subject to adverse effects from unrestricted levels of visitation or use. This will include (1) reviewing the park's purpose; (2) analyzing existing visitor use of and related impacts on the park's cultural resources and traditional resource users; (3) prescribing indicators and specific standards for acceptable and sustainable visitor use; and (4) identifying ways to address and monitor unacceptable impacts resulting from overuse. Studies to gather basic data and make recommendations on setting, enforcing, and monitoring carrying capacities for cultural resources will be conducted in collaboration with cultural resource specialists representing the appropriate disciplines.

(See Visitor Carrying Capacity 8.2.1)

5.3.1.7 Cultural Soundscape Management

Culturally appropriate sounds are important elements of the national park experience in many parks. The Service will preserve soundscape resources and values of the parks to the greatest extent possible to protect opportunities for appropriate transmission of cultural and historic sounds that are fundamental components of the purposes and values for which the parks were established. Examples of appropriate cultural and historic sounds include native drumming (at Yosemite National Park, for example), music (at New Orleans Jazz National Historical Park, for example), and bands, marching, cannon fire, or other military demonstrations at some national battlefield parks. The Service will prevent inappropriate or excessive types and levels of sound (noise) from unacceptably impacting the ability of the soundscape to transmit the cultural and historic resource sounds associated with park purposes.

(See Soundscape Management 4.9; Recreational Activities 8.2.2. Also see 36 CFR 2.12: Audio Disturbances)

5.3.2 Physical Access for Persons with Disabilities

The National Park Service will provide persons with disabilities the highest feasible level of physical access to historic properties that is reasonable, consistent with the preservation of each property's significant historical features. Access modifications for persons with disabilities will be designed and installed to least affect the features of a property that contribute to its significance. Modifications to some features may be acceptable in providing access once a review of options for the highest level of access has been completed. However, if it is determined that modification of particular features would impair a property's integrity and character in terms of the Advisory Council's regulations at 36 CFR 800.9, such modifications will not be made. To the extent possible, modifications for access will benefit the greatest number of visitors, staff, and the public, and be integrated with or close to the primary path of travel for entrances and from parking areas. In situations where access modifications cannot be made, alternative methods of achieving program access will be adopted.

(See Access to Interpretive and Educational Opportunities 7.5.2; Accessibility for Persons with Disabilities 8.2.4; Accessibility for Persons with Disabilities 9.1.2; Accessibility of Commercial Services 10.2.6.2. Also see Director's Order #42: Accessibility for Visitors with Disabilities in National Park Service Programs and Services)

5.3.3 Historic Property Leases and Cooperative Agreements

The National Park Service may permit the use of a historic property through a lease or cooperative agreement if the lease or cooperative agreement will ensure the property's preservation. Proposed uses must not unduly limit public appreciation of the property; interfere with visitor use and enjoyment of the park; or preclude use of the property for park administration, employee residences, or other management purposes judged more appropriate or cost-effective.

If a lease or cooperative agreement requires or allows the lessee or cooperator to maintain, repair, rehabilitate, restore, or build upon the property, the work must be done in accordance with applicable Secretary of the Interior's standards and guidelines and other NPS policies, guidelines, and standards.

(See Leases 8.12. Also see Director's Order #38: Real Property Leasing; NHPA [16 USC 470h-3]; 16 USC 460l-22(a); Omnibus Consolidated Appropriations Act, 1997 [16 USC 1g]; 36 CFR Part 18)

5.3.4 Stewardship of Human Remains and Burials

Marked and unmarked prehistoric and historic burial areas and graves will be identified, evaluated, and protected. Every effort will be made to avoid impacting burial areas and graves when planning park development and managing park operations. Such burial areas and graves will not knowingly be disturbed or archeologically investigated unless threatened with destruction.

The Service will consult with American Indian tribes, Alaska Natives, Native Hawaiians, and other individuals and groups linked by demonstrable ties of kinship or culture to potentially identifiable human remains when such remains may be disturbed or are inadvertently encountered on park lands. Reinterment at the same park may be permitted and may include remains that may have been removed from lands now within the park.

American Indian, Alaska Native, and Native Hawaiian human remains and photographs of such remains will not be exhibited. Drawings, renderings, or casts of such remains may be exhibited with the consent of culturally affiliated Indian tribes, Alaska Natives, and Native Hawaiian organizations. The exhibit of non-Native American human remains, or photographs, drawings, renderings, or casts of such remains, is allowed in consultation with traditionally associated peoples. The Service may allow access to and study, publication, and destructive analysis of human remains, but must consult with traditionally associated peoples and consider their opinions and concerns before making decisions on appropriate actions. In addition, such use of human remains will occur only with an approved research proposal that describes why the information cannot be obtained through other sources or analysis and why the research is important to the field of study and the general public.

(See Cultural Resources 6.3.8; Consultation 7.5.6; Cemeteries and Burials 8.6.10. Also see ARPA; NAGPRA; 36 CFR Part 79; 43 CFR Part 10)

5.3.5 Treatment of Cultural Resources

The Park Service will provide for the long-term preservation of, public access to, and appreciation of the features, materials, and qualities contributing to the significance of cultural resources. With some differences by type, cultural resources are subject to several basic treatments, including (1) preservation in their existing states; (2) rehabilitation to serve contemporary uses, consistent with their integrity and character; and (3) restoration to earlier appearances by the removal of later additions and replacement of missing elements. Decisions regarding which treatments will best ensure the preservation and public enjoyment of particular cultural resources will be reached through the planning and compliance process, taking into account

- the nature and significance of a resource and its condition and interpretive value
- the research potential of the resource
- the level of intervention required by treatment alternatives
- the availability of data and the terms of any binding restrictions
- the concerns of traditionally associated peoples and other groups and individuals

Except for emergencies that threaten irreparable loss without immediate action, no treatment project will be undertaken unless supported by an approved planning document appropriate to the proposed action.

The preservation of cultural resources in their existing states will always receive first consideration. Treatments entailing greater intervention will not proceed without the consideration of interpretive alternatives. The appearance and condition of resources before treatment and changes made during treatment will be documented. Such documentation will be shared with any appropriate state or tribal historic preservation office or certified local government and added to the park museum cataloging system. Pending treatment decisions reached through the planning process, all resources will be protected and preserved in their existing states.

As a basic principle, anything of historical appearance that the National Park Service presents to the public in a park will be either an authentic survival from the past or an accurate representation of that once existing there. Reconstructions and reproductions will be clearly identified as such.

The Service will holistically approach the treatment of related cultural resources in a park. All cultural resource and natural resource values will be considered in defining specific treatment and management goals. Research will be coordinated and sequenced so that decisions are not made in isolation. Each proposed action will be evaluated to ensure consistency or compatibility in the overall treatment of park resources. The relative importance and relationship of all values will be weighed to identify potential conflicts between and among resource preservation goals, park management and operation goals, and park user goals. Conflicts will be considered and resolved through the planning process, which will include any consultation required by 16 USC 470f.

Although each resource type is most closely associated with a particular discipline, an interdisciplinary approach is commonly needed to properly define specific treatment and management goals for cultural resources. Policies applicable to the various resource types follow.

(See Park Management 1.4; Levels of Park Planning 2.3; Planning 5.2; Cultural Resources 6.3.8. Also see NEPA; Secretary of the Interior's Standards for the Treatment of Historic Properties)

5.3.5.1 Archeological Resources

Archeological resources will be managed in situ, unless the removal of artifacts or physical disturbance is justified by research, consultation, preservation, protection, or interpretive requirements. Preservation treatments will include proactive measures that protect resources from vandalism and looting, and will maintain or improve their condition by limiting damage due to natural and human agents. Data recovery actions will be taken only in the context of planning, consultation, and appropriate decision-making. Preservation treatments and data recovery activities will be conducted within the scope of an approved research design. Archeological research will use nondestructive methods of testing and analysis wherever possible. The Park Service will incorporate information about archeological resources into interpretive, educational, and preservation programs. Artifacts and specimens recovered from archeological resources, along with associated records and reports, will be maintained together in the park museum collection.

(Also see Director's Order #28A: Archeology; 36 CFR Part 79; Secretary of the Interior's Standards and Guidelines for Archeological Documentation [48 FR 44734-737]; Museum Handbook)

5.3.5.1.1 Preservation

Archeological resources will be maintained and preserved in a stable condition to prevent degradation and loss. The condition of archeological resources will be documented, regularly monitored, and evaluated against initial baseline data. Parks are encouraged to enlist concerned local citizens in site stewardship programs to patrol and monitor the condition of archeological resources. The preservation of archeological components of cultural landscapes, structures, and ruins are also subject to the treatment policies for cultural landscapes, historic and prehistoric structures, and historic and prehistoric ruins.

(See Volunteers in the Parks 1.9.1.6)

5.3.5.1.2 Stabilization

Archeological resources subject to erosion, slumping, subsidence, or other natural deterioration will be stabilized using the least intrusive and destructive methods. The methods used will protect natural resources and processes to the maximum extent feasible. Stabilization will occur only after sufficient research demonstrates the likely success of the proposed stabilizing action and after existing conditions are documented.

5.3.5.1.3 Rehabilitation, Restoration, and Reconstruction

These terms are normally related to the treatment of historic structures and cultural landscapes. The Park Service will not normally undertake the rehabilitation, restoration, or reconstruction of archeological resources or features. Archeological studies undertaken in conjunction with the rehabilitation or restoration of cultural landscapes, structures, or ruins, or with the reconstruction of obliterated cultural landscapes or missing structures, will be guided by the treatment policies for archeological resources as well as those for the other associated resource types.

5.3.5.1.4 Protection

Archeological resources will be protected against human agents of destruction and deterioration whenever practicable. Archeological resources subject to vandalism and looting will be periodically monitored and, if appropriate, fencing, warning signs, remote-sensing alarms, and other protective measures will be installed. Training and public education programs will be developed to make park staff and the public aware of the value of the park's archeological resources and the penalties for destroying them. For public safety reasons, local citizens who are monitoring resources under site stewardship programs will be instructed to report incidents of vandalism and looting to law enforcement personnel for response.

(See Volunteers in Parks 7.6.1; Shared Responsibilities 8.3.3)

5.3.5.1.5 Archeological Data Recovery

Archeological data recovery is permitted if justified by research or interpretation needs. Significant archeological data that would otherwise be lost as a result of resource treatment projects or uncontrollable degradation or destruction will be recovered in accordance with appropriate research proposals and preserved in park museum collections. Data will be recovered to mitigate the loss of significant archeological data due to park development, but only after

- the redesign, relocation, and cancellation of the proposed development have all been considered and ruled out as infeasible through the planning process;
- the park development has been approved; and
- the project has provided for data recovery, cataloging, and the initial preservation of recovered collections.

(See Planning 5.2)

5.3.5.1.6 Earthworks

Appropriate and, when feasible, native vegetation will be maintained when necessary to prevent the erosion of prehistoric and historic earthworks, even when the historic condition might have been bare earth. Because earthwork restorations and reconstructions can obliterate surviving remains and are often difficult to maintain, other means of representing and interpreting the original earthworks will receive first consideration.

(See Management of Native Plants and Animals 4.4.2; Management of Exotic Species 4.4.4)

5.3.5.1.7 Submerged Cultural Resources

Historic shipwrecks and other submerged cultural resources will be protected, to the extent permitted by law, in the same manner as terrestrial archeological resources. Protection activities involve inventory, evaluation, monitoring, interpretation, and establishing partnerships to provide for the management of historic shipwrecks and other submerged cultural resources in units of the national park system. The Service will not allow treasure hunting or commercial salvage activities at or around historic shipwrecks or other submerged cultural resources located within park boundaries unless legally obligated to do so. Parks may provide recreational diving access to submerged cultural resources that are not susceptible to damage or the removal of artifacts. The Service will ensure that the activities of others in park waters do not adversely affect submerged cultural resources or the surrounding natural environment. The Service will consult with the owners of non-abandoned historic shipwrecks and enter into written agreements with them to clarify how the shipwrecks will be managed by the Park Service. Shipwrecks owned by a state government pursuant to the Abandoned Shipwreck Act of 1987 will be managed in accordance with the Abandoned Shipwreck Act Guidelines (55 FR 50116-145, 55 FR 51528, and 56 FR 7875).

(See Recreational Activities 8.2.2. Also see 36 CFR Part 2; 485 DM 27; Director's Order #4: Diving Management)

5.3.5.2 Cultural Landscapes

The treatment of a cultural landscape will preserve significant physical attributes, biotic systems, and uses when those uses contribute to historical significance. Treatment decisions will be based on a cultural landscape's historical significance over time, existing conditions, and use. Treatment decisions will consider both the natural and built characteristics and features of a landscape, the dynamics inherent in natural processes and continued use, and the concerns of traditionally associated peoples.

The treatment implemented will be based on sound preservation practices to enable long-term preservation of a resource's historic features, qualities, and materials. There are three types of treatment for extant cultural landscapes: preservation, rehabilitation, and restoration.

(See Decision-making Requirements to Identify and Avoid Impairments 1.4.7. Also see Secretary of the Interior's Standards for the Treatment of Historic Properties with Guidelines for the Treatment of Cultural Landscapes)

5.3.5.2.1 Preservation

A cultural landscape will be preserved in its present condition if

- that condition allows for satisfactory protection, maintenance, use, and interpretation; or
- another treatment is warranted but cannot be accomplished until some future time.

5.3.5.2.2 Rehabilitation

A cultural landscape may be rehabilitated for contemporary use if

- it cannot adequately serve an appropriate use in its present condition; and
- rehabilitation will retain its essential features and not alter its integrity and character or conflict with approved park management objectives.

5.3.5.2.3 Restoration

A cultural landscape may be restored to an earlier appearance if

- all changes after the proposed restoration period have been professionally evaluated and the significance of those changes has been fully considered;
- restoration is essential to public understanding of the park's cultural associations;
- sufficient data about that landscape's earlier appearance exist to enable its accurate restoration; and
- the disturbance or loss of significant archeological resources is minimized and mitigated by data recovery.

5.3.5.2.4 Reconstruction of Obliterated Landscapes

No matter how well conceived or executed, reconstructions are contemporary interpretations of the past rather than authentic survivals from it. The National Park Service will not reconstruct an obliterated cultural landscape unless

- there is no alternative that would accomplish the park's interpretive mission;
- sufficient data exist to enable its accurate reconstruction, based on the duplication of historic features substantiated by documentary or physical evidence, rather than on conjectural designs or features from other landscapes;
- reconstruction will occur in the original location;
- the disturbance or loss of significant archeological resources is minimized and mitigated by data recovery; and
- reconstruction is approved by the Director.

A landscape will not be reconstructed to appear damaged or ruined. General representations of typical landscapes will not be attempted.

5.3.5.2.5 Biotic Cultural Resources

Biotic cultural resources, which include plant and animal communities associated with the significance of a cultural landscape, will be duly considered in treatment and management. The cultural resource and natural resource components of the park's resource stewardship strategy will jointly identify acceptable plans for the management and treatment of biotic cultural resources. The park's resource stewardship strategy will anticipate and plan for the natural and human-induced processes of change. Before any major treatment of a cultural landscape is undertaken, there must be an understanding of the degree to which change contributes to or compromises the historic character of the landscape, and the way in which natural cycles influence the ecological processes within the landscape. Treatment and management of a cultural landscape will establish acceptable parameters for change and manage the biotic resources within those parameters.

(See Maintenance of Altered Plant Communities 4.4.2.5)

5.3.5.2.6 Land Use and Ethnographic Value

Many cultural landscapes are significant because of their historic land use and practices. When land use is a primary reason for the significance of a landscape, the objective of treatment will be to balance the perpetuation of use with the retention of the tangible evidence that represents its history. The variety and arrangement of cultural and natural features in a landscape often have sacred or other continuing importance in the ethnic histories and cultural vigor of associated peoples. These features and their past and present-day uses will be identified, and the beliefs, attitudes, practices, traditions, and values of traditionally associated peoples will be considered in any treatment decisions.

Contemporary use of a cultural landscape is appropriate if it

- does not adversely affect significant landscape characteristics and features; and
- either follows the historic use or does not impede public appreciation of it.

All uses of cultural landscapes are subject to legal requirements, policy, guidelines, and standards for natural and cultural resource preservation, public safety, and special park uses.

5.3.5.2.7 New Construction

Contemporary alterations and additions to a cultural landscape must not radically change, obscure, or destroy its significant spatial organization, materials, and features. New buildings, structures, landscape features, and utilities may be constructed in a cultural landscape if

- existing structures and improvements do not meet essential management needs;
- new construction is designed and sited to preserve the landscape's integrity and historic character; and
- the alterations, additions, or related new construction is differentiated from yet compatible with the landscape's historic character—unless associated with an approved restoration or reconstruction.

New additions will meet the Secretary of the Interior's Standards for Rehabilitation.

5.3.5.3 Ethnographic Resources

Park ethnographic resources are the cultural and natural features of a park that are of traditional significance to traditionally associated peoples. These peoples are the contemporary park neighbors and ethnic or occupational communities that have been associated with a park for two or more generations (40 years), and whose interests in the park's resources began before the park's establishment. Living peoples of many cultural backgrounds—American Indians, Inuit (Eskimos), Native Hawaiians, African Americans, Hispanics, Chinese Americans, Euro-Americans, and farmers, ranchers, and fishermen—may have a traditional association with a particular park.

Traditionally associated peoples generally differ as a group from other park visitors in that they typically assign significance to ethnographic resources—places closely linked with their own sense of purpose, existence as a community, and development as ethnically distinctive peoples. These places may be in urban or rural parks and support ceremonial activities or represent birthplaces of significant individuals, group origin sites, migration routes, or harvesting or collecting places. Although these places have historic attributes that are of great importance to the group, they may not necessarily have a direct association with the reason the park was established or be appropriate as a topic of general public interest. Some ethnographic resources might also be traditional cultural properties. A traditional cultural property is one that is eligible for inclusion in the National Register of Historic Places because of its association with cultural practices or beliefs of a living community that are (1) rooted in that community's history, and (2) important in maintaining the continuing cultural identity of the community.

The Service's primary interest in these places stems from its responsibilities under

- the NPS Organic Act—to conserve the natural and historic objects within parks unimpaired for the enjoyment of future generations;
- the National Historic Preservation Act (NHPA)—to preserve, conserve, and encourage the continuation of the diverse traditional prehistoric, historic, ethnic, and folk cultural traditions that underlie and are a living expression of our American heritage;
- the American Indian Religious Freedom Act (AIRFA)—to protect and preserve for American Indians access to sites, use and possession of sacred objects, and the freedom to worship through ceremonials and traditional rites;
- the Archeological Resources Protection Act (ARPA)—to secure, for the present and future benefit of the American people, the protection of archeological resources and sites that are on public lands and Indian Lands;
- the National Environmental Policy Act (NEPA)—to preserve important historic, cultural, and natural aspects of our national heritage; and
- Executive Order 13007 (Indian Sacred Sites)—to accommodate access to and ceremonial use of Indian sacred sites by Indian religious practitioners and avoid adversely affecting the physical integrity of such sacred sites.

The Service must therefore be respectful of these ethnographic resources and carefully consider the effects that NPS actions may have on them. When religious issues are evident, the Service must also consider constraints imposed on federal agency actions by the First and Fourteenth Amendments to the U.S. Constitution.

The National Park Service will adopt a comprehensive approach towards appreciating the diverse human heritage and associated resources that characterize the national park system. The Service will identify the present-day peoples whose cultural practices and identities were, and often still are, closely associated with each park's cultural and natural resources.

The Alaska National Interest Lands Conservation Act (ANILCA) recognizes the importance of maintaining Alaska Native and non-Native subsistence lifestyles and contains provisions that authorize activities by the Park Service to assist Alaska Natives in the preservation of cultural resources. For many rural Alaskans, the land and the way of life are inseparable. The Service will explore opportunities in Alaska to forge a mutually beneficial relationship between Alaska Natives, rural Alaskans, and the Service. In Alaska and elsewhere, the Service will try to strengthen the ability of traditional and indigenous peoples to perpetuate their culture and to enrich the parks with a deeper sense of place and applicable traditional knowledge held by associated groups.

Ethnographic information will be collected through collaborative research that recognizes the sensitive nature of such information. Cultural anthropologists/ethnographers will document the meanings that traditionally associated groups assign to traditional natural and cultural resources and the landscapes they form. The park's ethnographic file will include this information, as well as data on the traditional management practices and knowledge systems that affect resource uses and the short- and long-term effects of use on the resources.

(See Confidentiality 5.2.3. Also see Director's Order #28B: Ethnography Program)

5.3.5.3.1 Resource Access and Use

Consistent with the requirements of the Organic Act, the National Historic Preservation Act, American Indian Religious Freedom Act, the Archaeological Resources Protection Act, the National Environmental Policy Act, and Executive Order 13007 (Indian Sacred Sites) cited in section 5.3.5.3 above, the Service will strive to allow American Indians and other traditionally associated peoples access to and use of ethnographic resources. Continued access to and use of ethnographic resources is often essential to the survival of family, community, or regional cultural systems, including patterns of belief and sociocultural and religious life. However, the Service may not allow access and use if it would violate the criteria listed in section 8.1.

The Service generally supports traditional access and use when reasonable accommodations can be made under NPS authorities to allow greater access and use. Park superintendents may reasonably control the times when and places where specific groups may have exclusive access to particular areas of a park.

With regard to consumptive use of park resources, current NPS policy is reflected in regulations published at 36 CFR 2.1. These regulations allow superintendents to designate certain fruits, berries, nuts, or unoccupied seashells that may be gathered by hand for personal use or consumption if it will not adversely affect park wildlife, the reproductive potential of a plant species, or otherwise adversely affect park resources. The regulations do not authorize the taking, use, or possession of fish, wildlife, or plants for ceremonial or religious purposes except where specifically authorized by federal statute or treaty rights or where hunting, trapping, or fishing are otherwise allowed. These regulations are currently under review, and NPS policy is evolving in this area.

Regulations addressing traditional subsistence uses that are authorized in Alaska by the Alaska National Interest Lands Conservation Act are published at 36 CFR Part 13. Some park-specific enabling acts (for example, Big Cypress National Preserve and Kaloko-Honokohau National Historical Park) allow subsistence or other traditional uses of park resources.

(See Appropriate Use 8.1.1; Use by American Indians and Other Traditionally Associated Groups 8.5; Special Park Uses 8.6; Collecting Natural Products 8.8; Consumptive Uses 8.9)

5.3.5.3.2 Sacred Sites

The National Park Service acknowledges that American Indian tribes, including Native Alaskans, treat specific places containing certain natural and cultural resources as sacred places having established religious meaning and as locales of private ceremonial activities. Consistent with Executive Order 13007 (Indian Sacred Sites), the Service will, to the extent practicable, accommodate access to and ceremonial use of Indian sacred sites by religious practitioners from recognized American Indian tribes and Alaska Natives, and avoid adversely affecting the physical integrity of such sacred sites.

In consultation with the appropriate groups, the Service will develop a record about such places, and identify any treatments preferred by the groups. This information will alert superintendents and planners to the potential presence of sensitive areas and will be kept confidential to the extent permitted by law. The Service will collaborate with affected groups to prepare mutually agreeable strategies for providing access to ordinarily gated or otherwise inaccessible locales, and for enhancing the likelihood of privacy during religious ceremonies. Any strategies that are developed must comply with constitutional and other legal requirements. To the extent feasible and allowable by law, accommodations will also be made for access to and the use of sacred places when interest is expressed by other traditionally associated peoples (especially Native Hawaiians and other Pacific islanders) and by American Indian peoples and others who often have a long-standing connection and identity with a particular park or resource.

Various ethnic groups, local groups with recently developed ties to resources in neighboring parks, and visitors to family and national cemeteries and national memorials also might use park resources for traditional or individual religious ceremonies. Mutually acceptable agreements may be negotiated with known groups to provide access to and the use of such places, consistent with constitutional and other legal constraints.

(See Confidentiality 5.2.3; Resource Access and Use 5.3.5.3.1; Use by American Indians and Other Traditionally Associated Groups 8.5; First Amendment Activities 8.6.3. Also see Director's Orders #66: FOIA and Protected Resource Information, and #71B: Indian Sacred Sites; NHPA [16 USC 470w-3]; Executive Order 13007 (Indian Sacred Sites); 512 DM 3)

5.3.5.3.3 Research

The Park Service will maintain a program of professional cultural anthropological/ethnographic research designed to provide NPS managers with information about relationships between park resources and associated peoples. Research will be undertaken in cooperation with associated peoples in an interdisciplinary manner whenever reasonable, especially in studies of natural resource use and ethnographic landscapes. Research findings will be used to inform planning, cultural and natural resource management decision-making, and interpretation, as well as to help managers meet responsibilities to associated peoples and other stakeholders in the outcomes of NPS decisions.

Collaborative research dealing with recent or contemporary cultural systems and the resources of park-associated peoples will involve the groups in the design and implementation of the research and the review of research findings to the fullest possible extent. The Service will provide individuals or groups involved with or directly affected by the research with copies or summaries of the reports, as appropriate.

(See Levels of Park Planning 2.3; Studies and Collections 4.2; Consultation 7.5.6; Use by American Indians and Other Traditionally Associated Groups 8.5. Also see Secretary of the Interior's Standards for the Treatment of Historic Properties with Guidelines for the Treatment of Cultural Landscapes)

5.3.5.4 Historic and Prehistoric Structures

The treatment of historic and prehistoric structures will be based on sound preservation practice to enable the long-term preservation of a structure's historic features, materials, and qualities. There are three types of treatment for extant structures: preservation, rehabilitation, and restoration.

(Also see Secretary of the Interior's Standards for the Treatment of Historic Properties)

5.3.5.4.1 Preservation

A structure will be preserved in its present condition if

- that condition allows for satisfactory protection, maintenance, use, and interpretation; or
- another treatment is warranted but cannot be accomplished until some future time.

5.3.5.4.2 Rehabilitation

A historic structure may be rehabilitated (rehabilitation does not apply to prehistoric structures) for contemporary use if

- it cannot adequately serve an appropriate use in its present condition; and
- rehabilitation will retain its essential features and will not alter its integrity and character or conflict with approved park management objectives.

5.3.5.4.3 Restoration

A structure may be restored to an earlier appearance if

- all changes after the proposed restoration period have been professionally evaluated, and the significance of those changes has been fully considered;
- restoration is essential to public understanding of the park's cultural associations;
- sufficient data about that structure's earlier appearance exist to enable its accurate restoration; and
- the disturbance or loss of significant archeological resources is minimized and mitigated by data recovery.

5.3.5.4.4 Reconstruction of Missing Structures

No matter how well conceived or executed, reconstructions are contemporary interpretations of the past rather than authentic survivals from it. The National Park Service will not reconstruct a missing structure unless

- there is no alternative that would accomplish the park's interpretive mission;
- sufficient data exist to enable its accurate reconstruction based on the duplication of historic features substantiated by documentary or physical evidence rather than on conjectural designs or features from other structures;
- reconstruction will occur in the original location;
- the disturbance or loss of significant archeological resources is minimized and mitigated by data recovery; and
- reconstruction is approved by the Director.

A structure will not be reconstructed to appear damaged or ruined. Generalized representations of typical structures will not be attempted.

(See Environmental Monitoring and Control 5.3.1.4; Physical Access for Persons with Disabilities 5.3.2; Historic and Prehistoric Ruins 5.3.5.4.10)

5.3.5.4.5 Movement of Historic Structures

Proposals for moving historic structures will consider the effects of movement on the structures, their present environments, their proposed environments, and the archeological research value of the structures and their sites. No historic structure will be moved if its preservation would be adversely affected or until the appropriate recovery of significant archeological data has occurred. Prehistoric structures will not be moved.

A nationally significant historic structure may be moved only if

- it cannot practically be preserved on its present site; or
- the move constitutes a return to a previous historic location, and the previous move and present location are not important to the structure's significance.

A historic structure of less-than-national significance may be moved if

- it cannot practically be preserved on its present site; or
- its present location is not important to its significance, and its relocation is essential to public understanding of the park's cultural associations.

In moving a historic structure, every effort will be made to reestablish its historic orientation, immediate setting, and general relationship to its environment.

The Park Service will not acquire historic structures for relocation to parks unless those structures were removed from the park and are necessary to achieve the park purpose or authorized by legislation.

5.3.5.4.6 New Construction

In preference to new construction, every reasonable consideration will be given to using historic structures for park purposes compatible with their preservation and public appreciation. Additions may be made to historic structures when essential to their continued use and when new construction will not destroy historic materials, features, and spatial relationships that characterize the structure. Structural additions will harmonize in size, scale, proportion, and materials with, but be readily distinguishable from, the older work, and will not intrude upon the historic scene. New additions will meet the *Secretary of the Interior's Standards for Rehabilitation*.

In those areas of parks managed for the preservation, protection, and interpretation of cultural resources and their settings, new structures, landscape features, and utilities will be constructed only if

- existing structures and improvements do not meet essential park management needs; and
- new construction is designed and sited to preserve the integrity and character of the area.

Unless associated with an approved restoration or reconstruction, all alterations, additions, or related new construction will be differentiated from yet compatible with the historic character of the structure.

(See Rehabilitation 5.3.5.4.2; Use of Historic Structures 5.3.5.4.7; Adaptive Use 9.1.1.4. Also see Executive Order 13006 (Locating Federal Facilities on Historic Properties); National Historic Preservation Act)

5.3.5.4.7 Use of Historic Structures

NHPA (16 USC 470h-2(a)(1)) and Executive Order 13006 (Locating Federal Facilities on Historic Properties) require each federal agency—before acquiring, constructing, or leasing buildings—to use, to the maximum extent feasible, historic properties available to it whenever operationally appropriate and economically prudent. The *National Historic Preservation Act* also requires each agency to implement alternatives for the adaptive use of historic properties it owns if that will help ensure the properties' preservation. Therefore, compatible uses for structures will be found whenever possible. This policy will help prevent the accelerated deterioration of historic structures due to neglect and vandalism. Unused significant historic structures should be stabilized and protected through appropriate measures (such as mothballing) until long-term decisions are made through the planning process.

All uses of historic structures are subject to preservation and public safety requirements. No administrative or public use will be permitted that would threaten the stability or character of a structure, the museum objects within it, or the safety of its users, or that would entail alterations that would significantly compromise its integrity.

(See Fire Detection, Suppression, and Post-fire Rehabilitation and Protection 5.3.1.2; Physical Access for Persons with Disabilities 5.3.2; Adaptive Use 9.1.1.4; Energy Management 9.1.7; Historic Structures 9.4.3.3. Also see Executive Order 13287 (Preserve America))

5.3.5.4.8 Park Structures Owned or Managed by Others

Structures and related property owned or managed by others will be managed in accordance with NPS policies, guidelines, and standards to the extent permitted by the Service's interest. This includes structures and property owned but not occupied by the Service, and structures and property owned by others in which the Service has a less-than-fee interest or plays a major management or preservation role. Interests acquired or retained by the Service will enable the application of this policy.

(See Land Protection Plans 3.3; Historic Property Leases and Cooperative Agreements 5.3.3; Commercial Visitor Services Planning 10.2.2)

5.3.5.4.9 Damaged or Destroyed Historic Structures

Historic structures damaged or destroyed by fire, storm, earthquake, war, or any other accident may be preserved as ruins; be removed; or be rehabilitated, restored, or reconstructed in accordance with these policies.

5.3.5.4.10 Historic and Prehistoric Ruins

The stabilization of historic and prehistoric ruins will be preceded by studies leading to the recovery of any data that would be affected by stabilization work. Ruins and related features on unexcavated archeological sites will be stabilized only to the extent necessary to preserve research values or to arrest structural deterioration, recognizing that it is preferable to preserve archeological sites in situ than to excavate them. Archeological ruins to be exhibited will not be excavated until consultation has occurred with traditionally associated peoples and adequate provisions are made for data recovery and stabilization. Structures will not be deliberately reduced to ruins, and missing structures will not be reconstructed to appear damaged or ruined.

5.3.5.5 Museum Collections

The Service will collect, protect, preserve, provide access to, and use objects, specimens, and archival and manuscript collections (henceforth referred to collectively as "collections," or individually as "items") in the disciplines of archeology, ethnography, history, biology, geology, and paleontology to aid understanding among park visitors, and to advance knowledge in the humanities and sciences. As appropriate, the Service will consult with culturally affiliated or traditionally associated peoples before treating or reproducing items in NPS collections that are subject to the Native American Graves Protection and Repatriation Act.

(Also see Museum Handbook)

5.3.5.5.1 Preservation

An item in a museum collection will be preserved in its present condition through ongoing preventive care if

- that condition is satisfactory for exhibit or research; or
- another treatment is warranted but it cannot be accomplished until some future time.

An item will be stabilized if

- preventive measures are insufficient to reduce deterioration to a tolerable level; or
- the item is so fragile that it will be endangered under any circumstances.

Active conservation treatment (intervention) will be minimized to reduce the possibility of compromising the item's integrity. All active treatment will be documented.

5.3.5.5.2 Restoration

An item in a museum collection may be restored to an earlier appearance if

- restoration is required for exhibit or research purposes;
- sufficient data about that item's earlier appearance exist to enable its accurate restoration; and
- restoration will not modify that item's known original character.

Restoration will be accomplished using the techniques and materials that least modify the item and so that the materials can be removed at a later time with minimal adverse effect. Restored areas will be documented and distinguishable from original material. Restoration will take into account the possible importance of preserving signs of wear, damage, former maintenance, and other historical and scientific evidence.

5.3.5.5.3 Reproduction

Items needed for interpretive and educational presentations will be reproduced for such use when the originals (1) are unavailable, or (2) would be subject to undue deterioration or loss, or (3) are otherwise inappropriate for exhibit. If an object is inappropriate for exhibit because of its religious or spiritual significance to a traditionally associated people, it will be reproduced only after consultation with such people.

5.3.5.5.4 Acquisition, Management, Disposition, and Use

Collections and related documentation essential to achieving the purposes and objectives of parks will be acquired and maintained in accordance with approved scope of collection statements for each park. When museum objects, specimens, or archival documents become available and fall within a park's approved scope of collection statement, every reasonable effort will be made to acquire them if they can be managed and made accessible according to NPS standards.

Archeological objects systematically collected in a park, and natural history specimens systematically collected in a park for exhibit or permanent retention, will be managed as part of the park's museum collection. The management and care of museum collections will be addressed at all appropriate levels of planning. Requisite levels of care will be established through the interdisciplinary efforts of qualified professionals.

Museum collections will be acquired and disposed of in conformance with legal authorizations and current NPS procedures. The National Park Service will acquire only collections having legal and ethical pedigrees. Each park will maintain complete and current accession records to establish the basis for legal custody of the collections in its possession, including intellectual property rights when acquired. Each park will prepare museum catalog records to record basic property management data and other documentary information about the park's museum collection. Collections will be inventoried in accordance with current procedures. Archeological, cultural landscape, ethnographic, historic and prehistoric structure, historic furnishings, natural resource, and other projects that generate collections for parks will provide for cataloging and initial preservation of those collections in the project budget.

The Service may cooperate with qualified entities in the management, use, and exhibition of museum collections, and may loan items to or borrow items from such entities for approved purposes. The Service may deaccession items using means authorized in the Museum Act and the Native American Graves Protection and Repatriation Act.

Interested persons will be permitted to inspect and study NPS museum collections and records in accordance with standards for the preservation and use of collections, and subject to laws and policies regarding the confidentiality of resource data. At-cost copies of documents may be provided.

(See Natural Resource Collections 4.2.3; Paleontological Resources and Their Contexts 4.8.2.1; Confidentiality 5.2.3; Fire Detection, Suppression, and Post-fire Rehabilitation and Protection 5.3.1.2; Environmental Monitoring and Control 5.3.1.4; Consultation 7.5.6; Special Park Uses 8.6; Museum Collections Management Facilities 9.4.2. Also see 16 USC 18f; 43 USC 1460; 36 CFR Part 79; 43 CFR Part 10; and Museum Handbook)

5.3.5.5.5 Historic Furnishings

When historic furnishings are present in their original arrangement in a historic structure, every effort will be made to preserve them as an entity. Such historic furnishings will not be moved or replaced unless required for their protection or repair or unless the structure is designated for another use in an approved planning document. The original arrangement of historic furnishings will be properly documented. A structure may be refurnished in whole or in part if

- all changes after the proposed refurnishing period have been professionally evaluated, and their significance has been fully considered;
- a planning process has demonstrated that refurnishing is essential to public understanding of the park's cultural associations; and
- sufficient evidence of the design and placement of the structure's furnishings exists to enable its accurate refurnishing without reliance on evidence from comparable structures.

Generalized representations of typical interiors will not be attempted except in exhibit contexts that make their representative nature obvious. Reproductions may be used in place of historic furnishings, but only when photographic evidence or prototypes exist to ensure the accurate re-creation of historic pieces.

(See Levels of Park Planning 2.3; Nonpersonal Services 7.3.2)

5.3.5.5.6 Archives and Manuscripts

Archival and manuscript collections are museum collections; they will be preserved, arranged, cataloged, and described in finding aids. They will be maintained and used in ways that preserve the collections and their context (provenance and original order) intact while providing controlled access. With few legal exemptions, the Park Service will make archives and manuscripts available to researchers. Electronic documents that are to be preserved in archival and manuscript collections will be migrated so that their information remains accessible.

All documentation associated with natural and cultural resource studies and other resource management actions will be retained in the park's museum collection for use in managing park resources over time. Parks will retain notes or copies of records significant to their administrative histories when they periodically transfer their official records to federal record centers.

(See Managing Information 1.9.2; Confidentiality 5.2.3)

Wilderness Preservation and Management

All NPS lands will be evaluated for their eligibility for inclusion within the national wilderness preservation system. For those lands that possess wilderness characteristics, no action that would diminish their wilderness eligibility will be taken until after Congress and the President have taken final action. The superintendent of each park containing wilderness will develop and maintain a wilderness management plan or equivalent document. Wilderness considerations will be integrated into all planning documents to guide the preservation, management, and use of the park's wilderness area and ensure that wilderness is unimpaired for future use and enjoyment as wilderness.

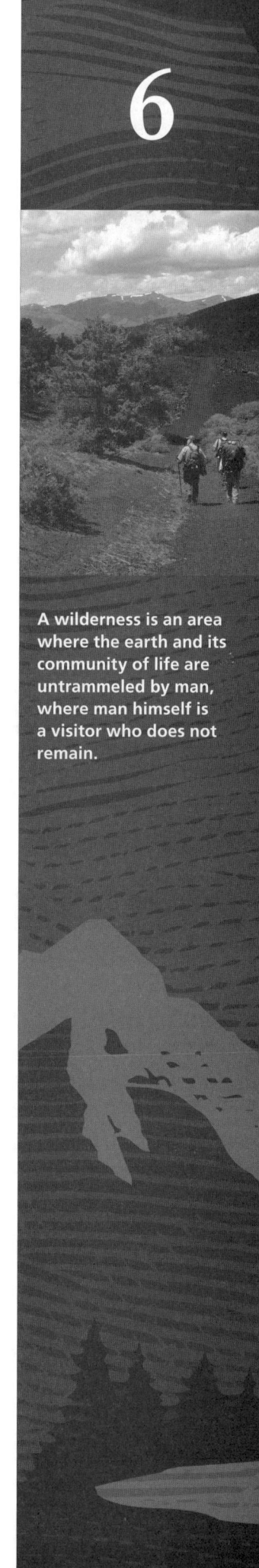

A wilderness is an area where the earth and its community of life are untrammeled by man, where man himself is a visitor who does not remain.

6.1 General Statement

The National Park Service will manage wilderness areas for the use and enjoyment of the American people in such a manner as will leave them unimpaired for future use and enjoyment as wilderness. Management will include the protection of these areas, the preservation of their wilderness character, and the gathering and dissemination of information regarding their use and enjoyment as wilderness. The purpose of wilderness in the national parks includes the preservation of wilderness character and wilderness resources in an unimpaired condition and, in accordance with the Wilderness Act, wilderness areas shall be devoted to the public purposes of recreational, scenic, scientific, educational, conservation, and historical use.

The policies contained in this chapter are supplemented by Director's Order #41: Wilderness Preservation and Management and Reference Manual 41, which accompanies the director's order. Those documents should be referred to for more detailed information on the topics covered in this chapter.

6.2 Identification and Designation of the Wilderness Resource

The National Park Service will use the following wilderness study process to consider NPS areas for inclusion within the congressionally designated national wilderness preservation system.

6.2.1 Assessment of Wilderness Eligibility or Ineligibility

All lands administered by the National Park Service, including new units or additions to existing units since 1964, will be evaluated for their eligibility[2] for inclusion in the national wilderness preservation system. Additionally, lands that were originally assessed as ineligible for wilderness because of nonconforming or incompatible uses must be reevaluated if the nonconforming uses have been terminated or removed. A wilderness eligibility assessment will consist of a brief memorandum from the regional director to the Director that makes a managerial determination as to the eligibility of the park lands for wilderness designation.

The assessment may include information important for other park planning purposes, and other park planning efforts may likewise produce information important to wilderness. The assessment should therefore be completed in a timely manner and thoughtfully coordinated with other planning activities. The assessment may be combined with the wilderness study described below if the combined document can be completed in a timely manner.

---

[2] *Management Policies 2001* used the term "suitability" to refer to the Park Service's initial screening assessment as to whether lands meet the minimum criteria for inclusion in the national wilderness preservation system. The Wilderness Act, however, uses "suitability" to refer to the Secretary's determinations in forwarding recommendations to the President. For purposes of clarity, the NPS initial screening assessment has been renamed an "eligibility" assessment. The change from "suitability" to "eligibility" in no way lessens the protected status of these lands.

6.2.1.1 Primary Eligibility Criteria

NPS lands will be considered eligible for wilderness if they are at least 5,000 acres or of sufficient size to make practicable their preservation and use in an unimpaired condition, and if they possess the following characteristics (as identified in the Wilderness Act):

- The earth and its community of life are untrammeled by humans, where humans are visitors and do not remain.

- The area is undeveloped and retains its primeval character and influence without permanent improvements or human habitation.

- The area generally appears to have been affected primarily by the forces of nature, with the imprint of humans' work substantially unnoticeable.

- The area is protected and managed so as to preserve its natural conditions.

- The area offers outstanding opportunities for solitude or a primitive and unconfined type of recreation.

6.2.1.2 Additional Considerations in Determining Eligibility

In addition to the primary eligibility criteria, the following considerations should be taken into account in determining eligibility:

- A wilderness area may contain significant ecological, geological, or other features of scientific, educational, scenic, or historical value, although it does not need these things to be considered eligible for wilderness designation.

- Lands that have been logged, farmed, grazed, mined, or otherwise used in ways not involving extensive development or alteration of the landscape may also be considered eligible for wilderness designation if, at the time of assessment, the effects of these activities are substantially unnoticeable or their wilderness character could be maintained or restored through appropriate management actions.

- An area will not be excluded from a determination of wilderness eligibility solely because established or proposed management practices require the use of tools, equipment, or structures if those practices are necessary to meet minimum requirements for the administration of the area as wilderness.

- In the process of determining wilderness eligibility, lands will not be excluded solely because of existing rights or privileges (e.g., mineral exploration and development, commercial operations, agricultural development, grazing, or stock driveways). If the National Park Service determines that these lands possess wilderness character, they may be included in the eligibility determination so that they can be considered for designation as wilderness or potential wilderness.

- Lands containing aboveground or buried utility lines will normally not be considered as eligible for wilderness designation, but they can be considered as eligible for "potential" wilderness designation if there is a long-term intent to remove the lines. No new utility lines may be installed in wilderness, and existing utility lines may not be extended or enlarged except as may be allowed pursuant to section 1106 of the Alaska National Interest Lands Conservation Act (16 USC 1133(c)).

◆ Historic features that are primary attractions for park visitors will generally not be recommended as eligible for wilderness designation. However, an area that attracts visitors primarily for the enjoyment of solitude and unconfined recreation in a primitive setting may also contain cultural resource features and still be included in wilderness. Historic trails may serve and be maintained as part of the wilderness trail system, as identified and coordinated within an approved wilderness management plan and the park's cultural resource plan. The presence of historic structures does not make an area ineligible for wilderness. A recommendation may be made to include a historic structure in wilderness if (1) the structure would be only a minor feature of the total wilderness proposal; and (2) the structure will remain in its historic state, without development.

◆ Dams within or affecting the area being studied do not make a waterway ineligible for wilderness designation. The nature and extent of impacts and the extent to which the impacts can be mitigated would need to be addressed in subsequent wilderness studies.

◆ The established use of motorboats, snowmobiles, or aircraft does not make an area ineligible for wilderness. The nature and extent of any impacts on the environment and on eligibility, and the extent to which the impacts can be mitigated would need to be addressed in subsequent wilderness studies, along with the possible need to discontinue the use.

◆ Overflights do not make an area ineligible for wilderness designation. The nature and extent of any overflight impacts and the extent to which the impacts can be mitigated would need to be addressed in subsequent wilderness studies.

6.2.1.3 The Assessment Process

The Service will involve the public in the wilderness eligibility assessment process through notification of its intentions to conduct the assessment and publication of the Director's determination, either as "eligible" or as "ineligible" for further wilderness study. Notification will include the issuance of news releases to local and regional news media and the publication of a final eligibility determination in the *Federal Register*. The final determination of an area's eligibility, or ineligibility, for further study must be approved by the Director before publication of the final eligibility determination in the *Federal Register*. For areas determined to be ineligible for wilderness designation, the wilderness preservation provisions in the NPS *Management Policies* are not applicable. However, ineligible lands will be managed in accordance with the NPS Organic Act and all other laws, executive orders, regulations, and policies applicable to units of the national park system.

6.2.2 Wilderness Studies

Lands and waters found to possess the characteristics and values of wilderness, as defined in the Wilderness Act and determined eligible pursuant to the wilderness eligibility assessment, will be formally studied to develop the recommendation to Congress for wilderness designation. The National Park Service will continue to undertake wilderness studies of all lands that have been determined to be eligible as a result of the wilderness eligibility assessment. Also, studies will be made of lands for which subsequent legislation directs that wilderness studies be completed.

Wilderness studies will be supported by appropriate documentation of compliance with the National Environmental Policy Act and the National Historic Preservation Act. The Council on Environmental Quality requires environmental impact statements for wilderness studies that will result in recommendations for designations (i.e., proposals for legislation to designate as wilderness).

6.2.2.1 Potential Wilderness

A wilderness study may identify lands that are surrounded by or adjacent to lands proposed for wilderness designation but that do not themselves qualify for immediate designation due to temporary nonconforming or incompatible conditions. The wilderness recommendation forwarded to the Congress by the President may identify these lands as "potential" wilderness for future designation as wilderness when the nonconforming use has been removed or eliminated. If so authorized by Congress, these potential wilderness areas will become designated wilderness upon the Secretary's determination, published in the *Federal Register*, that they have finally met the qualifications for designation by the cessation or termination of the nonconforming use.

6.2.2.2 Proposed Wilderness

The findings and conclusions of a formal wilderness study will be reviewed by the Director, who will then determine which lands will be forwarded to the Department of the Interior (Assistant Secretary's Office) as "proposed" wilderness. The Director's proposed wilderness will identify park lands that the Director believes the Secretary should recommend for immediate wilderness designation, as well as any other lands identified as "not proposed" or as "potential" wilderness.

6.2.3 Recommended Wilderness

The Secretary of the Interior is responsible for recommending to the President those lands under his/her jurisdiction that are suitable or nonsuitable for inclusion within the national wilderness preservation system. The Secretary performs this function through the Assistant Secretary's Office by reviewing NPS proposed wilderness and either approving or revising the proposal. The final result is forwarded by the Secretary for the President's consideration. The President is then responsible for transmitting his recommendations with respect to wilderness designation to both houses of Congress. These recommendations must be accompanied by maps and boundary descriptions. The National Park Service will track the status of the wilderness designation process in Congress.

6.2.4 Designated Wilderness

After the President's wilderness recommendation is formally sent to and considered by Congress, Congress may subsequently enact the legislation needed to include the area within the national wilderness preservation system as "designated" and/or "potential" wilderness. The National Park Service will assist the department and Congress in this process as requested. Lands released by Congress from further wilderness consideration will be managed in accordance with the NPS Organic Act and all other laws, executive orders, regulations, and policies applicable to nonwilderness areas of the national park system.

6.3 Wilderness Resource Management

6.3.1 General Policy

For the purposes of applying these policies, the term "wilderness" will include the categories of eligible, study, proposed, recommended, and designated wilderness. Potential wilderness may be a subset of any of these five categories. The policies apply regardless of category except as otherwise provided herein.

In addition to managing these areas for the preservation of the physical wilderness resources, planning for these areas must ensure that the wilderness character is likewise preserved. This policy will be applied to all planning documents affecting wilderness.

The National Park Service will take no action that would diminish the wilderness eligibility of an area possessing wilderness characteristics until the legislative process of wilderness designation has been completed. Until that time, management decisions will be made in expectation of eventual wilderness designation. This policy also applies to potential wilderness, requiring it to be managed as wilderness to the extent that existing nonconforming conditions allow. The National Park Service will apply the principles of civic engagement and cooperative conservation as it determines the most appropriate means of removing the temporary, nonconforming conditions that preclude wilderness designation from potential wilderness. All management decisions affecting wilderness will further apply the concept of "minimum requirement" for the administration of the area regardless of wilderness category. The only exception is for areas that have been found eligible, but for which, after completion of a wilderness study, the Service has not proposed wilderness designation. However, those lands will still be managed to preserve their eligibility for designation.

(See Minimum Requirement 6.3.5)

6.3.2 Responsibility

NPS responsibility for carrying out wilderness preservation mandates will be shared by the Director, regional directors, and superintendents of parks with eligible, study area,

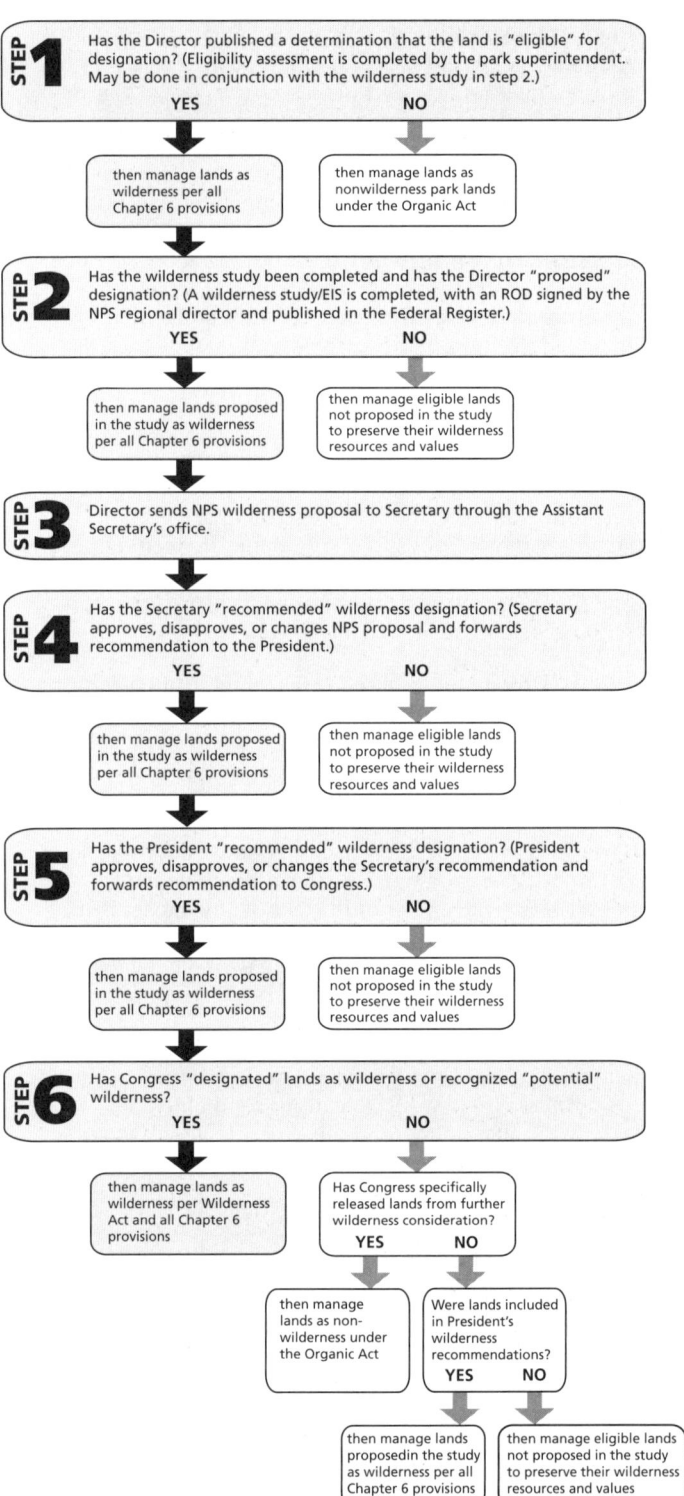

WILDERNESS REVIEW AND MANAGEMENT PROCESS

proposed, recommended, and designated wilderness. Interagency cooperation and coordination and training responsibilities will also be carried out at the Washington, D.C., region, and park levels. Specific wilderness management responsibilities will be assigned at each of these administrative levels to carry out these responsibilities effectively and to facilitate efforts for establishing agency and interagency consistency in wilderness management techniques.

Superintendents will provide the information needed to prepare an annual wilderness report to Congress and to report to the Director on the status of wilderness management in the national park system. Based on this information, the Associate Director for Visitor and Resource Protection will provide the Directorate with recommendations and advice to permanently establish a system of accountability, consistency, and continuity for NPS wilderness management.

6.3.3 Consistency

The National Park Service will seek to achieve consistency in wilderness management objectives, techniques, and practices on both an agency and an interagency basis. Accordingly, the National Park Service will seek to maintain effective intra-agency and interagency communications, and will encourage, sponsor, and participate in intra-agency and interagency training and workshops designed to promote the sharing of ideas, concerns, and techniques related to wilderness management. However, the need for interagency consistency will in no way diminish any established NPS wilderness standards and values.

6.3.4 Wilderness-related Planning and Environmental Compliance

Policies on wilderness planning and compliance include the following.

6.3.4.1 Zoning for Wilderness

When necessary, all categories of wilderness may be zoned for visitor experiences and resource conditions consistent with their wilderness values within the established management zoning system for each park. However, management zoning or other land use classifications cannot and will not diminish or reduce the maximum protection to be afforded lands with wilderness values. Transition zones adjacent to wilderness may be identified to help protect wilderness values, but no transitional or "buffer" zones are appropriate within wilderness boundaries.

6.3.4.2 Wilderness Management Planning

The superintendent of each park containing wilderness resources will develop and maintain a wilderness management plan or equivalent planning document to guide the preservation, management, and use of these resources. The wilderness management plan will identify desired future conditions, as well as establish indicators, standards, conditions, and thresholds beyond which management actions will be taken to reduce human impacts on wilderness resources.

The park's wilderness management plan may be developed as a separate document or as an action component of another planning document. Whether prepared as a stand-alone plan or as part of another planning document, all wilderness management plans must meet the same standards for process and content as specified in this section 6.3.4. Wilderness management plans will be supported by appropriate documentation of compliance with the National Environmental Policy Act and the National Historic Preservation Act. The plan will be developed with public involvement and will contain specific, measurable management objectives that address the preservation and management of natural and cultural resources within wilderness as appropriate to achieve the purposes of the Wilderness Act and other legislative requirements.

(See Visitor Carrying Capacity 8.2.1)

6.3.4.3 Environmental Compliance

Proposals having the potential to impact wilderness resources will be evaluated in accordance with NPS procedures for implementing the National Environmental Policy Act. Those procedures include the use of categorical exclusions, environmental assessments (EAs), or environmental impact statements (EISs). Administrative actions impacting wilderness must be addressed in either the environmental assessment or environmental impact statement accompanying the approved wilderness management plan or as a separate environmental compliance document.

Managers contemplating the use of aircraft or other motorized equipment or mechanical transportation within wilderness must consider impacts to the character, esthetics, and traditions of wilderness before considering the costs and efficiency of the equipment.

In evaluating environmental impacts, the National Park Service will take into account (1) wilderness characteristics and values, including the primeval character and influence of the wilderness; (2) the preservation of natural conditions (including the lack of man-made noise); and (3) assurances that there will be outstanding opportunities for solitude, that the public will be provided with a primitive and unconfined type of recreational experience, and that wilderness will be preserved and used in an unimpaired condition. Managers will be expected to appropriately address cultural resources management considerations in the development and review of environmental compliance documents impacting wilderness resources.

(Also see Director's Order #12: Conservation Planning, Environmental Impact Analysis, and Decision-making)

6.3.5 Minimum Requirement

All management decisions affecting wilderness must be consistent with the minimum requirement concept. This concept is a documented process used to determine if administrative actions, projects, or programs undertaken by the Service or its agents and affecting wilderness character, resources, or the visitor experience are necessary, and if so how to minimize impacts. The minimum requirement concept will be applied as a two-step process that determines

◆ whether the proposed management action is appropriate or necessary for administration of the area as wilderness and does not cause a significant impact to wilderness resources and character, in accordance with the Wilderness Act; and

- the techniques and types of equipment needed to ensure that impacts on wilderness resources and character are minimized.

In accordance with this policy, superintendents will apply the minimum requirement concept in the context of wilderness stewardship planning, as well as to all other administrative practices, proposed special uses, scientific activities, and equipment use in wilderness. The only exception to the minimum requirement policy is for eligible areas that the Service has not proposed for wilderness designation. However, those lands will still be managed to preserve their eligibility.

When determining minimum requirements, the potential disruption of wilderness character and resources will be considered before, and given significantly more weight than, economic efficiency and convenience. If a compromise of wilderness resources or character is unavoidable, only those actions that preserve wilderness character and/or have localized, short-term adverse impacts will be acceptable.

Although park managers have flexibility in identifying the method used to determine minimum requirement, the method used must clearly weigh the benefits and impacts of the proposal, document the decision-making process, and be supported by an appropriate environmental compliance document. Parks must develop a process to determine minimum requirement until the plan is finally approved. Parks will complete a minimum requirement analysis on those administrative practices and equipment uses that have the potential to impact wilderness resources or values. The minimum requirement concept cannot be used to rationalize permanent roads or inappropriate or unlawful uses in wilderness.

Administrative use of motorized equipment or mechanical transport will be authorized only

- if determined by the superintendent to be the minimum requirement needed by management to achieve the purposes of the area, including the preservation of wilderness character and values, in accordance with the Wilderness Act; or
- in emergency situations (for example, search and rescue, homeland security, law enforcement) involving the health or safety of persons actually within the area.

Such management activities will also be conducted in accordance with all applicable regulations, policies, and guidelines and, where practicable, will be scheduled to avoid creating adverse resource impacts or conflicts with visitor use.

While actions taken to address search and rescue, homeland security and law enforcement issues are subject to the minimum requirement concept, preplanning or programmatic planning should be undertaken whenever possible to facilitate a fast and effective response and reduce paperwork.

For more detailed guidance, see Director's Order #41 and the National Wilderness Steering Committee Guidance Paper #3: "What Constitutes the Minimum Requirements in Wilderness?"

(See Director's Order #12: Conservation Planning, Environmental Impact Analysis, and Decision-making)

6.3.6 Scientific Activities in Wilderness

The statutory purposes of wilderness include scientific activities, and these activities are encouraged and permitted when consistent with the Service's responsibilities to preserve and manage wilderness.

6.3.6.1 General Policy

The National Park Service has a responsibility to support appropriate scientific activities in wilderness and to use science to improve wilderness management. The Service recognizes that wilderness can and should serve as an important resource for long-term research into and study and observation of ecological processes and the impact of humans on these ecosystems. The National Park Service further recognizes that appropriate scientific activities may be critical to the long-term preservation of wilderness.

Scientific activities are to be encouraged in wilderness. Even those scientific activities (including inventory, monitoring, and research) that involve a potential impact to wilderness resources or values (including access, ground disturbance, use of equipment, and animal welfare) should be allowed when the benefits of what can be learned outweigh the impacts on wilderness resources or values. However, all such activities must also be evaluated using the minimum requirement concept and include documented compliance that assesses impacts against benefits to wilderness. This process should ensure that the activity is appropriate and uses the minimum tool required to accomplish project objectives. Scientific activities involving prohibitions identified in section 4(c) of the Wilderness Act (16 USC 1133(c)) may be conducted within wilderness when the following occur:

- The desired information is essential for the understanding health, management, or administration of wilderness, and the project cannot be reasonably modified to eliminate or reduce the nonconforming wilderness use(s); or if it increases scientific knowledge, even when this serves no immediate wilderness management purposes, provided it does not compromise wilderness resources or character. The preservation of wilderness resources and character will be given significantly more weight than economic efficiency and/or convenience.
- Compliance with the National Environmental Policy Act (including completion of documented categorical exclusions, environmental assessments/findings of no significant impact, or environmental impact statements/records of decision) and other regulatory compliance (including compliance with section 106 of the National Historic Preservation Act (16 USC 470f)) are accomplished and documented.

- All scientific activities will be accomplished in accordance with terms and conditions adopted at the time the research permit is approved. Later requests for exceptions to the Wilderness Act will require additional review and approval.

- The project will not significantly interfere with other wilderness purposes (recreational, scenic, educational, conservation, or historical) over a broad area or for a long period of time.

- The minimum requirement concept is applied to implementation of the project.

Research and monitoring devices (e.g., video cameras, data loggers, meteorological stations) may be installed and operated in wilderness if (1) the desired information is essential for the administration and preservation of wilderness and cannot be obtained from a location outside wilderness without significant loss of precision and applicability; and (2) the proposed device is the minimum requirement necessary to accomplish the research objective safely.

Park managers will work with researchers to make NPS wilderness area research a model for the use of low-impact, less intrusive techniques. New technology and techniques will be encouraged if they are less intrusive and cause less impact. The goal will be for studies in NPS wilderness to lead the way in "light on the resource" techniques.

Devices located in wilderness will be removed when determined to be no longer essential. Permanent equipment caches are prohibited within wilderness. Temporary caches must be evaluated using the minimum requirement concept.

All scientific activities, including the installation, servicing, removal, and monitoring of research devices, will apply minimum requirement concepts and be accomplished in compliance with *Management Policies*, director's orders, and procedures specified in the park's wilderness management plan.

(See Studies and Collections 4.2; Social Science Studies 8.11)

6.3.6.2 Monitoring Wilderness Resources

In every park containing wilderness, the conditions and long-term trends of wilderness resources will be monitored to identify the need for or effects of management actions. The purpose of this monitoring will be to ensure that management actions and visitor impacts on wilderness resources and character do not exceed standards and conditions established in an approved park plan.

As appropriate, wilderness monitoring programs may assess physical, biological, and cultural resources and social impacts. Monitoring programs may also need to assess potential problems that may originate outside the wilderness to determine the nature, magnitude, and probable source of those impacts.

6.3.7 Natural Resources Management

The National Park Service recognizes that wilderness is a composite resource with interrelated parts. Without natural resources, especially indigenous and endemic species, a wilderness experience would not be possible. Natural resources are critical, defining elements of the wilderness resource, but they need to be managed within the context of the whole ecosystem. Natural resource management plans will be integrated with and cross-reference wilderness management plans. Pursuing a series of independent component projects in wilderness, such as single-species management, will not necessarily accomplish the overarching goal of wilderness management. Natural resources management in wilderness will include and be guided by a coordinated program of scientific inventory, monitoring, and research.

The principle of nondegradation will be applied to wilderness management, and each wilderness area's condition will be measured and assessed against its own unimpaired standard. Natural processes will be allowed, insofar as possible, to shape and control wilderness ecosystems. Management should seek to sustain the natural distribution, numbers, population composition, and interaction of indigenous species. Management intervention should only be undertaken to the extent necessary to correct past mistakes, the impacts of human use, and influences originating outside of wilderness boundaries.

Management actions, including the restoration of extirpated native species, the alteration of natural fire regimes, the control of invasive alien species, the management of endangered species, and the protection of air and water quality, should be attempted only when the knowledge and tools exist to accomplish clearly articulated goals.

(See Chapter 4: Natural Resource Management. Also see Director's Order #77 series on natural resources management)

6.3.8 Cultural Resources

The Wilderness Act specifies that the designation of any area of the park system as wilderness "shall in no manner lower the standards evolved for the use and preservation of" such unit of the park system under the various laws applicable to that unit (16 USC 1133(a)(3)). Thus, the laws pertaining to historic preservation also remain applicable within wilderness but must generally be administered to preserve the area's wilderness character. The responsible decision-maker will include appropriate consideration of the application of these provisions of the Wilderness Act in analyses and decision-making concerning cultural resources.

Cultural resources that have been included within wilderness will be protected and maintained according to the pertinent laws and policies governing cultural resources using management methods that are consistent with the preservation of wilderness character and values. These laws include the Antiquities Act and the Historic Sites, Buildings and Antiquities Act, as well as subsequent historic preservation legislation, including the National Historic Preservation Act, the Archaeological Resources Protection Act, and the Native American Graves Protection and Repatriation Act. The *Secretary of the Interior's Standards and Guidelines for Archeology and Historic Preservation* projects provide direction for protection and maintenance. Cemeteries or commemorative features, such as plaques or memorials, that have been included in wilderness may be retained (including approved access to these sites), but no new cemeteries or additions to existing cemeteries may be made unless specifically authorized by federal statute, existing reservations, or retained rights.

(See Chapter 5: Cultural Resource Management)

6.3.9 Fire Management

All fire management activities conducted in wilderness areas will conform to the basic purposes of wilderness. Actions taken to suppress wildfires must use the minimum requirements concept unless the on-site decision-maker determines in his professional judgment that conditions dictate otherwise. Preplanning is critical to ensure that emergency response incorporates minimum requirements to the greatest extent possible. Fire suppression activities should be managed in ways that protect natural and cultural resources and minimize the lasting impacts of the suppression actions. Information on developing a fire management program in wilderness is contained in Director's Order #18: Wildland Fire Management.

Guidance on the need to suppress wildland fire or to use some wildland fires to achieve desired future conditions should appear in the park's planning documents (for example, in the wilderness management plan and fire management plan). Information in these documents will guide managers in the selection of fire management tactics that protect natural and cultural resources from fire and from fire suppression actions.

The park's fire management plan will provide guidance for responses to natural and human-caused wildland fires based on fuel conditions, climatic conditions, resources at risk, potential for damage to property or loss of life, both within and adjacent to the wilderness, as well as the availability of fire suppression resources.

If a wildland fire use program is implemented, planning documents will also include the prescriptions and procedures under which the program will be conducted within wilderness.

(See Fire Management 4.5)

6.3.10 Management Facilities

Part of the definition of wilderness as provided by the Wilderness Act is "undeveloped federal land retaining its primeval character and influence, without permanent improvements." Accordingly, authorizations of NPS administrative facilities in wilderness will be limited to the types and minimum number essential to meet the minimum requirements for the administration of the wilderness area. A decision to construct, maintain, or remove an administrative facility will be based primarily on whether or not the facility is required to preserve wilderness character or values, not on considerations of administrative convenience, economic effect, or convenience to the public or park staff. Maintenance or the removal of historic structures will also comply with cultural resource protection and preservation policies and directives, and with the concept of minimum requirement management techniques for wilderness.

6.3.10.1 Administrative Facilities

Administrative facilities (for example, ranger stations and/or patrol cabins, fire lookouts, radio and/or cellular telephone antennas, radio repeater sites, associated storage or support structures, drift fences, and facilities supporting trail stock operations) may be allowed in wilderness only if they are determined to be the minimum requirement necessary to carry out wilderness management objectives and are specifically addressed within the park's wilderness management plan or other appropriate planning documents. New roads will not be built in wilderness. Temporary vehicular access may be permitted only to meet the minimum requirements of emergency situations. As rapidly as possible, disturbed resources will be restored according to an approved restoration plan. Where abandoned roads have been included within wilderness, they may be used as trails, restored to natural conditions, or managed as a cultural resource.

No permanent heliports, helipads, or airstrips will be allowed in wilderness unless specifically authorized by statute or legislation. Temporary landing facilities may be used to meet the minimum requirements of emergency situations. Site improvements determined to be essential for safety reasons during individual emergency situations may be authorized, but no site markings or improvements of any kind may be installed to support nonemergency use. In Alaska, any prohibitions or restrictions on the use of fixed-wing aircraft should follow the procedures in 43 CFR 36.11(f).

Permanent storage caches are prohibited in wilderness unless necessary for health and safety purposes or when such caches are determined necessary, justified, documented, and approved through a minimum requirements analysis.

(See Overflights and Aviation Uses 8.4)

6.3.10.2 Trails in Wilderness

Trails will be permitted within wilderness when they are determined to be necessary for resource protection and/or for providing for visitor use for the purposes of wilderness. The identification and inventory of the wilderness trail system will be included as an integral part of the wilderness management plan or other appropriate planning document.

Trails will be maintained at levels and conditions identified within the approved wilderness management plan or other planning document. Trail maintenance structures (such as water bars, gabions) may be provided, under minimum requirement protocols, where they are essential for resource preservation or where significant safety hazards exist during normal use periods. Historic and/or prehistoric trails will be administered in keeping with approved cultural resource and wilderness management plan requirements.

Borrow pits are not permitted in wilderness areas, with the exception of small-quantity use of borrow material for trails, which must be in accordance with an approved minimum requirements analysis.

6.3.10.3 Shelters and Campsites

The construction of new shelters for public use will generally not be allowed, in keeping with the values and character of wilderness. An existing shelter may be maintained or reconstructed only if the facility is necessary to achieve specific wilderness management objectives as identified in the park's wilderness and cultural resources management plans. The construction, use, and occupancy of cabins and other structures in wilderness areas in Alaska are governed by applicable provisions of the Alaska National Interest Lands Conservation Act and by NPS regulations in 36 CFR Part 13; such structures may be permitted only under conditions prescribed in the park's wilderness management plan.

Although the development of facilities to serve visitors will generally be avoided, campsites may be designated when essential for resource protection and preservation or to meet other specific wilderness management objectives. In keeping with the terms of the park's wilderness management plan, campsite facilities may include a site marker, fire rings, tent sites, food storage devices, and toilets if these are determined by the superintendent to be the minimum facilities necessary for the health and safety of wilderness users or for the preservation of wilderness resources and values. Toilets will be placed only in locations where their presence and use will resolve health and sanitation problems or prevent serious resource impacts, especially where reducing or dispersing visitor use is impractical or has failed to alleviate the problems. Picnic tables will not be allowed in wilderness except in those limited circumstances when they are necessary for resource protection and when documented and approved through a minimum requirements analysis.

6.3.10.4 Signs

Signs detract from the wilderness character of an area and make the imprint of man and management more noticeable. Only those signs necessary for visitor safety or to protect wilderness resources, such as those identifying routes and distances, will be permitted. Where signs are used, they should be compatible with their surroundings and the minimum size possible.

6.3.11 Wilderness Boundaries

Policies related to wilderness boundaries include the following.

6.3.11.1 Legal Descriptions and Boundary Maps

Every park with designated wilderness will possess a written legal description of the wilderness area and a map (or maps) that illustrates the legal description of the wilderness. Each park will ensure that the legal description and map(s) are filed in the appropriate locations. Wilderness boundaries have the force of federal law and may only be modified through the legislative process—unless minor adjustments and corrections are specifically authorized within the wilderness designation enabling legislation.

6.3.11.2 Caves

All cave passages located totally within the surface wilderness boundary will be managed as wilderness. Caves that have entrances within wilderness but contain passages that may extend outside the surface wilderness boundary will be managed as wilderness. Caves that may have multiple entrances located both within and exterior to the surface wilderness boundary will be managed consistent with the surface boundary; those portions of the cave within the wilderness boundary will be managed as wilderness.

(See Caves 4.8.2.2)

6.3.11.3 Waters in Wilderness

In keeping with established jurisdictions and authorities, the Service will manage as wilderness all waters included within wilderness boundaries, and the lands beneath these waters (if owned by the United States).

(See Water Resource Management 4.6)

6.3.12 American Indian Access and Associated Sites

American Indian access rights and protection of sites associated with Indian tribes will be protected and maintained according to applicable laws and policies. The American Indian Religious Freedom Act reaffirms the First Amendment rights of Native Americans to access national park system lands for the exercise of their traditional religious practices. Native American human remains that were removed from wilderness areas and are subject to the NAGPRA repatriation may be reinterred at or near the site from which they were removed. American Indian religious areas and other ethnographic and cultural resources will be inventoried and protected. American Indians will be permitted access within wilderness for sacred or religious purposes consistent with the intent of the American Indian Religious Freedom Act, the Wilderness Act, and other applicable authorities provided by federal statues and executive orders.

(See also Executive Order 13007 (Indian Sacred Sites))

6.4 Wilderness Use Management

The National Park Service will encourage and facilitate those uses of wilderness that are in keeping with the definitions and purposes of wilderness and do not degrade wilderness resources and character. Appropriate restrictions may be imposed on any authorized activity in the interest of preserving wilderness character and resources or to ensure public safety.

When resource impacts or demands for use exceed established thresholds or capacities, superintendents may limit or redirect use. If these actions are determined to be the minimally required level of management, physical alterations, public education, general regulations, special regulations, permit systems, and the local restrictions, public use limits, closures, and designations implemented under the discretionary authority of the superintendent (36 CFR 1.5 and Part 13; 43 CFR Part 36 for Alaska units) may all be used in managing use and protecting wilderness.

6.4.1 General Policy

Park visitors need to accept wilderness on its own unique terms. Accordingly, the National Park Service will promote education programs that encourage wilderness users to understand and be aware of certain risks, including possible dangers arising from wildlife, weather conditions, physical features, and other natural phenomena that are inherent in the various conditions that comprise a wilderness experience and primitive methods of travel. The National Park Service will not modify the wilderness area to eliminate risks that are normally associated with wilderness, but it will strive to provide users with general information concerning possible risks, any recommended precautions, related user responsibilities, and applicable restrictions and regulations, including those associated with ethnographic and cultural resources.

6.4.2 Wilderness Interpretation and Education

In the context of interpretive and educational planning, national park system units with wilderness resources will (1) operate public education programs designed to promote and perpetuate public awareness of and appreciation for wilderness character, resources, and ethics while providing for acceptable use limits; (2) focus on fostering an understanding of the concept of wilderness that includes respect for the resource, willingness to exercise self-restraint in demanding access to it, and an ability to adhere to appropriate, minimum-impact techniques; and (3) encourage the public to use and accept wilderness on its own terms—that is, the acceptance of an undeveloped, primitive environment and the assumption of the potential risks and responsibilities involved in using and enjoying wilderness areas. NPS interpretive plans and programs for wilderness parks will address the primary interpretive themes for wilderness. Education is among the most effective tools for dealing with wilderness use and management problems and should generally be applied before more restrictive management tools.

(See Visitor Safety 8.2.5.1)

6.4.3 Recreational Use Management in Wilderness

Recreational uses of NPS wilderness are generally those traditionally associated with wilderness and identified by Congress in the legislative record for the development of the Wilderness Act and in keeping with the language provided by sections 2(a) and 2(c) of the act itself (16 USC 1131(a) and (c)). These recreational uses of wilderness will be of a type and nature that ensures that its use and enjoyment (1) will leave it unimpaired for future use and enjoyment as wilderness, (2) provides for the protection of the area as wilderness, and (3) provides for the preservation of wilderness character. Recreational uses in NPS wilderness areas will be of a nature that

- enables the areas to retain their primeval character and influence;
- protects and preserves natural conditions;
- leaves the imprint of man's work substantially unnoticeable;
- provides outstanding opportunities for solitude or primitive and unconfined types of recreation; and
- preserves wilderness in an unimpaired condition.

(See Management of Recreational Use 8.2.2.1)

6.4.3.1 Recreation Use Evaluation

Recreational uses—particularly new and emerging activities that compromise the stated purposes and definitions of wilderness or unduly impact the wilderness resource or the visitor experience within wilderness—will be evaluated to determine if these uses are appropriate or should be limited or disallowed through use of the superintendent's compendium in 36 CFR 1.5. Evaluation or reevaluation should be accomplished within wilderness management plans or similar implementation plans. Recreational uses that do not meet the purposes and definitions of wilderness should be prohibited in NPS wilderness.

Significant changes in patterns or increased levels of use will not be authorized by special permit, administrative discretion, or authorities under the superintendents' compendia, except in cases where sufficient information exists to adequately determine there is no significant impact on wilderness resources and values, including visitor experiences. These increased levels of use and changes in patterns of existing use will normally not qualify for a categorical exclusion under the National Environmental Policy Act. Decisions regarding significant changes in patterns and new levels of use will require environmental analysis and review, including opportunity for public comment, in accordance with the NEPA requirements.

(See Appropriate Use of the Parks 1.5; Visitor Carrying Capacity 8.2.1)

6.4.3.2 Outdoor Skills and Ethics

Leave-no-trace principles and practices will be applied to all forms of recreation management within wilderness, including commercial operations. Wilderness users will generally be required to carry out all refuse. Refuse is defined in 36 CFR 1.4.

6.4.3.3 Use of Motorized Equipment

Public use of motorized equipment or any form of mechanical transport will be prohibited in wilderness except as provided for in specific legislation. Operating a motor vehicle or possessing a bicycle in designated wilderness outside Alaska is prohibited (see NPS regulations in 36 CFR 4.30(d)(1)).

However, section 4(d)(1) of the Wilderness Act (16 USC 1133(d)(1)) authorizes the Secretary—where legislation designating the wilderness specifically makes this provision applicable—to allow the continuation of motorboat and aircraft use under certain circumstances in which those activities were established prior to wilderness designation. Section 4(d)(1) gives the Secretary the discretion to manage and regulate the activity in accordance with the Wilderness Act, the NPS Organic Act, and individual park enabling legislation. As authorized, the National Park Service will administer this use to be compatible with the purpose, character, and resource values of the particular wilderness area involved. The use of motorized equipment by the public in wilderness areas in Alaska is governed by applicable provisions of the Alaska National Interest Lands Conservation Act, NPS regulations in 36 CFR Part 13, and Department of the Interior regulations in 43 CFR Part 36. The specific conditions under which motorized equipment may be used by the public will be outlined in each park's wilderness management plan.

(See Soundscape Management 4.9; Use of Motorized Equipment 8.2.3)

6.4.4 Commercial Services

Wilderness-oriented commercial services that contribute to public education and visitor enjoyment of wilderness values or provide opportunities for primitive and unconfined types of recreation may be authorized if they meet the "necessary and appropriate" tests of the National Park Service Concessions Management Improvement Act of 1998 and section 4(d)(6) of the Wilderness Act (16 USC 1133(d)(5)), and if they are consistent with the wilderness management objectives contained in the park's wilderness management plan, including the application of the minimum requirement concept. Activities such as guide services for outfitted horseback, hiking, mountain climbing, or river trips and similar activities may be appropriate and may be authorized if conducted under the terms and conditions outlined in the park's wilderness management plan and/or in legislation authorizing these types of commercial uses.

The only structures or facilities used by commercial services that will be allowed in wilderness will be temporary shelters, such as tents, or other specifically approved facilities that may be required within the wilderness management plan for resource protection and the preservation of wilderness values. Temporary facilities will generally be removed from the wilderness after each trip, unless such removal will cause degradation of the wilderness resources. In Alaska, additional guidance for the management of temporary facilities for hunting and fishing guides is found in the Alaska National Interest Lands Conservation Act section 1316 (16 USC 3204). The use of permanent equipment and supply caches by commercial operators is prohibited within wilderness.

Managers will ensure that commercial operators are in compliance with established leave-no-trace protocols.

(See Visitor Use 8.2; Commercial Use Authorizations 10.3)

6.4.5 Special Events

The National Park Service will not sponsor or issue permits for special events to be conducted in wilderness if those events are inconsistent with wilderness resources and character or if they do not require a wilderness setting to occur. Permits will not be issued in NPS wilderness areas for commercial enterprises or competitive events, including activities involving animal, foot, or watercraft races; the physical endurance of a person or animal; organized survival exercises; war games; or similar exercises.

(See Special Events 8.6.2. Also see 36 CFR 2.50)

6.4.6 Existing Private Rights

Wilderness designation does not extinguish valid existing private rights (for example, fee-simple interest, less-than-fee-simple interest, valid mineral operations, rights-of-way, grazing permits). The validity of private rights within wilderness must be determined on a case-by-case basis. Valid private rights in wilderness must be administered in keeping with the specific conditions and requirements of the valid right.

6.4.7 Grazing and Livestock Driveways

Commercial grazing or driving of livestock in park wilderness will be allowed only as specifically authorized by Congress. Where these activities are authorized, they will be managed under conditions and requirements identified within the approved wilderness management plan and corresponding allotment management plans. The use of motorized vehicles, motorized equipment, or mechanical transport by grazing permittees will not be allowed except as provided for by a specific authority—that is, a valid existing right, the enabling legislation, or an NPS determination of minimum requirement. The construction of livestock management facilities other than those specifically authorized by legislation is prohibited.

Noncommercial grazing of trail stock used as part of an approved livestock management program within wilderness may be authorized in accordance with NPS regulations and conditions outlined in the wilderness management plan or stock use management plan. All approved livestock use must ensure the preservation of wilderness resources and character. Superintendents will be responsible for monitoring livestock use in wilderness to the same degree as human use, and may use the same management tools and techniques, including the application of the minimum requirement concept to manage livestock use that are available for managing other wilderness uses.

(See 8.6.8 Domestic and Feral Livestock)

6.4.8 Rights-of-Way

Existing rights-of-way that have been included in wilderness should be terminated or phased out where practicable. Rights-of-way subject to NPS administrative control should be administered under conditions outlined in the park's wilderness management plan that protect wilderness character and resources and limit the use of motorized or mechanical equipment. The Service will not issue any new rights-of-way or widen or extend any existing rights-of-way in wilderness. Rights-of-way and access procedures affecting wilderness areas in Alaska are governed by applicable provisions of the Alaska National Interest Lands Conservation Act and regulations in 43 CFR Part 36, and 36 CFR Part 13.

(See Existing Private Rights 6.4.6)

6.4.9 Mineral Development

The National Park Service will seek to remove or extinguish valid mining claims and nonfederal mineral interests in wilderness through authorized processes, including purchasing valid rights. In parks where Congress has authorized the leasing of federal minerals, the Park Service will take appropriate actions to preclude the leasing of lands or minerals within wilderness whenever and wherever it is authorized to do so. Lands included within wilderness will be listed as "excepted areas" under applicable regulations in 43 CFR Parts 3100 and 3500 (see section 3500.8).

Unless and until mineral interests and mining claims within NPS wilderness are eliminated, they must be managed pursuant to existing NPS regulations, policies, and procedures. (See 36 CFR Part 9, Subpart A, for mineral development on mining claims; 36 CFR Part 9, subpart B, for nonfederal oil and gas development; and 43 CFR Parts 3100 and 3500 for federal mineral leasing.). A validity examination of unpatented claims in wilderness affected by a proposed plan of operations must be conducted by a certified mineral examiner before plan approval. Motorized use in wilderness is allowed only with an approved plan of operations on valid mineral claims and where there is no reasonable alternative. Motorized use for access can occur only on existing or approved roads. There will be no new roads or improvement of existing roads unless documented as being necessary for resource protection. Any plan of operations that is approved will include stipulations on operations and reclamation that will ensure that long-term effects on the wilderness area are substantially unnoticeable. For access to mining claims in NPS wilderness in Alaska, see 43 CFR 36.10.

6.4.10 Accessibility for Persons with Disabilities

The National Park Service has legal obligations to make available equal opportunities for people with disabilities in all programs and activities. This requirement includes the opportunity to participate in wilderness experiences. Management decisions responding to requests for special consideration to provide wilderness use by persons with disabilities must be in accord with the Architectural Barriers Act of 1968, the Rehabilitation Act of 1973 (as amended in 1978), and section 507(c) of the Americans with Disabilities Act of 1990 (42 USC 12207(c)). Such decisions should balance the intent of access and wilderness laws and find a way of providing the highest level of protection to the wilderness resource.

Section 17.550 of the Secretary of the Interior's regulations regarding the enforcement of nondiscrimination on the basis of disability in Department of Interior programs (43 CFR Part 17, subpart E) states that agencies are not required to take any actions or provide access that would result in a fundamental alteration in the nature of a program or activity. However, the agency has the burden of proving that compliance would result in a fundamental alteration. This concept is also found in section 507 of the Americans with Disabilities Act.

(See Accessibility for Persons with Disabilities 1.9.3, 8.2.4, and 9.1.2. Also see Director's Order #42: Accessibility for Visitors with Disabilities in National Park Service Programs and Services)

Interpretation and Education

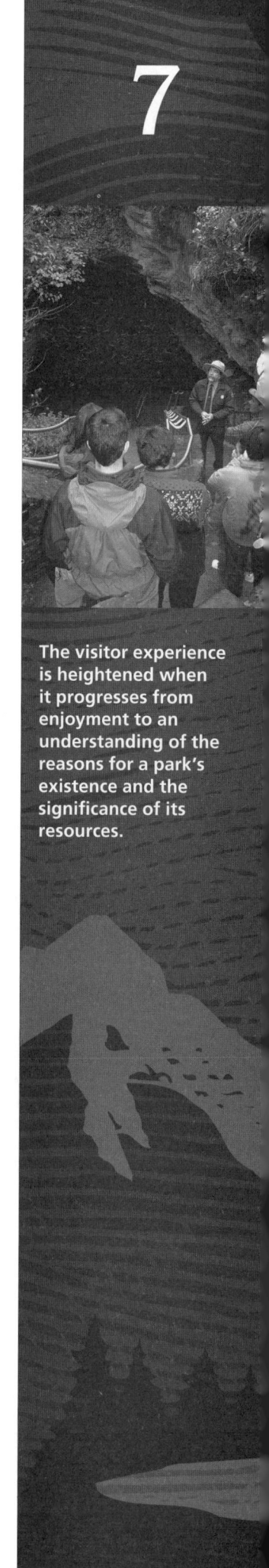

National parks are among the most remarkable places in America for recreation, learning, and inspiration. Interpretive programs are the methods the Service uses to connect people to their parks, with opportunities for all visitors to form their own intellectual, emotional, and physical connections to the meanings and values found in the parks' stories. Facilitating those opportunities through effective interpretive and educational programs will encourage the development of a personal stewardship ethic and broaden public support for preserving and protecting park resources so that they may be enjoyed by present and future generations.

The visitor experience is heightened when it progresses from enjoyment to an understanding of the reasons for a park's existence and the significance of its resources.

Introduction

The Organic Act of 1916 created the National Park Service to conserve park resources and "provide for the enjoyment of the same in such manner and by such means as will leave them unimpaired for future generations." The purpose of NPS interpretive and educational programs is to advance this mission by providing memorable educational and recreational experiences that will (1) help the public understand the meaning and relevance of park resources, and (2) foster development of a sense of stewardship. The programs do so by forging a connection between park resources, visitors, the community, and the national park system. That connection is made by linking a park's tangible resources to the intangible values and meanings found in those resources. An important outcome of the park experience is that visitors more readily retain information, grasp meanings, and adopt new behaviors and values because they are directly involved with cultural and natural heritage resources and sites.

As a result of technological advances, people can visit a national park "virtually" and connect with park resources at their convenience. Hence, for purposes of this chapter, the terms "visitor" and "park visitor" are defined as anyone who uses a park's interpretive and education services, regardless of where such use occurs.

The Service will maintain the capability to deliver visitor and interpretive services of the highest quality. Those services should provide understandable interpretation of the major features in the parks and the events that occurred there, with an emphasis on experiences that will lead visitors to appreciate the park's authentic qualities. Excellent and effective interpretation and education will be the shared responsibility of everyone, from the Washington and regional directorates, through park superintendents and chief interpreters, to field interpreters, noninterpretive staff, and partners. Excellence in interpretation and education will be achieved through specific visitor activities, interpretive media, ongoing scholarly research, planning, technical excellence in implementation, broad public input, continual reevaluation, sound business practices, and training to professional standards for all who provide interpretive services.

Enjoyment of the parks is a fundamental part of the visitor experience. That experience is heightened when it progresses from enjoyment to an understanding of the reasons for a park's existence and the significance of its resources. To determine the quality and quantity of the visitor experience, levels of visitor satisfaction, safety, understanding, and appreciation will be measured. Director's Order #6 and Reference Manual 6 provide additional guidance for the development of interpretive and educational programs.

7.1 Interpretive and Educational Programs

Since its inception, one of the chief functions of the national parks has been to serve educational purposes. The Service is committed to extend its leadership in education, build on what is in place, and pursue new relationships and opportunities to make national parks even more meaningful in the life of the nation. Within the rich learning environments of national parks and facilitation by NPS interpreters, visitors will be offered authentic experiences and opportunities to immerse themselves in places where events actually happened, experience the thrill of connecting with real objects used by previous generations, enjoy some of the most beautiful and historic places in America, and understand the difficult moments our nation has endured.

Every park will develop an interpretive and educational program that is grounded in (1) park resources, (2) themes related to the park's legislative history and significance, and (3) park and Service-wide mission goals. The intent will be to provide each visitor with an interpretive experience that is enjoyable and inspirational within the context of the park's tangible resources and the meanings they represent. In addition, visitors should be made aware of the purposes and scope of the national park system.

Interpretation will encourage dialogue and accept that visitors have their own individual points of view Factual information presented will be current, accurate, based on current scholarship and science, and delivered to convey park meanings, with the understanding that audience members will draw their own conclusions. Interpretation will also reach out to park neighbors, segments of the population that do not visit national parks, and community decision-makers to stimulate discussions about the park and its meanings in local, regional, and national contexts. In addition, interpretive services will help employees better understand the park's history, resources, processes, and visitors.

An effective park interpretive and educational program will include

- information and orientation programs that provide visitors with easy access to the information they need to have a safe and enjoyable park experience;

- interpretive programs that provide both on- and off-site presentations and are designed to encourage visitors to form their own intellectual or emotional connections with the resource. Interpretive programs facilitate a connection between the interests of visitors and the meanings of the park;

- curriculum-based educational programs that link park themes to national standards and state curricula and involve educators in planning and development. These programs include previsit and postvisit materials, address different learning styles, include an evaluation mechanism, and provide learning experiences that are linked directly to clear objectives. Programs develop a thorough understanding of a park's resources in individual, regional, national, and global contexts and of the park's place within the national park system; and

◆ interpretive media that provide visitors with relevant park information and facilitate more in-depth understanding of—and personal connection with—park stories and resources. This media will be continually maintained for both quality of content and condition based upon established standards.

(See Air Quality 4.7.1; Geologic Resource Management 4.8; Wilderness Interpretation and Education 6.4.2; Energy Management 9.1.7; Visitor Facilities 9.3. Also see Director's Order #6: Interpretation and Education)

7.2 Interpretive Planning

General management plans and comprehensive interpretive plans (CIPs) will serve as the backbone of interpretive and educational program planning and direction. The CIP process will guide park staff in defining themes, determining desired visitor experience opportunities, identifying challenges, and recommending which stories to tell, how to tell them, and how to reach specific audiences. All interpretive and educational services, including personal services, interpretive media, and partnerships that work to support the delivery of interpretive and educational programs, will be based on and coordinated with the comprehensive interpretive plan. The resulting parkwide interpretation and education program will thus communicate park significance and meanings in the most effective and efficient way. Recognition that concessioners, cooperating associations, friends groups, and other partners may have an important role in providing interpretive and educational services will be most important in planning for the overall visitor services program, and such entities should be included where appropriate in the planning process.

The CIP process will be initiated by superintendents. The life span of a CIP will be seven to ten years. Superintendents and chiefs of interpretation will be accountable to ensure that their parks have a completed and current comprehensive interpretive plan as defined in Director's Order #6 and Reference Manual 6. Harpers Ferry Center and regional offices will provide support.

(See also Director's Order #75A: Civic Engagement and Public Involvement)

7.3 Personal and Nonpersonal Services

7.3.1 Personal Services

Personal interpretive services feature contacts with visitors. Anyone who works in a park and makes contact with the public can and should provide an enjoyable, appropriate, and valuable visitor service. Superintendents and chiefs of interpretation will demand quality in the delivery of a multidimensional personal services program by park staff, volunteers, contractors, cooperating associations, concessioners, and other partners. In addition to basic information and orientation services, personal interpretive services can include walks, talks, tours, campfire programs, roving contacts, curriculum-based education programs, and Junior Ranger programs. These types of activities and programs will be designed to offer opportunities for greater enjoyment and in-depth understanding and appreciation of the park's resources.

Personal services will provide opportunities for diverse audiences to enjoy and connect to parks and nurture future stewards of America's national heritage. Park staff will help visitors have a safe, meaningful, and satisfying park experience; help them decide how to spend their time in the park, and inform them about the wonders that await their discovery. Personal services programs presented in parks will be recorded annually in the Service-wide interpretive report, which will document the number of programs offered, visitors served, and the costs associated with those programs. Park chiefs of interpretation will be responsible for submitting their park's portion of the report to the Washington Office Division of Interpretation and Education.

7.3.1.1 Curriculum-based Education Programs

Parks will be managed as places to demonstrate the principles of science, to illustrate the national experience as history, to engage learners throughout their lifetimes, and to do these things while challenging visitors in exciting and motivating settings. Schools represent a microcosm of society and present myriad opportunities for the Service to foster stewardship in future generations. Therefore, curriculum-based programs will be designed to link classroom learning with experiences in the parks. Programs will complement school curricula by matching a group's educational objectives with park resources. Curriculum-based programs will focus on the stories and meanings attached to park resources; the threats to the condition of those resources; and conservation or preservation issues relevant to the park, the national park system, and the park's place within that system. To continue to meet the demand from schools for NPS programs, parks will identify, in cooperation with park partners, alternative means for program delivery, such as publications, Internet deliveries, and distance learning.

7.3.2 Nonpersonal Services

Nonpersonal services are interpretive media (publications such as a unigrid brochure or park newspaper, films, exhibits, web-based programs). They do not require the presence of staff. Nonpersonal services, which can reach large audiences, must maintain a consistent quality of presentation over time. Used in conjunction with personal services, they will provide opportunities for visitor information, orientation, and personal connections to park resources. The Center for Media Services will establish Service-wide standards for all NPS informational media.

Harpers Ferry Center will also provide guidance and assistance to parks for interpretive media planning, design and production for museum and visitor center exhibits, wayside exhibits, audiovisual productions, publications, and directional signs. Plans or proposals to be accomplished by parks and regions, including privately funded projects, may be reviewed by the Center for Media Services for appropriateness and quality of design and execution. Proposals from concessioners, cooperating associations, and others may also be reviewed. To provide data for parks to maintain these assets, the condition of the NPS inventory of exhibits and interpretive trails (currently recorded in the Media Inventory Database System or MIDS) will be tracked through the Facilities Maintenance Management System.

Parks will be responsible for the conservation of historic furnishings and artifacts on exhibit in parks. They may obtain conservation services from the Center for Media Services or from outside contractors.

7.3.2.1 Park Brochures

Official park brochures are an important part of the NPS identity and a valuable and desired part of the park experience. Each brochure should provide a map of the park, address critical safety and resource protection issues, introduce park interpretive themes, and describe significant park resources. The Service's goal will be that 100% of parks have an adequate allotment of park brochures to meet demands and ensure that adequate numbers of brochures are available in other languages as needed.

7.3.3 Technology and Interpretation

Innovative use of existing and emerging technology can maximize both the visitor experience and employee effectiveness. Parks should use technological communications, such as the Internet and distance learning, to enhance their informational, orientation, interpretive, and educational programs. The National Park Service will maintain a site on the World Wide Web (nps.gov) to provide an opportunity for all parks and programs to reach beyond their borders to a worldwide audience. Each park will maintain a home page for the purpose of reaching this audience. Parks should link from their home pages to web pages of entities that support the NPS mission. Park home pages will comply with Director's Order #11C: Web Publishing and Department of the Interior policy, particularly as relates to security.

(See Managing Information 1.9.2)

7.3.4 Interpretive and Educational Services Beyond Park Boundaries

The Service will continually adjust to changing patterns of visitation and an increasingly multiracial, multiethnic, and multicultural society to ensure that the national park system remains high among societal concerns and relevant to future generations. Each park's interpretation and education program will reach out to park neighbors, those who are not visiting national parks, and community decision-makers to stimulate discussions about the park and its values in local, regional, and national contexts. Parks will use community programs and special events such as pageants, anniversaries, dedications, festivals, and other observances as opportunities to highlight meaningful connections between the park, its resources, the event, and the public. These activities, as well as other interpretive and educational services, support civic engagement and contribute to public understanding of the park's significance and the significance of the national park system.

National Park Service interpretive and educational programs must explore new and innovative approaches to inform a diverse constituency, many of whom may never set foot inside a park's boundaries. A planned outreach program will be employed to firmly establish each park as part of the local, national, and global community. Outreach will be used to disseminate park information and interpretive and educational programs beyond park boundaries. Everyone should have the opportunity to connect to the parks through NPS outreach services.

7.4 Interpretive Competencies and Skills

All interpretive services should be provided by highly trained personnel who have access to a continual supply of current information from research programs and other sources. All employees who provide interpretive services will be required to meet the Service's national standards of interpretation and education. To support that effort, the Service will develop a web-based distance learning and credentialing platform based on the interpretive development program (IDP) to teach interpretive and educational skills and competencies and test for knowledge of those skills and competencies.

NPS interpretation and education employees will be held to the most comprehensive standards and act as models and coaches for other NPS staff, especially law enforcement, volunteers, and other partners. Partners (including cooperating associations, contractors, and concessioners) will have access to and will be required to meet NPS national standards in the competency areas in which they work. Those who give formal programs will meet the appropriate national standards for such competencies. The cooperating association standard agreement, concession contracts, and other contracts that include interpretive services will require the demonstration of standards. Similarly, contractors for media projects will use the web-based distance learning and credentialing platform to both learn about NPS requirements and demonstrate their mastery of required standards. Permanent interpreters and seasonal interpreters will be required to certify in relevant and park-appropriate interpretive competencies of the interpretive development program. The certification will be designed to establish a consistent Service-wide professional standard and to fortify the full-performance interpretive ranger as a provider of interpretive services while also serving as standard bearer, coach, mentor, and facilitator for all others who provide those services.

7.5 Requirements for All Interpretive and Educational Services

The following factors must be considered in the development and review of all personal and nonpersonal services.

7.5.1 Interpretation and 21st Century Relevancy

Demographic trends in the United States indicate an ever increasing array of diversity within the population. The National Park Service must change its traditional approach of interpretation to improve relevancy in the 21st century to our visitors. To enact this change the National Park Service will implement new and innovative ways to reach out, engage, and cultivate the support of the increasingly diverse array of visitors. The unique qualities of the national parks—qualities that highlight, for example, America's diverse heritage and the principles of democracy—are what make them relevant. These qualities will be used to advantage in educating Americans and visitors to America about topics such as the civic experience of our country; the complex, diverse ecology of our nation and the world; and the influence of global climate change. Interpretation and education will seek to provide opportunities for more NPS audiences to have experiences that connect them to parks, so that they will come to value and enjoy these special places. The national park system and the Interpretation and Education program provide opportunities for facilitation of civic dialogue to engage Americans in understanding past and current issues of importance on a local-to-global basis. These opportunities should be pursued.

7.5.2 Access to Interpretive and Educational Opportunities

National parks belong to all of the nation's people and should have opportunities to enjoy them. Efforts will be made to ensure that interpretive and educational programs are available to all people and consider the special needs of children, senior citizens, non-English speaking visitors, and the economically disadvantaged. Foreign-language translations of park publications will be provided as needed in those parks visited by substantial numbers of non-English-speaking visitors.

The National Park Service will also ensure that persons with disabilities receive the same interpretive opportunities as those without disabilities. Interpretive and educational programs, exhibits, publications, and all other interpretive media will comply with Department of the Interior regulations at 43 CFR Part 17, subpart E, and with standards required by the Architectural Barriers Act. Accordingly, the Park Service will ensure that persons with disabilities have the opportunity to participate in all programs and activities in the most integrated setting appropriate. Additionally, the Service will take all feasible steps to ensure effective communication with individuals with hearing, visual, and cognitive disabilities. These steps should include but not be limited to providing sign language interpreters, audio/visual presentations, Braille, and large-print versions of printed materials.

(See Physical Access for Persons with Disabilities 5.3.2; Accessibility for Persons with Disabilities 8.2.4; Accessibility for Persons with Disabilities 9.1.2; Accessibility of Commercial Services 10.2.6.2. Also see Director's Order #42; Reference Manual 41; 43 CFR 17.550)

7.5.3 Resource Issue Interpretation and Education

Park managers are increasingly called upon to make difficult resource decisions, some of which may be highly controversial. Interpretation and education programs can provide opportunities for civic engagement with Indian tribes and residents and officials of gateway and neighboring communities, the region, and the state(s) surrounding a park and beyond. Such opportunities for civic dialogue about resource issues and broad initiatives are often the most effective means for eliminating resource threats and gaining input and feedback from stakeholder constituents. Therefore, parks should, in balanced and appropriate ways, thoroughly integrate resource issues and initiatives of local and Service-wide importance into their interpretive and educational programs. Whenever possible, the appropriate interpretive managers at the national, regional, or park level should be involved in the process.

In instances in which programming affects resources managed by other agencies, such agencies should be consulted during program planning. For interpretation of resource issues to be effective, frontline interpretive staff must be informed about the reasoning that guided the decision-making process, and interpreters must present balanced views. Acknowledging multiple points of view does not require interpretive and educational programs to provide equal time or disregard the weight of scientific or historical evidence. Resource issue interpretation should be integrated into both on- and off-site programs, as well as into printed and electronic media whenever deemed appropriate by the park manager.

7.5.4 Research and Scholarship

Interpretive and educational programs will be based on current scholarship and research about the history, science, and condition of park resources, and on research about the needs, expectations, and behavior of visitors. To accomplish this, a dialogue must be established and maintained among interpreters, education specialists, resource managers, scientists, archeologists, sociologists, ethnographers, historians, and other experts for the purpose of offering the most current and accurate programs to the public. When appropriate, parks are encouraged to use a master interpreter to foster, facilitate, and maintain this dialogue.

(See Levels of Park Planning 2.3)

7.5.5 Evaluation of Interpretation and Education Effectiveness

Evaluation is also critically important for continuous improvement of educational and interpretive programs that lead to achievement of the NPS mission. Evaluation, systematically applied, is necessary to ensure that the NPS interpretation and education program is cost-effective and financially accountable. The Service will maintain an evaluation strategy that fosters a Service-wide commitment to program planning and reflection, information sharing, and application of research-based results.

7.5.6 Consultation

The National Park Service will present factual and balanced presentations of the many American cultures, heritages, and histories. Diverse constituencies will be consulted to (1) ensure appropriate content and accuracy, and (2) identify multiple points of view and potentially sensitive issues. When appropriate, state and local agencies involved in heritage tourism and history (such as state historic preservation officers) should be included in consultations to foster coordination and partnerships. Acknowledging multiple points of view does not require interpretive and educational programs to provide equal time or disregard the weight of scientific or historical evidence.

Park managers will take culturally sensitive steps to preserve the knowledge of American Indian tribes and other traditionally associated peoples and secure the benefit of their deep understanding of the nature and spirit of places within the parks by encouraging their participation in park activities. A related goal will be to ensure that irreplaceable connections such as place names, migration routes, harvesting practices, prayers, and songs are cataloged for use in current and future activities.

The Service will respectfully consult traditionally associated peoples and other cultural and community groups in the planning, development, presentation, and operation of park interpretive programs and media relating to their cultures and histories. Cooperative programs will be developed with tribal governments and cultural groups to help the Service present accurate perspectives on their cultures. Ethnographic or cultural anthropological data and concepts will also be used in interpretive programs.

The Service will not display Native American human remains or photographs of those remains. Drawings, renderings, or casts of such remains will not be displayed without the consent of culturally affiliated Indian tribes, Alaska Natives, and Native Hawaiian organizations. The Service may exhibit non-Native American remains, photographs, drawings, renderings, or casts thereof, in consultation with appropriate traditionally associated peoples. The Service will consult with culturally affiliated or traditionally associated peoples to determine the religious status of any object whose sacred nature is suspected but not confirmed. These consultations will occur before an object is exhibited or any action is taken that may have an adverse effect on its religious qualities.

(See Relationship with American Indian Tribes 1.11; Evaluation and Categorization 5.1.3.2; Stewardship of Human Remains and Burials 5.3.4; Ethnographic Resources 5.3.5.3; Museum Collections 5.3.5.5)

7.5.7 Cultural Demonstrators

Cultural demonstrators can provide unique insights into their cultures. To facilitate their successful interaction with the public, parks may provide cultural demonstrators with training and direction. Cultural demonstrators (in parks outside the National Capital Region) who are not NPS employees may be permitted to sell self-made handcrafted items to park visitors, keeping the proceeds for themselves, where such handicrafts are related to the park's interpretive themes. This is allowed under 16 USC 1a-2(g), which authorizes the sale of products produced in the conduct of living exhibits, interpretive demonstrations, or park programs. When this practice is permitted, all materials used in creating such items must be the private property of the demonstrator, collected from outside the park. The superintendent may permit this practice through a cooperative agreement, special use permit, concession contract, or other legal instrument.

Titles 8 and 13 of the Alaska National Interest Lands Conservation Act regulate the taking of fish, wildlife, and other natural resources for subsistence and other purposes in the Alaska parks.

(See Reenactments 7.5.9; Special Events 8.6.2; Collecting Natural Products 8.8; Merchandise 10.2.4.5. Also see 36 CFR 5.3; 60 FR 17639)

7.5.8 Historic Weapons

All uses of historic weapons in parks will strictly comply with the Historic Weapons Demonstrations Safety Standards contained in Reference Manual 6, and will follow the procedures specified therein for the particular weapon(s) being used.

Weapons firing demonstrations conducted in NPS-administered areas are restricted to reproduction black powder weapons only. Original NPS museum weapons will not be used. Requests by outside groups or individuals to use non-NPS original weapons will follow the exemption request procedure prescribed in Reference Manual 6, and will be granted or denied in writing by the superintendent.

7.5.9 Reenactments

Battle reenactments and demonstrations of battle tactics that involve exchanges of fire between opposing lines, the taking of casualties, hand-to-hand combat, or any other form of simulated warfare are prohibited in all parks. Even the best-researched and most well-intentioned representation of combat cannot replicate the tragic complexity of real warfare. Respect for the memory of those whose lives were lost at these sites and whose unrecovered remains are often still interred in these grounds precludes the staging of inherently artificial battles at these memorial sites. Battle reenactments create an atmosphere that is inconsistent with the memorial qualities of the battlefields and other military sites placed in the Service's trust. The safety risks to participants and visitors, and the inevitable damage to the physical resource that occurs during such events are also unacceptably high when seen in light of the NPS mandate to preserve and protect park resources and values.

7.6 Interpretive and Educational Partnerships

The National Park Service will increase the effectiveness and accountability of park interpretation and education activities by collaborating with volunteers, cooperating associations, concessioners, and other partners to provide interpretive and educational services that adhere to Service-wide standards. To be successful, this will require all NPS interpretation and education practitioners, employees and partners, personal service providers, and media professionals to have access to training, coaching, and program evaluation results that meet national standards. NPS interpreters and educators will provide the leadership, example, and standards for all partners to deliver effective interpretation and education services.

Interpretation and education operational capacity will be improved in parks by actively pursuing additional partnerships. Partnerships for this purpose will be sought with willing and able organizations with compatible purposes, such as historical societies, museums, colleges and universities, school districts, tourism commissions, conservation groups, health organizations, libraries, and others.

7.6.1 Volunteers in Parks (VIPs)

Interpretation and education operational capacity will be increased in parks by actively pursuing volunteers and dedicating NPS staff time to coordinate volunteer programs in parks. Although the bulk of volunteer hours support interpretation and education, volunteer services may be used in various aspects of park operation under the authority of the Volunteers in the Parks Act of 1969. Pursuant to this legislation, volunteers may be recruited without regard to civil service regulations, are covered for tort liability and work-injury compensation, and may be reimbursed for out-of-pocket expenses while participating in the program. Volunteers will be accepted without regard to race, creed, religion, age, sex, color, national origin, disability, or sexual orientation. Volunteers will not displace NPS employees. NPS housing may be used for volunteers. Director's Order #7 and Reference Manual 7 provide additional guidance for the volunteer program.

(See Protection 5.3.5.1.4; Housing Management Plan 9.4.3.1. Also see Handbook 36 on Housing)

7.6.2 Cooperating Associations

The National Park Service will continue to nurture its relationship with nonprofit organizations that support park programs. Cooperating associations may provide publications and other items that enhance the interpretive story, allow visitors to explore particular interests, and enable them to take the park story home through their purchases.

When appropriate, cooperating associations will join the National Park Service in presenting interpretive and educational programs and supporting research efforts as authorized in 16 USC 1-3, 6, and 17j-(2)e. In accordance with the standard, nonnegotiable cooperating association agreement, cooperating associations may, consistent with a park's scope-of-sales statement, purchase for resale, or produce for sale, interpretive and educational items that are directly related to the understanding and interpretation of the park or the national park system. Associations may offer appropriate and approved interpretive services that support but do not supplant interpretive and educational services offered by the Park Service. Associations may accept donations on behalf of the Service when appropriate and when conducted through approved fund-raising efforts. Service housing may be used for cooperating association employees only if available and not needed for NPS employees. Guidance for managing NPS partnerships with cooperating associations is included in Director's Order #32 and Reference Manual 32.

(See Housing Management Plan 9.4.3.1. Also see Director's Order #21: Donations and Fundraising; Handbook 36 on Housing)

Use of the Parks

Many different types of uses take place in the hundreds of park units that make up the national park system. The Service must ensure that these uses are appropriate to the park in which they occur.

National parks belong to all Americans, and the National Park Service will welcome all Americans to experience their parks. The Service will focus special attention on visitor enjoyment of the parks while recognizing that the NPS mission is to conserve unimpaired each park's natural and cultural resources and values for the enjoyment, education, and inspiration of present and future generations. The Service will also welcome international visitors, in keeping with its commitment to extend the benefits of natural and cultural resource conservation and outdoor recreation throughout the world.

8.1 General

Many different types of uses take place in the hundreds of park units that make up the national park system. Some of those uses are carried out by the National Park Service, but many more are carried out by park visitors, permittees, lessees, and licensees. The 1916 Organic Act, which created the National Park Service, directs the Service to conserve park resources "unimpaired" for the enjoyment of future generations. The 1970 National Park System General Authorities Act, as amended in 1978, prohibits the Service from allowing any activities that would cause derogation of the values and purposes for which the parks have been established (except as directly and specifically provided by Congress). Taken together, these two laws establish for NPS managers (1) a strict mandate to protect park resources and values; (2) a responsibility to actively manage all park uses; and (3) when necessary, an obligation to regulate their amount, kind, time, and place in such a way that future generations can enjoy, learn, and be inspired by park resources and values and appreciate their national significance in as good or better condition than the generation that preceded them. (Throughout these *Management Policies*, the term "impairment" is construed to also encompass "derogation.")

8.1.1 Appropriate Use

The concept of appropriate use is especially important with regard to visitor enjoyment because, in accordance with the Organic Act, the fundamental purpose of all parks also includes providing for the enjoyment of park resources and values by present and future generations. The scope of enjoyment contemplated by the Organic Act is described in section 1.4.3. Appropriate forms of visitor enjoyment emphasize appropriate recreation consistent with the protection of the park. This includes interpretation of park resources and contemplation and understanding of the purposes for which a park unit's resources are being preserved. Many of these forms of enjoyment support the federal policy of promoting the health and personal fitness of the general public, as set forth in Executive Order 13266 (Activities to Promote Personal Fitness).

While providing opportunities for appropriate public enjoyment is an important part of the Service's mission, other park uses—unrelated to public enjoyment—may sometimes be allowed as a right or a privilege if they are not otherwise prohibited by law or regulation. In exercising its discretionary authority, the Service will allow only uses that are (1) appropriate to the purpose for which the park was established, and (2) can be sustained without causing unacceptable impacts. Recreational activities and other uses that would impair a park's resources, values, or purposes cannot be allowed. The only exception is when an activity that would cause impairment is directly and specifically mandated by Congress.

The fact that a park use may have an impact does not necessarily mean it will be unacceptable or impair park resources or values for the enjoyment of future generations. Impacts may affect park resources or values and still be within the limits of the discretionary authority conferred by the Organic Act. In these situations, the Service will ensure that the impacts are unavoidable and cannot be further mitigated. Even when they fall far short of impairment, unacceptable impacts can rapidly lead to impairment and must be avoided. For this reason, the Service will not knowingly authorize a park use that would cause unacceptable impacts.

When a use is mandated by law but causes unacceptable impacts on park resources or values, the Service will take appropriate management actions to avoid or mitigate the adverse effects. When a use is authorized by law but not mandated, and when the use may cause unacceptable impacts on park resources or values, the Service will avoid or mitigate the impacts to the point where there will be no unacceptable impacts; or, if necessary, the Service will deny a proposed activity or eliminate an existing activity.

(See Park Management 1.4; Unacceptable Impacts 1.4.7.1; Consumptive Uses 8.9. Also see Director's Order #12; 36 CFR 1.5; 36 CFR 2.1)

8.1.2 Process for Determining Appropriate Uses

All proposals for park uses will be evaluated for

- consistency with applicable laws, executive orders, regulations, and policies;
- consistency with existing plans for public use and resource management;
- actual and potential effects on park resources and values;
- total costs to the Service; and
- whether the public interest will be served.

Superintendents must continually monitor and examine all park uses to ensure that unanticipated and unacceptable impacts do not occur. Superintendents should also be attentive to existing and emerging technologies that might further reduce or eliminate impacts from existing uses allowed in parks. Unless otherwise mandated by statute, only uses that meet the criteria listed in section 8.2 may be allowed.

Specific park uses will be guided by the following subsections of this chapter, and must comply also with the other chapters of these *Management Policies*. The Service will coordinate with appropriate state authorities regarding activities that are subject to state regulation or to joint federal/state regulation. The regulatory framework for implementing NPS policies governing use of the parks, and for determining when and where activities may be allowed, is found in 36 CFR Parts 2, 3, 4, 5, 7, 12, and 13. Procedures for implementing or terminating a restriction, condition, public use limit, or closure within a park area are found in 36 CFR 1.5 (but see also 36 CFR 13.30 and 43 CFR 36.11(h) for procedures specific to park areas in Alaska). Some activities may be allowed in parks only after park-specific regulations have been published, which requires extensive analysis and opportunities for civic engagement.

The following illustration shows the process by which potential uses are evaluated for appropriateness.

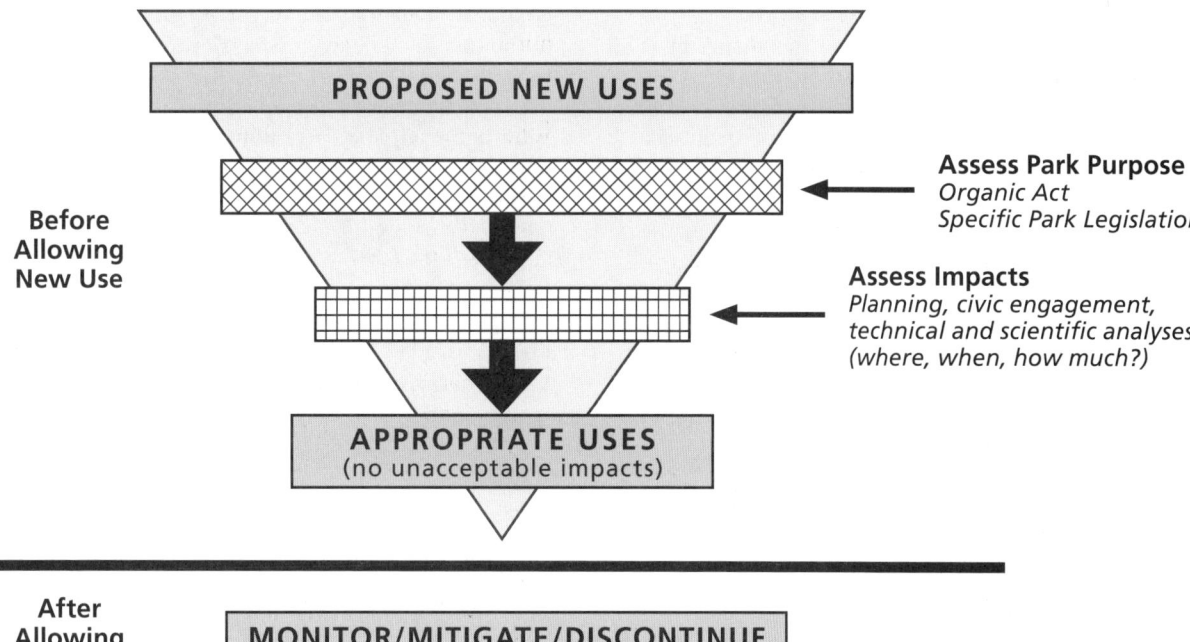

The National Park Service will always consider allowing activities that are appropriate to the parks, although conditions may preclude certain activities or require that limitations be placed on them. In all cases, impacts from park uses must be avoided, minimized, or mitigated through one or more of the following methods:

◆ visitor education and civic engagement

◆ temporal, spatial, or numerical limitations on the use

◆ the application of best available technology

◆ the application of adaptive management techniques

If, in monitoring a park use, unanticipated impacts become apparent, the superintendent must further manage or constrain the use to minimize the impacts, or discontinue the use if the impacts are unacceptable.

(See Park Purposes and Legislatively Authorized Uses 1.4.3.1; Park System Planning Chapter 2; Use of the Parks Chapter 8. Also see 36 CFR 1.5)

8.2 Visitor Use

Enjoyment of park resources and values by the people of the United States is part of the fundamental purpose of all parks. The Service is committed to providing appropriate, high-quality opportunities for visitors to enjoy the parks, and the Service will maintain within the parks an atmosphere that is open, inviting, and accessible to every segment of American society. However, many forms of recreation enjoyed by the public do not require a national park setting and are more appropriate to other venues. The Service will therefore

◆ provide opportunities for forms of enjoyment that are uniquely suited and appropriate to the superlative natural and cultural resources found in the parks;

◆ defer to local, state, tribal, and other federal agencies; private industry; and nongovernmental organizations to meet the broader spectrum of recreational needs and demands.

To provide for enjoyment of the parks, the National Park Service will encourage visitor activities that

◆ are appropriate to the purpose for which the park was established; and

◆ are inspirational, educational, or healthful, and otherwise appropriate to the park environment; and

◆ will foster an understanding of and appreciation for park resources and values, or will promote enjoyment through a direct association with, interaction with, or relation to park resources; and

◆ can be sustained without causing unacceptable impacts to park resources or values.

The primary means by which the Service will actively foster and provide activities that meet these criteria will be through its interpretive and educational programs, which are described in detail in chapter 7. The Service will also welcome the efforts of nongovernmental organizations, tour companies, guides, outfitters, and other private sector entities to provide structured activities that meet these criteria. In addition to structured activities, the Service will, to the extent practicable, afford visitors ample opportunity for inspiration, appreciation, and enjoyment through their own personalized experiences—without the formality of program or structure.

The Service may allow other visitor uses that do not meet all the above criteria if they are appropriate to the purpose for which the park was established and they can be sustained without causing unacceptable impacts to park resources or values. For the purposes of these policies, unacceptable impacts are impacts that, individually or cumulatively, would

- be inconsistent with a park's purposes or values, or
- impede the attainment of a park's desired conditions for natural and cultural resources as identified through the park's planning process, or
- create an unsafe or unhealthy environment for visitors or employees, or
- diminish opportunities for current or future generations to enjoy, learn about, or be inspired by park resources or values, or
- unreasonably interfere with
  - park programs or activities, or
  - an appropriate use, or
  - the atmosphere of peace and tranquility, or the natural soundscape maintained in wilderness and natural, historic, or commemorative locations within the park, or
  - NPS concessioner or contractor operations or services.

Management controls and conditions must be established for all park uses to ensure that park resources and values are preserved and protected for the future. If and when a superintendent has a reasonable basis for believing that an ongoing or proposed public use would cause unacceptable impacts to park resources or values, the superintendent must make adjustments to the way the activity is conducted to eliminate the unacceptable impacts. If the adjustments do not succeed in eliminating the unacceptable impacts, the superintendent may (1) temporarily or permanently close a specific area, or (2) place limitations on the use, or (3) prohibit the use. Restrictions placed on recreational uses that have otherwise been found to be appropriate will be limited to the minimum necessary to protect park resources and values and promote visitor safety and enjoyment.

Any closures or restrictions—other than those imposed by law—must be consistent with applicable laws, regulations, and policies, and (except in emergency situations) require a written determination by the superintendent that such measures are needed to

- protect public health and safety;
- prevent unacceptable impacts to park resources or values;
- carry out scientific research;
- minimize visitor use conflicts; or
- otherwise implement management responsibilities.

When practicable, restrictions will be based on the results of study or research, including (when appropriate) research in the social sciences. Any restrictions imposed will be fully explained to visitors and the public. Visitors will be given appropriate information on how to keep adverse impacts to a minimum, and how to enjoy the safe and lawful use of the parks.

(See Park Management 1.4; Management of Recreational Use 8.2.2.1. Also see 36 CFR 1.5: "Closures and Public Use Limits"; Director's Order #17: National Park Service Tourism)

8.2.1 Visitor Carrying Capacity

Visitor carrying capacity is the type and level of visitor use that can be accommodated while sustaining the desired resource and visitor experience conditions in the park. By identifying and staying within carrying capacities, superintendents can manage park uses that may unacceptably impact the resources and values for which the parks were established. Superintendents will identify visitor carrying capacities for managing public use. Superintendents will also identify ways to monitor for and address unacceptable impacts on park resources and visitor experiences.

When making decisions about carrying capacity, superintendents must use the best available natural and social science and other information, and maintain a comprehensive administrative record relating to their decisions. The decision-making process should be based on desired resource conditions and visitor experiences for the area, quality indicators and standards that define the desired resource conditions and visitor experiences, and other factors that will lead to logical conclusions and the protection of park resources and values. The level of analysis necessary to make decisions about carrying capacities is commensurate with the potential impacts or consequences of the decisions. The greater the potential for significant impacts or consequences on park resources and values or the opportunities to enjoy them, the greater the level of study and analysis and civic engagement needed to support the decisions.

The planning process will determine the desired resource and visitor experience conditions that are the foundation for carrying capacity analysis and decision-making. If the time frame for making decisions is insufficient to allow the application of a carrying capacity planning process, superintendents must make decisions based on the best available science, public input, and other information. In either case, such planning must be accompanied by appropriate environmental impact analysis, in accordance with Director's Order #12.

As park use changes over time, superintendents must continue to decide if management actions are needed to keep use at sustainable levels and prevent unacceptable impacts. If indicators and standards have been prescribed for an impact, the acceptable level is the prescribed standard. If indicators and standards do not exist, the superintendent must determine how much impact is acceptable before management intervention is required.

If and when park uses reach a level at which they must be limited or curtailed, the preferred choice will be to continue uses that are encouraged under the criteria listed in section 8.2, and to limit or curtail those that least meet those criteria. The Service will consult with tourism organizations and other affected service providers in seeking ways to provide appropriate types and levels of visitor use while sustaining the desired resource and visitor experience conditions.

(See Decision-making Requirements to Identify and Avoid Impairments 1.4.7; General Management Planning 2.3.1; Visitor Carrying Capacity 5.3.1.6; Management of Recreational Use 8.2.2.1. Also see Director's Order #2: Park Planning; 36 CFR 1.5)

8.2.2 Recreational Activities

The National Park Service will manage recreational activities according to the criteria listed in sections 8.1 and 8.2 (and 6.4 in wilderness areas). Examples of the broad range of recreational activities that take place in parks include, but are not limited to, boating, camping, bicycling, fishing, hiking, horseback riding and packing, outdoor sports, picnicking, scuba diving, cross-country skiing, caving, mountain and rock climbing, earth caching, and swimming. Many of these activities support the federal policy of promoting the health and personal fitness of the general public, as set forth in Executive Order 13266. However, not all of these activities will be appropriate or allowable in all parks; that determination must be made on the basis of park-specific planning.

Service-wide regulations addressing aircraft use, off-road bicycling, hang gliding, off-road vehicle use, personal watercraft, and snowmobiling require that special, park-specific regulations be developed before these uses may be allowed in parks. (The Alaska National Interest Lands Conservation Act statutory provisions (e.g., section 1110(a)) and regulatory provisions in 36 CFR Part 13 and 43 CFR 36.11(h) apply to snowmobile, motorboat, aircraft, and other means of access in units of the national park system in Alaska.)

The Service will monitor new or changing patterns of use or trends in recreational activities and assess their potential impacts on park resources. A new form of recreational activity will not be allowed within a park until a superintendent has made a determination that it will be appropriate and not cause unacceptable impacts. Restrictions placed on recreational uses that have been found to be appropriate will be limited to the minimum necessary to protect park resources and values and promote visitor safety and enjoyment.

Sounds that visitors encounter affect their recreational and/or educational experience. Many park visitors have certain expectations regarding the sounds they will hear as part of their experience. The type of park unit (for example, national battlefield, national seashore, national recreation area, national park) and its specific features often help shape those expectations. In addition to expectations of muted to loud sounds associated with nature (such as wind rustling leaves, elk bugling, waves crashing on a beach), park visitors also expect sounds reflecting our cultural heritage (such as cannons firing, native drumming, music) and sounds associated with people visiting their parks (such as children laughing, park interpretive talks, motors in cars and motorboats).

Park managers will (1) identify what levels and types of sounds contribute to or hinder visitor enjoyment, and (2) monitor, in and adjacent to parks, noise-generating human activities—including noise caused by mechanical or electronic devices—that adversely affect visitor opportunities to enjoy park soundscapes. Based on this information, the Service will take action to prevent or minimize those noises that adversely affect the visitor experience or that exceed levels that are acceptable to or appropriate for visitor uses of parks.

(See Soundscape Management 4.9; Cultural Soundscape Management 5.3.1.7. Also see 36 CFR 2.12: Audio Disturbances)

8.2.2.1 Management of Recreational Use

Superintendents will develop and implement visitor use management plans and take action, as appropriate, to ensure that recreational uses and activities in the park are consistent with its authorizing legislation or proclamation and do not cause unacceptable impacts on park resources or values. Depending on local park needs and circumstances, these plans may be prepared (1) as coordinated, activity-specific documents (such as a river use plan, a backcountry use plan, a wilderness management plan, an off-road vehicle use plan, a winter use plan); (2) as action-plan components of a resource management plan or general management plan; or (3) as a single integrated plan that addresses a broad spectrum of recreational activities. Regardless of their format or complexity, visitor use management plans will (1) contain specific, measurable management objectives related to the activity or activities being addressed; (2) be periodically reviewed and updated; and (3) be consistent with the carrying capacity decisions made in the general management plan.

The Service will seek consistency in recreation management policies and procedures on both a Service-wide and interagency basis to the extent practicable. However, because of differences in the enabling legislation and resources of individual parks, and differences in the missions of the Service and other federal agencies, an activity that is entirely appropriate when conducted in one location may be inappropriate when conducted in another. The Service will consider a park's purposes and the effects on park resources and visitors when determining the appropriateness of a specific recreational activity.

Superintendents will consider a wide range of techniques in managing recreational use to avoid adverse impacts on park resources and values or desired visitor experiences. Examples of appropriate techniques include visitor information and education programs, separation of conflicting uses by time or location, "hardening" sites, modifying maintenance practices, and permit and reservation systems. Superintendents may also use their discretionary authority to impose local restrictions, public use limits, and closures and designate areas for a specific use or activity (see 36 CFR 1.5). Any restriction of appropriate recreational uses will be limited to what is necessary to protect park resources and values, to promote visitor safety and enjoyment, or to meet park management needs. To the extent practicable, public use limits established by the Service will be based on the results of scientific research and other available support data. However, an activity will be restricted or prohibited when, in the judgment of the superintendent, its occurrence, continuation, or expansion would (1) violate the criteria listed in section 8.2, or (2) conflict with the findings of a carrying capacity analysis with no reasonable alternative that would avoid or satisfactorily mitigate the violation or conflict.

Recreational activities that are proposed as organized events or that involve commercialization, advertising, or publicity on the part of participants or organizers are defined as special events; these events are managed in accordance with the policies in section 8.6.2, regulations in 36 CFR 2.50, and criteria and procedures in Director's Order #53: Special Park Uses.

(See Levels of Park Planning 2.3; Wilderness Management Planning 6.3.4.2; General Policy 6.4.1; Visitor Carrying Capacity 8.2.1; Commercial Visitor Services 8.2.2.2; River Use 8.2.2.3, Backcountry Use 8.2.2.4; Fishing 8.2.2.5; Hunting and Trapping 8.2.2.6; Motorized Off-road Vehicle Use 8.2.3.1; Snowmobiles 8.2.3.2; Visitor Safety 8.2.5.1; Use by American Indians and Other Traditionally Associated Groups 8.5; Special Park Uses 8.6; Collecting Natural Products 8.8. Also see Director's Order #2: Park Planning, and #12: Conservation Planning, Environmental Impact Analysis, and Decision-making)

8.2.2.2 Commercial Visitor Services

For information on commercial visitor services, see Commercial Services 6.4.4, Commercial Visitor Services Planning 10.2.2, and Commercial Use Authorizations 10.3.

8.2.2.3 River Use

A river use management plan will be developed for each park having significant levels of river use unless the planning is accomplished through some other planning document. Appropriate types and levels of public uses will be identified and managed to prevent unacceptable impacts, particularly adverse impacts on aquatic resources, the riparian environment, and visitor enjoyment. Each river use management plan will include specific procedures for disposing of refuse and human waste. Using cooperating agency status where appropriate, plans should be coordinated with interested tribal, state and/or local governments and will include public participation.

(See Implementation Planning 2.3.4; National Wild and Scenic Rivers System 4.3.4; Water Resource Management 4.6; Floodplains 4.6.4; Wetlands 4.6.5; Domestic and Feral Livestock 8.6.8)

8.2.2.4 Backcountry Use

The Park Service uses the term backcountry to refer to primitive, undeveloped portions of parks. This is not a specific management zone, but rather refers to a general condition of land that may occur anywhere within a park. Backcountry use will be managed in accordance with a backcountry management plan (or other plan addressing backcountry uses) designed to avoid unacceptable impacts on park resources or adverse effects on the visitor enjoyment of appropriate recreational experiences. The Service will seek to identify acceptable limits of impacts, monitor backcountry use levels and resource conditions, and take prompt corrective action when unacceptable impacts occur. Strategies designed to guide the preservation, management, and use of the backcountry and to achieve the park's management objectives will be integrated into the park's backcountry management plan. Backcountry under study, proposed, or recommended for wilderness designation will be managed consistent with the wilderness stewardship policies in chapter 6.

The number and types of facilities to support visitor use in backcountry areas, including sanitary facilities, will be maintained at the minimum necessary to achieve a park's backcountry management objectives and to provide for the health and safety of park visitors. To avoid the need for sanitary facilities, public use levels will be managed, where practicable, in accordance with the natural system's ability to absorb human waste. The Service will not provide refuse containers in backcountry areas. All refuse must be carried out, except that combustible materials may be burned when authorized by the superintendent.

(See Water Resource Management 4.6, Management Facilities 6.3.10; Wilderness Use Management 6.4; Visitor Carrying Capacity 8.2.1; Waste Management 9.1.6.1; Comfort Stations 9.3.3. Also see Director's Order #83: Public Health).

8.2.2.5 Fishing

Recreational fishing will be allowed in parks when it is authorized or not specifically prohibited by federal law provided that it has been determined to be an appropriate use per section 8.1 of these policies. When fishing is allowed, it will be conducted in accordance with applicable federal laws and treaty rights, and nonconflicting state laws and regulations. The Service will manage fishing activities to achieve management objectives. Before the Service issues regulations or other restrictions, representatives of appropriate tribes and state and federal agencies will be consulted to ensure that all available scientific data are considered in the decision-making process. Any such regulations or other restrictions will be developed with public involvement and in consultation with fish and wildlife management agencies as appropriate, consistent with departmental policy at 43 CFR Part 24, and as described in section 4.4.3

For NPS units in Alaska, fishing will additionally be managed in accordance with the Alaska National Interest Lands Conservation Act.

Commercial fishing will be allowed only when specifically authorized by federal law or treaty right.

(See Implementation Planning 2.3.4; Planning for Natural Resource Management 4.1.1; Harvest of Plants and Animals by the Public 4.4.3; Facilities for Water Recreation 9.3.4.2)

8.2.2.6 Hunting and Trapping

Hunting, trapping, or any other methods of harvesting wildlife by the public will be allowed where it is specifically mandated by federal law. Where hunting activity is not mandated but is authorized on a discretionary basis under federal law, it may take place only after the Service has determined that the activity is an appropriate use and can be managed consistent with sound resource management principles.

Hunting and trapping, whether taking place as a mandated or a discretionary activity, will be conducted in accordance with federal law and applicable laws of the state or states in which a park is located. However, except for Alaska park units (which are subject to the Alaska National Interest Lands Conservation Act and regulations published at 36 CFR Part 13), the park in which hunting and trapping occur must also publish special regulations to govern the activity. Those regulations may be more restrictive than applicable state laws when necessary to prevent unacceptable impacts. Before the Service issues regulations or other restrictions, representatives of appropriate tribes and state and federal agencies will be consulted to ensure that all available scientific data are considered in the decision-making process. Any such regulations or other restrictions will be developed with public involvement.

The Service's cooperative consultation concerning fish and wildlife management will be consistent with departmental policy at 43 CFR Part 24. This policy recognizes the broad authorities and responsibilities of federal and state agencies with regard to the management of the nation's fish and wildlife resources, and promotes cooperative management relationships among these agencies. In particular, the policy calls on the Service to consult with state agencies on certain fish and wildlife management actions, and encourages the execution of memoranda of understanding as appropriate to ensure the conduct of programs that meet mutual objectives as long as they do not conflict with federal law or regulation.

(See Harvest of Plants and Animals by the Public 4.4.3; Genetic Resource Management Principles 4.4.1.2. Also see Director's Order #75A: Civic Engagement and Public Involvement)

8.2.2.7 Parachuting

Parachuting (or BASE jumping), whether from an aircraft, structure, or natural feature, is generally prohibited by 36 CFR 2.17(a)(3). However, if determined through a park planning process to be an appropriate activity, it may be allowed pursuant to the terms and conditions of a permit.

(See Appropriate Use 8.1.1)

8.2.2.8 Recreational Pack and Saddle Stock Use

Equine species such as horses, mules, donkeys and burros, and other types of animals (including llamas, alpacas, goats, oxen, dogs and reindeer) may be employed when it is an appropriate use to support backcountry transport of people and materials and will not result in unacceptable impacts. NPS regulations at 36 CFR 2.16 prohibit the use of animals other than those designated as "pack animals" for transporting equipment.

Planning for recreational stock use should be conducted in the context of visitor use planning to address social, biological, and physical carrying capacity considerations, and to make allocation decisions that minimize potential conflicts between and among user groups. The plan should (1) establish routes, trails, and areas of travel; and (2) identify the need for supporting infrastructure such as designated horse camps, hitch rails, corrals, and appropriate trailhead facilities designed for vehicles towing horse trailers. The plan should also identify sensitive natural and cultural resource areas and develop management strategies to protect these resources.

In areas where demand for available grazing for recreational and administrative stock exceeds allowable limits, alternative strategies must be developed. If available, and to prevent the spread of invasive exotic plant species, certified weed seed free hay or pellet rations should be considered as alternative feeding strategy to supplement grazing. Administrative stock use should generally follow the same rules and guidelines that are established for recreational stock use.

(See Domestic and Feral Livestock 8.6.8)

8.2.3 Use of Motorized Equipment

The variety of motorized equipment—including visitor vehicles, concessioner equipment, and NPS administrative or staff vehicles and equipment—that operates in national parks could adversely impact park resources, including the park's natural soundscape and the flow of natural chemical information and odors that are important to many living organisms. In addition to their natural values, natural sounds (such as waves breaking on the shore, the roar of a river, and the call of a loon), form a valued part of the visitor experience. Conversely, the sounds of motor vehicle traffic, an electric generator, or loud music can greatly diminish the solemnity of a visit to a national memorial, the effectiveness of a park interpretive program, or the ability of a visitor to hear a bird singing its territorial song. Many parks that appear as they did in historical context no longer sound the way they once did.

The Service will strive to preserve or restore the natural quiet and natural sounds associated with the physical and biological resources of parks. To do this, superintendents will carefully evaluate and manage how, when, and where motorized equipment is used by all who operate equipment in the parks, including park staff. Uses and impacts associated with the use of motorized equipment will be addressed in park planning processes. Where such use is necessary and appropriate, the least impacting equipment, vehicles, and transportation systems should be used, consistent with public and employee safety. The natural ambient sound level—that is, the environment of sound that exists in the absence of human-caused noise—is the baseline condition, and the standard against which current conditions in a soundscape will be measured and evaluated.

To meet its responsibilities under Executive Order 13149 (Greening the Government through Federal Fleet and Transportation Efficiency), the Service will develop and implement a strategy to reduce its vehicle fleet's annual petroleum consumption.

(See Soundscape Management 4.9; Chemical Information and Odors 4.11)

8.2.3.1 Motorized Off-road Vehicle Use

Off-road motor vehicle use in national park units is governed by Executive Order 11644 (Use of Off-road Vehicles on Public Lands, as amended by Executive Order 11989), which defines off-road vehicles as "any motorized vehicle designed for or capable of cross-country travel on or immediately over land, water, sand, snow, ice, marsh, swampland, or other natural terrain" (except any registered motorboat or any vehicle used for emergency purposes). Unless otherwise provided by statute, any time there is a proposal to allow a motor vehicle meeting this description to be used in a park, the provisions of the executive order must be applied.

In accordance with 36 CFR 4.10(b), routes and areas may be designated only in national recreation areas, national seashores, national lakeshores, and national preserves, and only by special regulation. In accordance with the executive order, they may be allowed only in locations where there will be no adverse impacts on the area's natural, cultural, scenic, and esthetic values, and in consideration of other existing or proposed recreational uses. The criteria for new uses, appropriate uses, and unacceptable impacts listed in sections 8.1 and 8.2 must also be applied to determine whether off-road vehicle use may be allowed. As required by the executive order and the Organic Act, superintendents must immediately close a designated off-road vehicle route whenever the use is causing or will cause unacceptable impacts on the soil, vegetation, wildlife, wildlife habitat, or cultural and historic resources.

NPS administrative off-road motor vehicle use will be limited to what is necessary to manage the public use of designated off-road vehicle routes and areas; to conduct emergency operations; and to accomplish essential maintenance, construction, and resource protection activities that cannot be accomplished reasonably by other means.

(See Park Management 1.4; Minimum Requirement 6.3.5. Also see 36 CFR 4.10)

8.2.3.2 Snowmobiles

Snowmobile use is a form of off-road vehicle use governed by Executive Order 11644 (Use of Off-road Vehicles on Public Lands, as amended by Executive Order 11989), and in Alaska also by provisions of the Alaska National Interest Lands Conservation Act (16 USC 3121 and 3170). Implementing regulations are published at 36 CFR 2.18, 36 CFR Part 13, and 43 CFR Part 36. Outside Alaska, routes and areas may be designated for snowmobile and oversnow vehicle use only by special regulation after it has first been determined through park planning to be an appropriate use that will meet the requirements of 36 CFR 2.18 and not otherwise result in unacceptable impacts. Such designations can occur only on routes and water surfaces that are used by motor vehicles or motorboats during other seasons. In Alaska, the Alaska National Interest Lands Conservation Act provides additional authorities and requirements governing snowmobile use.

NPS administrative use of snowmobiles will be limited to what is necessary (1) to manage public use of snowmobile or oversnow vehicles routes and areas; (2) to conduct emergency operations; and (3) to accomplish essential maintenance, construction, and resource protection activities that cannot be accomplished reasonably by other means.

(See Unacceptable Impacts 1.4.7.1; Minimum Requirement 6.3.5; Management Facilities 6.3.10; General Policy 6.4.1; Process for Determining New Appropriate Uses 8.1.2; Visitor Use 8.2; Recreational Activities 8.2.2)

8.2.3.3 Personal Watercraft Use

Personal watercraft use is generally prohibited by 36 CFR 3.24. However, it may be allowed within a park by special regulation if it has first been determined through park planning to be an appropriate use that will not result in unacceptable impacts.

(See Unacceptable Impacts 1.4.7.1; Process for Determining New Appropriate Uses 8.1.2; Visitor Use 8.2; Recreational Activities 8.2.2. Also see 36 CFR Part 3: Boating and Water Use)

8.2.4 Accessibility for Persons with Disabilities

All reasonable efforts will be undertaken to make NPS facilities, programs, and services accessible to and usable by all people, including those with disabilities. This policy reflects the commitment to provide access to the widest cross section of the public, and to ensure compliance with the intent of the Architectural Barriers Act of 1968 and the Rehabilitation Act of 1973. The Service will also comply with section 507 of the Americans with Disabilities Act

(42 USC 12207), which relates specifically to the operation and management of federal wilderness areas. Specific guidance for implementing these laws is found in the Secretary of the Interior's regulations regarding enforcement of nondiscrimination on the basis of disability in Department of the Interior programs (43 CFR Part 17, Subpart E), and General Service Administration regulations adopting accessibility standards for the Architectural Barriers Act (41 CFR Part 102-76, Subpart C).

One primary tenet of accessibility is that, to the highest degree reasonable, people with disabilities should be able to participate in the same programs and activities available to everyone else. In choosing among methods for providing accessibility, higher priority will be given to those methods that offer programs and activities in the most integrated setting appropriate. Special, separate, or alternative facilities, programs, or services will be provided only when existing ones cannot reasonably be made accessible. The determination of what is reasonable will be made only after careful consultation with persons with disabilities or their representatives. Any decision that would result in less than equal opportunity is subject to the filing of an official disability rights complaint under the departmental regulations cited above.

(See Accessibility for Persons with Disabilities 1.9.4; Physical Access for Persons with Disabilities 5.3.2; Accessibility for Persons with Disabilities 6.4.10; Accessibility for Persons with Disabilities 9.1.2. Also see Director's Order #16A: Reasonable Accommodation for Applicants and Employees with Disabilities; Director's Order #42: Accessibility for Visitors with Disabilities in National Park Service Programs and Services; Americans with Disabilities Act and Architectural Barriers Act Accessibility Standards)

8.2.5 Visitor Safety and Emergency Response
8.2.5.1 Visitor Safety

The saving of human life will take precedence over all other management actions as the Park Service strives to protect human life and provide for injury-free visits. The Service will do this within the constraints of the 1916 Organic Act. The primary—and very substantial—constraint imposed by the Organic Act is that discretionary management activities may be undertaken only to the extent that they will not impair park resources and values.

While recognizing that there are limitations on its capability to totally eliminate all hazards, the Service and its concessioners, contractors, and cooperators will seek to provide a safe and healthful environment for visitors and employees. The Service will work cooperatively with other federal, tribal, state, and local agencies; organizations; and individuals to carry out this responsibility. The Service will strive to identify and prevent injuries from recognizable threats to the safety and health of persons and to the protection of property by applying nationally accepted codes, standards, engineering principles, and the guidance contained in Director's Orders #50B, #50C, #58, and #83 and their associated reference manuals. When practicable and consistent with congressionally designated purposes and mandates, the Service will reduce or remove known hazards and apply other appropriate measures, including closures, guarding, signing, or other forms of education. In doing so, the Service's preferred actions will be those that have the least impact on park resources and values.

The Service recognizes that the park resources it protects are not only visitor attractions, but that they may also be potentially hazardous. In addition, the recreational activities of some visitors may be of especially high-risk, high-adventure types, which pose a significant personal risk to participants and which the Service cannot totally control. Park visitors must assume a substantial degree of risk and responsibility for their own safety when visiting areas that are managed and maintained as natural, cultural, or recreational environments.

These management policies do not impose park-specific visitor safety prescriptions. The means by which public safety concerns are to be addressed is left to the discretion of superintendents and other decision-makers at the park level who must work within the limits of funding and staffing. Examples include decisions about whether to install warning signs or artificial lighting, distribute weather warnings or advisories, initiate search-and-rescue operations or render emergency aid, eliminate potentially dangerous animals, close roads and trails or install guardrails and fences, and grant or deny backcountry or climbing permits. Some forms of visitor safeguards typically found in other public venues—such as fences, railings, and paved walking surfaces—may not be appropriate or practicable in a national park setting.

(See Air Quality 4.7.1; Lightscape Management 4.10; General Policy 6.4.1; Siting Facilities to Avoid Natural Hazards 9.1.1.5; Waste Management and Contaminant Issues 9.1.6; Risk Management Program 10.2.4.8; Food Service Sanitation Inspections 10.2.4.14)

8.2.5.2 Emergency Preparedness and Emergency Operations

The National Park Service will develop a program of emergency preparedness in accordance with title VI of the Robert T. Stafford Disaster Relief and Emergency Assistance Act (42 USC 5195-5197g); National Security Decision Directive 259 (February 4, 1987); Department of the Interior policy; and other considerations at the Washington headquarters, regional, and park levels. The program will (1) provide guidance for incident management at the park level and management and relief for emergency incidents and events beyond park capabilities; (2) ensure the agency complies with the Presidential Homeland Security Directives, the National Emergency Response Plan, and the National Incident Management System standards; and (3) support interagency and national response to major incidents. The purpose of the program will be to provide for visitor and employee safety and the protection of resources and property to the extent possible. This program will include a systematic method for alerting visitors about potential disasters and evacuation procedures.

Superintendents may assist other agencies with emergencies outside of parks, as authorized by 16 USC 1b(1). To the extent practicable and in accordance with Director's Order #20, written agreements with other agencies must first be in effect. NPS employees who are outside the area of their jurisdiction and who are directed by their supervisors to provide emergency assistance to other agencies will be considered to be acting within the scope of their employment.

NPS emergency operations will be conducted using the Incident Command System of the National Interagency Incident Management System (NIIMS). The Unified Command System (within the Incident Command System) will be used when other agencies are involved. Each park superintendent will develop and maintain an emergency operations plan to ensure an effective response to all types of emergencies that can be reasonably anticipated.

As one element of the emergency operations plan, or as a separate document, each park must have an oil and chemical spill response management plan for spills that result from NPS activities or from activities that are beyond NPS control (such as commercial through-traffic on roads that pass through a park). The plans will place first priority on responder and public safety.

Employees will not be permitted to respond to hazardous material spills unless they are properly qualified and certified in accordance with Director's Order #30B: Hazardous Spill Response. The Service will seek to recover all allowable direct and indirect costs for responding to oil or hazardous materials spills.

Parks that have their own aircraft or contract for the use of aircraft must have an aircraft crash rescue response plan or other planning document in place.

(See Compensation for Injuries to Natural Resources 4.1.6; Emergency Management 5.3.1.1. Also see Director's Order #55: Incident Management Program; Director's Order #60: Aviation Management)

8.2.5.3 Search and Rescue

To provide for the protection and safety of park visitors, the Service will make reasonable efforts to search for lost persons and rescue sick, injured, or stranded persons. This responsibility may be fulfilled by NPS staff or by qualified search-and-rescue organizations or agencies that are capable of responding to life-threatening emergencies pursuant to the terms of a formal agreement. Deceased persons will be evacuated unless the level of risk to the rescue party is found to be unacceptably high. Search managers and superintendents will jointly determine when to terminate a search. The Service will not charge visitors for search-and-rescue operations. Search-and-rescue operations will be conducted using the Incident Command System.

(See Management Facilities 6.3.10; General Policy 6.4.1. Also see Director's Order #59: Search and Rescue)

8.2.5.4 Dive Operations

NPS dive operations in rivers, lakes, reservoirs, and oceans will be used to support other park operations, including scientific inquiry, search and rescue, law enforcement, public education, and resource and facility management. The level of service provided within a park will be determined through a dive program needs assessment. Personal safety of those engaged in diving activities is of primary importance and will not be compromised for any reason. NPS diving activities will not be permitted in any park that does not have an approved safe practices manual (dive safety plan).

(See Director's Order #4: Diving Management. Also see 29 CFR 1910, subpart T, 485 DM 28)

8.2.5.5 Public Health Program

The Service will work to identify public health issues and disease transmission potential in the parks and to conduct park operations in ways that reduce or eliminate these hazards. Park managers will pursue these goals with technical assistance provided under the auspices of a Service-wide public health program. The public health program will use the consultation services of commissioned officers of the U.S. Public Health Service.

(See Pest Management 4.4.5. Also see Director's Order #83: Public Health)

8.2.5.6 Emergency Medical Services

The Service will make reasonable efforts to provide appropriate emergency medical services for persons who become ill or injured. An emergency medical services program will be maintained, where appropriate, to provide transportation and prehospital care of the sick and injured, which may range from minor first aid to advanced life support in various environmental settings. Transportation may include everything from patrol cars and ambulances to fixed-wing planes and helicopter air ambulances, consistent with departmental policies regarding aircraft use.

Qualified emergency medical services in local communities may be used if such services can respond rapidly enough in life-threatening emergencies. When such services are not available, the Park Service will make a reasonable effort to provide a level of emergency medical service commensurate with park needs and in response to an emergency medical needs assessment. Each superintendent will develop and implement a program to meet those needs in accordance with Director's Order #51: Emergency Medical Services. Extended emergency medical services operations will be conducted using the Incident Command System.

(Also see Director's Order #55: Incident Management Program)

8.2.6 Recreation Fees and Reservations

The National Park Service may charge a recreation entrance or expanded amenity recreation (use) fee at parks when authorized by law. Although these fees may provide for the support of the overall management and operation of parks, as set forth in the Federal Lands Recreation Enhancement Act and other relevant statutes, they are not intended to offset the operational costs associated with a park. Such services include protection; resource management; information and orientation; maintenance of park facilities; and interpretation to foster an understanding and appreciation of each park's resources, management procedures, regulations, and programs. Fees may be instituted for secondary or special services that the Service cannot or elects not to offer because of economic constraints or the need for special skills or equipment or because they are purely supplemental programs. The Service may also contract or enter into an agreement for the collection of recreational fees if there is a demonstrated benefit to the collecting park unit. In all cases, fee programs will support park purposes and comply with appropriate Service policies and standards and federal law.

(See Commercial Use Authorizations 10.3. Also see Director's Order #22: Fee Program)

8.2.6.1 Recreation Fees

Visitors who use federal facilities and services for recreation may be required to pay a greater share of the cost of providing those opportunities than the population as a whole. Under the guidelines and criteria established by law and regulation, the Service will collect recreation fees of the appropriate type for its parks, facilities, and programs. No fees will be collected in circumstances in which the costs of collection would exceed revenue or where fee collection is prohibited by law or regulation. Fees charged for recreational activities will be collected only in accordance with the applicable authority, and recreation fee revenues will be managed according to law and policy. Fee rates will be reasonable and equitable and consistent with criteria and procedures contained in law and NPS guidance documents. Those who lawfully enter or use a park for activities not related to recreation will not be charged an entrance fee, expanded amenity recreation use fee, or special recreation permit fee. Examples of nonrecreation exemptions include persons entering parks for

- First Amendment activities, which are exempt from all fees;
- special park uses such as agricultural, grazing, and commercial filming activities (all of which are subject to special park use fees);
- NPS-authorized research activities;
- federal, state, tribal, and local government business;
- hospital in-patients involved in medical treatment or therapy;
- a leaseholder or property owner accessing their property;
- outings conducted for noncommercial educational purposes by schools and other bona fide academic institutions.

Current law (the Federal Lands Recreation Enhancement Act) prohibits charging entrance fees to persons 15 years of age and younger. In Alaska, the Alaska National Interest Lands Conservation Act prohibits charging entrance fees to all national parks except Denali National Park.

(See Fees 8.6.1.2; First Amendment Activities 8.6.3)

8.2.6.2 National Recreation Reservation Service

Superintendents are encouraged to participate in a reservation service for campgrounds and other facilities, and for tours or other services operated or provided by the Park Service for visitors when doing so will

- better serve park visitors, or
- ensure the protection of park resources, or
- increase public awareness of lesser-known parks, or
- improve the efficiency of park operations or administration.

To avoid duplicative costs and confusion, if a reservation service will be employed in a park, the Service-wide recreation reservation vendor will be the preferred provider of that service. The vendor's services may be expanded or new services may be developed based on NPS needs and the vendor's capacity to accommodate the needs. If a superintendent wishes to participate in a different reservation system, a determination must first be made that the Service-wide vendor will not accommodate the park's reservation needs. Authorization must be obtained from the Director before participating in a different reservation system. Concessioners who manage lodging and camping services are not required to transfer their existing reservation services to the NPS reservation system. However, they are encouraged to do so when it is administratively, operationally, and financially feasible, in order to provide more seamless reservation services to the public.

(See Chapter 7: Interpretation and Education)

8.2.7 Tourism

The Service will support and promote appropriate visitor use through cooperation and coordination with the tourism industry. As part of this effort, the Service will

- develop and maintain a constructive dialogue and outreach effort with public and private organizations and businesses, including state and local tourism and travel offices;
- establish positive and effective working relationships with park concessioners and others in the tourism industry to ensure a high quality of service to park visitors;
- collaborate with industry professionals to promote sustainable and informed tourism that incorporates socioeconomic and ecological concerns and supports long-term preservation of park resources and quality visitor experiences; and
- use this collaboration as an opportunity to encourage and showcase environmental leadership by the Service and by the tourism industry, including park concessioners.

(Also see Director's Order #17: National Park Service Tourism)

8.3 Law Enforcement Program

8.3.1 General

The law enforcement program is an important tool in carrying out the NPS mission. The objectives of the NPS law enforcement program are (1) the prevention of criminal activities through resource education, public safety efforts, and deterrence; and (2) the detection and investigation of criminal activity and the apprehension and successful prosecution of criminal violators. In carrying out the law enforcement program, the Service will make reasonable efforts to protect the natural and cultural resources entrusted to its care and to provide for the protection, safety, and security of park visitors, employees, concessioners, and public and private property.

Law enforcement is characterized by high risks and inherent dangers to enforcement officers, and by high public expectations that law enforcement activities will be performed in a lawful and professional manner. It is therefore essential that the Service issue clear policies and procedures to guide the law enforcement program, and that commissioned employees receive the training and equipment necessary to perform their duties successfully. The NPS law enforcement program will be managed and supervised in accordance with all applicable laws and regulations; Part 446 of the *Department of the Interior Manual*; all applicable Secretarial directives, these Management Policies; and Director's Order #9: Law Enforcement Program and Reference Manual #9 (or U. S. Park Police General Orders, as appropriate). To help sustain the high level of public trust necessary for an effective law enforcement program, commissioned employees will adhere to the Department of the Interior's law enforcement code of conduct and the standards of ethical conduct found in Reference Manual 9.

All necessary and appropriate steps will be taken to ensure that the Park Service maintains a professional law enforcement program. The authority and responsibility to manage the NPS Commissioned Park Ranger program and U.S. Park Police operations will flow in a logical order from the Director and in accordance with departmental policy.

8.3.2 The Context for Law Enforcement

Park law enforcement activities will be managed by superintendents as part of a comprehensive, interdisciplinary effort to protect resources, manage public use, and promote public safety and appropriate enjoyment. This is in keeping with guidance provided by Congress in 1976 when it amended the General Authorities Act (16 USC 1a-6):

> The Committee intends that the clear and specific enforcement authority contained in this subsection, while necessary for the protection of the Federal employees so involved, will be implemented by the Secretary to ensure that law enforcement activities in our National Park System will continue to be viewed as one function of a broad program of visitor and resource protection. (House Report No. 94-1569, September 16, 1976)

8.3.3 Shared Responsibilities

Congress has authorized the designation of certain employees as law enforcement officers, with the responsibility to "maintain law and order and protect persons and property within areas of the National Park System" (16 USC 1a 6(b)). Only employees who meet the standards prescribed by and who are designated by the Secretary of the Interior may perform law enforcement duties. The duties of these commissioned employees will not be limited to just law enforcement; they will also continue to incorporate a diversity of other protection concerns, as stipulated in House Report No. 94-1569.

The Service recognizes that effective enforcement requires a cooperative community effort. Therefore, employees without law enforcement commissions will continue to share responsibility for the protection of park resources and visitors, and they will be expected to report any apparent violations or suspicious activities. All park employees will be trained to recognize, observe, and record criminal acts and illegal activities. The Service will also encourage and assist park neighbors in the development of cooperative crime prevention and detection programs.

Extended law enforcement operations will be conducted using the Incident Command System of the National Interagency Incident Management System.

8.3.4 Enforcement Authority

Within national park system boundaries, the Service will fulfill its law enforcement responsibilities using NPS employees. However, the Park Service is authorized by 16 USC 1a-6(c) to appoint (deputize) another agency's qualified law enforcement personnel as special police when it will benefit the administration of a park area. Deputations may be issued for the purpose of obtaining supplemental law enforcement assistance when deemed economical and in the public interest, and with the concurrence of the other agency. All such appointments must be approved by the senior NPS law enforcement official or his/her designee and supported by a written agreement with the other agency at the park or national level, except when there is insufficient time because of an emergency law enforcement situation. While deputations may be used to supplement NPS law enforcement capabilities, they may not be used to transfer NPS law enforcement responsibilities to state or local governments.

The Service is authorized to use appropriated funds for "rendering of emergency rescue, fire fighting, and [other] cooperative assistance to nearby law enforcement and fire prevention agencies and for related purposes outside of the National Park System"(16 USC 1b(1)). Further, insofar as 16 USC 1b(1) does not confer arrest authority to NPS personnel who act outside park boundaries, state arrest authority is first needed before NPS personnel can enforce state law or engage in law enforcement activity outside national park system boundaries.

This authority will be used in emergency situations, only after first determining that such actions will facilitate the administration of the park or be an effective management tool for obtaining mutual assistance from other agencies. Furthermore, the authority is intended for use only in response to an unexpected occurrence that requires immediate action, which may include one or more of the following:

- emergency responses such as life-or-death incidents, serious injury/fatality accident/incident scenes, crime scenes involving the protection of human life, officer needs assistance, threats to health or safety of the public;
- emergency or law enforcement incidents directly affecting visitor safety or resource protection;
- probable-cause felonies and felonies committed in the presence of and observed by U.S. Park Rangers, Special Agents, or U.S. Park Police;
- misdemeanors committed in the presence of U.S. Park Rangers, Special Agents, or U.S. Park Police that present an immediate threat to the health and safety of the public.

Except where specifically provided by acts of Congress codified in the District of Columbia Code, sections 5-201 to 5-208 (2001), the Service may not assume law enforcement responsibility outside of a park in lieu of the legitimate responsibilities of nearby agencies. Cooperative assistance rendered to nearby law enforcement agencies outside park boundaries should be limited to only those actions or efforts that support or assist those agencies.

8.3.5 Jurisdiction

The term jurisdiction defines the sphere of authority and outlines the boundaries or territorial limits within which any particular authority may be exercised. Jurisdiction may be either exclusive, partial, concurrent, or proprietary. Insofar as is practicable, the Service will seek to acquire concurrent legislative jurisdiction for all units of the national park system, as required by the 1976 amendment to the General Authorities Act. Concurrent jurisdiction allows the Service to enforce federal criminal statutes and also to assimilate state law under 18 USC 13 when no applicable federal law or regulation exists. Concurrent jurisdiction will allow for the more efficient conduct of both state and federal law enforcement functions within the parks.

8.3.6 Use of Force

Commissioned employees may use a wide variety of defensive equipment and force options in response to various threats and other enforcement situations. The primary consideration is the timely and effective application of the appropriate level of force required to establish and maintain lawful control.

8.3.7 Law Enforcement Public Information and Media Relations

The National Park Service will provide information to the public and the news media in accordance with applicable laws, departmental policy, and Director's Order #75B: Media Relations. Superintendents should identify appropriate opportunities to (1) enhance deterrence by publicizing arrests, weapons seizures, and successful prosecutions; (2) highlight cooperation and assistance activities (e.g., Park Watch); and (3) educate the public about the full range of threats to and the difficulty in protecting park resources.

The right of the public to obtain information about government operations and activities is subject to the requirements of the Freedom of Information Act and the Privacy Act.

(See Civic Engagement 1.7. Also see Director's Order #66: FOIA and Protected Resource Information; Director's Order #75A: Civic Engagement and Public Involvement)

8.3.8 Homeland Security

The Park Service will work cooperatively with the Department of the Interior; Department of Homeland Security; and other federal, state, and local agencies to prevent and respond to foreign and domestic attacks on American soil. The Park Service will maintain a capacity to rapidly move law enforcement personnel to critical asset and infrastructure or other identified areas in the event of a terrorist attack, elevated threat level, or other major emergency incident.

(See National Emergency Response Plan)

8.4 Overflights and Aviation Uses

A variety of aircraft, including military, commercial, general aviation, and aircraft used for NPS administrative purposes, fly in the airspace over national parks. Although there are many legitimate aviation uses, overflights can adversely affect park resources and values and interfere with visitor enjoyment. The Service will take all necessary steps to avoid or mitigate unacceptable impacts from aircraft overflights.

Because the nation's airspace is managed by the Federal Aviation Administration (FAA), the Service will work constructively and cooperatively with the Federal Aviation Administration and national defense and other agencies to ensure that authorized aviation activities affecting units of the national park system occur in a safe manner and do not cause unacceptable impacts on park resources and values and visitor experiences. The Service will build and maintain a cooperative and problem-solving relationship with national defense agencies to address the congressionally mandated mission of each agency and prevent or mitigate unacceptable impacts of military training or operational flights on park resources, values and the visitor experience. Cooperation is essential because the other agencies involved have statutory authorities and responsibilities that must be recognized by the Service.

(See Soundscape Management 4.9. Also see Director's Orders #47: Soundscape Preservation and Noise Management; #60: Aviation Management)

8.4.1 Alaska and Remote Areas

Aviation can provide an important, and in some cases the preferred, means of access to remote areas in certain parks, especially in Alaska. In such cases, access by aircraft may make an important contribution to the protection and enjoyment of those areas. Dependence on aviation will be fully considered and addressed in the planning process for those parks. Alaska parks have specific regulations concerning fixed-wing aircraft, published at 36 CFR Part 13 and 43 CFR 36.11(f).

8.4.2 Education

For the general public and for aviation interests, the Service will develop educational materials describing the importance of the natural soundscape and tranquility to park visitors, as well as the need for cooperation from the aviation community.

(See Chapter 7: Interpretation and Education; Soundscape Management 4.9)

8.4.3 General Aviation

The Service will work closely with the Federal Aviation Administration and with general aviation organizations to ensure that general aviation operations over units of the national park system are conducted in accordance with applicable FAA advisories and "fly-friendly" techniques and procedures designed to help pilots minimize impacts on national parks. The Service will seek the assistance of these organizations in problem resolution if general aviation concerns arise over national parks.

8.4.4 Administrative Use

Aviation is a necessary and acceptable management tool in some parks when used in a manner consistent with the NPS mission. Aviation activities will comply with all applicable policies and regulations issued by the Department of the Interior, the Federal Aviation Administration, and the National Park Service. In its administrative use of aircraft, the Service will

- use, to the maximum extent practicable, the quietest aircraft available for its aviation operations;
- limit official use of flights over parks to those needed to support or carry out emergency operations or essential management activities in cases where there are no practical alternatives or when alternative methods would be unreasonable;
- give full consideration to safety; wilderness management implications; impacts on resources, values, and opportunity for visitor enjoyment; impacts on other administrative activities; and overall cost-effectiveness;
- plan, schedule, and consolidate flights so as to avoid or minimize unacceptable impacts on park resources and values and visitor enjoyment;
- work cooperatively with other agencies using aircraft and airspace over parks to adhere to the above standards.

(Also see Director's Order #60: Aviation Management)

8.4.5 Military Aviation

The Service will work cooperatively with agencies of the Department of Defense to address the congressionally mandated missions of all agencies. In addition, the Service will prevent or strive to mitigate any unacceptable impacts of overflights related to military training or operational low-level overflights. Superintendents are responsible for opening lines of communication with base commanders controlling military training routes or military operations areas that may affect their parks, and for developing formal agreements that mitigate identified impacts.

8.4.6 Commercial Air Tour Management

The National Parks Air Tour Management Act of 2000 and implementing FAA regulations provide for a joint FAA/NPS planning process that will lead to the management by the Federal Aviation Administration of commercial air tours over national parks (with the exception of parks in Alaska and Rocky Mountain National Park, which are specifically excluded from the process). The Service, as a cooperating agency, will assist the Federal Aviation Administration in developing an air tour management plan (ATMP) for each park with existing or proposed air tours. Superintendents will work cooperatively with the Federal Aviation Administration, air tour operators, and other stakeholders in the development of these plans and will determine the nature and extent of impacts on natural and cultural resources and visitor experience opportunities inside park boundaries. The Federal Aviation Administration, with responsibility for ensuring the safe and efficient use of the nation's airspace and protecting the public health and welfare from aircraft noise, will implement the air tour management plans and regulate commercial air tours in accordance with it.

8.4.7 Permitted Overflights

When issuing permits for activities such as filming or research in which the use of aircraft is proposed, the superintendent will determine whether use is appropriate and apply conditions to protect park resources and values from unacceptable impacts. Permit requests will be denied if the activity will have unacceptable impacts on a park's resources, values, or desired visitor experiences.

8.4.8 Airports and Landing Sites

Private or commercial aircraft may be operated in parks only on lands or water surfaces designated by the Park Service as landing sites through special regulation. (See section 8.4.1 regarding Alaska and some remote areas.) The Service will evaluate and manage aircraft landing sites under its jurisdiction to ensure that the use of the sites will have no unacceptable impacts on park resources and values, public safety, or visitor enjoyment. Existing sites that meet these criteria and that have been designated as a result of previously established use may be retained as long as the administrative need for them continues. New sites will be designated only where essential to provide administrative access to remote areas (other than wilderness), and only where the site can be established, used, and maintained without the need for new construction or major site improvements.

The National Park Service will also work with entities having jurisdiction over landing sites and airports adjacent to parks for the purpose of preventing, reducing, or otherwise mitigating the effects of aircraft operations. Whether landing sites or airports are situated within or adjacent to parks, the objective will be to minimize noise and other impacts and confine them to the smallest and most appropriate portion of the park, consistent with safe aircraft operations.

(Also see 36 CFR 2.17; 43 CFR 36.11 (f))

8.5 Use by American Indians and Other Traditionally Associated Groups

The National Park Service will develop and implement its programs in a manner that reflects knowledge of and respect for the cultures of American Indian tribes or groups with demonstrated ancestral ties to particular resources in parks. Evidence of such ties will be established through systematic archeological or anthropological studies, including ethnographic oral history and ethnohistory studies or a combination of these sources. For purposes of these policies, the term American Indian tribe means any tribe, band, nation, or other organized group or community of Indians, including any Alaska Native Village, which is recognized as eligible for the special programs and services provided by the United States to Indians because of their status as Indians. Other groups of people with traditional associations to park lands or resources include native peoples of the Caribbean; Native Hawaiians and other native Pacific islanders; and state-recognized tribes and other groups who are defined by themselves and known to others as members of a named cultural unit that has historically shared a set of linguistic, kinship, political, or other distinguishing cultural features.

The Service will regularly and actively consult with American Indian tribal governments and other traditionally associated groups regarding planning, management, and operational decisions that affect subsistence activities, sacred materials or places, or other resources with which they are historically associated. Information about the outcome of these consultations will be made available to those consulted.

In developing its plans and carrying out its programs, the Service will ensure the following:

◆ NPS general regulations governing access to and use of natural and cultural resources in parks will be applied in an informed and balanced manner consistent with park purposes that (1) does not unreasonably interfere with American Indian tribal use of traditional areas or sacred resources, and (2) does not violate the criteria listed in section 8.2 for use of the parks.

◆ Superintendents will establish and maintain consulting relationships with potentially affected American Indian tribes or traditionally associated groups.

◆ Management decisions will reflect knowledge about and understanding of potentially affected American Indian cultures and people, gained through research and consultations with the potentially affected groups.

The American Indian Religious Freedom Act (42 USC 1996) states that

> Henceforth it shall be the policy of the United States to protect and preserve for American Indians their inherent right to freedom to believe, express, and exercise the traditional religions of the American Indians, Eskimo, Aleut, and Native Hawaiians, including but not limited to access to sites, use and possession of sacred objects, and the freedom to worship through ceremonials and traditional rites.

The National Park Service recognizes that site-specific worship is vital to Native American religious practices. As a matter of policy and in keeping with the spirit of the law, and provided the criteria listed in section 8.2 for use of the parks are not violated, the Service will be as unrestrictive as possible in permitting Native American tribes access to park areas to perform traditional religious, ceremonial, or other customary activities at places that have been used historically for such purposes. In allowing religious access by other entities, including nonrecognized Indian groups, the Service will consider requests individually, being mindful not to take actions that will either advance or inhibit religion. The Service will not direct visitor attention to the performance of religious observances unless the Native American group so wishes.

With regard to consumptive use of park resources, current NPS policy is reflected in regulations published at 36 CFR 2.1 and 36 CFR Part 13. These regulations allow superintendents to designate certain fruits, berries, nuts, or unoccupied seashells that may be gathered by hand for personal use or consumption if it will not adversely affect park wildlife, the reproductive potential of a plant species, or otherwise adversely affect park resources. The regulations do not authorize the taking, use, or possession of fish, wildlife, or plants for ceremonial or religious purposes, except where specifically authorized by federal statute or treaty rights or where hunting, trapping, or fishing are otherwise allowed.

When authorized under National Historic Preservation Act, the Archeological Resources Protection Act or other provisions of law, the Service will protect sacred resources to the extent practicable and in a manner consistent with the goals of American Indian tribes or other traditionally associated groups. The location and character of sacred sites will be withheld from public disclosure if disclosure will cause significant invasion of privacy, risk harm to the historic resource, or impede the use of a traditional religious site by practitioners.

Members of American Indian tribes or traditionally associated groups may enter parks for traditional nonrecreational activities without paying an entrance fee.

The ceremonial use of peyote will be limited to members of the Native American Church during religious ceremonies, in accordance with regulations of the Department of Justice, Drug Enforcement Administration ("Special Exempt Persons, Native American Church," 21 CFR 1307. 31).

(See Relationship with American Indian Tribes 1.11; Consultation 5.2.1; Ethnographic Resources 5.3.5.3; first Amendment Activities 8.6.3; Consumptive Uses 8.9. Also see Executive Order 13007 (Indian Sacred Sites); Director's Orders #71A: Government-to-government Relationships with Tribal Governments, and #71B: Indian Sacred Sites)

8.6 Special Park Uses

8.6.1 General

A special park use is defined as an activity that takes place in a park area, and that

- provides a benefit to an individual, group, or organization rather than the public at large;
- requires written authorization and some degree of management control from the Service in order to protect park resources and the public interest;
- is not prohibited by law or regulation;
- is not initiated, sponsored, or conducted by the Service; and
- is not managed under a concession contract (see chapter 10), a recreation activity for which the NPS charges a fee, or a lease (see chapter 5).

8.6.1.1 Requests for Permits

Using criteria and procedures outlined in Director's Order #53: Special Park Uses, each request to permit a special park use or renew authorization of an existing use will be reviewed and evaluated by the superintendent according to the terms of applicable legislation, regulations, and management planning documents. When considering permit requests, superintendents will take into account the Service-wide implications of their decisions. A superintendent must deny initial requests or requests for renewal upon finding that the proposed activity would cause unacceptable impacts. The superintendent likewise must terminate previously authorized special park uses based on such a finding.

(See Appropriate Use of the Parks 1.5; Unacceptable Impacts 1.4.7.1; Process for Determining New Appropriate Uses 8.1.2)

8.6.1.2 Fees

Cost recovery and performance bond and liability insurance requirements will be imposed, consistent with applicable statutory authorities and regulations. All costs incurred by the Service in receiving, writing, and issuing the permit, monitoring the permitted use, restoring park areas, or otherwise supporting a special park use may be paid by the permittee. The money will be retained by the park as reimbursement.

When appropriate, the Service will also collect a fee for the use of the land or facility based on a market evaluation. Fees collected for use of the land or facility will be deposited into the U.S. Treasury.

Based on the published schedule, commercial filming and still photography activities requiring a permit are subject to a location fee. The money will be retained by the Park Service in accordance with the fee demonstration program.

(See Park Management 1.4; Recreation Fees and Reservations 8.2.6.; Special Events 8.6.2)

8.6.2 Special Events
8.6.2.1 General

Special events—such as sports, pageants, regattas, public spectator attractions, entertainment, ceremonies, and encampments—may be permitted by the superintendent when (1) there is a meaningful association between the park area and the event, and (2) the event will contribute to visitor understanding of the significance of the park area. However, a permit must be denied if the event would be disallowed under the criteria listed for unacceptable impacts in sections 1.4.7.1 and 8.2.

Superintendents must ensure that appropriate permit conditions are imposed for special events. Permit conditions are intended to mitigate damage to park resources and values while ensuring that any necessary resource restoration and rehabilitation is completed. Permit conditions should include conditions on resource protection as well as requirements for cost recovery and fees, a hold-harmless clause, liability insurance, and bonding.

The Park Service will not permit the staging of an event in an area that is open to the public, or the closure of an area that is open to the public, when the event

- is conducted primarily for the material or financial benefit of a for-profit entity; or
- awards participants an appearance fee or prizes of more than nominal value; or
- requires in-park advertising or publicity (unless the event is co-sponsored by the Service); or
- charges a separate public admission fee.

However, park buildings or specially designated locations that are suitable and appropriate may be made available for private, invitation-only events. Admission fees or any other monies associated with the event will not be collected by the permittee on park premises.

Large-scale events will be managed using the Incident Command System. Donor recognition associated with special events is addressed in Director's Order #21: Donations and Fundraising.

(See Special Events 6.4.5; Personal Services 7.3.1; Cultural Demonstrators 7.5.7; Facilities for Arts and Culture 9.3.1.7. Also see Director's Order #55: Incident Management Program; 36 CFR 2.50; 36 CFR 7.96)

8.6.2.2 Helium-filled Balloons

Helium-filled balloons pose a danger to the health and safety of marine wildlife (such as sea turtles and sperm whales) and create a litter problem. Therefore, no releases of helium-filled balloons into the atmosphere within a park will be authorized, except for research or planning purposes. Releasing balloons indoors where they can be retrieved may be authorized under permit.

8.6.2.3 Fireworks Displays

Fireworks displays will be considered unless they pose an unacceptable risk of wildland or structural fire or will cause unacceptable impacts on park resources or values or jeopardize public safety. In all instances, the decision to approve or deny a request will be made by the superintendent following consultation with the regional safety officer. Fireworks displays will be conducted in compliance with the National Fire Protection Association Code for the Display of Fireworks (NFPA 1123).

8.6.2.4 Sale of Food or Merchandise

The sale of food and merchandise in the parks may be allowed when managed under a commercial use authorization that does not conflict with a concession contract and that complies with applicable public health codes and Director's Order #83: Public Health. The sale of printed matter as defined in 36 CFR 2.52, 36 CFR 7.96(k) and Reference Manual 53 is allowed under a special use permit. The sale of products produced as part of living exhibits, interpretive demonstrations, or park programs is addressed in section 7.5.7.

(See Commercial Use Authorizations 10.3)

8.6.3 First Amendment Activities

The National Park Service will authorize the use of park land for public assemblies, meetings, demonstrations, religious activities, and other public expressions of views protected under the First Amendment of the U. S. Constitution, in accordance with 36 CFR 2.51 or 36 CFR 7.96. To ensure public safety and the protection of park resources and values, and to avoid assigning the same location and time to two or more activities, the Service may manage these activities by issuing a permit to regulate the time, location, number of participants, use of the facilities, and number and type of equipment used, but not the content of the message presented.

For all parks except those within designated portions of the National Capital Region, locations that are available for public assemblies and other First Amendment activities, including the sale and distribution of printed matter, will be so designated by the superintendent on a map in accordance with procedures and criteria found in NPS regulations (36 CFR 1.5, 1.7, 2.51, and 2.52), unless the sites are otherwise protected from public disclosure, such as sites sacred to American Indians or sites with vulnerable natural and cultural resources. Selected National Capital Region parks are subject to special demonstration regulations found at 36 CFR 7.96(g)(4)(iii) and do not have such areas designated by the superintendent.

When the Service allows one group to use an area or facility for expressing views, it must provide other groups with a similar opportunity, if requested. No group wishing to assemble lawfully may be discriminated against or denied the right of assembly provided that all permit conditions are met. Whenever religious activities are conducted in parks, any NPS actions pertaining to them must reflect a clearly secular purpose, must have a primary effect that neither advances nor inhibits religion, and must avoid "excessive governmental entanglement with religion."

NPS staff on duty in an area in which a First Amendment activity is being conducted will be neutral toward the activity, but will remain responsible for the protection of participants, spectators, private property, public property, and park resources. On-duty staff may not participate in a First Amendment activity. NPS employees exercising their First Amendment rights when off-duty must not in any way imply any official NPS endorsement of the activity.

When a permit is requested for the exercise of First Amendment rights, including freedom of assembly, speech, religion, and the press, the superintendent will issue the permit without any requirement for fees, cost recovery, bonding, or insurance. The superintendent will issue or deny a First Amendment permit request under 36 CFR 2.51 within two (2) business days after receiving a proper application. In National Capital Parks subject to special demonstration regulations found at 36 CFR 7.96(g)(3), permits are deemed granted subject to all applicable limitations and restrictions, unless denied within 24 hours of receipt.

(See Confidentiality 5.2.3. Also see Reference Manual 53)

8.6.4 Rights-of-Way for Utilities and Roads
8.6.4.1 General

A right-of-way is a special park use allowing a utility to pass over, under, or through NPS property. It may be issued only pursuant to specific statutory authority, and generally only if there is no practicable alternative to such use of NPS lands. The criteria listed in section 8.2 must also be met. New roads may not be permitted with a right-of-way permit, but require specific statutory authority. Procedures for roads are addressed in section 8.6.4.4.

Before a written application is submitted to the park, potential applicants for a right-of-way permit should meet with the staff to discuss the proposed project. Once an application for a right-of-way is submitted, a compliance analysis must be conducted according to NEPA, NHPA, and other statutory compliance requirements as appropriate. Due to the potentially high costs and values associated with rights-of-way, special attention will be paid to charges and a fair market value for use of the land. Permits will be drafted by park staff and should include terms and conditions necessary to protect park resources and values. New right-of-way permits will be executed by the regional director; conversions from other authorizing documents, amendments, and renewals of existing permits may be signed by the superintendent. A right-of-way permit issued by the Park Service is considered a temporary document and does not convey an interest in the land. The permit is subject to termination for cause or at the discretion of the regional director.

NPS regulations pertaining to the issuance of rights-of-way are in 36 CFR Part 14; Department of the Interior regulations pertaining to rights-of-way in Alaska are found in 43 CFR Part 36. Additional guidance can be found in Director's Order #53 and Reference Manual 53: Special Park Uses. A utility or road right-of-way proposed for a park in Alaska is subject to the authorities and procedural requirements of title XI of the Alaska National Interest Lands Conservation Act.

(See Park Management 1.4, Rights-of-way 6.4.8. Also see Director's Order #53)

8.6.4.2 Utilities

Utility rights-of-way over lands administered by the Park Service are governed by statutory authorities in 16 USC 5 (electrical power transmission and distribution, radio and TV, and other forms of communication facilities) and 16 USC 79 (electrical power, telephone, and water conduits). If not incompatible with the public interest, rights-of-way issued under 16 USC 5 or 79 are discretionary and conditional upon a finding by the Service that the proposed use will not cause unacceptable impacts on park resources, values, or purposes.

8.6.4.3 Telecommunication Sites

Requests to site non-NPS telecommunication antennas and related facilities on NPS lands will be considered in accordance with the Telecommunications Act of 1996 (47 USC 332 note), which authorizes but does not mandate a presumption that such requests be granted absent unavoidable conflict with the agency mission, or the current or planned use of the property or access to that property. The currently applicable government-wide procedures are contained in GSA Bulletin FPMR D-242.

Superintendents will accept an application for a telecommunications site only from a Federal Communications Commission licensee or from an agency regulated by the Department of Commerce through the National Telecommunications and Information Administration. In recognition of the growing prevalence of wireless telecommunications, the manner in which the park will manage the technology and related facilities should be addressed in an appropriate planning document.

As with other special park uses, telecommunication proposals must meet the criteria listed in sections 1.4.7.1 and 8.2 to prevent unacceptable impacts. In addition, when considering whether to approve, deny, or renew permits, superintendents will

- hold preliminary meetings with telecommunication facility applicants to discuss pending applications and policy and procedural issues (such as the application process, impact analysis, estimated cost recovery charges and fees) and other NPS concerns. Similar meetings should be held during the decision-making process, as necessary, particularly if the superintendent is considering denying the application;

- conduct NEPA and NHPA analysis expeditiously and consistent with all applicable statutes and Director's Order #12, and within timetables established pursuant to Director's Order #53;

- consider the potential benefit of having telephone access to emergency law enforcement and public safety services;

- consider whether the proposal would cause unavoidable conflict with the park's mission, in which case the permit will be denied.

New facilities frequently require the installation of new electrical and telephone lines and vehicular access to the site. Superintendents will therefore evaluate the entire footprint of the new facilities when evaluating requests.

Superintendents will avoid or minimize potential impacts of current and future telecommunications facilities by ensuring that the facilities and their supporting infrastructure

- are located where they would have the least impact on park resources and values;

- are not located in scenic, historic, and/or sensitive areas integral to the park's mission;

- include maximum potential for future co-location.

Superintendents will require the best technology available. For example, consideration should be given first to co-locating new facilities, constructing towers that are camouflaged to blend in with their surroundings, and installing micro-sites. New traditional towers (i.e., monopole or lattice) should be approved only after all other options have been explored. If a traditional tower is necessary, it should not be visible from any significant public vantage point.

As appropriate, superintendents should consider making use of available interpretive media to caution park users of the limited (or nonexistent) cellular service and their personal responsibility to plan accordingly.

When construction of telecommunication facilities on nonpark lands might adversely impact park resources and values, superintendents will actively participate in the applicable planning and regulatory processes and seek to prevent or mitigate the adverse impacts.

(See Decision-making Requirements to Identify and Avoid Impairments 1.4.7; Cooperative Conservation Beyond Park Boundaries 1.6; Integration of Facilities into the Park Environment 9.1.1.2; Signs 9.3.1.1)

8.6.4.4 Roads and Highways and Petroleum-based Pipelines

There are no general NPS statutory authorities for non-NPS roads or for gas pipelines. However, such authorization is sometimes contained in park-specific enabling legislation. Roads and highways within the federal aid highway system are generally authorized by statutes found at 23 USC 107(d) or 317. The Service will generally object to proposals for the use of park lands for highway purposes that do not directly benefit a park. A request for lands for road or highway purposes is subject to compliance with 23 USC 138—commonly referred to as 4(f). The 4(f) evaluation is completed by the Secretary of Transportation and requires the concurrence of the Secretary of the Interior. Approved road or highway requests are authorized by a highway easement deed (not a right-of-way permit).

(See Fees 8.6.1.2; Non-NPS Roads 9.2.1.2, Construction and Expansion Proposals 9.2.1.2.2. Also see Director's Order #87D: Non-NPS Roads)

8.6.5 Access to Private Property

The Park Service will allow access to the private property of adjacent landowners and property of landowners within park boundaries, when

- it would contribute in a material way to the park's mission without causing unacceptable impacts on park resources or values or the purposes for which the park was established; or
- access is the landowner's right by law or by deed reservation.

When one of these circumstances exists, commercial vehicles will be allowed access to private property only in accordance with 36 CFR 5.6, "Commercial Vehicles." Access to nonfederal lands in Alaska that requires access across NPS-administered lands will be provided in accordance with the applicable regulations implementing title 11 of the Alaska National Interest Lands Conservation Act.

8.6.6 Filming and Photography
8.6.6.1 General

The Service's policies and procedures governing filming and photography are governed by Public Law 106-206 (16 USC 460l-6d), which distinguishes filming from photography in that filming involves movement or motion of the subject, whereas photography does not (thus still photography is simply photography). Filming and photography activities—whether commercial or noncommercial—will be allowed in parks provided that the activities do not cause unacceptable impacts under sections 1.4.7.1 or 8.2. For the purposes of NPS policy, filming and photography encompass any technology that may be used for recording images or the sound tracks associated with them.

8.6.6.2 Permits and Fees

A permit will not be required for a visitor's personal, noncommercial filming and photography activities within normal visitation areas and hours. (Outside normal visitation areas and hours, a permit may be required.) However, all commercial filming activities will require a permit. Commercial filming means filming that involves the digital or film recording of a visual image or sound recording by a person, business, or other entity for a market audience. This includes recordings such as those used for a documentary, television or feature film, advertisement, or similar project.

In accordance with Public Law 106-206, still photography (whether commercial or noncommercial) will not require a permit unless

- it takes place at a location(s) where or when members of the public are generally not allowed, or
- it uses model(s) or prop(s) that are not a part of the location's natural or cultural resources or administrative facilities, or
- the Park Service would need to provide management and oversight to prevent unacceptable impacts.

Notwithstanding the above policies, commercial media coverage of breaking news never requires a permit. However, it is subject to the restrictions and conditions necessary to protect park resources from unacceptable impacts.

Performance bond and liability insurance requirements must be met, and all costs incurred by the Service in writing the permit, monitoring, providing protection services, or otherwise supporting filming or photography activities will be reimbursed by the permittee as a condition of the permit. A location fee will also be required as a condition of the permit. The amount of the fee will be based on the fee schedule current at the time the permit is approved. Neither the location fee nor the cost recovery charges may be waived.

8.6.6.3 NPS Participation

The Service's participation is governed by the following:

- The Service will encourage and may actively assist filming and photography activities that promote public understanding and appreciation of the national park system, and the Director may authorize use of the arrowhead symbol for such filming projects.
- A superintendent may request a credit line, provided that the content or subject matter of the filming project would not reflect adversely on the National Park Service.
- NPS employees, while on duty or in uniform, will not be employed by filming permittees.
- Identifiable NPS equipment, uniforms, or insignia must not be portrayed in any way that would imply Service endorsement of a product or service.
- The Service will not censor the content of any filming project, or require finished film products for review, files, or documentation purposes. However, a superintendent may review a story board or other material if requested by the applicant to help determine whether (1) the information about the park is accurate,

(2) a credit line would be appropriate, or (3) it would be appropriate for the Service to actively assist a filming activity or authorize use of the arrowhead symbol.

Additional guidance is provided by Director's Order #53: Special Park Uses; and by Reference Manual 53.

(Also see Director's Order #52D: Use of the Arrowhead Symbol)

8.6.7 Agricultural Uses

Agricultural uses and activities are authorized in parks in accordance with the direction provided by a park's enabling legislation and general management plan. Agricultural practices and techniques, including the use of pesticides and other biocontrol agents such as genetically modified or engineered organisms, should be specified in an approved resource stewardship strategy, and are subject to review and approval by the NPS integrated pest management (IPM) program manager. These practices and techniques are also subject to the provisions of federal and state laws, NPS regulations and policies, and Director's Orders #53: Special Park Uses and #77-7: Integrated Pest Management. In general, agricultural activities should be conducted in accordance with accepted best management practices.

Agricultural activities, including demonstration farms, prescribed to meet a park's management objectives will be allowed if (1) they do not result in unacceptable impacts on park resources, values, or purposes; (2) they conform to activities that occurred during the historic period; and (3) they support the park's interpretive themes. Agricultural uses that do not conform to those in practice during the historic period may be allowed if (1) they are authorized by the park's enabling legislation, (2) they are retained as a right subsequent to NPS land acquisition, (3) they contribute to the maintenance of a cultural landscape, or (4) they are carried out as part of a living exhibit or interpretive demonstration.

The Service may issue leases or special use permits to individuals or organizations to conduct agricultural activities that are allowed on park lands under the criteria listed in the preceding paragraph. The use of a lease (versus a special use permit) is appropriate only when (1) specifically authorized by the park's enabling legislation, or (2) it is part of an historic leasing program authorized by 16 USC 470h-3, or (3) it is associated with a building that is leased pursuant to 16 USC 1a-2(k). NPS and concession employees living in parks may cultivate gardens for personal use under the terms and conditions established by the superintendent. Such use will not be permitted if it would have unacceptable impacts on park resources, values, or purposes or visitor enjoyment thereof. In urban parks, areas may be designated for community recreational gardening under the same conditions.

(See Levels of Park Planning 2.3; Biological Resource Management 4.4; Pest Management 4.4.5; Cultural Landscapes 5.3.5.2; Personal Services 7.3.1; Process for Determining New Appropriate Uses 8.1.2. Also see Director's Order #77-7: Integrated Pest Management)

8.6.8 Domestic and Feral Livestock
8.6.8.1 General

Livestock uses in parks fall into four categories: (1) recreational pack and saddle stock use, (2) administrative stock use, (3) agricultural (commercial and administrative) grazing, and (4) trespass and feral stock. Grazing that is incidental to the recreational use of stock is regulated by the horse and pack stock regulations at 36 CFR 2.16, and the policy direction for such use is discussed in section 8.2.2.8. Agricultural stock use regulations are found at 36 CFR 2.60.

8.6.8.2 Managing Agricultural Grazing

Agricultural (commercial and administrative) grazing occurs in some parks. The Park Service will only allow agricultural grazing in parks where it is

- specifically authorized by federal law, or
- required under a reserved right of use arising from the acquisition of a tract of land, or
- required to maintain an historic scene, or
- carried out as part of a living exhibit or interpretive demonstration; or
- used to achieve resource conditions (e.g., using sheep to remove leafy spurge) as part of an IPM plan, and
- does not cause unacceptable impacts on park resources and values.

The National Park Service must manage its resources in a manner that conserves them for future generations. Parks with agricultural livestock use, including parks where such use is administered by another agency, must address this use in an appropriate planning document. Agricultural livestock grazing will use best management practices to protect park resources, with particular attention being given to protecting wetland and riparian areas, sensitive species and their habitats, water quality, and cultural resources. Managers must regulate livestock so that (1) ecosystem dynamics and the composition, condition, and distribution of native plants and animal communities are not significantly altered or otherwise threatened; and (2) cultural values are protected. A comprehensive monitoring program must be implemented, and adaptive management practices must be used to protect park resources.

Integrated pest management methods must conform to NPS pest management policy in section 4.4.5.

8.6.8.2.1 Permitting Agricultural Grazing

Agricultural livestock activities by parties other than the Park Service will be conducted only pursuant to the terms and conditions of a special use permit or lease. The use of a lease is appropriate only when (1) specifically authorized by the park's enabling legislation, or (2) it is part of an historic preservation program authorized by 16 USC 470h-3, or (3) the livestock use is associated with a building that is leased pursuant to 16 USC 1a-2(k).

In addition to any other penalty provisions, violation of the terms and conditions of the permitting instrument may result in revocation of the livestock use privilege. In parks where the Park Service shares livestock allotment management with another government agency, or where through legislation another government agency administers the use, a general agreement between agencies is necessary to describe the relationship and responsibilities.

8.6.8.2.2 Structures for Agricultural Grazing

Appropriate structures may be approved by the National Park Service and may be allowed in parks when the structures

- ◆ are consistent with a livestock management plan or another appropriate management plan;
- ◆ are consistent with park purposes and other applicable laws, regulations, or policies; and
- ◆ will not cause unacceptable impacts on park resources and values.

The Service will not expend funds to construct or maintain livestock structures unless there is a direct benefit to the protection of park resources. The permittee will generally be required to remove structures when livestock activities are no longer authorized.

(See Chapter 2: Park System Planning; Management of Exotic Species 4.4.4; Water Resource Management 4.6; Identification and Designation of the Wilderness Resource 6.2; Grazing and Livestock Driveways 6.4.7; Equestrian Trails 9.2.2.3; Miscellaneous Management Facilities 9.4.5. Also see Director's Order #77-3: Domestic and Feral Livestock Management, and Reference Manual 77-3; Director's Order #53: Special Park Uses, and Reference Manual 53; Director's Order #77-7: Integrated Pest Management)

8.6.8.3 Trespass and Feral Livestock

Livestock trespassing on park lands may be impounded and disposed of pursuant to the provisions of 36 CFR 2.60, with the owner charged for expenses incurred. Wild living or feral livestock having no known owner may also be disposed of in accordance with 36 CFR 2.60.

Parks having shared jurisdiction with state fish and wildlife agencies should coordinate with their counterparts in the determination of how a particular animal is classified in that state. Good communication with state and other officials will be fostered to minimize conflicts.

8.6.9 Military Operations

In general, military activities are discouraged in parks, except for study of military history at related NPS sites. Periodically, an armed services unit may request the use of park areas for noncombat exercises such as search-and-rescue and outdoor survival. Determining when and where military units may conduct such activities is a discretionary decision of the superintendent.

A permitted military activity must conform to the following conditions:

- ◆ A permit will be issued that clearly states all necessary conditions or stipulations to protect park resources and visitor safety.
- ◆ All applicable park rules and regulations will be followed.
- ◆ No weaponry will be carried, displayed, or used, except for ceremonial purposes or authorized public demonstrations.
- ◆ The activity will be conducted away from visitor use locations and out of public view (except where a public demonstration is specifically authorized).
- ◆ The military organization will designate a liaison officer who will be available to the superintendent throughout the exercise.
- ◆ Permittees will be educated about how the purpose, mission, and regulations of the park differ from their own missions, especially in regard to resource protection and visitor use and enjoyment.

National security and law enforcement agencies, such as the Central Intelligence Agency, Federal Bureau of Investigation, Secret Service, Department of Homeland Security, and state police, may wish to conduct similar exercises. These requests should be evaluated in the same way as military special use requests.

8.6.10 Cemeteries and Burials
8.6.10.1 National Cemeteries

All NPS-administered national cemeteries will be managed as historically significant resources and as integral parts of larger historical parks. Burials in national cemeteries will be permitted, pursuant to applicable regulations, until available space has been filled. The management and preservation of national cemeteries are subject to the provisions of the National Cemeteries Act of 1973; NPS "National Cemetery Regulations" (36 CFR Part 12); and Director's Order #61: National Cemeteries.

The enlargement of a national cemetery for additional burials constitutes a modern intrusion, compromising the historical character of both the cemetery and the historical park, and will not be permitted.

8.6.10.2 Family Cemeteries

The burial of family members in family cemeteries that have been acquired by the Park Service in the course of establishment of parks will be permitted to the extent practicable, pursuant to applicable regulations, until space allotted to the cemeteries has been filled. Family members (or their designees) will be allowed access for purposes of upkeep and commemoration (such as wreath-laying and religious rituals) that do not jeopardize safety or resource protection. Whenever applicable, park managers will keep active files on cemeteries for the purpose of responding to requests and inquiries.

(Also see Director's Order #19: Records Management)

8.6.10.3 Other Burials and the Scattering of Ashes

Other burials or reinterments outside established cemeteries in parks will be prohibited except where permitted by cultural resource policies. The scattering of ashes from cremation may be permitted by a superintendent, in accordance with NPS general regulations in 36 CFR 2.62 and applicable state laws. Authorization to scatter ashes must take into account potential conflicts with the spiritual or cultural practices of the indigenous people associated with the area.

(See Stewardship of Human Remains and Burials 5.3.4; Cultural Resources 6.3.8, Consultation 7.5.6)

8.6.11 Other Special Park Uses

Other special park uses that may be allowed under permit or special regulations include the use of explosives and the use of portable power equipment. Specific guidance is provided in 36 CFR Part 2; Director's Order #53: Special Park Uses; and Reference Manual 53.

8.7 Mineral Exploration and Development

Mineral exploration and development include exploration, extraction, production, storage, and transportation of minerals. Mineral exploration or development may be allowed in parks only when prospective operators demonstrate that they hold rights to valid mining claims, federal mineral leases, or nonfederally owned minerals. If this right is not clearly demonstrated, the National Park Service will inform the prospective operator that, until proof of a property right is documented, the Service will not further consider the proposed activity. Unless otherwise directed by Congress, if the Service determines that the proposed mineral development would impair park resources or values, or that such development is not consistent with park purposes or does not meet approval standards under applicable NPS regulations and cannot be sufficiently modified to meet those standards, the Service will seek to extinguish the associated mineral right through acquisition. In some parks, all or certain types of mineral development are specifically prohibited by law.

All persons who conduct mineral development within parks will do so only in conformance with applicable statutes, regulations, and NPS policies. These statutes include the Mining in the Parks Act, the Mineral Leasing Act, the Acquired Lands Mineral Leasing Act, the Surface Mining Control and Reclamation Act of 1977, the National Park System General Authorities Act, the Alaska National Interest Lands Conservation Act, and enabling statutes for individual parks. Applicable regulations include 36 CFR Part 9, Subpart A and Subpart B; 43 CFR Parts 3100-3500; and special use regulations.

Persons may not use or occupy surface lands in a park for purposes of removing minerals outside the park unless provided for in law. General management plans, land protection plans, and other planning documents for parks with mining claims, federal mineral leases, or nonfederally owned mineral interests will address these nonfederal property interests as appropriate. Lands with mineral interests will be zoned according to their anticipated management and use—based on their resource values, park management objectives, and park-specific legislative provisions relating to mineral interests.

(See Levels of Park Planning 2.3; Land Protection Plans 3.3; Identification and Designation of the Wilderness Resource 6.2; Mineral Development 6.4.9)

8.7.1 Mining Claims

The location of new mining claims pursuant to the General Mining Act of 1872 is prohibited in all park areas. Under the Mining in the Parks Act, the National Park Service may permit mineral development only on existing patented and valid unpatented mining claims in conformance with the park's enabling legislation and the regulations for mining claims in 36 CFR Part 9, Subpart A. The Service may initiate a validity examination on unpatented mining claims at any time. The Service will require a validity examination of all unpatented mining claims before approving any operations on such claims in accordance with 36 CFR Part 9, Subpart A. However, a validity examination is not required before NPS authorization of activities that are conducted only to reclaim a site. All mineral development and use of resources in connection with a claim will be confined to the boundaries of the claim itself, except for the access and transport that are permitted under 36 CFR Part 9, Subpart A; or, for Alaska, 43 CFR Part 36.

8.7.2 Federal Mineral Leases

All parks are closed to new federal mineral leasing except for three national recreation areas (Lake Mead, Whiskeytown, and Glen Canyon) where Congress has explicitly authorized federal mineral leasing in each area's enabling legislation. Through park planning documents, the National Park Service has closed portions of these areas to federal mineral leasing because of the presence of sensitive resources. No person may explore for federal minerals in any of these areas except under a lease issued pursuant to regulations in 43 CFR Part 3100 or a prospecting permit pursuant to 43 CFR 3500. Before consenting to a federal mineral lease or subsequent mineral development connected with a lease, the regional director must find, in writing, that leasing and subsequent mineral development will not result in a significant adverse effect on park resources or administration.

Some park areas contain leases that existed at the time the park was created or expanded. These leases are valid existing rights and will continue to exist until they expire under the regulations that govern federal mineral leasing (43 CFR Parts 3100 and 3500).

8.7.3 Nonfederally Owned Minerals

Nonfederal mineral interests in park units consist of oil and gas interests, rights to mineral interests other than oil and gas (such as private outstanding mineral rights, mineral rights through general land grant patents, homestead patents, or other private mineral rights that did not derive from the General Mining Act). The Park Service governs activities associated with these two categories of nonfederal mineral rights under separate regulatory schemes.

The Park Service may approve operations associated with nonfederal oil and gas interests under the standards and procedures in 36 CFR Part 9, Subpart B. If an operator's plan fails to meet the approved standards of these regulations, the Park Service generally has authority to deny the operation and may initiate acquisition. Absent a decision to acquire the property, application of the regulations is not intended to result in a taking of the property interest, but rather to impose reasonable regulation of the activity.

Operations associated with nonfederal mineral interests, other than oil and gas, are subject to the requirements of 36 CFR Part 5, "Commercial and Private Operations," and 36 CFR 1.6.

The Service must determine that operations associated with these mineral interests would not adversely impact "public health and safety, environmental or scenic values, natural or cultural resources, scientific research, implementation or management responsibilities, proper allocation and use of facilities, or the avoidance of conflict among visitor use activities …." If the impacts from the operation on the resource cannot be sufficiently mitigated to meet this standard, the Park Service may seek to acquire the mineral interest.

8.8 Collecting Natural Products

The collection of natural products for personal use or consumption is governed by NPS general regulations contained in 36 CFR 2.1 and 36 CFR Part 13. A superintendent may designate certain fruits, berries, nuts, or unoccupied seashells that can be gathered by hand for personal use or consumption upon a written determination by the superintendent that such an activity will not adversely affect park wildlife or the reproductive potential of a plant species or otherwise adversely affect park resources. In some cases, peer-reviewed scientific information may be needed to support the determination. The regulations do not authorize the taking, use, or possession of fish, wildlife, or plants for ceremonial or religious purposes, except where specifically authorized by federal statute or treaty rights or where hunting, trapping, or fishing are otherwise allowed. The collection of minerals or rocks for personal use will be allowed only when specifically authorized by federal law or treaty rights.

The gathering of firewood will be allowed only where subsistence use is authorized by federal law, or in specific areas designated by a superintendent in which dead and down wood may be collected for campfires or in small quantities for other uses within the park. Natural resource products that accumulate as a result of site clearing for development, hazard tree removal, vista clearing, or other management actions will be recycled through the ecosystem when practicable. When recycling is not practicable, the products may be disposed of by other means. Disposal may be accomplished by contract, if the result of the work done under contract and the value are calculated in the contract cost, or by sale at fair market value in accordance with applicable laws and regulations. Wood that accumulates as a result of the management actions described above may also be used for park purposes, such as heating public buildings or offices or for interpretive campfire programs.

(See Consumptive Uses 8.9, Natural and Cultural Studies, Research, and Collection Activities 8.10. Also see Director's Order #18: Wildland Fire Management)

8.9 Consumptive Uses

Consumptive uses of park resources may be allowed only when they are

◆ specifically authorized by federal law or treaty rights (such as hunting, trapping, or mining, or subsistence use in specifically identified parks);

◆ specifically authorized pursuant to other existing rights (such as a right retained by a donor of the land on which the use would occur);

◆ grazing activities authorized in accordance with section 8.6.8.1; or

◆ traditional visitor activities, such as fishing or berry picking, that are authorized in accordance with NPS general regulations.

As a matter of policy, the Service generally supports the limited and controlled consumption of natural resources for traditional religious and ceremonial purposes and is moving toward a goal of greater access and accommodation. As a general matter, a superintendent may not allow consumptive use of park resources by any particular group to the exclusion of others.

Current NPS policy is reflected in regulations published at 36 CFR Part 13. The general regulations at 36 CFR 2.1 allow superintendents to designate certain fruits, berries, nuts, or unoccupied seashells that may be gathered by hand for personal use or consumption if it will not adversely affect park wildlife, the reproductive potential of a plant species, or otherwise adversely affect park resources. The regulations do not authorize the taking, use, or possession of fish, wildlife, or plants for ceremonial or religious purposes, except where specifically authorized by federal statute or treaty rights or where hunting, trapping, or fishing are otherwise allowed.

The 36 CFR Part 13 regulations address the consumptive use of park resources for subsistence purposes in Alaska, where it is allowed in the 10 parks and "expanded areas" established by the Alaska National Interest Lands Conservation Act. Some park-specific enabling acts (e.g., Big Cypress National Preserve and Kaloko-Honokohau National Historical Park) also allow subsistence or other traditional uses of park resources.

(See Park Management 1.4; Harvest of Plants and Animals by the Public 4.4.3; Resource Issue Interpretation and Education 7.5.3; General 8.; Use by American Indians and Other Traditionally Associated Groups 8.5. Also see 36 CFR Part 13, Subpart B)

8.10 Natural and Cultural Studies, Research, and Collection Activities

Studies, research, and collection activities by non-NPS personnel involving natural and cultural resources will be encouraged and facilitated when they otherwise comport with NPS policies. Scientific activities that involve field work or specimen collection, or that have the potential to disturb resources, the visitor experience, or park operations, require a permit issued by the superintendent that prescribes appropriate conditions for protecting park resources, visitors, and operations. Such studies may require additional permits from other jurisdictions.

(See Studies and Collections 4.2; Independent Research 5.1.2; Independent and Commercial Studies 8.11.3)

8.11 Social Science Studies

8.11.1 General

Understanding the changing demographics of our nation is critical to the future of the National Park Service. The Park Service will actively seek to better understand the values and connections the changing U.S. population has, or does not have, for our natural and cultural heritage so that the Service can be responsive and relevant to public needs and desires. This includes understanding why people do or do not visit national parks.

The National Park Service will facilitate social science studies that support the NPS mission by providing an understanding of park visitors, the nonvisiting public, gateway communities and regions, and human interactions with park resources. This approach will provide a scientific basis for park planning, development, operations, management, education, and interpretive activities. Investigators will be encouraged to use the parks for scientific studies whenever such use is consistent with NPS policies that recognize the scientific value of parks as laboratories. Specific guidance is provided in Director's Orders #75A: Civic Engagement and Public Involvement, and #78: Social Science.

Studies include short- or long-term scientific investigations in NPS areas that may involve social science surveys and research. The data and information acquired through scientific activities conducted in the parks will be made broadly available to park managers, the scientific community, and the public, except where legal restrictions apply. Studies may include both internally and externally conducted projects by researchers and scholars with universities; foundations and other nongovernmental organizations; federal, state and local agencies; chambers of commerce; industry organizations; and NPS staff. The Park Service will promote cooperative relationships with educational and scientific institutions and qualified individuals (1) when specialized expertise exists that can be of significant assistance to the Service in obtaining information, and (2) when the opportunity for research and study in the parks offers institutions a significant benefit to their programs. NPS facilities and assistance may be made available to qualified researchers conducting NPS-authorized studies. NPS or other federally funded studies that rely on survey instruments or focus groups are strictly regulated and must be approved by the Park Service, the Department of the Interior, and the Office of Management and Budget before they can be used to gather information directly from visitors or the general public.

(See Managing Information 1.9.2; Studies and Collections 4.2; Research 5.1, Planning 5.2; Appropriate Use 8.1.1; Special Park Uses 8.6; NPS-supported Studies 8.11.2; Independent and Commercial Studies 8.11.3; Department of the Interior Interim Guidelines for Collection of Information from the Public. Also see Director's Order #17: Tourism))

8.11.2 NPS-supported Studies

The National Park Service is responsible for the identification and acquisition of needed inventory, monitoring, and research, as well as for the interpretation of the management and operational implications of such studies. The Service will use the best available science to assist park managers in addressing management needs and objectives that have been identified in legislation and planning documents.

The Service will support studies to

- reach a level of understanding that will minimize "crisis" management;
- ensure a systematic and fully adequate park information base;
- provide a sound basis for policy, planning, and decision-making;
- develop effective strategies, methods, and technologies to predict, avoid, or minimize unacceptable impacts on resources, visitors, and related activities;
- determine causes of resource management problems;
- further understand park ecosystems and related human social systems, and document their components, condition, and significance;
- evaluate visitor satisfaction with services, facilities, and recreational opportunities;
- ensure that the interpretation of park resources and issues reflects current standards of scholarship for the history, science, and condition of the resources;
- evaluate performance measures in support of strategic plan goals;
- establish economic measures and impact indicators of interest or importance;
- improve understanding of local, regional, and national demographics and trends.

Superintendents may authorize park staff to carry out routine duties without requiring a research/collecting permit. NPS-supported research will rely on high-quality methods and undergo peer review. NPS-supported scientists will be expected to publish their findings in refereed journals, among other outlets.

8.11.3 Independent and Commercial Studies

Non-NPS social science studies conducted in parks are not required to address specifically identified NPS management issues or information needs. However, these studies (excluding research in museum collections) require an NPS research/collecting permit. Pursuant to the terms and conditions of the permit, the studies must conform to NPS policies and other guidance regarding activities such as the collection and publication of data, conduct of studies, and wilderness restrictions. NPS research/collecting permits may also include requirements that permittees provide parks, within reasonable time-frames, with the appropriate field notes (subject to ethical guidelines of the appropriate discipline), data, information about the data, catalog data, progress reports, interim and final reports, and publications derived from the permitted activities. Projects will be administered and conducted only by fully qualified personnel, and will conform to current standards of scholarship.

The collection of data from the public and employees to support the research, development, and marketing of commercial products or services may be permitted only in limited circumstances. Such activity will not be permitted when the superintendent determines that it would impose an undue burden on visitors and/or employees, and/or when it has the potential to adversely impact park resources or detract from visitors' experiences in the park. All necessary data collection permits must be obtained, including a scientific research and collecting permit and the permission of the superintendent. Names and addresses and any other unique identifying information collected from park visitors and/or employees cannot be distributed, shared, or sold for commercial purposes.

(Also see Director's Order #84: Library Management)

8.11.4 Management and Conduct of Studies

All studies in parks will employ nondestructive methods to the maximum extent possible to avoid the irretrievable commitment of park resources. Studies will be preceded by an approved scope of work, proposal, or other detailed written description of the work to be performed.

(See Studies and Collections 4.2. Also see Director's Order #74: Studies and Collecting)

8.12 Leases

In accordance with 36 CFR Part 18, the National Park Service may enter into a lease for the use of any park property—historic or nonhistoric (except nonhistoric land)—if the following determinations are first made by the appropriate regional director (who may redelegate this authority to superintendents):

(1) The lease will not result in degradation of the purposes and values of the park area.

(2) The lease will not deprive the park area of property necessary for appropriate park protection, interpretation, visitor enjoyment, or administration.

(3) The lease contains such terms and conditions as will ensure that the leased property will be used for an activity and in a manner that are consistent with the purposes established by law for the park area in which the property is located.

(4) The lease is compatible with NPS programs.

(5) The lease is for rent at least equal to the fair market value rent of the leased property.

(6) The proposed activities under the lease are not subject to authorization through a concession contract, commercial use authorization, or similar instrument.

(7) If the lease includes historic property, the lease will adequately ensure the preservation of the historic property. (In addition, a lease that includes historic property may be executed by the Park Service only after compliance with the CFR Part 800, the commenting procedures of the Advisory Council on Historic Preservation).

It is likely that lease uses will be permissible under paragraph (6) if

- the leased property where the proposed services are to be provided is not near a particular visitor destination of the park area, and
- the patrons of the lessee are expected to be primarily persons who come to the park area only to use the lessee's services.

8.12.1 Additional Criteria

- All leases must be at fair market value.
- The term of the lease will be the shortest time needed for the proposed use, taking into account required lessee investments and other factors related to determining an appropriate lease term.
- No lease will exceed 60 years.
- Lease terms may not be extended except that leases with a term of one (1) year or more may be extended once for a period not to exceed one (1) additional year if it is determined that an extension is necessary because of circumstances beyond NPS control.

8.12.2 Prior Approval

No lease instrument may be awarded or amended without prior written approval by the Solicitor's Office.

Prior to their execution by a regional director or superintendent, the Director must approve—

- proposed leases with terms of more than ten (10) years;
- proposed leases or lease amendments that provide for a leasehold mortgage or similar encumbrance; and
- proposed amendments of existing leases that required the Director's approval prior to execution.

8.12.3 Noncompetitive Awards

The Service generally may not enter into a Part 18 lease without issuing a Request for Bids or a Request for Proposals. The Service may, however, enter into Part 18 leases on a noncompetitive basis in two circumstances:

(1) The Part 18 lease is with a nonprofit organization or a unit of government and the Service determines that the nonprofit or governmental use of the property will contribute to the purposes and programs of the park area; or

(2) The lease is short-term (sixty (60) continuous days or less) and the Service determines that to award the lease noncompetitively is in the best interests of the administration of the park area. This authority is not limited to nonprofit organizations or units of government; any qualified person or entity may be awarded a lease with a term of sixty (60) days or less. These leases cannot require any rehabilitation or improvements to the applicable property.

Noncompetitive leases must in all other ways meet the requirements of 36 CFR Part 18 and Director's Order #38: Real Property Leasing.

8.12.4 Historic Properties

If a lease agreement requires or allows the lessee to maintain, repair, rehabilitate, restore, or build upon historic property, the work must be done in accordance with the Secretary of the Interior's Standards and Guidelines for Archeology and Historic Preservation and other NPS policies, guidelines, and standards.

Park Facilities

9

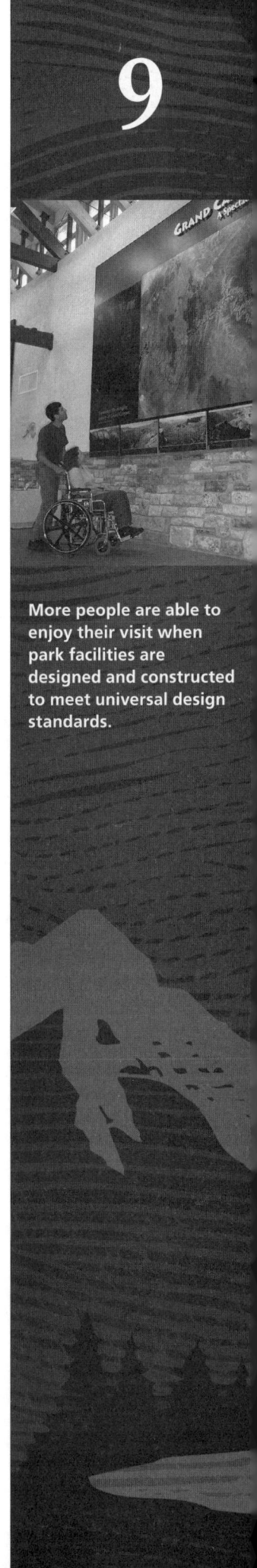

More people are able to enjoy their visit when park facilities are designed and constructed to meet universal design standards.

The National Park Service will provide visitor and administrative facilities that are necessary, appropriate, and consistent with the conservation of park resources and values. Facilities will be harmonious with park resources, compatible with natural processes, esthetically pleasing, functional, energy- and water-efficient, cost-effective, universally designed, and as welcoming as possible to all segments of the population. NPS facilities and operations will demonstrate environmental leadership by incorporating sustainable practices to the maximum extent practicable in planning, design, siting, construction, and maintenance.

9.1 General

The Organic Act, which created the National Park Service in 1916, directs the Service to conserve park resources "unimpaired" for the enjoyment of future generations. The 1970 National Park System General Authorities Act, as amended in 1978, prohibits the Service from allowing any activities that would cause derogation of the values and purposes for which the park units have been established. Taken together, these two laws impose on NPS managers a strict mandate to protect park resources and values. (Throughout Management Policies, "impairment" is construed to also encompass "derogation.") In protecting park resources and values, the Service will demonstrate environmental leadership and a commitment to the principles of sustainability and asset management in all facility developments and operations. This commitment will be made obvious to the public in the choices and decisions that are made, and through appropriate educational opportunities.

Support facilities necessary to house, transport, inform, and serve visitors and staff require proper planning, design, programming, construction, operation, and maintenance. The Service must avoid the construction of buildings, roads, and other development that will cause unacceptable impacts on park resources values. The Service must also avoid the future operation and maintenance costs of unnecessary or ineffective facilities, regardless of how the asset investment is funded. The Service must also recognize the ongoing operations and maintenance costs of its facilities and be able to sustain them over time. Therefore, the Service will not develop or redevelop a facility within a park until a determination has been made that the facility is necessary and appropriate, and that it would not be practicable for the facility to be developed or the service to be provided outside the park. This policy recognizes, for example, that a gas station or a grocery store may be necessary to park use and enjoyment, but that it may not need to be located within the park. Special considerations may be necessary in Alaska, given section 1306 of the Alaska National Interest Lands Conservation Act (16 USC 3196).

Partnership construction projects will be held to the same standards articulated above. In addition, where donated funds are used, the Service will follow the requirements of Director's Order #21: Donations and Fundraising.

(See Park Management 1.4; Decision-making Requirements to Identify and Avoid Impairments 1.4.7; Evaluating Impacts on Natural Resources 4.1.3; Planning 5.2; Commercial Visitor Services Planning 10.2.2; Director's Order #80: Asset Management; Director's Order #21: Donations and Fundraising)

9.1.1 Facility Planning and Design

The protection of each park's resources and values will be the primary consideration in facility development decisions. Facilities for visitor use and park management will be consistent with each park's authorizing legislation, and with approved general management plans, development concept plans, and associated planning documents. The planning and design of park facilities will be accomplished by interdisciplinary teams constituted to meet the resource stewardship, programmatic, and technical requirements of the project. Public input will be sought at the earliest stage of planning and design, particularly in those cases where controversy is likely.

The Park Service will meet its facility development needs in a cost-effective manner, ensuring that value is returned for every decision made. Only development projects that are shown to be an appropriate use of funds and economically feasible will be approved. Value analysis and value engineering techniques, such as functional analysis and cost evaluation, will be applied to achieve the lowest life-cycle cost that is consistent with environmental, energy performance, reliability, quality, safety, and resource protection requirements. Construction and operational cost estimates will be continually reviewed throughout the planning and development processes to avoid excessive, unwarranted, or unnecessary costs. Development projects will also be continually reviewed for opportunities to add value and benefits that will help achieve the NPS mission.

Designs for park facilities, regardless of their origin (NPS, contractor, concessioner, or other), will use NPS facility models for space and function requirement and will be harmonious with and integrated into the park environment. They will also be subject throughout all phases of design and construction to the same code compliance; the same high standards of sustainable design, universal design, and functionality; and the same review and approval processes. NPS requirements for sustainable design and functionality include protection of the natural and cultural environments, resource conservation, energy conservation, pollution prevention, defensible space for fire safety, and fostering education about sustainable design and practices.

The Service will issue, and update as necessary, guiding principles for sustainable design to be applied throughout the national park system, consistent with federal regulations such as Executive Order 13123 (Greening the Government through Efficient Energy Management), Executive Order 13101 (Greening the Government through Waste Prevention, Recycling and Federal Acquisition), and Executive Order 13327 (Federal Real Property Asset Management).

(See Levels of Park Planning 2.3; General Management Concepts 4.1; Lightscape Management 4.10. Also see Director's Orders #13A: Environmental Management Systems; and #90: Value Analysis; NPS Guiding Principles of Sustainable Design)

9.1.1.1 Life-cycle Costs

The total cost of a system, facility, or other product will be considered in its planning, design, and construction. Total cost will be computed over a product's or system's useful life or other specified period of time using economic analysis. Life-cycle costs include acquisition, shipping, initial construction or installation, operation and maintenance, environmental and energy consumption, water, wastewater, and the costs of eventual disposal or deconstruction of the system, facility, and/or product. To the extent practicable, the waste implications of materials, products, and by-products (including product life-cycle pollution) should be considered as part of life-cycle costs. When the cost of facility deconstruction is included in the life-cycle cost analysis, deductions may be factored in for the salvage value of the recyclable materials.

(Also see Director's Orders #13A: Environmental Management Systems; and #90: Value Analysis)

9.1.1.2 Integration of Facilities into the Park Environment

Whenever feasible and authorized by Congress, major park facilities—especially those that can be shared with other entities—should be developed outside park boundaries. The Service will encourage the private sector to meet facility needs in gateway communities and thus contribute to local economic development, encourage competition, increase choices for visitors, and minimize the need for in-park construction. Where possible, appropriate, and authorized, the Park Service will cooperatively establish and maintain administration/information facilities with other federal, state, or local entities.

If facilities must be located inside park boundaries, the preferred locations will be those that minimize impacts on park resources and are situated to stimulate the use of alternative transportation systems, bicycle routes, and pedestrian walkways. Major facilities within park boundaries will be placed only in locations identified in an approved general management plan or implementation planning document as being suitable and appropriate. Facility siting will take into account the need for protection from fires and take maximum advantage of factors such as solar energy, wind direction and speed, natural landscaping, and other natural features.

When structures are no longer functional in their present locations or are determined to be inappropriately placed in important resource areas, they will be removed subject to appropriate compliance.

When the determination has been made through a planning process that it is appropriate for a facility to be constructed within park boundaries, all facilities will be integrated into the park landscape and environs with sustainable designs and systems to minimize environmental impact. Development will not compete with or dominate park features or interfere with natural processes, such as the seasonal migration of wildlife or hydrologic activity associated with wetlands.

If a cohesive design theme is desired, recommended, or required, the theme will reflect the purpose and character of the park, or in a large park the theme will reflect an individual developed area. Standard designs and components may be used, but they will be adapted as appropriate to the specific site and conditions as part of the design process.

The full integration of facilities into the park environment will involve

- sensitivity to cultural, regional, esthetic, and environmental factors (e.g., solar orientation, prevailing winds, landscaping, vulnerability to wildfire and other natural hazards) in the selection of site, construction materials, and forms;
- innovative concepts for grouping facilities and activities, both in the design of new development and in the redesign of existing complexes while building on the architectural and landscape elements already present;
- thorough interdisciplinary resource, user, and short- and long-term structure maintenance analyses;
- the long-term need for and sustainable use of water, energy, and waste disposal resources;
- assessment of the transportation and mobility needs of park visitors and concessioner and NPS employees, and of access to the park from gateway communities; and
- knowledge about the values and sociocultural interests of American Indians and other groups traditionally associated with the park.

(See Environmental Leadership 1.8; General Management Planning 2.3.1; Lightscape Management 4.10; Historic and Prehistoric Structures 5.3.5.4; Protection of Cultural Values 9.1.1.3; Siting Facilities to Avoid Natural Hazards 9.1.1.5; Visitor Centers 9.3.1.3; Commercial Visitor Services Planning 10.2.2)

9.1.1.3 Protection of Cultural Values

When important cultural resources are present, efforts will be made to use existing contributing structures. New visitor or administration structures will harmonize with the area and the cultural resources in proportion, color, and texture. No attempt will be made to duplicate or mimic a historic design, nor will any modern construction be portrayed to the public as being historic. However, vernacular styles of architecture are appropriate when they provide visual compatibility with the cultural landscape. Application of the criteria of effect promulgated by the Advisory Council on Historic Preservation and compliance with the council's regulations on "Protection of Historic Properties" (36 CFR Part 800) will precede any development. These criteria apply to all historic properties.

(See Identification and Evaluation of Resources 5.1.3; Planning 5.2; Treatment of Cultural Resources 5.3.5. Also see Secretary of the Interior's Standards and Guidelines for Archeology and Historic Preservation)

9.1.1.4 Adaptive Use

The National Historic Preservation Act and Executive Order 13006 (Locating Federal Facilities on Historic Properties) require each federal agency— before acquiring, constructing, or leasing buildings— to use, to the maximum extent feasible, historic properties available to it whenever operationally appropriate and economically prudent. (16 USC 470h-2(a)(1)). The act also requires each agency to implement alternatives for the adaptive use of historic properties it owns if that will help ensure the properties' preservation. Therefore, the adaptive use of historic and nonhistoric buildings for operations such as visitor centers, hostels, and administrative offices will be considered first, before new construction, provided that (1) it can meet park objectives and current code requirements, (2) its use will not be an intrusion on significant natural or cultural resources, and (3) a cost savings will be realized. Even when the cost of adaptive use is greater than new construction, it may still be justified. Use of historic buildings will comply with all laws, regulations, and policies regarding the treatment and use of cultural resources.

(See Physical Access for Persons with Disabilities 5.3.2; Use of Historic Structures 5.3.5.4.7; Leases 8.12))

9.1.1.5 Siting Facilities to Avoid Natural Hazards

The Service will strive to site facilities where they will not be damaged or destroyed by natural physical processes. Natural hazard areas include sites with unstable soils and geologic conditions, fault zones, thermal areas, floodplains, flash-flood zones, fire-prone vegetation, and coastal high-hazard areas. Park development that is damaged or destroyed by a hazardous or catastrophic natural event will be thoroughly evaluated for relocation or replacement by new construction at a different location. If a decision is made to relocate or replace a severely damaged or destroyed facility, it will be placed, if practicable, in an area that is believed to be free from natural hazards. In areas where dynamic natural processes cannot be avoided, such as seashores, developed facilities should be sustainably designed (e.g., removable in advance of hazardous storms or other conditions). When it has been determined that facilities must be located in such areas, their design and siting will be based on

- a thorough understanding of the nature of the physical processes; and
- avoiding or mitigating (1) the risks to human life and property, and (2) the effect of the facility on natural physical processes and the ecosystem.

Requirements for development in floodplains and wetlands are contained in Executive Order 11988 (Floodplain Management); Executive Order 11990 (Protection of Wetlands); Director's Orders #77-1: Wetland Protection and #77-10: Natural Resource Inventorying and Monitoring; and other NPS guidance documents.

(See Levels of Park Planning 2.3; Floodplains 4.6.4; Wetlands 4.6.5; Shorelines and Barrier Islands 4.8.1.1; Geologic Hazards 4.8.1.3; Visitor Safety and Emergency Response 8.2.5; Concession Facilities 10.2.6)

9.1.1.6 Sustainable Energy Design

Any facility development, whether it is a new building, a renovation, or an adaptive reuse of an existing facility, must include improvements in energy efficiency and reduction in greenhouse gas emissions for both the building envelope and the mechanical systems that support the facility. Maximum energy efficiency should be achieved using solar thermal and photovoltaic applications, appropriate insulation and glazing strategies, energy-efficient lighting and appliances, and renewable energy technologies. Energy-efficient construction projects should be used as an educational opportunity for the visiting public.

All projects that include visitor centers or major visitor services facilities must incorporate LEED (Leadership in Energy and Environmental Design) standards to achieve a silver rating.

9.1.2 Accessibility for Persons with Disabilities

The Service will design, construct, and operate all buildings and facilities so they are accessible to and usable by persons with disabilities to the greatest extent reasonable, in accord with all applicable laws, regulations, and standards. This means that all new and altered buildings and facilities will comply with the General Services Administration's regulations adopting accessibility standards for the Architectural Barriers Act of 1968 (41 CFR Part 102-76, Subpart C), and 43 CFR, Part 17, Subpart E, Enforcement of Nondiscrimination on the Basis of Handicap in Programs or Activities Conducted by the Department of Interior. It also means that some buildings and facilities will be modified to ensure that programs can be provided in an accessible location.

Accessibility will be provided consistent with preserving park resources and providing visitor safety and high-quality visitor experiences. In most instances, the degree of accessibility provided will be proportionately related to the degree of human-made modifications in the area surrounding the facility and the importance of the facility to people visiting or working in the park. Accordingly, most administrative offices, some overnight visitor accommodations, some employee housing, and most interpretive and visitor service facilities will be accessible. Undeveloped areas, such as those outside the immediate influence of buildings and roads, will not normally be modified, nor will special facilities be provided for the sole purpose of providing access to all segments of the population. Accessibility to facilities in threshold areas will be determined on the basis of topography, the significance of the attraction, the number of physical modifications being made to the environment, and the modifications necessary to ensure programmatic accessibility.

Transportation systems in parks, including water transportation, will have a sufficient percentage of fully accessible vehicles or watercraft to provide effective services to persons with disabilities. In the case of existing systems, the necessary vehicles will be provided on a replacement or retrofit basis. Until the transportation system has been made fully accessible, a separate accessible vehicle will be provided, or disabled persons will be allowed to drive their personal vehicles on otherwise-restricted roadways. In meeting the goal of accessibility, emphasis will be placed on ensuring that persons with disabilities are afforded experiences and opportunities along with other visitors to the greatest extent reasonable. Separate facilities for people with disabilities are not a substitute for full accessibility to other park facilities, but they may be allowed where the need for specialized services is clearly demonstrated.

(See Physical Access for Persons with Disabilities 5.3.2; Accessibility for Persons with Disabilities 8.2.4; Accessibility of Commercial Services 10.2.6.2. Also see Director's Order #42: Accessibility for Visitors with Disabilities in National Park Service Programs and Services)

9.1.3 Construction

The Service will incorporate sustainable principles and practices into design, siting, construction, building materials, utility systems, recycling of all unusable materials, and waste management. Best management practices will be used for all phases of construction activity, including preconstruction, actual construction, and postconstruction. Although construction of new assets is often a viable alternative for meeting visitor needs or protecting resources, the Service will consider nonbuild alternatives to meet its needs. The nonbuild alternative is developed and evaluated as part of the early facility planning and design process.

9.1.3.1 Construction Sites

Construction sites will be limited to the smallest feasible area. The selection of construction sites will consider opportunities for taking advantage of natural sources of lighting, heating, and cooling (e.g., near an existing or potential stand of deciduous trees) to maximize energy conservation. Ground disturbance and site management will be carefully controlled to prevent undue damage to vegetation, soils, and archeological resources and to minimize air, water, soil, and noise pollution. Protective fencing and barricades will be provided for safety and to preserve natural and cultural resources. Effective storm water management measures specific to the site will be implemented, and appropriate erosion and sedimentation control measures will be in place at all times. Solid, volatile, and hazardous wastes will be avoided when possible. When they cannot be avoided, they will be properly stored, transported, and disposed of in compliance with federal, state, and local laws and regulations. All materials will be recycled whenever possible.

A review and approval of any "hot work" (e.g., welding, use of open flame, grinding) will be done to ensure fire safety at the construction site. Visual intrusions will be kept to a minimum. Construction equipment will be in satisfactory condition; i.e., it will be equipped with required safety components and not be leaking hazardous liquids or emitting hazardous or undesirable fumes above allowable legal limits. Care will be exercised to ensure that construction equipment and all construction materials imported into the park are free of undesirable species. The cost of restoring areas impacted by construction will be considered part of the cost of construction, and funding for restoration will be included in construction budgets.

(See Air Resource Management 4.7; Water Resource Management 4.6; Soil Resource Management 4.8.2.4. Also see Denver Service Center specifications section 01570)

9.1.3.2 Revegetation and Landscaping

The selection of plant materials and cultivation practices will be guided by the policies for management of plant materials in section 4.4 and the need for fire-resistant vegetation for defensible space. To the maximum extent possible, plantings will consist of species that are native to the park or that are historically appropriate for the period or event commemorated. The use of exotic plant species is restricted to situations that conform to the exotic species policy in section 4.4.4. Irrigation to maintain exotic plantings will be avoided, except when it is part of an approved management program essential to achieve park objectives and when adequate and dependable supplies of water are available. Low water use practices that measure soil moisture content and other technologies (such as drip irrigation and appropriate timing of water applications) should be employed.

Prior to using soil fertilizers or other soil amendments in park natural or altered landscapes, parks must develop a prescription to ensure that the amendments will not unacceptably alter the physical, chemical, or biological characteristics of the soil, biological community, or surface or groundwaters.

Wherever practicable, soils and plants affected by construction will be salvaged for use in site restoration. Any surplus soils and plants may be used, as appropriate, for the restoration of other degraded areas in the park. Surplus soils not used in this way should be stockpiled for future use. If additional soil and plants are needed to restore disturbed sites, they may be obtained from other sites in the park if it is determined that the use of an in-park source will not significantly affect cultural or natural resources or ecological processes. In any case, imported soils must (1) be compatible with existing soils, (2) be free of undesired seeds and organisms, and (3) fulfill the horticultural requirements of plants used for restoration.

(See Management of Native Plants and Animals 4.4.2; Genetic Resource Management Principles 4.4.1.2; Management of Exotic Species 4.4.4; Water Resource Management 4.6; Soil Resource Management 4.8.2.4; Cultural Landscapes 5.3.5.2; Water Supply Systems 9.1.5.1; Wastewater Treatment Systems 9.1.5.2. Also see Executive Order 13148 (Greening the Government through Leadership in Environmental Management) section 207, "Environmentally and Economically Beneficial Landscaping")

9.1.3.3 Borrow Pits and Spoil Areas

Materials from borrow pits, quarries, and other clay, stone, gravel, or sand sources on NPS lands, including submerged lands, will be extracted and used only

- by the Park Service or its agents or contractors;
- for in-park administrative uses;

- after compliance with the National Environmental Policy Act and National Historic Preservation Act, including written findings that
  - extraction and use of in-park borrow materials does not or will not impair park resources or values; and
  - it is the park's most reasonable alternative based on economic, environmental, and ecological considerations; and
  - no outside sources are reasonably available;
- after compliance with other applicable federal, state, and local requirements.

Parks should use existing pits, quarries, or sources, or create new pits, quarries, or sources in the park only after developing and implementing a parkwide borrow management plan that addresses the cumulative effects of borrow site extraction, restoration, and importation. NPS guidance documents, as well as natural and cultural resources and facilities management staff, should be consulted during plan development and the review of specific proposals.

In designated wild and scenic rivers, no new sources may be established, and existing sources should be closed and reclaimed. Borrow material may be extracted in proposed or designated wilderness areas only in small quantities for trail use and in accordance with an approved wilderness management plan.

Spoil may be used for beach nourishment or another resource management activity only if the superintendent first finds that the proposed nourishment or activity will not impair park resources and values and that the proposed activity is consistent with park planning documents.

All existing spoil areas within park units that meet the definition of "solid waste disposal site" (36 CFR Part 6) will be brought into compliance with NPS solid waste regulations in 36 CFR 6.5. The development of new spoil areas or borrow pits, or the expansion of existing ones, will be analyzed through the NEPA and NHPA processes. In addition, superintendents will comply with NPS solid waste regulations and other specific NPS requirements.

Proposed borrow pits and spoil areas outside parks will also be evaluated to ensure that use by the Service or its contractors does not impair resources or values inside the park, and that extraction operations comply with all applicable statutes and regulations, including the National Environmental Policy Act and National Historic Preservation Act.

(See Decision-making Requirements to Identify and Avoid Impairments 1.4.7; Geologic Resource Management 4.8; Nonfederally Owned Minerals 8.7.3; Revegetation and Landscaping 9.1.3.2)

9.1.4 Maintenance
9.1.4.1 General

There is a maintenance responsibility and cost for every asset that is administered by the National Park Service. A regular, periodic inventory and condition assessment of park assets will be performed to identify deficiencies and to ensure the cost-effective maintenance of all facilities. The costs of operation and the useful life of facilities and equipment are directly related to the type and level of maintenance provided. Therefore, the Service will conduct a program of preventive and rehabilitative maintenance and preservation to (1) provide a safe, sanitary, environmentally protective, and esthetically pleasing environment for park visitors and employees; (2) protect the physical integrity of facilities; and (3) preserve or maintain facilities in their optimum sustainable condition to the greatest extent possible. Preventive and rehabilitative maintenance programs will incorporate sustainable design elements and practices to ensure that water and energy efficiency, pollution prevention, and waste prevention and reduction are standard practice.

(Also see NPS Solid Waste Management Handbook; Executive Order 13101 (Greening the Government through Waste Prevention, Recycling, and Federal Acquisition); Executive Order 13148 (Greening the Government through Leadership in Environmental Management); Executive Order 13149 (Greening the Government through Federal Fleet and Transportation Efficiency); Executive Order 13327 (Federal Real Property Asset Management); and Director's Order #80: Asset Management)

9.1.4.2 Acquisition of Environmentally Preferable and Energy-Efficient Products

In carrying out its maintenance responsibilities, the Park Service will acquire environmentally preferable and energy-efficient products, as required by the Solid Waste Disposal Act, federal regulations, and executive orders, and will strive to meet and exceed any Department of the Interior affirmative acquisition goals that are established. The Service will consider a variety of attributes when purchasing products, including cost, energy efficiency, biodegradability, toxicity, recovered material content, packaging, transport cost, and other life-cycle environmental impacts, such as disposal. The Service will actively pursue opportunities to test and demonstrate environmentally preferable and energy-efficient products, consistent with its goal of demonstrating sustainable practices that avoid or minimize environmental impacts.

(See Environmental Leadership 1.8; Concession Operations 10.2.4. Also see Director's Order #13A: Environmental Management Systems)

9.1.5 Utilities

Energy, water, and wastewater systems will be sited outside park boundaries whenever possible. In-park utilities will be as unobtrusive as possible and have the least possible resource impact. The Service will use municipal or other utility systems outside parks whenever economically and environmentally practicable, and it may participate, when authorized, in cost-sharing with municipalities and others in meeting new, expanded, or replacement park utility needs. The Service will use the least polluting power supply options, either through on-site generation or through power purchases, where appropriate, available, and cost-effective, or where such purchase helps meet federal or state emissions goals or alternative energy goals.

(See Utilities and Services 10.2.6.4. Also see Director's Order #35A: Sale or Lease of Park Services, Resources, or Water in Support of Activities Outside the Boundaries of National Park Areas; and Director's Order #35B: Sale of National Park Service-produced Utilities)

9.1.5.1 Water Supply Systems

The National Park Service will use water efficiently and sustainably. Water systems will be designed to maximally conserve water and the energy used in its treatment and distribution. Water supply and delivery systems will be designed and maintained to provide sufficient water to operate fire sprinkler systems and fire hydrants. Water efficient devices will be installed in retrofitting structures and building new structures. New water systems, or extensions to existing systems, will be constructed only if reasonable conservation measures will not be sufficient to cover park needs. Where a new system or an expansion is justified, the system must be properly sized, and the available or projected water supply must be sufficient for expected needs. Where feasible and appropriate, and given resource availability, groundwater sources will generally be developed rather than surface water diversions in parks.

Water supply systems and their operators must comply with all applicable state and federal health standards. Outdoor use of water will be limited to those applications deemed essential to park operations or to protect park values. Consistent with native plant policies, the Service will use efficient methods for outdoor irrigation. Where appropriate, rainwater should be collected for uses such as maintenance of landscape features and general cleaning.

(See Water Resource Management 4.6; Campgrounds 9.3.2.1; Comfort Stations 9.3.3. Also see Director's Order #83: Public Health)

9.1.5.2 Wastewater Treatment Systems

New wastewater systems, or extensions or expansions of existing systems, will be constructed only if a determination has first been made that reasonable conservation measures will not be sufficient to cover park needs. In the selection of an appropriate method of wastewater treatment, factors such as all-season reliability, regulatory and public health issues, cost-effectiveness, and minimum adverse impact on the environment will all be considered. Alternatives to traditional methods may be used, especially in environmentally sensitive regions or in areas where water is in short supply. Where alternative technologies are used, such as composting toilets, there should be interpretation for visitors regarding the value of recycling organic solid waste. Wastewater will be adequately treated so that on its return to water courses or when recycled it meets or exceeds applicable state and federal water quality standards.

Water and wastewater systems and their operators are subject to state and federal health standards. Superintendents must ensure that operators are certified and that operations are inspected and conducted in accordance with all laws, regulations, and policies.

(See Water Resource Management 4.6; Campgrounds 9.3.2.1; Comfort Stations 9.3.3; Miscellaneous Management Facilities 9.4.5. Also see Director's Order #83: Public Health)

9.1.5.3 Utility Lines

Where feasible, NPS utility lines will be placed underground, except where such placement would cause significant damage to natural or cultural resources (such as historic structures or cultural landscapes). When placed aboveground, utility lines and appurtenant structures will be located and designed to minimize their impact on park resources and values. Whenever possible and visually acceptable, all utilities will share a common corridor and be combined with transportation corridors. Cost-effectiveness, reliability of service, and visual impact will be considered when deciding whether to install utility lines aboveground or underground. To minimize the impact of on-grid utility lines, consideration will be given to long-term, cost-effective, renewable-energy applications, such as the use of photovoltaic, wind, fuel cell, and/or bio-fuel technologies (either as stand-alones or as hybrid systems), particularly in remote areas.

(See Potential Wilderness 6.2.2.1)

9.1.5.4 Historic Utilities

Utilities that were present during the historic period will be managed as cultural resources and governed by the same policies as other cultural resources. Where current aboveground needs require upgraded lines and facilities, they will conform insofar as possible to the appearance and location of the historic utilities.

(See Treatment of Cultural Resources 5.3.5; Utility Lines 9.1.5.3)

9.1.6 Waste Management and Contaminant Issues

The National Park Service recognizes the far-reaching impacts that waste products, contaminants, and wasteful practices have, not only on national park resources, but also on biotic and abiotic resources elsewhere in the nation and around the world. The Service will therefore demonstrate environmental leadership and serve as a model for others to follow in managing wastes and contaminants.

9.1.6.1 Waste Management

The Service will implement solid and hazardous waste management practices that integrate waste reduction, reuse, and recycling programs to minimize the generation and disposal of solid and hazardous waste at and from NPS sites.

For purposes of this section, solid and hazardous wastes include any materials that are so defined in the Solid Waste Disposal Act, as amended. The Service will require the use of biodegradable materials, the reuse and recycling of materials, and other appropriate measures to minimize solid waste and conserve natural resources to the fullest extent possible. Innovation in the use of recyclable or reusable materials is encouraged. For example, the Service may encourage the remanufacturing of recyclable materials into acceptable sales items for willing markets, including the Park Service.

The disposal in parks of solid wastes generated by non-NPS activities is, in most cases, incompatible with national park values. All disposal of solid waste on lands and waters within the boundaries of a unit of the park system, whether federally or nonfederally owned, must comply with NPS regulations in 36 CFR Part 6, which implement Public Law 98-506 (16 USC 460l-22(c)). These regulations are designed to ensure that all activities associated with the operation of solid waste disposal sites within the boundaries of national park units are conducted in a manner that will (1) prevent the deterioration of air and water quality; (2) prevent the degradation of natural and cultural resources; and (3) reduce adverse effects on visitor enjoyment. In accordance with the spirit and intent of these requirements, the Park Service will, to the extent practicable, avoid the use of park lands for landfills by such means as (1) implementing waste minimization and substitution practices, (2) diverting material to recycling facilities or other appropriate locations, and (3) using storage or treatment facilities that meet or exceed DOI and all legal and regulatory standards for any generated waste that is not diverted.

The Park Service will remove landfill operations and associated impacts from parks where feasible. Cooperative waste management solutions that minimize adverse impacts on park resources are also encouraged for areas where alternatives to landfilling are scarce for both parks and adjacent communities.

Open burning for solid waste disposal will not be permitted in parks, except in the very limited circumstances described in Director's Order #18: Wildland Fire Management.

Any hazardous waste that the Service generates will be disposed of separately from solid waste, in full accord with all applicable legal requirements.

(See Air Quality 4.7.1; River Use 8.2.2.3; Backcountry Use 8.2.2.4; Miscellaneous Management Facilities 9.4.5. Also see Director's Order #18: Wildland Fire Management; Director's Order #30A: Damage Assessments)

9.1.6.2 NPS Response to Contaminants

The Service will make every reasonable effort to prevent or minimize the release of contaminants on or that will affect NPS lands or resources, and the Service will take all necessary actions to control or minimize such releases when they occur. For purposes of this section, contaminants include any substance that may pose a risk to NPS resources or is regulated or governed by statutes referenced in this subsection. Prevention and minimization will include, but not be limited to, (1) the acquisition, use, and selection of non-toxic or less toxic materials; (2) implementation of safe use, storage, and disposal practices; (3) recycling of spent materials; (4) implementation of effective hazard communication programs for employees, contractors, concessioners, and visitors; (5) development and extension of appropriate emergency response programs; and (6) ensuring that parties responsible for contamination or threatened contamination of NPS property bear the responsibility for addressing such contamination.

Activities pertaining to contaminants, including response actions or handling, acquisition, storage, transportation, and disposal of such substances, will comply with federal, state, and local laws and regulations including, but not limited to, (1) the Solid Waste Disposal Act, including the Resource Conservation and Recovery Act of 1976 and the Hazardous and Solid Waste Amendments of 1984, as amended; (2) the Comprehensive Environmental Response, Compensation and Liability Act of 1980; (3) the Oil Pollution Act of 1990; (4) the Clean Water Act; (4) the Hazardous Materials Transportation Act; and (5) the Toxic Substances Control Act. Such activities will also comply with the NPS integrated pest management program.

The Service will identify, assess, and take response actions as promptly as possible to address releases and threatened releases of contaminants into the environment. Each park will have an oil and chemical spill response management plan for spills that result from NPS activities or from activities that are beyond NPS control (such as commercial through-traffic on roads that pass through a park). The plans will place first priority on responder and public safety. Employees will not be permitted to respond to hazardous materials spills unless they are properly qualified and certified in accordance with Director's Order #30B: Hazardous Spill Response.

The Service will take affirmative and aggressive action to ensure that all NPS costs and damages associated with the release of contaminants are borne by those responsible for the contamination of NPS property. In addition, when lands are proposed for acquisition by the Park Service, the Service will take steps to avoid or minimize its liability for the contamination of NPS property caused by other parties. The Service will include in the preacquisition environmental assessment process the identification of recognizable environmental conditions, such as those associated with prior or existing commercial facilities, mining sites, and landfills. Any recognizable existing or potential environmental contamination of lands proposed for inclusion in a park will be brought to the attention of the regional director as soon as they are identified.

(See Criteria for Inclusion 1.3; Chapter 3: Land Protection; Pest Management 4.4.5; Emergency Preparedness and Emergency Operations 8.2.5.2. Also see Director's Orders #25: Land Protection; #30A: Damage Assessments; #30B: Hazardous Spill Response)

9.1.7 Energy Management

The National Park Service will conduct its activities in ways that use energy wisely and economically. Park resources and values will not be degraded to provide energy for NPS purposes. The Service will adhere to all federal policies governing energy and water efficiency, renewable resources, use of alternative fuels, and federal fleet goals as established in the Energy Policy Act of 1992. The Service will also comply with applicable executive orders, including Executive Order 13123 (Greening the Government through Efficient Energy Management), and Executive Order 13149 (Greening the Government through Federal Fleet and Transportation Efficiency).

All facilities, vehicles, and equipment will be operated and managed to minimize the consumption of energy, water, and nonrenewable fuels. Full consideration will be given to the use of alternative fuels. Alternative transportation programs and the use of bio-based fuels will be encouraged, where appropriate. Renewable sources of energy and new developments in energy-efficiency technology, including products from the recycling of materials and waste, will be used where appropriate and cost-effective over the life cycle. However, energy efficiencies will not be pursued if they will cause adverse impacts on park resources and values.

To conserve energy, park personnel and visitors may be provided with opportunities for in-park public transportation or trails and walks for nonmotorized transport. As an environmental leader, the Service will interpret for the public the overall resource protection benefits from the efficient use of energy, and will actively educate and motivate park personnel and visitors to use sustainable practices in conserving energy. The Service will also pursue partnership efforts with the Department of Energy and others to further develop and meet NPS energy conservation goals.

(See Air Quality 4.7.1; Lightscape Management 4.10; Resource Issue Interpretation and Education 7.5.3; Maintenance 9.1.4; Transportation Systems and Alternative Transportation 9.2; Trails and Walks 9.2.2; Sustainable Energy Design 9.1.1.6. Also see Director's Order #13A: Environmental Management Systems)

9.1.8 Structural Fire Protection and Suppression

Superintendents will manage structural fire activities as part of a comprehensive interdisciplinary effort to protect resources and promote the safe and appropriate public enjoyment of those resources. Fire prevention, protection, and suppression will be primary considerations in the design, construction, rehabilitation, maintenance, and operation of all facilities. Structural fires will be suppressed to prevent the loss of human life and minimize damage to property and resources. The Service's structural fire protection and suppression program will provide, through Director's Order #58: Structural Fire Management and Reference Manual 58, additional policy, standards, operational procedures, and accountability to meet the diverse needs and complexities of individual park units. The goal is to ensure that all national park areas receive an appropriate level of fire protection that is provided in a safe and cost-effective manner by qualified personnel.

Each superintendent will complete a structural fire assessment and develop a structural fire plan to meet park needs. Structural fire protection and suppression capabilities will be maintained in accordance with those plans. Prevention priorities will focus on occupied structures and cultural resources, with emphasis placed evenly on code compliance, early warning detection, suppression systems, and employee training and awareness.

Fire prevention through code-compliant new construction, upgrading of existing structures, standardized and regularly scheduled fire inspections, and properly installed and maintained detection and suppression systems will be the primary means of addressing and correcting NPS structural fire deficiencies. Where these measures are not sufficient to meet park needs, agreements will be entered into with non-NPS entities capable of providing requisite fire suppression assistance. Support from neighboring fire protection organizations is encouraged, and superintendents should enter into appropriate agreements whenever possible to enhance fire-fighting capabilities. Development of a park fire brigade will be considered only when all other options have been explored and found unacceptable.

(See Fire Management 4.5; Fire Detection, Suppression, and Postfire Rehabilitation and Protection 5.3.1.2; Water Supply Systems 9.1.5.1. Also see Director's Order #58: Structural Fire Management)

9.2 Transportation Systems and Alternative Transportation

The location, type, and design of transportation systems and their components (e.g., roads, bridges, trails, and parking areas), and the use of alternative transportation systems, all strongly influence the quality of the visitor experience. These systems also affect, to a great degree, how and where park resources will be impacted. For these reasons, management decisions regarding transportation facilities require a full, interdisciplinary consideration of alternatives and a full understanding of their consequences. Traditional practices of building wider roads and larger parking areas to accommodate more motor vehicles are not necessarily the answer. The Service must find transportation solutions that will preserve the natural and cultural resources in its care while providing a high-quality visitor experience.

Early NPS participation in transportation studies and planning processes is crucial to the long-term strategy of working closely with other federal agencies; tribal, state and local governments; regional planning bodies; citizen groups; and others to enhance partnering and funding opportunities. The Service will participate in all transportation planning forums that may result in links to parks or impacts on park resources. Working with federal, tribal, state, and local agencies on transportation issues, the Service will seek reasonable access to parks and connections to external transportation systems. The Service will also advocate corridor crossings for terrestrial and aquatic wildlife and other accommodations to promote biodiversity and avoid or mitigate (1) harm to individual animals, (2) the fragmentation of plant and animal habitats, and (3) the disruption of natural systems.

Depending on a park unit's size, location, resources, and level of use, the Service will, where appropriate, emphasize and encourage alternative transportation systems, which may include a mix of buses, trains, ferries, trams, and—preferably—nonmotorized modes of access to and moving within parks. In general, the preferred modes of transportation will be those that contribute to maximum visitor enjoyment of, and minimum adverse impacts on, park resources and values.

Before a decision is made to design, construct, expand, or upgrade access to or within a park, nonconstruction alternatives—such as distributing visitors to alternative locations—must be fully explored. If nonconstruction alternatives will not achieve satisfactory results, then a development solution should consider whether the project

- is appropriate and necessary to meet park management needs or to provide for visitor use and enjoyment;
- is designed with extreme care and sensitivity to the landscape through which it passes;
- will not cause unacceptable impacts on natural and cultural resources and will minimize or mitigate those impacts that cannot be avoided;
- will reduce traffic congestion, noise, air pollution, and adverse effects on park resources and values;
- will not cause use in the areas it serves to exceed the areas' visitor carrying capacities;
- will incorporate the principles of energy conservation and sustainability;
- is able to demonstrate financial and operational sustainability;
- will incorporate universal design principles to provide for accessibility for all people, including those with disabilities;
- will take maximum advantage of interpretive opportunities and scenic values;
- will not violate federal, state, or local air pollution control plans or regulations;
- is based on a comprehensive and multidisciplinary approach that is fully consistent with the park's general management plan and asset management plan;
- will enhance the visitor experience by offering new or improved interpretive or recreational opportunities, by simplifying travel within the park, or by making it easier or safer to see park features.

All transportation systems may be considered conceptually. Before advancing beyond the conceptual stage, appropriate approvals must be obtained from the Director.

If a decision is made to construct, expand, or reconstruct a park transportation system, the Service will address the need for terrestrial and aquatic wildlife corridor crossings and other accommodations to avoid or mitigate harm to individual animals, the fragmentation of plant and animal habitats, and the disruption of natural systems.

(See Environmental Leadership 1.8; General Management Planning 2.3.1; Implementation Planning 2.3.4; Air Quality 4.7.1; General 9.1; Accessibility for Persons with Disabilities 9.1.2; Energy Management 9.1.7. Also see Director's Orders #87A: Park Roads and Parkways; #87B: Alternative Transportation Systems; #87C: Transportation System Funding; #87D: Non-NPS Roads)

9.2.1 Road Systems
9.2.1.1 Park Roads

Park roads will be well constructed, sensitive to natural and cultural resources, reflect the highest principles of park design, and enhance the visitor experience. Park roads are generally not intended to provide fast and convenient transportation; rather, they are intended to enhance the quality of a visit while providing for safe and efficient travel with minimal or no impacts on natural and cultural resources. For most parks, a road system is already in place. When plans for meeting the transportation needs of these parks are updated, a determination must be made as to whether the road system should be maintained as is, reduced, expanded, reoriented, eliminated, or supplemented by other means of travel. Before roads are chronically at or near capacity, the use of alternative destination points or transportation systems or limitations on use will be considered as alternatives to road expansion.

Park road designs are subject to NPS Park Road Standards, which are adaptable to each park's unique character and resource limitations. Although some existing roads do not meet current engineering standards, they may be important cultural resources whose values can and should be preserved with attention to visitor safety.

(Also see Director's Order #87A: Park Roads and Parkways)

9.2.1.2 Non-NPS Roads

Many parks contain roads that were not constructed by the Park Service and may not be under NPS jurisdiction. Most often, these roads existed before the areas became part of the national park system, and the Park Service must rely heavily on tribal, state, or local authorities to maintain the roads consistent with park management goals. These other government authorities sometimes propose to expand an existing road or construct a new road within a park, with significant potential for adversely affecting park resources and values. Superintendents must consider road proposals in strict accordance with section 9.2.1.2.2, and Director's Order #87D: Non-NPS Federal Aid Roads. Where practicable, and after concurrence of the entity with road jurisdiction, non-NPS roads that are no longer needed will be closed or removed, and the area will be restored to a natural condition. The Service will not permit the public or private construction of new roads for access to inholdings unless specifically authorized by law.

Access to inholdings in Alaska will be managed in accordance with the provisions of section 1110(b) of the Alaska National Interest Lands Conservation Act (16 USC 3170 (b)) and 43 CFR Part 36.

(See General 8.6.4.1)

9.2.1.2.1 Existing Commercial and Other Through-Traffic

The Service will work with appropriate governments and private organizations and individuals to minimize the impacts of traffic on park resources and values. Whenever possible, commercial traffic will be prohibited on roads within parks, except for the purpose of serving park visitors and park operations. However, in accordance with section 8.6.5 and applicable NPS regulations (36 CFR 5.6)

- superintendents will permit commercial vehicles to use park roads when necessary for access to private lands within or adjacent to a park area to which access is otherwise not available; and

- superintendents may issue permits for commercial vehicle traffic to pass through the park in emergencies.

When a determination is made that existing through-traffic routes have adverse impacts on park resources and values, the Service will work with the appropriate government authorities to minimize these impacts, or to have the traffic flow rerouted over an alternative route. Where feasible and practicable, roads that are no longer needed will be closed or removed, and the area will be restored to a natural condition.

9.2.1.2.2 Construction and Expansion Proposals

Superintendents must take an active role in overall community and transportation planning activities to educate all parties about the NPS mandate to protect park resources. The Park Service will work closely with the U. S. Department of Transportation and state departments of transportation when new highways or roads or expansions of existing road corridors that may impact park lands are proposed. In accordance with 23 USC 138 and the Organic Act, the Service will object to any proposal to route a state or local road through national park lands, or to increase the size of a right-of-way for an existing road, unless the Service first determines (or concurs with a DOT determination) the following:

- There is no feasible and prudent alternative.

- All possible planning has taken place to minimize and mitigate harm to the park.

- It will not be contrary to the public interest, or inconsistent with the purposes for which the park was established.

- It will not cause health and safety risks to visitors or park staff.

- It will conform to NPS standards and practices for road design, engineering, and construction.

In making these determinations, the Service will take into account the factors listed in section 9.2.

Responsibility for future maintenance—meeting NPS standards—must be identified before NPS approval of a proposal.

(Also see Director's Order #87D: Non-NPS Roads)

9.2.2 Trails and Walks

Trails and walks provide the only means of access into many areas within parks. These facilities will be planned and developed as integral parts of each park's transportation system and incorporate principles of universal design. Trails and walks will serve as management tools to help control the distribution and intensity of use. All trails and walks will be carefully situated, designed, and managed to

- reduce conflicts with automobiles and incompatible uses;

- allow for a satisfying park experience;

- allow accessibility by the greatest number of people; and

- protect park resources.

Heavily used trails and walks in developed areas may be surfaced as necessary for visitor safety, accessibility for persons with impaired mobility, resource protection, and/or erosion control. Surface materials should be carefully selected, taking into account factors such as the purpose and location of a trail or walk and the potential for erosion and other environmental impacts.

The visitor use and management aspects of trails and walks are addressed in section 8.2.2, "Recreational Activities." In addition, trail planning will take into account NPS interest in cooperating with federal, state, local, and tribal governments, as well as individuals and organizations, to advance the goal of a seamless networks of parks. These partnership activities are intended to establish corridors that link together, both physically and with a common sense of purpose, open spaces such as those found in parks, other protected areas, and compatibly managed private lands.

(See Cooperative Conservation Beyond Park Boundaries 1.6; Chapter 7: Interpretation and Education; Accessibility for Persons with Disabilities 9.1.2. Also see Director's Order #42: Accessibility for Visitors with Disabilities in National Park Service Programs and Services)

9.2.2.1 Cooperative Trail Planning

The Park Service will cooperate with other land managers, nonprofit organizations, and user groups to facilitate local and regional trail access to parks. When parks abut other public lands, the Service will participate in interagency, multi-jurisdictional trail planning. When an effective trail system exists, and when otherwise permitted, hostels or similar low-cost overnight facilities may be provided if they are consistent with the park's general management plan and harmonize with the natural and/or cultural resources.

(See Hostels and Shelters 9.3.2.3)

9.2.2.2 Hiking Trails

Trail design will vary to accommodate a wide range of users and be appropriate to user patterns and site conditions. Wetlands will generally be avoided, and where possible they will be spanned by a boardwalk or other means, using sustainable materials that will not disturb hydrologic or ecological processes. Backcountry trails will offer visitors a primitive outdoor experience, and these trails will be unsurfaced and modest in character except where a more durable surface is needed. The use of nonnative materials is generally not permitted on backcountry trails.

(See Trails in Wilderness 6.3.10.2; General Policy 6.4.1; Backcountry Use 8.2.2.4)

9.2.2.3 Equestrian Trails

Equestrian trails and related support facilities, such as feed boxes and hitch rails, may be provided when they are consistent with park objectives and when site conditions are suitable. Horse camps should be designed with user interest in mind and consistency with NPS policy. Photovoltaic systems should be evaluated to power any necessary water systems. Ramps for mounting the animals must be provided for persons with disabilities.

(See Grazing and Livestock Driveways 6.4.7; Domestic and Feral Livestock 8.6.8; Accessibility of Commercial Services 10.2.6.2)

9.2.2.4 Bicycle Trails

Bicycle routes may be considered as an alternative to motor vehicle access. Bicycle travel may be integrated with park roads when determined to be safe and feasible. Bicycle trails may be paved or stabilized for the protection of resources and for the safety and convenience of travelers. In accordance with 36 CFR 4.30, bicycle use is allowed on park roads, in parking areas, and on routes designated for bicycle use. The designation of bicycle routes is allowed in developed areas and in special use zones based on a written determination that such use is (1) consistent with the protection of a park's natural, cultural, scenic, and esthetic values; (2) consistent with safety considerations; (3) consistent with management objectives; and (4) will not disturb wildlife or other park resources. A similar determination may be made to designate routes outside developed areas and special use zones; however, the designation must be made by promulgating a special regulation.

(See General Policy 6.4.1; Backcountry Use 8.2.2.4. Also see 36 CFR 4.30)

9.2.2.5 Water Trails

Water access and use may be provided when consistent with resource protection needs. Appropriate locations and levels of use will be determined in the park's general management plan. The Park Service will work with other agencies and organizations, as appropriate, to develop and provide education and interpretation for water trails that access parks; to promote understanding and enjoyment; and to protect waterways and adjacent lands.

9.2.2.6 Interpretive Trails

Interpretive trails and walks, both guided and self-guiding, may be used for purposes of visitor appreciation and understanding of park values.

9.2.2.7 National Trails

Several components of the National Trails System which are administered by the Service, have been designated as units of the national park system. These trails are therefore managed as national park areas and are subject to all the policies contained herein, as well as to any other requirements specified in the National Trails System Act.

Other scenic, historic, connecting/side, and recreational trails designated under the National Trails System Act are in or adjacent to park units. Some of these may also be administered by the Service, though not as units of the national park system. In all cases, the Service will cooperate with other land managers, nonprofit organizations, and user groups to facilitate appropriate trail use in accordance with the laws and policies applicable to such trails, and to the extent that trail management and use would not cause unacceptable impacts.

(See Cooperative Conservation Beyond Park Boundaries 1.6. Also see Director's Order #45-1: National Scenic and Historic Trails; National Trails System Act)

9.2.2.8 Trailheads

Trailheads, and trail access points from which trail use can begin, will be carefully tied into other elements of the park development and circulation system to facilitate safe and enjoyable trail use and efficient management.

9.2.2.9 Trail Bridges

Trail bridges may be used for crossing swift waters areas prone to flash-flooding, and other places that present potential safety hazards. Less obtrusive alternatives to bridges (such as, fords) and trail relocation will be considered before a decision is made to build a bridge. A bridge may be the preferred alternative when necessary to prevent stream bank erosion or protect wetlands or fisheries. If a bridge is determined to be appropriate, it will be kept to the minimum size needed to serve trail users, and it will be designed to harmonize with the surrounding natural scene and be as unobtrusive as possible.

(See Water Resource Management 4.6)

9.2.3 Traffic Signs and Markings

Signs will be limited to the minimum necessary to meet information, warning, and regulatory needs and to avoid confusion and visual intrusion. Signs should be planned to provide a pleasing, uniform appearance. Traffic signs and pavement markings on park roads will be consistent with the standards contained in the Manual on Uniform Traffic Control Devices, as supplemented by the NPS Sign Manual. All roadside signs and markings will conform to good traffic engineering practices. Park signs—especially those that display the NPS arrowhead—are an important part of the total identity system for the Park Service and must conform to the standards contained in Director's Order #52C: Park Signs.

(See Navigation Aids 9.2.5; Signs 9.3.1.1)

9.2.4 Parking Areas

Parking areas and overlooks will be located to not unacceptably intrude, by sight, sound, or other impact, on park resources or values. When parking areas are deemed necessary, they will be limited to the smallest size appropriate, and they will be designed to harmoniously accommodate motor vehicles and other appropriate users. When large parking areas are needed, appropriate plantings and other design elements will be used to reduce negative visual and environmental impacts. When overflow parking is provided to meet peak visitation, it should be in areas that have been stabilized or are otherwise capable of withstanding the temporary impacts of parking without causing unacceptable impacts on park resources. Permanent parking areas will not normally be sized for the peak use day, but rather for the use anticipated on the average weekend day during the peak season of use.

(See Management of Native Plants and Animals 4.4.2; General 9.1; Transportation Systems and Alternative Transportation 9.2)

9.2.5 Navigation Aids

Necessary aircraft and water navigation aids will be planned in collaboration with the Federal Aviation Administration and U. S. Coast Guard, respectively, and will be installed, maintained, and used in conformance with the standards established by these agencies only if there are no appropriate alternatives outside park boundaries. Exceptions to the standards may be authorized when necessary to meet specific park and public safety needs, provided the exceptions are jointly agreed to by the Park Service and the agency having primary jurisdiction.

(See Overflights and Aviation Uses 8.4; Traffic Signs and Markings 9.2.3)

9.3 Visitor Facilities

While striving for excellence in visitor services, the Park Service will limit visitor facility development to that which is necessary and appropriate. Facilities like gas stations and grocery stores may be necessary to park use and enjoyment, but it does not necessarily follow that these facilities must be located inside a park. The Park Service will encourage the development of private sector visitor services in gateway communities to contribute to local economic development, encourage competition, increase choices for visitors, and minimize the need for in-park facilities. When visitor facilities are found to be necessary and appropriate within a park, they will be designed, built, and maintained in accordance with accepted NPS standards for quality and the NPS commitment to visitor satisfaction.

9.3.1 Informational and Interpretive Facilities

Informational and interpretive facilities may be provided to assist park visitors in appreciating and enjoying the park and understanding its significance, provided that the facilities can be developed without impairing the park's natural or cultural resources.

(See Chapter 7: Interpretation and Education; Accessibility for Persons with Disabilities 9.1.2)

9.3.1.1 Signs

Signs will be carefully planned and designed to fulfill their important roles of conveying an appropriate NPS and park image and providing information and orientation to visitors. Each park should have an approved parkwide sign plan based on Service-wide design criteria and tailored to meet individual park needs. Entrance and other key signs will be distinctively designed to reflect the character of the park while meeting Service-wide standards for consistency.

Signs will be held to the minimum number, size, and wording required to serve their intended functions and to minimally intrude upon the natural and historic settings. They will be placed where they do not interfere with park visitors' enjoyment and appreciation of park resources. Roadside information signs are subject to the standards established in the National Park Service Sign Manual. Interpretive signs will be guided by sign and wayside exhibit plans.

(See Signs 6.3.10.4; Visitor Safety 8.2.5.1; Traffic Signs and Markings 9.2.3; Navigation Aids 9.2.5. Also see Director's Order #52C: Park Signs)

9.3.1.2 Entrance Stations

Entrance and fee collection stations will be harmonious with the park environment, and these stations should reflect the architectural character of the park. Entrance and fee collection stations should (1) reasonably accommodate the average peak season visitor traffic, (2) incorporate best available technology, and (3) use best management practices to minimize delays—thus reducing vehicle emissions at the entrance station and enhancing the visitor experience.

9.3.1.3 Visitor Centers

When necessary to provide visitor information and interpretive services, visitor centers may be constructed at locations identified in approved plans. To minimize visual intrusions and impacts on major park features, visitor centers will generally not be located near such features. Where an in-park location would create unacceptable environmental impacts, authorization should be obtained to place a visitor center outside the park.

Visitor centers are not substitutes for personal or self-guiding on-site interpretation. They will be constructed only when it has been determined that indoor media are the most effective means of communicating major elements of the park story and that a central public contact point is needed.

As appropriate, a visitor center may include information services, sales of educational materials and theme-related items, audiovisual programs, museums, museum collections storage, exhibits, and other staffed or self-help programs and spaces necessary for a high-quality visitor experience. Additionally, the need for restrooms, drinking fountains, and other basic visitor requirements will be considered during the planning and design stage. The size and scope of all visitor centers will be evaluated using the Visitor Center Planning Model or similar tool before submitting any visitor center project to the Director for approval.

(See Park Management 1.4; Environmental Leadership 1.8; Nonpersonal Services 7.3.2; Integration of Facilities into the Park Environment 9.1.1.2; Accessibility for Persons with Disabilities 9.1.2; Museum Collections Management Facilities 9.4.2)

9.3.1.4 Amphitheaters

Amphitheaters may be provided in campgrounds and in other locations where formal interpretive programs are desirable. Campfire circles may be provided in campgrounds to accommodate evening programs and informal social gatherings. Artificial lighting must be carefully directed and kept to a minimum, with due regard for natural night sky conditions.

(See Lightscape Management 4.10; Campgrounds 9.3.2.1)

9.3.1.5 Wayside Exhibits

Wayside exhibits may be provided along roads and heavily used walks and trails to interpret on-site resources.

(See Nonpersonal Services 7.3.2)

9.3.1.6 Viewing Devices

Viewing devices, such as pedestal binoculars or telescopes, may be provided at appropriate locations when the superintendent determines that such devices are desirable for the meaningful interpretation or understanding of park resources. Such devices may be provided by the Service or by others under a concession contract or commercial use authorization.

9.3.1.7 Facilities for Arts and Culture

Various cultural events (such as concerts, films, lectures, plays, craft shows, and art exhibits) are permitted when they will support a park's purposes and objectives. However, permanent facilities may be built specifically for cultural activities only when all of the following criteria are met:

◆ The permanent facility is required for programs of major importance in conveying the park story.

◆ It would be impossible or impractical to use demountable or temporary facilities.

◆ It would be impossible to adaptively use other park facilities.

◆ Neither the facility nor its operation would impair cultural or natural resources or hinder the use of the park for its intended purposes.

◆ It would not be feasible for others outside the park to provide the facility.

(See Use of Historic Structures 5.3.5.4.7; Special Events 8.6.2)

9.3.2 Overnight Accommodations and Food Services

Overnight facilities and food services will be restricted to the kinds and levels necessary and appropriate to achieve each park's purposes. In many cases, overnight accommodations and food services are not needed within a park. In general, they should be provided only when the private sector or other public agencies cannot adequately provide them in the park vicinity. However, in-park facilities or services may be justified when the distance and travel time to accommodations and services outside the park are too great to permit reasonable use, or when leaving the park to obtain incidental services would substantially detract from the quality of the visitor experience. Certain activities, such as backcountry use, may require overnight stays. Types of overnight accommodations may vary from unimproved backcountry campsites to motel- or hotel-type lodging, as appropriate. Commercial facilities run by concessioners are addressed in greater detail in chapter 10.

(See Accessibility for Persons with Disabilities 9.1.2; Commercial Visitor Services Planning 10.2.2)

9.3.2.1 Campgrounds

When campgrounds are determined to be necessary, their design will accommodate the differences between recreation-vehicle camping and tent camping, and cultural landscapes, terrain, soils, vegetation, wildlife, climate, special needs of users, visual and auditory privacy, and other relevant factors will be considered.

The Service will determine the range of amenities and utility hookups that are appropriate to each campground based on the park's mission, campground location and size, availability of commercial campgrounds in the area, cost of installing and maintaining the amenities and utilities, and other considerations. To eliminate the need for generators, electric utilities may be provided on a limited basis. Shower facilities may be provided where feasible. Modestly sized play areas for small children are permissible, as are informal areas for field sports associated with organized group camps. Wood fires in fire rings are generally permissible; however, whenever it is necessary to restrict such fires at individual campsites because of fire danger, air pollution, or other hazards, alternatives may be provided or allowed—such as facilities for the use of charcoal or other fuels or central cook sheds. When a need exists, sanitary dump stations will be provided in or near campgrounds that accommodate recreation vehicles.

When necessary for basic safety requirements, pathways and the exteriors of buildings and structures may be lighted. Such lighting will be energy efficient and shielded as much as possible so that visitors have the opportunity to experience the natural darkness and night skies.

Campgrounds intended to accommodate large recreation vehicles or buses will be located only where existing roads can safely accommodate such vehicles and the resulting increased traffic load.

No campground will exceed 250 sites unless a larger number of sites has been approved by the Director.

When desirable for purposes of management, tent camping may be accommodated in separate campgrounds or in separately designated areas within campgrounds. Provision may also be made for accommodating organized groups in separate campgrounds or in separately designated areas.

Boating campgrounds may be provided in parks with waters used for recreational boating. The need for campgrounds—and their sizes, locations, and numbers—will be determined by (1) the type of water body (for example, river, lake, reservoir, saltwater); (2) the availability and resiliency of potential campsites; (3) the feasibility of providing and maintaining docking, beaching, mooring, camping, and sanitary facilities; and (4) the potential for unacceptable impacts on park resources or values.

(See Soundscape Management 4.9; Lightscape Management 4.10; Recreation Fees 8.2.6.1; National Recreation Reservation Service 8.2.6.2; Collecting Natural Products 8.8; Water Supply Systems 9.1.5.1; Wastewater Treatment Systems 9.1.5.2; Concession Facilities 10.2.6. Also see Director's Order #47: Soundscape Preservation and Noise Management; Director's Order #83: Public Health)

9.3.2.2 Backcountry Campsites

Backcountry and wilderness campsites may be permitted, but only within the acceptable limits of use determined by the park's wilderness management plan, resource management plan, or other pertinent planning document.

(See Wilderness Use Management 6.4; Backcountry Use 8.2.2.4)

9.3.2.3 Hostels and Shelters

Hostels are low-cost, supervised accommodations that encourage and facilitate the energy-efficient, nonmotorized enjoyment of parks and their surrounding regions by individuals and families. Such facilities, along with hostel-like accommodations such as huts and shelters, will be considered in the planning process if overnight use is determined to be an appropriate use of the park, particularly as a means of encouraging and facilitating the use of trails and backcountry areas. The Service will cooperate with other agencies, nonprofit organizations, park concessioners, and others to plan and develop hostels, where appropriate. If a decision is reached to develop a hostel accommodation, it will be managed by others under the provisions of concession policies and procedures.

Hostels will, at a minimum, contain sheltered overnight accommodations and sanitary facilities, and they will usually contain cooking, eating, and recreation spaces. Hostels may be used for other park programs, such as environmental education or interpretation. Although nonmotorized access to hostels is emphasized, motorized transportation may also be available.

(See Facility Planning and Design 9.1.1; Chapter 10: Commercial Visitor Services)

9.3.3 Comfort Stations

Comfort facilities will have waste disposal systems that meet Public Health Service standards. Levels of use will determine the size and nature of the utility systems provided. Low-water use or waterless (oil and composting) toilets will be considered in locations where there are water-supply and wastewater-disposal problems. Chemical toilets in portable enclosures may be used for temporary purposes when necessary. Vault toilets and composting toilets that meet public health standards may be used where development or expansion of utilities may not be practical or cost-effective. Pit privies that meet public health standards may suffice in areas of infrequent use and when utility services are not readily available.

(See General Policy 6.4.1; Backcountry Use 8.2.2.4; Accessibility for Persons with Disabilities 8.2.4; Water Supply Systems 9.1.5.1; Wastewater Treatment Systems 9.1.5.2; Campgrounds 9.3.2.1. Also see Director's Order #83: Public Health)

9.3.4 Other Visitor Facilities

Other visitor facilities may be provided when necessary for visitor enjoyment of the area and when consistent with the protection of park values. Visitor facilities determined to be detrimental to park resources or values will not be permitted.

9.3.4.1 Picnic and Other Day Use Areas

Picnic areas and other day use areas to be used for specific purposes (such as play areas) may be provided on a limited basis as appropriate to meet existing visitor needs.

9.3.4.2 Facilities for Water Recreation

Boating facilities (such as access points, courtesy docks, boat ramps, floating sewage pump-out stations, navigational aids, and marinas), breakwaters, and fish cleaning stations may be provided as appropriate for the safe enjoyment by visitors of water recreation resources, when (1) they are consistent with the purposes for which the park was established, and (2) there is no possibility that adequate private facilities will be developed. Facilities must be carefully sited and designed to avoid unacceptable adverse effects on aquatic and riparian habitats and minimize conflicts between boaters and other visitors who enjoy use of the park. A decision to develop water-based facilities must take into account not only the primary impacts (such as noise, air, and water pollution) of the development, but also the secondary impacts (including cumulative effects over time) that recreational use associated with the development may have on park resources and visitor enjoyment.

(See Park Management 1.4; Soundscape Management 4.9; Visitor Use 8.2; River Use 8.2.2.3; Fishing 8.2.2.5; Campgrounds 9.3.2.1; Water Trails 9.2.2.5. Also see Director's Order #47: Soundscape Preservation and Noise Management)

9.3.4.3 Skiing Facilities

The Park Service will not permit new downhill skiing facilities or associated structures in any unit of the national park system. Downhill skiing is an activity that requires extensive development with resulting significant environmental impacts, and it should only be provided outside park areas. When such facilities have been provided based on previous policy, their use may continue unless the development and use have caused or may cause impairment of park resources or values. Any proposal to eliminate or change the capacity of existing facilities will be accomplished through the NPS planning process, and will involve public participation and an environmental assessment of impacts.

(See Decision-making Requirements to Identify and Avoid Impairments 1.4.7; Recreational Activities 8.2.2)

9.3.5 Advertising

Commercial notices or advertisements will generally not be displayed, posted, or distributed on the federally owned or federally controlled land, water, or airspace of a park. A superintendent may permit advertising only if the notice or advertisement is for goods, services, or facilities available within the park, and if such notices and advertisements are found to be desirable and necessary for the convenience and guidance of the public. Acceptable forms of advertising will be addressed, as necessary, in concession contracts and cooperating association agreements.

Billboard advertising will in no case be permitted within a park and, in general, will be discouraged on approach roads outside of parks when it would adversely affect a park's scenic values.

NPS policy allows donor recognition, which occurs when the Park Service publicly thanks an individual, corporation, or some other entity for their gift or service to the Park Service. Such recognition must be consistent with the provisions of Director's Order #21: Donations and Fundraising.

In accordance with Part 470 of the DOI manual, the Service will not use paid advertising in any publication in connection with its programs and activities, except where special legal requirements and authority exist. If a superintendent believes paid advertising is necessary because of the significant benefits it affords in enhancing public participation, prior approval must be obtained from the Washington Office of Public Affairs.

(See Cooperating Associations 7.6.2; Concession Contracting 10.2.3. Also see Director's Order #21: Donations and Fundraising, 36 CFR 5.1)

9.4 Management Facilities

Where authorized by Congress, management facilities will be located outside park boundaries whenever the management functions being served can be adequately supported from such a location. When management facilities must be located inside the park, they will be located away from primary resources and features of the park and sited so as to not adversely affect park resources or values or detract from the visitor experience. Historic properties will be used to the maximum extent practicable, provided that the use will not affect their significance.

Modular, precut, or prefabricated structures may be used for management facilities, including administrative offices, employee housing, and maintenance structures, when products meeting design requirements are available. Standard plans will be modified to (1) reflect regional and park design themes and harmonize with the natural surroundings; (2) preserve the natural and cultural environments; (3) provide for resource conservation; (4) provide for energy efficiency or the use of renewable energy sources; (5) limit chemical emissions; and (6) foster education about sustainable design.

(See Park Management 1.4; Environmental Leadership 1.8; Use of Historic Structures 5.3.5.4.7; Accessibility for Persons with Disabilities 8.2.4; Facility Planning and Design 9.1.1; Accessibility for Persons with Disabilities 9.1.2. Also see Director's Orders #89: Acquisition and Management of Leased Space; and #90: Value Analysis)

9.4.1 Administrative Offices

The location of administrative offices will be determined by conditions specific to each park, including impacts on park resources, availability and adequacy of leasable space outside the park, relationship to adjacent communities, convenience to visitors, weather, energy consumption, comparative costs, commuting distance for employees, and management effectiveness.

(See Facility Planning and Design 9.1.1; Energy Management 9.1.7)

9.4.2 Museum Collections Management Facilities

Park curatorial facilities should be adapted to the needs of each park. They may share space in visitor centers or administrative office buildings, or be housed in completely separate buildings. Incorporation with facilities in which there would be a heightened danger of fire, chemical spills, and similar accidents should be avoided. Curatorial facilities will meet each collection's special requirements for security, fire suppression, and environmental controls.

The operation of environmental control systems to meet the temperature, relative humidity, particulate, and, as necessary, pollutant control specifications for museum collections are typically more energy intensive than those for structures with staff and offices. To ensure energy efficiency and the correct performance of the systems to protect the resource, the thermal performance of the building envelope and the efficiency of the systems must be addressed in facility planning and design. Before planning a collections management facility, the park, in consultation with subject-matter specialists, must complete a value analysis that evaluates various options for addressing the collections management needs of the park, including on-site and off-site locations and joint facilities with other NPS units and entities outside the Park Service.

(See Museum Collections 5.3.5.5; Fire Detection, Suppression, and Post-fire Rehabilitation and Protection 5.3.1.2; Environmental Monitoring and Control 5.3.1.4. Also see Director's Order #24: NPS Museum Collections Management)

9.4.3 Employee Housing

The Park Service will generally rely on the private sector to provide housing for NPS employees. If reasonable price and quality housing is not available in the private sector, the Service will provide only the number of housing units necessary to support the NPS mission.

Occupancy may be permitted or may be required to provide for timely response to park protection needs, to ensure reasonable deterrence to prevent threats to resources, and to protect the health and safety of visitors and employees. Acceptable and appropriate locations for employee housing will be determined based on these prevention or response services provided for the benefit of the government in meeting the NPS mission.

9.4.3.1 Housing Management Plan

A housing management plan will be prepared and updated every three to five years to determine the necessary number of housing units in a park. Park superintendents are accountable to their regional directors for employee housing in their parks. Regional directors are responsible for approval of park housing management plans and ensuring the consistent application of Service-wide housing policy.

9.4.3.2 Eligible Residents

Park housing will be provided for persons who are essential to the management and operation of the park. These may include not only NPS employees, but also concession employees, volunteers in the parks, Student Conservation Association volunteers, researchers, essential cooperators (for example, schoolteachers, health personnel, contractors, state or county employees), and employees of another federal agency.

9.4.3.3 Historic Structures

The use of historic structures for housing is encouraged when NPS managers determine that this use contributes to the preservation of these structures, and after feasible cost-effective alternatives have been considered.

(See Use of Historic Structures 5.3.5.4.7; Adaptive Use 9.1.1.4)

9.4.3.4 Design and Construction

Because of location, use, and other unique factors, special design concerns must be considered for housing constructed in parks. Housing must be designed to be as much a part of the natural or cultural setting as possible, yet it must be well built, functional, energy efficient, and cost-effective. The design of park housing will minimize impacts on park resources and values, comply with the standards for quality design, and consider regional design and construction influences. Value analysis principles will be applied in all NPS housing construction projects. Design costs will be kept to a minimum by using designs from the NPS Standard Design Catalog and a cost model.

(See Facility Planning and Design 9.1.1. Also see Director's Orders #36: Housing Management, and #90: Value Analysis)

9.4.4 Maintenance Structures

Maintenance structures will be consistent in design, scale, texture, and details with other park facilities. Optimally, they will be screened or located in areas remote from public use. Wherever feasible, NPS and concessioner maintenance facilities will be adjacent and integrated in design to facilitate operations and reduce impacts on park resources.

9.4.5 Miscellaneous Management Facilities

When installations such as landing sites and airstrips, security structures, protection devices, fire towers, weather monitors, research stations, communication towers, and pump houses are necessary, they will be located and designed to minimize their impact on resources and their intrusion on the visitor experience. Whenever possible and practicable, such installations will be located within developed park areas or outside park boundaries. When totally utilitarian facilities such as maintenance storage yards, sewage lagoons, and solid waste disposal sites absolutely must be developed inside a park, they will be screened from view, sited to avoid adverse impacts on resources, and not detract from the visitor experience. Facilities that illustrate technologies important to interpretive and educational objectives may be located in more visible areas. Examples include alternative energy applications and sustainable wastewater treatment facilities, such as aquaculture ponds, wetlands, and rootzone beds.

(See Environmental Leadership 1.8; Studies and Collections 4.2; General Policy 6.3.1; Airports and Landing Sites 8.4.8; Facility Planning and Design 9.1.1; Water Supply Systems

9.1.5.1; *Wastewater Treatment Systems 9.1.5.2; Waste Management 9.1.6.1; Maintenance Structures 9.4.4)*

9.5 Dams and Reservoirs

Dams and reservoirs will not be constructed in parks. The National Park Service will not seek to acquire and operate dams and will seek to deactivate existing structures unless they contribute to the cultural, natural, or recreational resource bases of the area or are a necessary part of a park's water supply system.

All dams will be subject to annual safety inspections. Each park with a dam or reservoir will prepare an emergency action plan. The emergency action plan will also address potential hazards posed by dams outside the park and beyond the Service's control. The National Park Service inventory of dams will be used to record all NPS and non-NPS dams and reservoirs, and any other type of stream flow control structures affecting units of the national park system, including those that are proposed or have been deactivated.

(See Water Quality 4.6.3; Floodplains 4.6.4; Wetlands 4.6.5; Watershed and Stream Processes 4.6.6; Emergency Preparedness and Emergency Operations 8.2.5.2; Water Supply Systems 9.1.5.1; Wastewater Treatment Systems 9.1.5.2. Also see Director's Order #40: Dams and Appurtenant Works—Maintenance, Operation, and Safety)

9.6 Commemorative Works and Plaques

9.6.1 General

For the purpose of this section, the term "commemorative work" means any statue, monument, sculpture, memorial, plaque, or other structure or landscape feature, including a garden or memorial grove, designed to perpetuate in a permanent manner the memory of a person, group, event, or other significant element of history. It also includes the naming of park structures or other features—including features within the interior of buildings. Within the District of Columbia and its environs, the Commemorative Works Act prohibits the establishment of commemorative works unless specifically authorized by an act of Congress. Outside of the District of Columbia and its environs, commemorative works will not be established unless authorized by Congress or approved by the Director (36 CFR 2.62). The consultation process required by section 106 of the National Historic Preservation Act must be completed before the Director will make a decision to approve a commemorative work.

To be permanently commemorated in a national park is a high honor, affording a degree of recognition that implies national importance. At the same time, the excessive or inappropriate use of commemorative works—especially commemorative naming—diminishes its value as a tool for recognizing people or events that are truly noteworthy. This situation can also divert attention from the important resources and values that park visitors need to learn about. Therefore, the National Park Service will discourage and curtail the use and proliferation of commemorative works except when

- ◆ Congress has specifically authorized their placement; or
- ◆ there is compelling justification for the recognition, and the commemorative work is the best way to express the association between the park and the person, group, event, or other subject being commemorated.

In general, compelling justification for a commemorative work will not be considered unless

- ◆ the association between the park and the person, group, or event is of exceptional importance; and
- ◆ in cases where a person or event is proposed for commemoration, at least five years have elapsed since the death of the person (or the last member of a group), or at least 25 years have elapsed since the event. (Within the District of Columbia and its environs, refer to the Commemorative Works Act for more specific requirements.)

Simply having worked in a park, or having made a monetary or other type of donation to a park, does not necessarily meet the test of compelling justification. In these and similar cases other forms of recognition should be pursued.

With regard to the naming of park structures, names that meet the criteria listed above may be approved by the Director. Names that do not meet those criteria will require legislative action. All donor recognition must be consistent with Director's Order #21: Donations and Fundraising. In accordance with Director's Order #21, the naming of rooms, features, or park facilities will not be used to recognize monetary or in-kind donations to a park or to the National Park Service.

9.6.2 Interpretive Works That Commemorate

The primary function of some commemorative works—most often in the form of a plaque presented by an outside organization—is to describe, explain, or otherwise attest to the significance of a park's resources. These devices are not always the most appropriate medium for their intended purpose, and their permanent installation may not be in the best long-term interests of the park. Therefore, permanent installations of this nature will not be allowed unless it can be clearly demonstrated that the work will substantially increase visitors' appreciation of the significance of park resources or values, and do so more effectively than other interpretive media.

With regard to Civil War parks, new commemorative works will not be approved, except where specifically authorized by legislation. However, consideration may be given to proposals that would commemorate groups that were not allowed to be recognized during the commemorative period.

In those parks where there is legislative authorization to erect commemorative works, superintendents will prepare a plan to control their size, location, materials, and other factors necessary to protect the overall integrity of the park.

The plan may include a requirement for an endowment to cover the costs of maintaining the commemorative work.

9.6.3 Approval of Commemorative Works

Before being approved, a determination must be made, based on consultation with qualified professionals that the proposed commemorative work will

- be designed and sited to avoid disturbance of natural and cultural resources and values;
- be located in surroundings relevant to its subject;
- be constructed of materials suitable to and compatible with the local environment;
- meet NPS design and maintenance standards;
- not encroach on any other preexisting work or be esthetically intrusive;
- not interfere significantly with open space and existing public use;
- not divert attention from a park's primary interpretive theme; and
- not be affixed to the historic fabric of a structure.

The Director may order the removal or modification of commemorative works that were installed without proper authorization, or that are inconsistent with the policies in this section. Temporary forms of in-park recognition, and permanent forms that will not be installed within park boundaries, do not require the Director's approval.

The naming of geographic features is subject to approval by the U. S. Board on Geographic Names. NPS proposals for naming geographic features will follow the procedures described in Director's Order #63: Geographic Names.

(Also see Director's Order #67: Copyright and Trademarks; U. S. Board on Geographic Names "Principles, Policies, and Procedures: Domestic Geographic Names")

9.6.4 Preexisting Commemorative Works

Many commemorative works have existed in the parks long enough to qualify as historic features. A key aspect of their historical interest is that they reflect the knowledge, attitudes, and tastes of the persons who designed and placed them. These works and their inscriptions will not be altered, relocated, obscured, or removed, even when they are deemed inaccurate or incompatible with prevailing present-day values. Any exceptions from this policy require specific approval by the Director.

9.6.5 Donated Commemorative Works

Although commemorative works and other forms of in-park permanent recognition will not be used to recognize monetary contributions or other donations to a park or the Service, there may be occasions when an authorized or approved commemorative work will be offered or provided by a private donor. Placing donor names on commemorative works will be discouraged. If they do appear, donor names will be conspicuously subordinate to the subjects commemorated. Donations of commemorative works should include sufficient funds to provide for their installation, and an endowment for their permanent care.

(See Nonpersonal Services 7.3.2; Cemeteries and Burials 8.6.10. Also see Director's Order #64: Commemorative Works and Plaques)

9.6.6 Commemorative Works in National Cemeteries

Regulations governing commemorative works associated with national cemeteries are found in 36 CFR Part 12; and Director's Order #61: National Cemetery Operations.

Commercial Visitor Services

Through the use of concession contracts or commercial use authorizations, the National Park Service will provide commercial visitor services that are necessary and appropriate for public use and enjoyment. Concession operations will be consistent to the highest practicable degree with the preservation and conservation of resources and values of the park unit. Concession operations will demonstrate sound environmental management and stewardship.

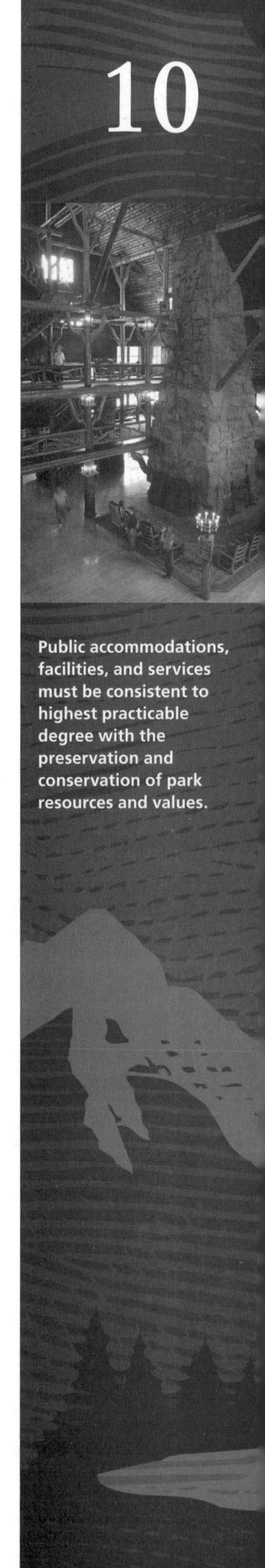

Public accommodations, facilities, and services must be consistent to highest practicable degree with the preservation and conservation of park resources and values.

10.1 General

Commercial visitor services will be authorized through concession contracts or commercial use authorizations, unless otherwise provided by law. Section 10.2 below addresses concession authorizations; section 10.3 addresses commercial use authorizations.

(See Leases 8.12. Also see Director's Orders #48A: Concession Management, and #48B: Commercial Use Authorizations)

10.1.1 Leasing
See Section 8.12.

10.2 Concessions

10.2.1 Concession Policies
Concession operations are subject to the provisions of the National Park Service Concessions Management Improvement Act of 1998; NPS regulations published at 36 CFR Part 51; this chapter of NPS Management Policies; Director's Order #48A: Concession Management; and other specific guidance that may be issued under the Director's authority. In Alaska, concession operations are also subject to the provisions of the Alaska National Interest Lands Conservation Act and 36 CFR Part 13.

10.2.2 Commercial Visitor Services Planning
Commercial visitor services planning will identify the appropriate role of commercial operators in helping parks to provide opportunities for visitor use and enjoyment. This planning will be integrated into other plans and planning processes and will comply with all Service policies regarding planning and environmental analysis. The number, location, and sizes of facilities and sites assigned through concession authorizations will be the minimum necessary for proper and satisfactory operation of the facilities.

A park commercial services strategy must be in place to ensure that concession facilities and services are necessary and appropriate, financially viable, and addressed in an approved management plan. Commercial services plans may be developed to further implement a park's commercial services strategy and to guide decisions on whether to authorize or expand concessions. A decision to authorize or expand a park concession will consider the effect on, or need for, additional infrastructure and management of operations and be based on a determination that the facility or service

- is consistent with enabling legislation, and
- is complementary to a park's mission and visitor service objectives, and
- is necessary and appropriate for the public use and enjoyment of the park in which it is located, and
- is not, and cannot be, provided outside park boundaries, and
- incorporates sustainable principles and practices in planning, design, siting, construction, and maintenance, and
- adopts appropriate energy and water conservation, source reduction, and environmental purchasing standards and goals, and
- will not cause unacceptable impacts.

Prior to initiating new services authorized under a concession contract, a market and financial viability study/analysis will be completed to ensure the overall contract is feasible.

For information about leasing structures for appropriate uses, see section 8.12 and Director's Order #38: Real Property Leasing.

(See Unacceptable Impacts 1.4.7.1)

10.2.3 Concession Contracting
Approved standard contract language will be used in all NPS concession contracts. Any deviations from such language must be approved in writing by the Director.

10.2.3.1 Terms and Conditions of Contracts
Concession services will be authorized under concession contracts unless otherwise authorized by law. The term of a concession contract will generally be 10 years or less. However, the Director may award a contract for a term of up to 20 years if the Director determines that the contract terms and conditions, including the required construction of capital improvements, warrant a longer term. In this regard, the term of concession contracts should be as short as is prudent, taking into account the financial requirements of the concession contract, the required construction of capital improvements, resource preservation and conservation, visitor needs, and other factors that the Director may deem appropriate. Proposed concession operations must be economically feasible and supported by a feasibility study prepared by a qualified individual.

10.2.3.2 Modifications/Amendments
Concession contracts may be modified only by written amendment. Amendments developed after the issuance of a concession contract must be consistent with current NPS policies and orders. Unless otherwise authorized by the contract, a concession contract may be amended to provide minor additional visitor services that are a reasonable extension of the existing services.

10.2.3.3 Extension
Concession contracts may be extended only in accordance with the requirements of 36 CFR Part 51, subpart D. The signature authority for contract extensions or amendments must be consistent with delegations of authority from the Director.

10.2.3.4 Competition
To obtain the best service provider and maximize benefits to the government, the National Park Service encourages competition in the awarding of concession contracts. Through outreach, the National Park Service also encourages the participation of American Indian, minority,

and women-owned businesses when new business activities occur.

10.2.3.5 Third-party Agreements and Subconcessions

Unless specified in the contract, sub-concession or other third-party agreements (including management agreements) for the provision of visitor services that are required and/or authorized under concession contracts are not permitted. The Park Service may also advertise for a new concession contract to provide these additional services.

10.2.3.6 Multipark Contracts

Concessioners operating in more than one park unit must have separate contracts for each park unit. When approved by the Director, an exception may be made in the case of those park units having common NPS management or where service is provided in contiguous park areas (for example, a pack trip that crosses the boundary of two adjoining parks, or where lack of opportunity for profit, geographic location, and type of service is not feasible within a single location).

10.2.3.7 Termination

The Service may terminate concession contracts for default and under any other circumstances specified in the concession contract.

10.2.4 Concession Operations
10.2.4.1 Operating Plans

The operating plan is an exhibit to the concession contract; the plan will describe operational responsibilities authorized in the contract between the concessioner and the Park Service. The plan is reviewed and updated annually by the Service in accordance with the terms of the contract. Operating plans are considered an integral part of a concessioner's contractual performance compliance. Some aspects of a concessioner's operating requirements may also be contained in general or specific provisions unique to that contract.

10.2.4.2 Service Type and Quality

It is the objective of the National Park Service that park visitors be provided with high-quality facilities and services. Where appropriate, the concession contract will specify a range of facility, accommodation, and service types that are to be provided at reasonable rates and standards to ensure optimal facility maintenance and quality services to visitors. Concessioners are not permitted to use or encourage pseudo-ownership concepts such as time shares or long-term rental agreements.

10.2.4.3 Evaluation of Concession Operations

Concession operations will be regularly evaluated to ensure that park visitors are provided with high-quality services and facilities that are safe and sanitary and meet NPS environmental, health, safety, and operational standards. As outlined in the concessioner operational evaluation program, the evaluation results will provide a basis for NPS management to determine (1) whether to continue or terminate a concession contract, and (2) whether a concessioner is eligible to exercise a right of preference in the award of a qualified new concession contract for those categories of contracts where such a right is available by law.

10.2.4.4 Interpretation by Concessioners

Concessioners will be required to appropriately train their employees and, through their facilities and services, to instill in their guests an appreciation of the park, its purpose and significance, its proper and sustainable management, and the stewardship of its resources. When the provision of interpretive services is required by the contract, concessioners will provide formal interpretive training, approved by the Park Service, for their employees, or will participate in formal interpretive training that is either offered by the Park Service or cosponsored by the concessioner.

Visitor appreciation of the park can be instilled in many ways. For example, it can be accomplished through guided activities; the design, architecture, landscape, and decor of facilities; educational programs; interpretive menu design and menu offerings; and involvement in the park's overall interpretive program. Gift shop merchandise and displays also present opportunities to educate visitors about park history; natural, cultural, and historical resources; and sustainable environmental management.

Concession contracts will require the concessioner to provide all visitor services in a manner that is consistent with and supportive of the interpretive themes, goals, and objectives articulated in each park's planning documents, mission statement, and/or interpretive prospectus.

(See Interpretive Competencies and Skills 7.4)

10.2.4.5 Merchandise

The National Park Service will approve the nature, type, and quality of merchandise to be offered by concessioners. Although there is no Service-wide list of specific preferred merchandise, priority will be given to sale items that foster awareness, understanding, and appreciation of the park and its resources and that interprets those resources. Merchandise should have interpretive labeling or include other information to indicate how the merchandise is relevant to the park and its interpretive program and themes.

Each concession operation with a gift shop will have a mission statement based on the park's concession service plan or general management plan. Concessioners will develop and implement a merchandise plan based on the park's gift shop mission statement. The merchandise plan must be satisfactory to the Director, and should ensure that merchandise sold or provided reflects the significance of the park and promotes the conservation of the park's geological resources, wildlife, plant life, archeological resources, local Native American culture, local ethnic and traditional culture, historical significance, and other park resources and values. The plan should also integrate pollution prevention and waste-reduction objectives and strategies for merchandise and packaging.

Merchandise must be available at a range of prices. Theme-related merchandise manufactured or handcrafted in the United States—particularly in a park's geographic vicinity—will be encouraged. The revenue derived from the sale of United States Indian, Alaska Native, native Samoan, and Native Hawaiian handicrafts is exempt from any franchise fee payments.

10.2.4.6 Artifacts and Specimens

Concessioners will not be permitted to sell any merchandise in violation of laws, regulations, or NPS policies. The park superintendent may prohibit the sale of some items for retail sale because the merchandise is locally sensitive or inappropriate for sale. The sale of original objects, artifacts, or specimens of a historic, archeological, paleontological, or biological nature is prohibited. Replicated historic, archeological, paleontological, or biological objects, artifacts, or specimens may be sold if they are obvious replicas and clearly labeled.

Any geological merchandise approved for sale or exhibit by concessioners must be accompanied by appropriate educational material and a written disclaimer clearly stating that such items were not obtained from inside park boundaries. The proposed sale of any replicas, or of geological merchandise, must be addressed in the gift shop merchandise plan.

10.2.4.7 Rates

The National Park Service must approve all rates charged to visitors by concessioners. The reasonableness of a concessioner's rates and charges to the public will, unless otherwise provided in the contract, be judged primarily on the basis of comparison with current rates and charges for facilities and services of comparable character under similar conditions. Due consideration will be given to length of season, provision for peak loads, average percentage of occupancy, accessibility, availability and costs of labor and materials, type of patronage, and other factors deemed significant by the NPS Director.

10.2.4.8 Risk Management Program

Concession contracts require each concessioner to develop a risk management program that is (1) appropriate in scope to the size and nature of the operation, (2) in accord with the Occupational Safety and Health Act of 1970 and the NPS concession risk management program, and (3) approved by the superintendent. Concessioners are responsible for managing all of their operations to minimize risk and control loss due to accident, illness, or injury. To ensure compliance, the Service will include a risk management evaluation as part of its standard operational review of concession operations.

10.2.4.9 Natural and Cultural Resource Management Requirements

Concessioners are required to comply with applicable provisions of all laws, regulations, and policies that apply to natural and cultural resource protection. The use, maintenance, repair, rehabilitation, restoration, or other modification of concession facilities that are listed in or eligible for the National Register of Historic Places are subject to the applicable provisions of all laws, executive orders, regulations, and policies pertaining to cultural properties. The National Park Service will assist concessioners in understanding and complying with regulations for the protection of historic properties (36 CFR Part 800) promulgated by the Advisory Council on Historic Preservation. Historic structures and their contents and museum objects that are in the control of concessioners will be treated in accordance with the appropriate standards contained in NPS guidance documents. The Service will work closely with concessioners to integrate into concession activities the policies, procedures, and practices of Executive Order 13287 (Preserve America).

(See Chapter 4: Natural Resource Management; Use of Historic Structures 5.3.5.4.7. Also see Reference Manual 24: the Museum Handbook; Director's Order #28: Cultural Resource Management; #38: Real Property Leasing, and #48A: Concession Management)

10.2.4.10 Environmental Program Requirements

In the operation of visitor services, concessioners will be required by contract to meet environmental compliance objectives by

- complying with all applicable laws pertaining to the protection of human health and the environment; and
- incorporating best management practices in all operations, construction, maintenance, acquisition, provision of visitor services, and other activities under the contract.

Concessioners will also be required by contract to develop, document, implement, and comply fully with—to the satisfaction of the Director—a comprehensive, written environmental management program (EMP) to achieve environmental management objectives. The EMP

- should be appropriate to the nature and size of the operation;
- must account for all activities with potential environmental impacts conducted by the concessioner, or to which the concessioner contributes;
- must be updated at least annually; and
- must be approved by the superintendent.

The scope and complexity of the EMP may vary based on the type, size, and number of concessioner activities. Exceptions to the requirement for an EMP must be approved by the Director.

The National Park Service will review concessioner compliance with the EMP under the contract. The Park Service will also

- assist concessioners in understanding environmental program requirements;
- conduct environmental compliance audits of all commercial visitor services at least every three years

in accordance with the concessions environmental audit program (the concessioner will be responsible for corrective actions required by law and identified during the environmental compliance audits); and

- include an environmental management evaluation as part of its annual standard operational reviews of concession operations.

(See Compensation for Injuries to Natural Resources 4.1.6; Integrated Pest Management Program 4.4.5.2; Compensation for Injuries to Cultural Resources 5.3.1.3; Overnight Accommodations and Food Services 9.3.2. Also see Director's Order #48A: Concession Management; Director's Order #83: Public Health)

10.2.4.11 Insurance

Concession contracts will identify the types and minimum amounts of insurance coverage required of concessioners to

- provide reasonable assurance that concessioners have the ability to cover bona fide claims for bodily injury, death, or property damage arising from an action or omission of the operator;
- protect the government against potential liability for claims based on the negligence of the operators; and
- enable rapid repair or replacement of essential visitor facilities located on park lands that are damaged or destroyed by fire or other hazards.

Concessioners will not be permitted to operate without liability insurance. Under limited conditions, concessioners may operate without property insurance, as described in Director's Order #48A: Concession Management.

10.2.4.12 Food Service Sanitation Inspections

Concessioners who prepare food on or off park lands or serve food on park lands will be subject to inspection for compliance with all applicable health and sanitation requirements of local and state agencies, the U.S. Public Health Service, and the Food and Drug Administration.

(Also see Director's Order #83: Public Health)

10.2.4.13 Smoking

Generally, all NPS concession facilities will be smoke free. The only exceptions—which the Service does not encourage—will be specifically designated smoking areas and rooms if allowed by state and local law. The sale of tobacco products through vending machines is prohibited.

(Also see Director's Order #50D: Smoking Policy; Executive Order 13058 (Protecting Federal Employees and the Public from Exposure to Tobacco Smoke in the Federal Workplace))

10.2.4.14 Wireless Local Area Networks

Concessioners may be authorized to provide wireless local area network access for park visitors and for administrative and employee use within concessioner assigned facilities. If this type of service is found to be necessary and appropriate and otherwise in accord with the park's planning and other guidance documents, the concession authorization's operating plan must identify the need for the service and the standards for offering the service. A request to construct telecommunications equipment and infrastructure outside the concessioner's assigned facilities must be processed in accordance with section 8.6.4.3.

10.2.5 Concessions Financial Management

Concession contracts must provide for payment to the government of a franchise fee, or other monetary consideration as determined by the Secretary, upon consideration of the probable value to the concessioner of the privileges granted by the particular contract involved. Such probable value will be based upon a reasonable opportunity for net profit in relation to capital invested and the obligations of the contract. Consideration of revenue to the United States is subordinate to the objectives of protecting and preserving park areas and providing necessary and appropriate services for visitors at reasonable rates.

10.2.5.1 Franchise Fees

The amount of the franchise fee or other monetary consideration paid to the United States for the term of the concession contract must be specified in the concession contract and may only be modified to reflect extraordinary unanticipated changes from the conditions expected as of the effective date of the contract. Contracts with a term of more than five years will include a provision that allows reconsideration of the franchise fee at the request of the Director or the concessioner in the event of such extraordinary unanticipated changes. Such provision will provide for binding arbitration in the event that the Director and the concessioner are unable to agree upon an adjustment to the franchise fee in these circumstances.

10.2.5.2 Franchise Fee Special Account

All franchise fees and other monetary considerations will be deposited into a Department of the Treasury special account. In accordance with the NPS Concessions Management Improvement Act of 1998, twenty percent (20%) will be available to support activities throughout the national park system, and eighty percent (80%) will be available to the park unit in which it was generated for visitor services and funding high-priority and urgently necessary resource management programs and operations.

10.2.5.3 Record-keeping System

All concessioners will establish and maintain a system of accounts and a record-keeping system that use written journals and general ledger accounts to facilitate the preparation of annual concessioner financial reports.

10.2.5.4 Annual Financial Reports

For each concession contract, concessioners will be required to submit a separate annual financial report that reflects only the operations they are authorized to provide under that particular contract.

10.2.5.5 Donations to the National Park Service

The National Park Service will not solicit or accept direct donations or gifts from entities that have or are seeking to obtain a concessions contract. The Park Service will not require any concessioner to donate or make contributions to the Service under any circumstance, including the incorporation of such a requirement in concession contracts. Further guidance on donations is available in Director's Order #21: Donations and Fundraising.

10.2.6 Concession Facilities

All buildings under a concession contract are U.S. government/Service-owned structures and are part of the overall facility inventory at each park. Depending on the contract, the concessioner may have a contractual right of compensation in the form of a leasehold surrender interest or possessory interest in one, some, or all of the buildings. Responsibilities for maintenance, environmental management, and other operational issues must be included in each concession contract. Park facility managers will work closely with the park's concession program managers to ensure that these government buildings are part of the overall park inventory and tracking systems. Park managers will ensure that possessory interests and leasehold surrender interest valuations conform to the terms and conditions of the concession contract.

10.2.6.1 Design

Concession facilities will be of a size and at a location that the Service determines to be necessary and appropriate for their intended purposes. All concession facilities must comply with applicable federal, state, and local construction codes, and meet accessibility requirements as set forth in applicable accessibility guidelines. Proposed concession facilities must conform to NPS standards for sustainable design, universal design, and architectural design. Concession development or improvement proposals must undergo review for compliance with the National Environmental Policy Act of 1969 and section 106 of the National Historic Preservation Act (16 USC 470f), and proposals must be carried out in a manner consistent with applicable provisions of the *Secretary of the Interior's Standards and Guidelines for Archeology and Historic Preservation* and other applicable legal requirements.

In addition to general park design requirements, the Park Service will apply value analysis during the design process to analyze the functions of facilities, processes, systems, equipment, services, and supplies. Value analysis must be used to help achieve essential functions at the lowest life-cycle cost, consistent with required performance, reliability, environmental quality, and safety criteria and standards.

(See Facility Planning and Design 9.1.1)

10.2.6.2 Accessibility of Commercial Services

Concessioners share the National Park Service's responsibility to provide employees and visitors with the greatest degree of access to programs, facilities, and services that is reasonable, within the terms of existing contracts and agreements. Applicable laws include, but are not limited to (1) regulations issued under the authority of section 504 of the Rehabilitation Act of 1973, as amended (43 CFR Part 17), which prohibits discrimination on the basis of disability in programs or activities conducted by federal executive agencies; and (2) the Architectural Barriers Act of 1968, which requires physical access to buildings and facilities. Where there is no specific language identifying applicable accessibility laws in an existing concession contract, the Park Service will address the issue of compliance in the annual concession operating plan.

(See Physical Access for Persons with Disabilities 5.3.2; Accessibility for Persons with Disabilities 1.9.3, 8.2.4 and 9.1.2. Also see Director's Order #42: Accessibility for Visitors with Disabilities in National Park Service Programs and Services)

10.2.6.3 Maintenance

Concession contracts will require concessioners to be responsible for all maintenance and repair of facilities, lands, and utility systems assigned for their use, in accordance with standards acceptable to the Service. Exceptions will be made only in extraordinary circumstances, as determined by the Director. All concession contracts must include a current maintenance plan as specified in the concession contract. Maintenance plans are an exhibit to the concession contract and will be considered an integral part of a concessioner's contractual performance compliance.

Maintenance of historic properties and cultural landscapes will be carried out in a manner consistent with applicable provisions of the *Secretary of the Interior's Standards and Guidelines for Archeology and Historic Preservation*.

10.2.6.4 Utilities and Services

Utilities include, but are not limited to, electricity, fuel, natural gas, water, disposal of wastewater and solid waste, and communication systems. When available, the Service may provide utilities to the concessioner for use in connection with the operations required or authorized under the contract at rates to be determined in accordance with applicable laws. If the Service does not provide utilities to the concessioner, the concessioner will, with the written approval of the Director and under any requirements prescribed by the Director, (1) secure necessary utilities at its own expense from sources outside the area; or (2) install the utilities within the area, subject to conditions of the contract.

(Also see Director's Order #35B: Sale of National Park Service-produced Utilities)

10.2.6.5 Closure of Commercial Operations during Government Shutdown

The Anti-Deficiency Act requires federal agencies to suspend all nonessential activities whenever there is a failure to enact an appropriations bill or adopt a continuing resolution. All concessioner-operated programs and services must cease, and visitors must be asked to leave within 48 hours. All commercial facilities and services in a park will be closed to protect the safety of visitors and the integrity of park resources. Exceptions to this policy include concessions that are required for health and safety purposes or protection of the environment, or that are necessary to support park operations that are deemed essential, such as law enforcement.

Commercial facilities located on through-roads (roads or public highways that begin and end outside of a park, plus parkways) and public highways may remain open if doing so does not result in additional costs to the park (for example, the staffing of entrance stations). These commercial facilities may include operations such as service stations, food services, stores, and lodging, or portions of such operations. The commercial facility in question should have access directly from the road or highway and not require the reopening of park roads having other destinations. More specific aspects of closures may be guided by a Service-wide shutdown plan.

10.2.7 Concessioner Employees and Employment Conditions
10.2.7.1 Nondiscrimination

Concessioners will comply with all applicable laws and regulations relating to nondiscrimination in employment and the provision of services to the public. As the National Park Service strives to achieve workforce diversity, so too will concessioners be encouraged to recognize workforce diversity as a sound business practice.

10.2.7.2 Substance Abuse

In compliance with state and federal regulations condemning substance abuse, the Park Service prohibits the unlawful possession, use, or distribution of illicit drugs and alcohol. The Service also prohibits the unlawful manufacture, cultivation, processing, or transportation of illicit drugs. This policy applies to concessioners and their employees, at any facility or in any activity taking place on NPS lands. Concessioners are required to provide and advise employees about the availability of employee assistance programs addressing substance abuse problems.

10.2.8 NPS Employees
10.2.8.1 Accepting Gifts and Reduced Rates from Concessioners

NPS employees may not receive concessioner goods or services at a discount unless it is in connection with official business, is to the government's advantage, and is provided for under the terms of a concession contract. However, employees may accept reduced rates or discounts offered by the concessioner when those same reduced rates or discounts are available to the general public.

NPS employees may not solicit or accept, directly or indirectly, any gift, gratuity, favor, entertainment, loan, or any other thing of monetary value from a concessioner or other person who conducts operations and activities that are regulated by the Department of the Interior. Employees should consult with their ethics counselor regarding the limited exceptions to the general prohibition on accepting gifts from outside sources.

10.2.8.2 Employment of NPS Personnel or Family Members by Concessioners

Federal law prohibits government employees from making recommendations, decisions, or approvals relating to applications, contracts, controversies, or other matters in which the employee or the employee's spouse or minor child has a financial interest. Park employees may not make decisions, approvals, or recommendations related to concession activities when their spouse or dependent child is employed by a park concessioner in that particular park. For example, the spouse or dependent child of the superintendent, assistant superintendent, concession staff, environmental manager, or public health specialist may not be employed by a concessioner in the specific park in which the NPS employee works.

(Also see Director's Order #37: Home Businesses in Park Housing)

10.2.8.3 NPS Employee Ownership or Investment in Concession Businesses

Department of the Interior policy prohibits employees and their spouses and minor children from acquiring or retaining for commercial purposes any permit, lease, or other rights granted by the Department for conducting commercial services on federal lands. Therefore, no NPS concession contract or commercial use authorization to conduct commercial services in a park will be issued to NPS employees or their spouses and minor children who are owners, partners, corporate officers, or general managers of any business seeking such a contract in federal land managed by the Department of the Interior. Further, to avoid the appearance of partiality and conflicts of interest, and to comply with ethics laws that apply to all federal employees, NPS employees may not work on any matter involving a business in which they, their spouse, or their minor children have a financial interest.

10.2.8.4 Concession Management Personnel Qualifications

To effectively carry out the concession management program, managers and supervisors will make every effort to ensure that personnel selected for positions meet the essential competencies established for the position being filled. When concession management personnel lack the full complement of essential competencies or require refresher training for their position, managers and supervisors will ensure that those employees are trained and certified as competent. All personnel vacancy announcements issued for concession management must include program competencies.

10.3 Commercial Use Authorizations

Commercial use authorizations (CUAs), which are not considered as concession contracts, may be issued pursuant to section 418 of the National Park Service Concessions Management Improvement Act of 1998 (16 USC 5966). A commercial use authorization is a permit that authorizes suitable commercial services to park area visitors in limited circumstances as described in 10.3.1. A concession contract may be issued instead of the commercial use authorization when the Director determines that the services are necessary and appropriate, and/or provision of the services require certain protections such as legal, financial, and resource provisions that are more typical of a concession contract. A more detailed discussion of commercial use authorizations is included in Director's Order #48B: Commercial Use Authorizations.

10.3.1 General

Commercial use authorizations may be issued only to authorize services that (1) are determined to be an appropriate use of the park; (2) will have minimal impact on park resources and values; and (3) are consistent with the purpose for which the unit was established, as well as all applicable management plans and park policies and regulations.

10.3.2 Requirements

By law, a commercial use authorization must provide for

- payment of a reasonable fee, such fees to be used, at a minimum, to recover associated management and administrative costs;
- provision of services in a manner consistent to the highest practicable degree with the preservation and conservation of park resources and values; and
- limitation of liability of the federal government arising from the commercial use authorization.

No park may issue commercial use authorizations in a quantity inconsistent with the preservation and proper management of park resources and values. Each park issuing commercial use authorizations will ensure that it contains provisions for the protection of visitors and the resources and values of the park.

10.3.3 Limitations

By law, commercial use authorizations may be issued only for

- commercial operations with annual gross receipts of not more than $25,000 resulting from services originating and provided solely within a unit of the national park system pursuant to such authorization;
- the incidental use of resources of the unit by commercial operations that provide services originating and terminating outside of the boundaries of the park unit; or
- such uses by organized children's camps, outdoor clubs, nonprofit institutions (including backcountry use), and such other uses as the Secretary of the Interior deems appropriate.

Nonprofit institutions will be required to obtain commercial use authorizations only when they generate taxable income from the authorized use.

10.3.4 Construction Prohibition

By law, under no circumstances will a commercial use authorization provide for or allow construction of any structure, fixture, or improvement on federally owned land within any unit of the national park system.

10.3.5 Duration

By law, the maximum term for any commercial use authorization is two years in length. No rights of renewal are associated with commercial use authorizations.

10.3.6 Other Contracts

Holding or seeking to obtain a commercial use authorization does not preclude a person, corporation, or other entity from submitting proposals for concessions contracts.

Appendix A
Laws Cited in Text

Abandoned Shipwreck Act of 1987
43 USC[1] 2101—2106; PL[2] 100-298

(popularly known as) Acquired Lands Mineral Leasing Act
30 USC 301—306; May 21, 1930, ch. 307, 46 Stat. 373

Administrative Procedure Act (APA)
5 USC 551 et seq.[3], June 11, 1946, ch. 324, 60 Stat. 237

Alaska National Interest Lands Conservation Act (ANILCA)
16 USC 3101—3233; PL 96-487

American Indian Religious Freedom Act (AIRFA)
42 USC 1996—1996a; PL 95-341, 103-344

Americans with Disabilities Act of 1990 (ADA)
42 USC 12101—12213; PL 101-336

Animal Welfare Act
7 USC 2131—2159; PL 89-544; 94-279

Anti-Deficiency Act
31 USC 1341; July 12, 1870, ch. 251, 16 Stat. 251, PL 97-258

Antiquities Act of 1906
16 USC 431—433; June 8, 1906, ch. 3060, 34 Stat. 225

Archaeological Resources Protection Act of 1979 (ARPA)
16 USC 470aa—470mm; PL 96-95

Architectural Barriers Act of 1968
42 USC 4151—4157; PL 90-480

Clean Air Act (CAA)
42 USC 7401—7671q; PL 88-206

Coastal Zone Management Act of 1972 (CZMA)
16 USC 1451—1465; PL 89-454, 92-583

Commemorative Works Act
40 USC 8901—8909; PL 99-652, 107-217

Comprehensive Environmental Response, Compensation and Liability Act of 1980 (CERCLA)
42 USC 9601—9675; PL 96-510

Endangered Species Act of 1973
16 USC 1531—1544; PL 93-205

Energy Policy Act of 1992
42 USC 13201—13556; PL 102-486

Equal Employment Opportunity Act of 1972
42 USC 2000e-16(a)[4]; PL 92-261

Federal Advisory Committee Act (FACA)
5 USC App. 1—16; PL 92-463

Federal Cave Resources Protection Act of 1988 (FCRPA)
16 USC 4301—4310; PL 100-691

Federal Insecticide, Fungicide and Rodenticide Act
7 USC 136—136y; PL 92-516

Federal Lands Recreation Enhancement Act (FLREA)
16 USC 6801—6814; PL 108-447[5]

Federal Managers' Financial Integrity Act of 1982
31 USC 3512(d); PL 97-255, 97-452[6]

Federal Water Pollution Control Act (commonly known as the Clean Water Act)
33 USC 1251—1387; PL 92-500, 95-217

Freedom of Information Act (FOIA)
5 USC 552; PL 89-554, 90-23

General Mining Act of 1872
30 USC 22 et seq.[7]; May 10, 1872, ch. 152, 17 Stat. 91

Geothermal Steam Act of 1970
30 USC 1001—1028; PL 91-581, 100-443

Government Performance and Results Act of 1993 (GPRA)
31 USC 1115[8] et seq. ; PL 103-62

Hazardous Materials Transportation Act
49 USC 5101—5127; PL 93-633, 101-615, 103-311

---

[1] The United States Code (USC) can be accessed on the Internet, e.g., at <http://www4.law.cornell.edu/uscode/>, or <http://www.gpoaccess.gov/uscode/index.html>.

[2] The text of any Public Law (PL) enacted by the 101st or a later Congress (1989 onward) can be accessed at the Library of Congress's THOMAS website, <http://thomas.loc.gov/>.

[3] Act of June 11, 1946, ch. 324, has been codified to 5 USC §§551—559, 701—706, 1305, 3105, 3344, 4301, 5335, 5372, and 7521.

[4] PL 92-261 was codified to 42 USC §§2000e—2000e-6, 2000e-8, 2000e-9, 2000e-13, 2000e-14, 2000e-16 and 2000e-17, and 5 USC §§5108 and 5314—5316.

[5] The Federal Lands Recreation Enhancement Act is division J, title VIII of PL 108-447, the Consolidated Appropriations Act, 2005.

[6] PL 97-452, the Jan. 12, 1983 revision of title 31, in particular section 1(12), redesignated 16 USC 3512(b) as 16 USC 3512(d).

[7] The General Mining Act of 1872 was the basis of 30 USC §§22-24, 26-30, 33-35, 37, 39-43, and 47.

[8] PL 103-62 was codified to: 5USC 306; 31 USC 1105(a)(29); 1115—1119, 9703, 9704; and 39 USC 2801—2805.

(popularly known as) Historic Sites, Buildings and Antiquities Act
16 USC 461—467; Aug. 21, 1935, ch. 593, 49 Stat. 666

Land and Water Conservation Fund Act of 1965
16 USC 460l-4—460l-11; PL 88-578

Mineral Leasing Act
30 USC 181—287; Feb. 25, 1920, ch. 85, 41 Stat. 437

Mining in the Parks Act
16 USC 1901—1912; PL 94-429

(popularly known as) Museum Act
16 USC 18f—18f-3; July 1, 1955, ch. 259, 69 Stat. 242, PL 104-333[9]

National Cemeteries Act of 1973
38 USC 2400—2410; PL 93-43

National Environmental Policy Act of 1969 (NEPA)
42 USC 4321—4370d; PL 91-190

National Historic Preservation Act (NHPA)
16 USC 470—470x-6; PL 89-665, 96-515

National Parks Air Tour Management Act of 2000
114 Stat. 61; PL 106-181 (title VIII)

National Parks Omnibus Management Act of 1998
16 USC 5901—6011[10]; PL 105-391

National Park Service Concessions Management Improvement Act of 1998
16 USC 5951—5966; PL 105-391 (title IV)

National Park Service Organic Act
16 USC 1—4; Aug. 25, 1916, ch. 408, 39 Stat. 535[11]

National Park System General Authorities Act
16 USC 1a-1 et seq.[12]; PL 91-383, 94-458, 95-250[13]

(popularly known as) National Park System Resource Protection Act
16 USC 19jj—19jj-4; PL 101-337, 104-333

National Trails System Act
16 USC 1241—1251; PL 90-543, 98-11

Native American Graves Protection and Repatriation Act (NAGPRA)
25 USC 3001—3013; PL 101-601

Occupational Safety and Health Act of 1970
29 USC 651—678; PL 91-596[14]

Oil Pollution Act of 1990
33 USC 2701—2761; PL 101-380

(popularly known as) Omnibus Consolidated Appropriations Act, 1997
16 USC 1g et seq.[15]; PL 104-208

Privacy Act of 1974
5 USC 552a; PL 93-579

Rehabilitation Act of 1973
29 USC 701—797b; PL 93-112, 105-220

Rivers and Harbors Appropriation Act of 1899
33 USC 401 et seq.[16]; Mar. 3, 1899, ch. 425, 30 Stat. 1121

Robert T. Stafford Disaster Relief and Emergency Assistance Act
42 USC 5121—5204c[17]; PL 93-288, 100-707, 103-337

Solid Waste Disposal Act
42 USC 6901—6992k; PL 89-272, 94-580[18], 98-616[19]

Surface Mining Control and Reclamation Act of 1977
30 USC 1201—1328; PL 95-87

Telecommunications Act of 1996
47 USC 332 note; PL 104-104[20]

Toxic Substances Control Act
15 USC 2601—2692; PL 94-469

Volunteers in the Parks Act of 1969
16 USC 18g—18j; PL 91-357

Wild and Scenic Rivers Act
16 USC 1271—1287; PL 90-542

Wilderness Act
16 USC 1131—1136; PL 88-577

---

[9] Section 804 of division 1, title VIII of PL 104-333, the Omnibus Parks and Public Lands Management Act of 1996, amended 16 USC 18f, and enacted §§18f-2 and 18f-3

[10] In addition to enacting §§19o and 5901—6011 of title 16, PL 105-391 amended 16 USC 1a-2, 1a-5, 1a-7, and 3, and repealed 16 USC 17b-1, 20, 20a—20g.

[11] See also §10(a) of PL 108-352.

[12] PL 91-383, as originally enacted, added §§1a-1 and 1a-2, and amended §§1b and 1c, of title 16.

[13] PL 95-250, an act expanding Redwood National Park, also amended the National Park System General Authorities Act by adding the second and third sentences to 16 USC 1a-1. See also, §10(b) of PL 108-352.

[14] PL 91-596 enacted 29 USC 651—678 and 42 USC 3142-1, and amended 29 USC 553, 5 USC 5108, 5314, 5315, and 7902, 15 USC 633 and 636, 18 USC 1114, and §1421 of former title 49.

[15] The Omnibus Consolidated Appropriations Act, 1997 enacted §§1g and 1011 of title 16, and amended §§773 ,773c, 917, 917a, 971, 971b, 971d, 971e, 972c, 973a, 1362, 1371, 1383a, 1387, 1417, 1432, 1445a, 1827, 2803, 2804, 3125, 3343, 3373, 3377, 3631, 4120, 5102, 5103, 5106, 5107a, 5107b, 5503, 5504 and 5609 of the same title.

[16] The Rivers and Harbors Appropriation Act of 1899 was codified to 33 USC §§401, 403, 404, 406—409, 411—416, 418, 502, 549 note, 686, and 687.

[17] The Federal Civil Defense Act of 1950, 50 USC App. 2251—2303, was repealed, and restated in title VI (42 USC 5195—5197g) of the Robert T. Stafford Disaster Relief and Emergency Assistance Act, by PL 103-337.

[18] The Solid Waste Disposal Act was amended and essentially re-written by PL 94-580, the Resource Conservation and Recovery Act of 1976.

[19] PL 98-616, the Hazardous and Solid Waste Amendments of 1984, enacted §§6917, 6936 to 6939a, 6949a, 6979b, and 6991 to 6991i of title 42 of the US Code (and provisions set out as notes to §§6905, 6921 and 6926), and amended §§6901, 6902, 6905, 6912, 6915, 6916, 6921 to 6933, 6935, 6941 to 6945, 6948, 6956, 6962, 6972, 6973, 6976, 6982 and 6984 of the same title.

[20] The provision of the Telecommunications Act of 1996 dealing with the granting of rights-of-way, etc., by federal departments and agencies to wireless telecommunications providers is §704(c), title VII, of PL 104-104.

Appendix B

Executive Orders and Memoranda Cited in Text

Executive Order No. 11644 (Use of Off-road Vehicles on the Public Lands)
February 8, 1972, 37 FR 2877, as amended by **Ex. Ord. No. 11989**, May 24, 1977, 42 FR 26959; **Ex. Ord. No. 12608**, September 9, 1987, 52 FR 34617 [42 USC 4321][1]

Executive Order No. 11988 (Floodplain Management)
May 24,1977, 42 FR 26951, as amended by **Ex. Ord. No. 12148**, July 20, 1979, 44 FR 43239 [42 USC 4321]

Executive Order No. 11990 (Protection of Wetlands)
May 24, 1977, 42 FR 26961, as amended by **Ex. Ord. No. 12608**, September 9, 1987, 52 FR 34617 [42 USC 4321]

Executive Order No. 12898 (Federal Actions to Address Environmental Justice in Minority Populations and Low Income Populations)
February 11, 1994, 59 FR 7629, as amended by **Ex. Ord. No. 12948**, January 30, 1995, 60 FR 6381 [42 USC 4321]

Memorandum on Government-to-Government Relations with Native American Tribal Governments
April 29, 1994, 59 FR 22951 [25 USC 450]

Executive Order No. 13006 (Locating Federal Facilities on Historic Properties in Our Nation's Central Cities)
May 21, 1996, 61 FR 26071 [40 USC 3306]

Executive Order No. 13007 (Indian Sacred Sites)
May 24, 1996, 61 FR 26771 [42 USC 1996]

Executive Order No. 13058 (Protecting Federal Employees and the Public from Exposure to Tobacco Smoke in the Federal Workplace)
August 9, 1997, 62 FR 43451 [5 USC 7301]

Executive Order No. 13101 (Greening the Government Through Waste Prevention, Recycling and Federal Acquisition)
September 14, 1998, 63 FR 49643 [42 USC 6961]

Executive Order No. 13112 (Invasive Species)
February 3, 1999, 64 FR 6183, as amended by **Ex. Ord. No. 13286**, February 28, 2003, 68 FR 10619 [42 USC 4321]

Executive Order No. 13123 (Greening the Government Through Efficient Energy Management)
June 3, 1999, 64 FR 30851 [42 USC 8251]

Executive Order No. 13148 (Greening the Government Through Leadership in Environmental Management)
April 21, 2000, 65 FR 24595 [42 USC 4321]

Executive Order No. 13149 (Greening the Government Through Federal Fleet and Transportation Efficiency)
April 21, 2000, 65 FR 24607 [42 USC 13212]

Executive Order No. 13175 (Consultation and Coordination with Indian Tribal Governments)
November 6, 2000, 65 FR 67249 [25 USC 450]

Executive Order No. 13266 (Activities to Promote Personal Fitness)
June 20, 2002, 67 FR 42467 [42USC 300u]

Executive Order No. 13287 (Preserve America)
March 3, 2003, 68 FR 10635 [16 USC 470h-2]

Executive Order No. 13327 (Federal Real Property Asset Management)
February 4, 2004, 69 FR 5897 [40 USC 121]

Executive Order No. 13352 (Facilitation of Cooperative Conservation)
August 26, 2004, 69 FR 52989 [42 USC 4332]

---

[1] The citation in brackets indicates where the Executive Order or Memorandum may be found in notes to the US Code.

Appendix C

Director's Orders

Director's Orders provide guidance for implementing certain aspects of NPS *Management Policies*, and are used as a vehicle for updating Management Policies between publishing dates.

In many cases, Director's Orders are further supplemented by handbooks or reference manuals.

Director's Orders marked with an asterisk (*) in this list have not been completed as of the publication date of Management Policies. Copies of those that have been completed and those that are completed or added in the future may be obtained by contacting the NPS Office of Policy or the appropriate NPS program office, or by accessing the NPS World Wide Web site at <http://www.nps.gov/policy>.

Please note that the numbers assigned to some of the Director's Orders on this list may be revised as the Directives system evolves in the future. A status chart at the web site should be consulted for the most current listing of Director's Orders.

1. National Park Service Directives System
2. Park Planning
2-1. Resource Stewardship Planning*
3. Delegations of Authority*
4. Diving Management
5. Paper and Electronic Communications
6. Interpretation and Education
7. Volunteers in Parks
8. Budget and Programming*
9. Law Enforcement Program
10A. Design and Construction Drawings
10B. Drawing and Map Numbers*
11A. Information Technology Management*
11B. Ensuring Quality of Information Disseminated by the NPS
11C. Web Publishing*
12. Conservation Planning, Environmental Impact Analysis, and Decision-making
13A. Environmental Management Systems
13B. Solid and Hazardous Waste Management*
14. Resource Damage Assessment and Restoration
15. NPS Wireless Spectrum Management
16A. Reasonable Accommodation for Applicants and Employees with Disabilities
16B. Diversity in the Workplace*
16C. Discrimination Complaints Process*
16D. Equal Employment Opportunity and Zero Tolerance for Discrimination
16E. Sexual Harassment
17. National Park Service Tourism
18. Wildland Fire Management
19. Records Management
20. Agreements
21. Donations and Fundraising
22. Fee Program*
23. (reserved)
24. NPS Museum Collections Management
25. Land Protection
26. Youth Programs
27. Challenge Cost-share Program*
28. Cultural Resource Management
28A. Archeology
28B. Ethnography Program*
28C. Oral History*
29. (reserved)
30. (reserved)
31. Travel Procedures*
32. Cooperating Associations
33. (reserved)
34. (reserved)
35A. Sale or Lease of Park Services, Resources, or Water in Support of Activities Outside the Boundaries of National Park Areas
35B. Sale of National Park Service-Produced Utilities*
36. Housing Management*
37. Home Businesses in Park Housing*
38. Real Property Leasing
39. (reserved)
40. Dams and Appurtenant Works—Maintenance, Operation, and Safety*
41. Wilderness Preservation and Management

42. Accessibility for Visitors with Disabilities in National Park Service Programs and Services	60. Aviation Management	77-5. Bioengineered Organisms*
43. Uniform Program	61. National Cemetery Operations*	77-6. Cooperative Research and Development Agreements*
44. Personal Property Management	62. Property Acquisition*	77-7. Integrated Pest Management*
45-1. National Scenic and Historic Trails*	63. Geographic Names*	77-8. Endangered Species*
46A. Wild and Scenic Rivers Within the National Park System*	64. Commemorative Works and Plaques*	77-9. In-park Borrow Material*
47. Soundscape Preservation and Noise Management	65. Explosives Use and Blasting Safety	77-10. Natural Resource Inventorying and Monitoring
48A. Concession Management*	66. FOIA and Protected Resource Information*	78. Social Science
48B. Commercial Use Authorizations*	67. Copyright and Trademarks*	79. Relocation Policies and Procedures*
49. (reserved)	68. Notification Protocol for Conduct of Employee Investigations	80. Asset Management*
50A. Worker's Compensation Case Management	69. Serving on Boards of Directors*	81. (reserved)
50B. Occupational Safety and Health	70. (See 11 C)	82. Public Use Data Collecting and Reporting Program*
50C. Public Risk Management Program*	71A. Government-to-Government Relationships with Tribal Governments*	83. Public Health
50D. Smoking Policy	71B. Indian Sacred Sites*	84. Library Management*
51. Emergency Medical Services	72. Receiving or Generating Individual Indian Trust Data	85. Garnishments and Levies*
52A. Communicating the National Park Service Mission	73. (reserved)	86. (reserved)
52B. Graphic Design Standards*	74. Studies and Collecting*	87A. Park Roads and Parkways*
52C. Park Signs	75A. Civic Engagement and Public Involvement	87B. Alternative Transportation Systems*
52D. Use of the Arrowhead Symbol*	75B. Media Relations*	87C. Transportation System Funding*
53. Special Park Uses	76. Legislative and Congressional Affairs	87D. Non-NPS Roads
54. Management Accountability*	77-1. Wetland Protection	88. Documents Needed for Litigation*
55. Incident Management Program*	77-2. Floodplain Management	89. Acquisition and Management of Leased Space
56. International Affairs*	77-3. Domestic and Feral Livestock Management*	90. Value Analysis
57. Occupational Medical Standards, Health and Fitness	77-4. Use of Pharmaceuticals for Wildlife*	91. Advisory Committees*
58. Structural Fire Management		92. Human Resources*
59. Search and Rescue*		93. Conflict Resolution
		94. Appeals and Hearings*

Glossary

Some of the words, terms, and concepts used in these Management Policies will have different meanings for different readers. For the purposes of understanding and applying these policies, their meanings are as shown below.

Accessibility—occurs when individuals with disabilities are able to reach, use, understand, or appreciate NPS programs, facilities, and services, or to enjoy the same benefits that are available to persons without disabilities. See also, "universal design."

Accession— a transaction whereby a museum object or specimen is acquired for a museum collection. Accessions include gifts, exchanges, purchases, field collections, loans, and transfers.

Adaptive management—a system of management practices based on clearly identified outcomes, monitoring to determine if management actions are meeting outcomes, and, if not, facilitating management changes that will best ensure that outcomes are met or to re-evaluate the outcomes. Adaptive management recognizes that knowledge about natural resource systems is sometimes uncertain and is the preferred method of management in these cases. *(Source: Departmental Manual 516 DM 4.16)*

Administrative record— the "paper trail" that documents an agency's decision making process and the basis for the agency's decision. It includes all materials directly or indirectly considered by persons involved in the decision making process, including opinions or information considered but rejected. These are the documents that a judge will review to determine whether the process and the resulting agency decision were proper, and that future managers will use to understand the evolution of the issue(s) and how decisions were reached and made.

American Indian tribe— any band, nation, or other organized group or community of Indians, including any Alaska Native Village, which is recognized as eligible for the special programs and services provided by the United States to Indians because of their status as Indians.

Appropriate use—a use that is suitable, proper, or fitting for a particular park, or to a particular location within a park.

Archeological resource— any material remains or physical evidence of past human life or activities which are of archeological interest, including the record of the effects of human activities on the environment. An archeological resource is capable of revealing scientific or humanistic information through archeological research.

Asset—a physical structure or grouping of structures, land features, or other tangible property which has a specific service or function.

Asset management—a systematic process of maintaining, upgrading, and operating assets cost-effectively by combining engineering principles with sound business practices and economic theory.

Backcountry— primitive, undeveloped portions of parks, some of which may be managed as "wilderness."

Best available technology—technology that will help achieve efficient and economically viable facilities and services, while offering the greatest protection and environmental benefit for park visitors, employees, resources and values.

Best management practices (BMPs)— practices that apply the most current means and technologies available to not only comply with mandatory environmental regulations, but also maintain a superior level of environmental performance. See also, "sustainable practices/principles."

Carrying capacity—the maximum population of a particular species that a particular region can support without hindering future generations' ability to maintain the same population. A visitor, or user, carrying capacity is the type and level of use that can be accommodated while sustaining the desired resource and visitor experience conditions.

Civic Engagement— as a philosophy, a discipline, and a practice, it can be viewed as a continuous, dynamic conversation with the public on many levels that reinforces the commitment of the NPS and the public to the preservation of park resources and strengthens understanding of the full meaning and contemporary relevance of these resources. Civic engagement is the philosophy of welcoming people into the parks and building relationships around a shared stewardship mission, whereas public involvement (also called public participation) is the specific, active involvement of the public in NPS planning and other decision-making processes.

Commemorative work— any statue, monument, sculpture, plaque, memorial, or other structure or landscape feature, including a garden or memorial grove, designed to perpetuate the memory of a person, group, event, or other significant element of history.

Conserve—to protect from loss or harm; preserve. Historically, the terms conserve, protect, and preserve have come collectively to embody the fundamental purpose of the NPS—preserving, protecting and conserving the national park system.

Consultation— a discussion, conference, or forum in which advice or information is sought or given, or information or ideas are exchanged. Consultation generally takes place on an informal basis; formal consultation requirements for compliance with section 106 of NHPA are published in 36 CFR Part 800. Consultation with recognized tribes is done on a government-to-government basis.

Cooperating associations— private, nonprofit corporations established under state law which support the educational, scientific, historical, and interpretive activities of the NPS in a variety of ways, pursuant to formal agreements with the Service.

Cooperative conservation—as defined in Executive Order 13352, actions that relate to use, enhancement, and enjoyment of natural resources, protection of the environment, or both, and that involve collaborative activity among federal, state, local, and tribal governments, private for-profit and nonprofit institutions, other nongovernmental entities and individuals. It is one of several "tools" or authorities that park managers may employ as they use the full scope of NPS authorities to protect park resources and values, while encouraging others to use theirs toward the same purpose. As with civic engagement, the Service applies the principles of cooperative conservation to cultural resources as well as natural resources.

Critical habitat— specific areas within a geographical area occupied by a threatened or endangered species which contain those physical or biological features essential to the conservation of the species, and which may require special management considerations or protection; and specific areas outside the geographical area occupied by the species at the time of its listing, upon a determination by the Secretary of the Interior that such areas are essential for the conservation of the species. (See 16 USC 1342)

Cultural landscape— a geographic area, including both cultural and natural resources and the wildlife or domestic animals therein, associated with a historic event, activity, or person, or exhibiting other cultural or esthetic values. There are four non-mutually exclusive types of cultural landscapes: historic sites, historic designed landscapes, historic vernacular landscapes, and ethnographic landscapes.

Cultural resource— an aspect of a cultural system that is valued by or significantly representative of a culture, or that contains significant information about a culture. A cultural resource may be a tangible entity or a cultural practice. Tangible cultural resources are categorized as districts, sites, buildings, structures, and objects for the National Register of Historic Places, and as archeological resources, cultural landscapes, structures, museum objects, and ethnographic resources for NPS management purposes.

Defensible space— the space needed for firefighters to adequately defend structures from oncoming wildland fires, or to stop a structural fire before it ignites wildland vegetation. Defensible space describes the desired result of planning, siting, landscaping and constructing developed facilities in a way that minimizes their vulnerability to wildfire threats and maximizes their protection against wildfire hazards.

Derogation— see "impairment."

Decision-maker—the managerial-level employee who has been delegated authority to make decisions or to otherwise take an action that would affect park resources or values. Most often it refers to the park superintendent or regional director, but may at times include, for example, a resource manager, facility manager, or chief ranger to whom authority has been re-delegated.

Desired conditions— a park's natural and cultural resource conditions that the NPS aspires to achieve and maintain over time, and the conditions necessary for visitors to understand, enjoy, and appreciate those resources. These conditions are identified through a park's planning process.

Developed area— an area managed to provide and maintain facilities (e.g., roads, campgrounds, housing) serving visitors and park management functions. Includes areas where park development or intensive use may have substantially altered the natural environment or the setting for culturally significant resources.

Directives system— policy guidance system established by Director's Order #1 in 1996. The system replaces and updates guidance documents formerly known as NPS Guidelines, Special Directives, and Staff Directives. The system consists of 3 levels:

> Level 1— NPS Management Policies— the primary policy document for managing the national park system.
>
> Level 2— Director's Orders— operational policies and procedures that supplement Level 1.
>
> Level 3— Reference Manuals and other detailed guidance on how to implement Service-wide policies and procedures.

Ecosystem— a system formed by the interaction of a community of organisms with their physical and biological environment, considered as a unit.

Environmental assessment— a brief NEPA document that is prepared, with public involvement, (a) to help determine whether the impact of a proposed action or its alternatives could be significant; (b) to aid the NPS in compliance with NEPA by evaluating a proposal that will have no significant impacts, but may have measurable adverse impacts; or (c) as an evaluation of a proposal that is either not described on the list of categorically excluded actions, or is on the list, but exceptional circumstances apply.

Environmental impact statement— a detailed NEPA analysis document that is prepared, with extensive public involvement, when a proposed action or alternatives have the potential for significant impact on the human environment.

Environmental leadership— advocating, on a personal and organizational level, cooperative conservation, best management practices, best available technology, adaptive management, and the principles of sustainability, and making collaborative decisions that demonstrate a commitment to those practices and principles.

Ethnographic landscape— an area containing a variety of natural and cultural resources that traditionally associated people define as heritage resources. The area may include plant and animal communities, structures, and geographic features, each with their own special local names.

Ethnographic resources— objects and places, including sites, structures, landscapes, and natural resources, with traditional cultural meaning and value to associated peoples. Research and consultation with associated people identifies and explains the places and things they find culturally meaningful. Ethnographic resources eligible for the National Register of Historic Places are called traditional cultural properties.

Foundation statement—a statement that begins a park's planning process and sets the stage for all future planning and decision-making by identifying the park's mission, purpose, significance, special mandates and the broad, park-wide mission goals. Incorporated into a park's GMP, but may also be produced as a stand-alone document for a park.

Gateway community— a community that exists in close proximity to a unit of the national park system whose residents and elected officials are often affected by the decisions made in the course of managing the park, and whose decisions may effect the resources of the park. Because of this, there are shared interests and concerns regarding decisions. Gateway communities usually offer food, lodging, and other services to park visitors. They also provide opportunities for employee housing, and a convenient location to purchase goods and services essential to park administration.

Geologic resources— features produced from the physical history of the earth, or processes such as exfoliation, erosion and sedimentation, glaciation, karst or shoreline processes, seismic, and volcanic activities.

General management plan (GMP)— a plan which clearly defines direction for resource preservation and visitor use in a park, and serves as the basic foundation for decision making. GMPs are developed with broad public involvement.

Historic property—a district, site, building, structure, or object significant in the history of American archeology, architecture, culture, engineering, or politics at the national, state, or local level.

Impact— the likely effect of an action or proposed action upon specific natural, cultural or socioeconomic resources. Impacts may be direct, indirect, individual, cumulative, beneficial, or adverse. (Also see Unacceptable impacts.)

Impairment— An impact that, in the professional judgment of a responsible NPS manager, would harm the integrity of park resources or values and violate the 1916 NPS Organic Act's mandate that park resources and values remain unimpaired.

Implementation plan—a plan that focuses on how to implement an activity or project needed to achieve a long-term goal. An implementation plan may direct a specific project or an ongoing activity.

Integrated pest management— a decision-making process that coordinates knowledge of pest biology, the environment, and available technology to prevent unacceptable levels of pest damage, by cost-effective means, while posing the least possible hazard to people, resources, and the environment.

Leave-no-trace— principles and practices that emphasize the ethic of leaving a place clear of the residual evidence of human presence; applied to all forms of recreational activities within wilderness, backcountry, and frontcountry areas.

Life cycle costing (analysis)— an accounting method that analyzes the total costs of a product or service, including construction, maintenance, manufacturing, marketing, distribution, useful life, salvage, and disposal.

Lightscape management (natural ambient)— the effective use of good design to appropriately light areas and minimize or eliminate light clutter, the spill over of light into areas where light is not wanted, and light pollution, all of which wastes energy and impacts park visitors, neighbors and resources.

Manager— the managerial-level employee who has authority to make decisions or to otherwise take an action that would affect park resources or values. Most often it refers to the park superintendent or regional director, but may at times include, for example, a resource manager, facility manager, or chief ranger to whom authority has been redelegated.

Management prescriptions— a planning term referring to statements about desired resource conditions and visitor experiences, along with appropriate kinds and levels of management, use, and development for each park area.

Minimum requirement— a documented process used by the NPS to determine the appropriateness of all actions affecting wilderness.

Minimum tool— a use or activity, determined to be necessary to accomplish an essential task, which makes use of the least intrusive tool, equipment, device, force, regulation, or practice that will achieve the wilderness management objective.

Mission-critical— something that is essential to the accomplishment of an organization's core responsibilities.

Mitigation— a modification of a proposal to lessen the intensity of its impact on a particular resource.

National park system— the sum total of the land and water now or hereafter administered by the Secretary of the Interior through the National Park Service for park, monument, historic, parkway, recreational or other purposes.

Native American— of or relating to, a tribe, people, or culture that is or was indigenous to the United States.

Native Hawaiian— any individual who is a descendant of the aboriginal people who, prior to 1778, occupied and exercised sovereignty in the area that now constitutes the State of Hawaii.

NEPA process— the objective analysis of a proposed action to determine the degree of its impact on the natural, physical, and human environment; alternatives and mitigation that reduce that impact; and the full and candid presentation of the analysis to, and involvement of, the interested and affected public –as required of federal agencies by the National Environmental Policy Act of 1969.

New use— a use that has not previously taken place within a particular park, or that has taken place previously and been discontinued due to public disinterest or as a result of a management action.

Organic Act (NPS)— the 1916 law (and subsequent amendments) that created the National Park Service and assigned it responsibility to manage the national parks.

Paleontological/paleoecological resources— resources such as fossilized plants, animals, or their traces, including both organic and mineralized remains in body or trace form. Paleontological resources are studied and managed in their paleoecological context (that is, the geologic data associated with the fossil that provides information about the ancient environment).

Park— any one of the hundreds of areas of land and water administered as part of the national park system. The term is used interchangeably in this document with "unit," "park unit," and "park area."

Practicable— capable of being done or put into practice. Practicable reflects not only what is possible to do, but also what is reasonable, after considering all of the consequences.

Prescribed burning— the deliberate ignition of fires to accomplish specified resource management objectives and under an identified range of conditions documented in a prescribed burn plan.

Preserve— to protect from loss or harm; conserve. Historically, the terms preserve, protect and conserve have come collectively to embody the fundamental purpose of the NPS— preserving, protecting and conserving the national park system. (See also "preservation.")

Preservation— for the purposes of the Secretary of the Interior's Standards for the Treatment of Historic Properties, preservation means the act or process of applying measures necessary to sustain the existing form, integrity and materials of an historic property.

Professional judgment— a decision or opinion that is shaped by study and analysis and full consideration of all the relevant facts, and that takes into account

- the decision-maker's education, training, and experience;
- advice or insights offered by subject matter experts and others who have relevant knowledge and experience;
- good science and scholarship; and, whenever appropriate,
- the results of civic engagement and public involvement activities relating to the decision.

Public involvement (also called public participation)— the active involvement of the public in NPS planning and decision-making processes. Public involvement occurs on a continuum that ranges from providing information and building awareness, to partnering in decision-making.

Record of decision (ROD)—the document which is prepared to substantiate a decision based on an analysis of a range alternatives (e.g., an EIS). When applicable, it includes a detailed discussion of rationale and reasons for not adopting all mitigation measures analyzed.

Sacred sites— certain natural and cultural resources treated by American Indian tribes and Alaska Natives as sacred places having established religious meaning, and as locales of private ceremonial activities.

Scholarship— knowledge resulting from study and research in a particular field, or the mastery of a particular area of learning reflected in a scholar's work. A scholar is a learned person; someone who by long study has gained mastery in one or more disciplines and practices, and whose mastery is recognized by a peer group.

Soundscape (natural)— the aggregate of all the natural, nonhuman-caused sounds that occur in parks, together with the physical capacity for transmitting natural sounds.

Special Regulation— a regulation that is prescribed for a specific park area. A special regulation may amend, modify, relax or make more stringent the "general" regulations that are applicable to all areas of the national park system.

Stakeholder— an individual, group or other entity that has a strong interest in decisions concerning park resources and values. Stakeholders may include, for example, recreational user groups, permittees, and concessioners. In the broadest sense, all Americans are stakeholders in the national parks.

Stewardship— the cultural and natural resource protection ethic of employing the most effective concepts, techniques, equipment, and technology to prevent, avoid, or mitigate unacceptable impacts.

Strategic plan— a Service-wide, 5-year plan required by GPRA (5 USC 306) in which the NPS states (1) how it plans to accomplish its mission during that time, and (2) the value it expects to produce for the tax dollars expended. Strategic plans serve as "performance agreements" with the American people.

Superintendent— the senior on-site NPS official in a park. Used interchangeably with "park superintendent," "park manager," or "unit manager."

Sustainable design— design that applies the principles of ecology, economics, and ethics to the business of creating necessary and appropriate places for people to visit, live in, and work. Development that has a sustainable design sits lightly upon the land, demonstrates resource efficiency, and promotes ecological restoration and integrity, thus improving the environment, the economy, and society.

Sustainable practices/principles— those choices, decisions, actions and ethics that will best achieve ecological/ biological integrity; protect qualities and functions of air, water, soil, and other aspects of the natural environment; and preserve human cultures. Sustainable practices allow for use and enjoyment by the current generation, while ensuring that future generations will have the same opportunities. See also, "environmental leadership" and "best management practices."

Traditional— pertains to recognizable, but not necessarily identical, cultural patterns transmitted by a group across at least two generations. Also applies to sites, structures, objects, landscapes, and natural resources associated with those patterns. Popular synonyms include "ancestral" and "customary."

Traditionally associated peoples— social/cultural entities such as tribes, communities, and kinship units, as well as park neighbors, traditional residents, and former residents who remain attached to a park area despite having relocated, are "traditionally associated" with a particular park when (1) the entity regards park resources as essential to its development and continued identity as a culturally distinct people; (2) the association has endured for at least two generations (40 years); and (3) the association began prior to establishment of the park.

Traditional cultural property— a property associated with cultural practices, beliefs, the sense of purpose, or existence of a living community that is rooted in that community's history or is important in maintaining its cultural identity and development as an ethnically distinctive people. Traditional cultural properties are ethnographic resources eligible for listing in the National Register.

Unacceptable impacts— impacts that, individually or cumulatively, would

- be inconsistent with a park's purposes or values, or
- impede the attainment of a park's desired future conditions for natural and cultural resources as identified through the park's planning process, or
- create an unsafe or unhealthful environment for visitors or employees, or
- diminish opportunities for current or future generations to enjoy, learn about, or be inspired by park resources or values, or
- unreasonably interfere with
  - park programs or activities, or
  - an appropriate use, or
  - the atmosphere of peace and tranquility, or the natural soundscape maintained in wilderness and natural, historic, or commemorative locations within the park.
  - NPS concessioner or contractor operations or services.

Unit—see "park."

Universal design— the design of products and environments to be usable by all people to the greatest extent possible, without the need for adaptation or specialized design.

Value analysis/value engineering— an organized, multi-disciplined team effort that analyzes the functions of facilities, processes, systems, equipment, services, and supplies for the purpose of achieving essential functions at the lowest life-cycle cost consistent with required performance, reliability, quality, and safety.

Visitor— anyone who physically visits a park for recreational, educational or scientific purposes, or who otherwise uses a park's interpretive and educational services, regardless of where such use occurs (e.g., via Internet access, library, etc.).

Visitor Experience and Resource Protection (VERP) framework— a visitor carrying capacity planning process applied to determine the desired resource and visitor experience conditions, and used as an aid to decision-making.

Waiver (of policy)— an exemption from a particular policy provision. A waiver may be granted only by the Director of the National Park Service or a higher authority (e.g., the Secretary of the Interior).

Wilderness (designated)—federal land that has been designated by Congress as a component of the National Wilderness Preservation System.

Wilderness (eligible, study, proposed and recommended)—federal lands that have been found to possess wilderness character based on the criteria specified in the Wilderness Act. The four categories reflect different stages of the wilderness review process, and all are managed to preserve the wilderness resources and values that make them eligible for wilderness designation. Differences in the management of these categories are specified in Chapter 6.

Wilderness (potential)— federal lands that are surrounded by, or adjacent to, lands proposed for wilderness designation but that do not themselves qualify for designation due to temporary, non-conforming uses or incompatible conditions. Potential wilderness is a subset of the other wilderness categories (it can be eligible, study, proposed, recommended or designated potential wilderness).

Wildland fires— unplanned fires that burn vegetation in parks. Wildland fires occur from both natural and human sources of ignition, and may contribute to or hinder the achievement of park management objectives.

Wildland fire use— the application of an appropriate, prescribed management response to naturally ignited wildland fires under prescribed circumstances to accomplish resource management objectives in predefined areas outlined in approved fire management plans.

Index

A

Access and circulation systems
    See Transportation
Access to private property 8.6.5
Accessibility for disabled persons 1.9.3;5.3.2; 6.4.7; 7.5.2; 8.2.4; 9.1.2; 10.2.6.2
    to concessions 10.2.6.2
    to historic properties 5.3.2
    to interpretive programs 7.5.2
    to transportation systems 9.1.2; 9.2; 9.3
    to undeveloped areas 9.1.2
    to visitor and management facilities 9.1.2
    to wilderness 6.4.7
Accountability *Introduction*; 1.9.5
Adaptive use of historic structures 5.3.5.4.6, 5.3.5.4.7; 9.1.1.4; 9.4.3.3
Adjacent lands and land protection plans 3.3
    donation of 3.6
    encouragement of compatible land uses 3.4
    managing fires 4.1.4; 4.5
    need for park awareness of land usage 3.4
    owners involved in planning 2.1.3; 2.3.1.4; 2.3.1.7
    partnerships to improve natural resource management 4; 4.1.4
Administrative facilities
    in wilderness 6.3.10.1
    offices 9.4.1
Administrative history of the national park system
    depositories for 5.3.5.5.6
Advertising 9.3.5
    at special events 8.6.2.1
Advisory committees 1.10; 2.3.1.5; 5.2.1
Advisory Council on Historic Preservation
    consultation with 5.2.1
Affiliated areas 1.3.4
Agreements 1.9; 4.1.4; 5.2.2;, 8.12 9.1.8
Agriculture
    agricultural use of parks 8.6.7
    in cultural landscapes 5.3.5.2; 5.3.5.2.6;
    also see 4.4.2.5
Air quality
    air quality related values 4.7.1
    effect of fire management plan on 4.5
    management of class I areas 4.7.1
    partnerships to improve 4.1.4
    review of permits 4.7.1
Aircraft use 8.4
    administrative 8.4.4
    in Alaska 6.3.10.1; 8.4.1
    in wilderness 6.2.1.2
    landing sites 8.4.8
    military aviation 8.4.5
    navigation aids 9.2.5
    overflights 8.4.7
Airstrips
    in wilderness 6.3.10.1
    Alaska
    Park Units 2.3.1.10
    Alaska National Interest Lands Conservation Act
    cultural resources 5.3.5.3
    general exceptions to policy *Introduction*
    provisions related to rights-of-way 8.6.4.1
    provisions related to snowmobiles 8.2.3.2
    provisions related to subsistence 7.5.7
    provisions related to wilderness 6.2.1.2; 6.3.10.1; 6.3.10.3; 6.4.6.1
Alternative transportation systems 9.2
American Indians
    Also see Native Americans
    access to and activities in wilderness 6.3.12
    collection of natural products in parks 5.3.5.3.1; 8.8
    confidentiality of information 5.2.3
    consultation regarding burials 5.3.4
    consultation regarding cultural interpretation 7.5.6
    consultation regarding cultural resources 5.2.1
    consultation regarding ethnographicresources see 5.3.5.3.1
    consultation regarding game harvest regulations 4.4.3
    consultation regarding government-to-government relationship 1.11.2
    consultation regarding museum objects 5.3.5.5
    cultural demonstrators 7.5.7
    definition of 8.5
    exhibit of sacred objects 5.3.5.5; 7.5.6
    fee waivers for 8.5
    participation in interpretive programs 7.5.6
    repatriation of cultural items or human remains 5.2.1; 5.3.5.5.4
    relationship with American Indian tribes 1.11
    resource access and use 5.3.5.3.1; 8.5
    trust resources 1.11.3
    use of traditional areas or sacred resources 5.3.5.3.2
American Indian Religious Freedom Act 5.3.5.3
Amphitheaters 9.3.1.4
Animals
    biological resource management 4.4
    corridor crossings 9.2
    disposal of carcasses 4.4.2.1
    exotic species 4.4.4
    harvest of, by the public 4.4.3
    livestock 8.6.8
    migratory species 4.4.1.1
    native species 4.4.1.3; 4.4.2; 4.4.2.1; 4.4.2.2
    population management 4.4.1.1
    recreational stock use 8.2.2.8
    removing 4.4.2.1
    threatened and endangered species 4.4.2.3
Appropriate Use 1.5, 8.1.1, 8.1.2, Glossary
Archeological Resource Protection Act 5.3.5.3
Archeological resources
    data recovery 5.3.5.1.5
    display and storage of collections 5.3.5.5.4
    in wilderness 6.3.8
    inventory of 5.1.3.1
    relocation of 5.3.5.1; 5.3.5.4.5
    sale of in concessions 10.2.4.6
    treatment of 5.3.5.1.1–5.3.5.1.4
Archives and Manuscripts 5.3, 5.5.6
Art and cultural facilities
    See Facilities for arts and culture
Asset management 1.9.5.3; 9.1; 9.4.1
Aviation 8.4

B

Backcountry use and management 8.2.2.4
Base Jumping 8.2.2.7
Balloons, use of 8.6.2.2
Best management practices
    and agricultural use of parks 8.6.7
    and livestock use 8.6.8.2
    by concessioners 10.2.4.10
    during construction 9.1.3
Bicycles
    bicycle trails 9.2.2.4
    in wilderness 6.4.3.3
    off-road use of 8.2.2
Biodegradable materials 9.1.6.1
Bio-engineered products 4.4.5.4
Biological Resources 4.4.1.0
Biosphere reserves 4.3.6
Black-powder weapons 7.5.7
Boating 8.2.2
    navigation aids 9.2.5
    support facilities 9.3.4.2
Borrow pits 9.1.3.3
Boundary studies
    authority for 1.3.4; 1.5
Burials
    historic burial areas and graves 5.3.4
    in family cemeteries 8.6.10.2
    in national cemeteries 8.6.10.1
    other burials and scattering of ashes 8.6.10.3

C

Campfires 8.8; 9.3.2.1
    firewood gathering 8.8
Campgrounds 9.3.2.1
    reservation systems for 8.2.6.2
Camping 8.2.2
    in wilderness 6.3.10.3
Carrying capacity 5.3.1.6; 8.2.1
Caves 4.8.2.2
    in wilderness 6.3.11.2
Caving 4.8.2.2
Cemeteries and Burials 8.6.10.
    Also see Burials
Chemicals 4.11
Civic Engagement 1.7
Closures 8.2
Coastal zone management program 4.8.1.1
Collecting
    and development of commercial
        products 4.2.4
    natural products 8.8
    research specimens 4.2; 5.1.2; 8.10
Collections 133
    acquisition, management, and
        disposition of 5.3.5.5.4
    archives and manuscripts 5.3.5.5.6
    curatorial facilities 9.4.2
    loan of museum objects 5.3.5.5.4
    museum catalog records 5.3.5.5.4
    museum collections 5.3.5.5
    National Catalog of Museum Objects 5.1.3.1
    natural products 8.8
    of natural resources 4.2.3
    of paleontologic resources 4.8.2.1
    of submerged archeological resources 5.3.5.1.7
    preservation of items in 5.3.5.5.1
    repatriation of museum objects 5.3.5.5; 5.3.5.5.4
    reproduction of objects in 5.3.5.5.3
    restoration of objects in 5.3.5.5.2
    specimens 4.2.3
Comfort stations 9.3.3. Also see Toilets
Commemorative works 9.6
Commercial activities 6.4.4; 8.6.2.1
Commercial use authorizations 10.3
Communication towers.
    Also see Telecommunications antennas
    in wilderness 6.3.10.1

Compensation for damages
    to cultural resources 5.3.1.3
    to natural resources 4.1.6
Compliance and accountability 7
Concession contracts 10.2.3
    extension of 10.2.3.3
    length of term 10.2.3.1
    modifications 10.2.3.2
Concessioners
    construction by 10.2.2; 10.2.3.1; 10.2.4.10; 10.2.6.1
    donations and contributions 10.2.5.5
    employment of NPS personnel 10.2.8.2
    financial management 10.2.5
    franchise fees 10.2.5; 10.2.5.1; 10.2.5.2
    housing 9.4.3.1, 9.4.3.2
    insurance 10.2.4.11
    interpretation by 7.6; 10.2.4.4
    liability insurance requirements 10.2.4.11
    minority businesses 10.2.3.4
    preference given to satisfactory concessioners 10.2.4.3
    risk management program 10.2.4.8
    subconcessioners 10.2.3.5
Concessions 10.2
    accessibility of 10.2.6.2
    criteria for 10.2.2
    design of 10.2.6.1
    environmental compliance 10.2.4.10
    facilities 10.2.6
    maintenance of 10.2.6.3
    rates charged 10.2.4.7
    sales merchandise 10.2.4.5
    utilities 10.2.6.4
Condemnation of nonfederal lands 3.2; 3.7, 3.8
Confidential information 1.7.1.3; 4.1.2; 5.2.3
Construction 9.1.3
    controls to avoid introduction of
        exotics 9.1.3.2
    project supervision 9.1.1
    roads 9.2.1.2.2
    sites 9.1.3.1
Consultation
    See Cooperation and consultation
Consumptive use 8.9
Contaminants 9.1.6.2
Cooperating associations
    interpretation by 7.6.2
    sales by 8.6.2.4
Cooperation and consultation.
    Also see American Indians and Native Americans
    during planning 2.1.3
    conservation 1.6
    hunting, trapping, and fishing 4.4.3, 8.2.2.6
    interpretation of ethnographic resources 7.5.6
    land protection 3.2; 3.4
    law enforcement 8.3.3
    management of aircraft overflights 8.4; 8.4.6
    management of animal populations 4.1.4; 4.4.3
    management of cemeteries and burial sites 5.3.4
    management of cultural resources 5.2.1
    management of ethnographic resources 5.3.5.3
    management of museum objects 5.3.5.5
    management of natural resources 4
    management of submerged resources 5.3.5.1.7
    management of threatened or endangered
        species 4.4.2.3
    national trails 9.2.2.7
    protection of air quality 4.1.4; 4.7.1
    protection of water resources 4.6.2; 4.6.3
    research 4.2, 4.2.1; 5.1.2; 5.2.1; 8.11
    response to emergencies 8.2.5.2
    sacred sites 5.3.5.3.2
    trail planning 9.2.2.1
    transportation planning and services 9.2
    visitor safety 8.2.5.1
    wilderness preservation 6.3.2
Cooperative management 1.9
Cooperative research 8.11.1
Criteria for affiliated areas 1.3.4

Criteria for national parks 1.3
Cultural events 9.3.1.7
Cultural landscapes 5.3.5.2
    biotic cultural resources 5.3.5.2.
    construction 5.3.5.2.7
    inventory of 5.1.3.1
    preservation of 5.3.5.2.1
    reconstruction of 5.3.5.2.4
    rehabilitation of 5.3.5.2.2
    restoration of 5.3.5.2.3
Cultural Landscapes Inventory 5.1.3.1
Cultural resources
    Also see individual resource categories, such as Historic structures
    agreements 5.2.2
    carrying capacity 5.3.1.6
    categorization 5.1.3.2
    conservation of 5.3.1
    damaged by natural forces 5.3.5.4.9
    designation of National Historic Landmarks 5.1.3.2.2
    evaluation of 5.1.3, 5.1.3.2
    in wilderness 6.3.8
    inventories of 5.1.3.1
    movement of 5.3.5.4.5
    nominations to Natural Register of Historic Places 5.1.3.2.1
    planning and proposal formulation 5.2
    protection from fire 5.3.1.1
    protection from exotic species 4.4.4.2
    protection from pests 5.3.1.5
    protection of 5.3.1
    rescue of, in event of emergency 5.3.1.1
    research 5.1
    security for 5.3.5.1.4; 8.3.3
    submerged 5.3.5.1.7
    treatment of 5.3.5
    World Heritage List designation 5.1.3.2.3
Curatorial facilities 9.4.2

D

Damage Assessment and Recovery 4.1.6; 5.3.1.3
Dams and reservoirs 9.5
Demonstrators (cultural) 7.5.7
Derogation 1.4.2
Design
    duplication of historic design 9.1.1.3
    parkwide themes 9.1.1.2
    signs 9.3.1.1
    standard plans and designs 9.1.1.2
    sustainable energy design 9.1.1.7
Desired Park Conditions 2.1.4, 2.2
Development.
    Also see Construction
    accessibility for disabled persons 9.1.2
    adaptive re-use of historic structures 9.1.1.4
    avoiding natural hazards 9.1.1.6
    in floodplains 4.6.4
    in shoreline areas 4.8.1.1
    in wetlands 4.6.5
    in wilderness 6.2.1.2; 6.3.10.3
    life-cycle costs 9.1.1; 9.1.1.1; 10.2.6.1
    location of 9.1.1.5
    management facilities 9.4
    outside park boundaries 3.4; 9.1
    planning and design 2.2; 2.3.1.1; 4.4.2.5; 9.1.1
    principles 9.1; 9.1.1.2; 9.1.1.3; 9.1.1.4; 9.1.7
    replacement/relocation of 4.1.5; 4.4.2.4
    soil protection 4.8.2.4
    transportation 9.2
    utilities 9.1.5
    facilities 1.9.5.2; 9.3
Directives system *Introduction*
Director of the National Park Service
    authorities related to policy *Introduction*
Disabled persons. Also see Accessibility for disabled persons
    interpretive programs for 7.5.2
    special facilities for 9.1.2
Disease control
    See Pests
Domestic and feral livestock 8.6.8
Donations
    from concessioners 10.2.5.5

E

Earthworks 5.3.5.1.6
Education
    Also see Interpretation
    curriculum-based educational programs 7.1
    outreach services 7.3.4
    resource issues 7.5.3
    wilderness 6.4.2
Emergencies
    emergency operations plan 8.2.5.2
    emergency preparedness 8.2.5.2
    in wilderness see 6.3.5
    involving cultural resources 5.3.1.1
    medical services 8.2.5.4
    outside park boundaries 8.2.5.2
    search and rescue 8.2.5.3
    temporary access to wilderness 6.3.5; 6.3.10.1
    use of off-road vehicles 8.2.3.1
Employees
    employment by a concessioner 10.2.8.2; 10.2.8.3
    gardens 8.6.7
    housing 9.4.3
    participation in First Amendment activities 8.6.3
    safety 8.2.5.1
    training 1.9.1.1
Energy management 9.1.7
    alternative energy 9.1.5; 9.2; 9.4.5
    charges to concessioners 10.2.6.4
    conservation 9.1.1; 9.1.3.1; 9.1.7; 9.2
    efficiency 9.1.4.1; 9.1.4.2; 9.1.7; 9.3.2.1; 9.3.2.3
    performance 9.1.1
    sustainable design 9.1.7
Endangered species
    See Threatened or endangered species
Entrance stations 9.3.1.2; 10.2.6.5
Environmental Analysis 2.3.1.7, 2.3.4.1
Environmental auditing program 1.6
Environmental monitoring and control 5.3.1.4
Environmental impact statements
    for general management plans 2.3.1.5
    for natural resources 4.1.3
    for wilderness studies 6.2.2
Environmental leadership 1.6; 9.1.6
Equestrian trails 9.2.2.3
Ethnographic resources 5.3.5.3
    in exhibits 7.5.6
    inventory of 5.1.3.1
    resource access and use 5.3.5.3.1
    sacred sites 5.3.5.3.2
Executive Order 13007 5.3.5.3
Exhibits 7.3.2
    ethnographic resources in 7.5.6
Exotic species
    management of 4.4.4
    definition of 4.4.1.3
    fish stocking with exotics 4.4.4.1
    found in soils 4.8.2.4
    introduction of 4.4.4.1
    removal of 4.4.4.2
Experimental research areas 4.3.2
External influences on parks 1.5.; 3.4

F

Facilities
    See Development
Facilities for arts and culture 9.3.1.7
Federal Advisory Committee Act 1.9; 2.3.1.4; 5.2.1
Fees
    entrance fees 8.2.6
    franchise fees 10.2.5.1
    recreation fees 8.2.6.1

reimbursement of costs associated with special use permits 8.6.1.2
Fertilizer 4.4.2.4; 4.4.2.5; 4.8.2.4; 9.1.3.2
Filming and photography 8.6.6
Financial sustainability 1.9.5.1
Fire management 4.5
 cultural resources 5.3.1.2
 in wilderness 6.3.9
 prescribed fires 4.5
 wildland fires 4.5
Fire pits, for campers 9.3.2.1
Fire prevention and suppression
 agreements with local fire departments 9.1.8
 compliance with fire codes 5.3.1.2; 9.1.8
 in wilderness 6.3.9
 special provisions for cultural resources 5.3.1.2
 structural fires 9.1.8
Fire towers 9.4.5
Firewood 8.8
Fireworks 8.6.2.3
First Amendment activities 8.6.3
Fish stocking 4.4.3
Fishing 8.2.2; 8.2.2.5
 commercial fishing 4.4.3; 8.2.2.5
 restrictions on 8.2.2.5
 sport fishing 4.4.3; 8.2.2.5
 support facilities 9.3.4; 9.3.4.2
Floodplains 4.6.4
Food sales 8.6.2.4
Food services 9.3.2; 10.2.4.12
Foreign-language publications 7.5.2
Fossils
 See Paleontologic resources
Franchise fees 10.2.5.1; 10.2.5.2
Future
 Alternative Evaluation 2.3.1.6
Fund raising 7.6.2
Fundamental purpose of NPS 1.4.3

G

Gardens 8.6.7
General Authorities Act 1.4
General management plan
 See Plans
Generators
 for recreation vehicles 9.3.2.1
Genetic resources 4.2.4; 4.3.1; 4.3.6; 4.4.1.2
Geologic resources 4.8
 hazards 4.8.1.3
 management of 4.8.3
 process, protection of 4.8.1
Geothermal resources 4.8.2.3
Government Performance and Results Act 1.7.4.1; 2.3.3
Graves
 See Burials, Cemeteries and burials
Grazing 4.4.4.1; 8.6.8.2
 Also see Domestic and feral livestock
 commercial 4.4.3
 criteria for 8.6.8.1
 in wilderness 6.4.6.3
 management plans 8.6.8.2
 support facilities 8.6.8.2.2
Groundwater
 See Water resources
Guidelines.
 See Directives system
Guides and outfitters
 operations in wilderness 6.4.4

H

Handcrafts
 sale by concessioners 10.2.4.4
 sale by cultural demonstrators 7.5.7
Hang-gliding 8.2.2
Harvested species
 management of 4.4.3
Hazardous materials 9.1.6.1; 9.1.6.2

Hazards
 floodplains 4.6.4
 geologic 4.8
 landscape restoration following 4.1.5
 shorelines 4.8.1.1
 siting development to avoid 4.8.1.3; 9.1.1.6
Heritage area 1.3.4
Hiking 8.2.2
 hiking trails 9.2.2.2
Historic districts
 See Cultural landscapes
Historic furnishings 5.3.5.5.5
Historic landscapes 5.3.5.2
Historic objects
 See Collections
Historic resources
 See Cultural resources
Historic ships
 See Historic structures. Also see Shipwrecks
Historic structures 5.3.5.4
 accessibility for disabled persons 5.3.2
 acquisition of 5.3.5.4.5
 adaptive use of 5.3.5.4.7
 additions to 5.3.5.4.6
 damaged or destroyed 5.3.5.4.9
 in shoreline areas 4.8.1.1; 5.3.5.4.5; 5.3.5.4.9
 in wilderness 6.2.1.2; 6.3.8
 leasing of 5.3.3
 movement of 5.3.5.4.5; 5.3.5.4.9
 new construction in conjunction with 5.3.5.4.6
 owned or managed by others 5.3.5.4.8
 preservation of 5.3.5.4.1
 reconstruction of 5.3.5.4.4
 refurnishing of 5.3.5.5.5
 rehabilitation of 5.3.5.4.2
 restoration of 5.3.5.4.3
 use for employee housing 5.3.1.2; 5.3.5.4.7; 9.4.3.3
Historic trails
 in wilderness 6.2.1.2
 national trails 9.2.2.7
Historic utilities 9.1.5.4
Historic weapons 7.5.8
Homeland Security 8.3.8
Horseback riding 8.2.2
 equestrian trails 9.2.2.3
 trail stock 8.6.8
Hostels 9.3.2.3
Housing 9.4.3
 concessioner 9.4.3.2
 eligible residents 9.4.3.2
 use of historic structures 5.3.5.4.7; 9.4.3.3
Human health and safety 8.2.5
 concessioner responsibilities for 10.2.4.8
 removal of hazards 8.2.5.1
Hunting and trapping
 cooperative management of 4.4.3
 federal regulation of 8.2.2.6
 genetic resource management principles 4.4.1.2

I

Impairment pg. 4 1.4, 4.1, 4.1.3
 decision-making to avoid 1.4.7
 definition of 1.4.5
 how to treat existing impairment 1.4.7
 how to treat potential impairment 1.4.7
 prohibition of 1.4.4
 versus derogation 1.4.2
Incineration 9.1.6.1
Indians
 See American Indians. Also see Native Americans
Information
 See Public information
Information base 1.7.1; 2.3.1; 2.3.1.4; 4.1.1; 4.1.2; 4.2.1; 5.1.1; 5.1.3.1
Insect control.
 See Pests
Insurance
 for concessions 10.2.4.11

Integrated pest management 4.4.5.2
Interpretation
    Also see Education
    balance and accuracy 7.5.3; 7.5.6
    by concessioners 7.6
    by cooperating associations 7.6.2
    consultation 7.5.6
    cultural demonstrations 7.5.7
    electronic 7.3.3
    elements of 7.1
    exhibit of sacred objects 7.5.6
    for special populations 7.5.2
    nonpersonal services 7.3.2
    of resource issues 7.5.3
    outreach programs 7.3.4
    personal services 7.3.1
    reenactments 7.5.9
    research and scholarship 7.5.4
    special needs 7.5.2
    training 7.4
    wilderness 6.4.2
Interpretive competencies and skills 7.4
Interpretive planning 7.2
Invasive species 4.4.1.3
Inventories
    of cultural resources 5.1.3.1
    of natural resources 4.2.1
Irrigation 4.6.2; 9.1.3.2; 9.1.5.1
Islands 4.8.1.1

K

Karst 4.8.1.2

L

Land acquisition 3.6; 3.7
Land protection 3
    addressing external threats 3.4
    boundary adjustments 3.5
    land acquisition authority 3.6
    land acquisition funding 3.7
    land protection plans 3.3
    land protection methods 3.2
Landfills 9.1.6.1; 9.4.5
Landscape management
    at construction sites 9.1.3.1; 9.1.3.2
    of cultural landscapes 5.3.5.2
    of natural landscapes 4.4.2.4
    prescribed burns 4.5
Law enforcement 8.3, 8.3.1
    authority 8.3.4
    jurisdiction 8.3.5
    public information 8.3.6
Leasing 8.12
    agricultural land 8.6.7
    federal mineral leases 8.7.2
    for livestock 8.6.8.2
    historic structures 5.3.3
Legislative authorized use 1.4.3.1
Legislative exceptions to policy 6; 1.4.4
Life-cycle costs
    and value analysis 9.1.1; 10.2.6.1
    computation of 9.1.1.1
    facility planning and design 9.1.1
Light, artificial 4.10
    control of light pollution 4.10
List of Classified Structures 5.1.3.1
Livestock 4.4.4.1; 8.6.8

M

Maintenance 9.1.4
    in general 9.1.4.1
    support facilities 9.4.4; 9.4.5
    use of environmentally friendly and energy efficient products 9.1.4.2
Man and the Biosphere program 4.3.6
Management
    accountability 1.9.5
    facilities 9.4
    in wilderness 6.3.10
    of parks 1.3.4; 1.4
    for resource conservation 1.4.7.1
    plans 2.2
    zoning 2.3.1.2
    for wilderness 6.3.4.1
Management Excellence 1.9
Marina operations 9.3.4.2
    controls to avoid water pollution 4.6.3
Medical services 8.2.5.4
Media 1.9.4
Memorials 9.6
Merchandise 10.2.4.5
Meteorological stations
    in wilderness 6.3.6.1
Migratory species
    management of 4.4.1.1
Military Use and Operation 8.6.9
Mineral development 8.7
Mineral interests
    addressed in planning 8.7
    federal mineral leases 8.7.2
    in wilderness 6.4.6; 6.4.6.2
    mining claims 8.7.1
    non-federal mineral interests 8.7.3
Minimum requirement 6.3.5
Mining claims 8.7.1
Monuments 9.6
Motion picture filming 8.6.6
Motorized equipment and vehicles 8.2.3
Mountain and rock climbing 8.2.2
Museum collections
    See Collections

N

National Catalog of Museum Objects 5.1.3.1
National Environmental Policy Act 5.3.5.3
National historic landmarks 5.1.3.2.2
National Historic Preservation Act 5.3.5.3
National Interagency Incident Management System 8.2.5.2
National natural landmarks 4.3.5
National Park Service Organic Act 1.1; 1.4; 4; 4.4.2.3; 4.7.1; 5.3.5.3; 8.2.5.1
National Park System Resource Protection Act 5.3.1.3
National park system
    criteria for additions to 1.3
    extent of 1.2
    legislation governing management of 1.4
National Register of Historic Places 5.1.3.2.1
National significance criteria for new areas 1.3;1.3.1
National trails 9.2.2.7
National wild and scenic rivers 1.2; 2.3.1.8; 4.3.4
Native Americans
    Also see American Indians
consultation regarding natural resource
    management 4.1.4
    involvement in planning 2.1.3; 2.3.1.4
    participation in interpretive programs 7.5.6
    preference given to sales of Native American handcrafts 10.2.4.5
    preference to, in removing animals from parks 4.4.2.1
Native Hawaiians, Pacific Islanders, and Caribbean Islanders 1.12
Native plants and animals
    definition of 4.4.1.3
    management of 4.4.2
    removal of 4.4.2.1; 5.3.5.3.1
    restoration of 4.4.2.2
Natural landmarks 4.3.5
Natural resources 4
    change caused by natural phenomena 4.1
    compensation for injuries to 4.1.6
    disturbance by human activities, and restoration of natural processes/systems 4.1;4.1.5
    management planning 4.1.1
    park resources and values 1.4.6
Navigation aids 9.2.5

New park units 1.3
Noise 8.2.3
    Also see Soundscape management
Nonfederal lands
    acquisition of 3.6, 3.7

O

Odors 4.11
Off-road vehicle use 8.2.3.1
Oil and gas development.
    See Mineral development, Mineral interests
Outdoor sports 8.2.2
Overflights 8.4.7
Overnight accommodations 9.3.2

P

Paleontological resources
    management of 4.8.2; 4.8.2.1
    protection of 4.1.2; 4.8.2.1
    sale of in concessions 10.2.4.6
Park Uses Preferred 1.5
Parking areas 9.2.4
Parkways 9.2.1.1
Partnerships 1.10, 4.1.4, 7.6
Performing arts 7.3.1
    Also see Facilities for arts and culture
Permits 8.6.1.1
Personal watercraft 8.2.3.3
Pesticides 4.4.5.3, 4.4.5.5
Pests
    management of 4.4.5
    and cultural resources 5.3.1.5
    definition of 4.4.5.1
Photography and filming 8.6.6
Picnic areas 9.3.4.1
Picnicking 8.2.2
Planning
    assessment of alternatives 2.1.2; 2.3.1.5
    consultation with American Indians 5.2; 7.5.6
    cooperative planning 2.3.1.8
    cooperative trail planning 9.2.2.1
    decision making 2.1.1
    environmental analysis 2.3.1.7, 2.3.4.1
    for concessions 10.2.2
    for cultural resource management 5.2
    for natural resource management 4.1.1
    for park development 9.1.1
    general principles 2.1
    identification of issues and problems 7.5.3
    implementation planning 2.3.4
    in a regional context 2.3.1.7
    information base 2.3.1
    interpretive 7.2
    major elements of 2.2
    planning team 2.3.1; 2.3.1.3
    tiers of 2.2
    public participation in 2.1.3; 2.3.1.4
    succession 1.9.1.2
    workforce 1.9.1.3
Plans
    air tour management plan 8.4.6
    Alaska units 2.3.1.10
    annual performance plan 2.2, 2.3.4, 2.3.4.2
    annual performance report 2.2
    backcountry management plan 8.2.2.4
    cave management plan 4.8.2.2
    comprehensive interpretive plan 7.2
    concession management plan 10.2.2
    development concept plan 9.1.1
    emergency plans 5.3.1.1; 8.2.5.2; 9.5
    exotic species management plans 4.4.4.2
    fire management plan 4.5; 5.3.1.1; 5.3.1.2; 9.1.8
    foundation document 2.2
    general management plan 2.2, 2.3.2.1, 2.3.1.11
    implementation plan 2.3.3
    land protection plan 3.3
    livestock management plan 8.6.8.2
    park-wide sign plan 9.3.1.1
    program management plan 2.2, 2.3.2
    relationship between strategic plan and GMP 2.3.2.1
    river management plan 8.2.2.3
    strategic plan 2.2, 2.3.2.1, 2.3.3
    structural fire plan 5.3.1.2
    visitor use management plans 8.2.2.1
    wayside exhibit plan 9.3.1.1
    wilderness management plan 6.3.10; 6.3.10.2; 6.4.3.1; 6.4.3.3; 6.4.4; 6.4.6.1; 6.4.6.3
Plants
    altered communities 4.4.2.5
    and earthworks 5.3.5.1.6
    cultural landscapes 5.3.5.2
    disposal of cut vegetation 8.8
    exotic species 4.4.4; 5.3.1.5
    natural landscapes 4.4.2.4
    native species 4.4.1.3
    population management 4.4.1.1
    revegetation 9.1.3.2
    threatened and endangered species 4.4.2.3
Plaques 9.6
Playgrounds 9.3.2.1
Policy *Introduction*
Predators 4.4.1
Prescribed burning
    See fire management
Private Property 8.6.5
Professional judgment 1.4.7, 1.5, 1.9, Glossary
Public assemblies 8.6.3
Public information
    access to museum collections 5.3.5.5.4
    and law enforcement 8.3.6
    confidentiality 1.9.2.3
    confidentiality of ethnographic information 5.2.3; 5.3.5.3
    confidentiality of sensitive resource information 5.2.3
    sharing and management of 1.9.2
Public participation
    in developing hunting regulations 8.2.2.6
    in facility planning 9.1.1
    in land protection planning 2.1.3; 2.3.1.4; 3.3
    in planning 2.1.3; 2.3.1.4; 5.2
    in wilderness assessment and studies 6.2.1.3; 6.2.2
    in wilderness planning 6.3.4.2; 6.3.4.3
Public transportation systems 9.2
Public use 8.2
    controls on 5.3.1.6; 8.2
    consumptive uses 8.9
    management of recreational use 8.2.2.1
    special park uses 8.6
Publications 7.3.2

R

Reconstructions and reproductions
    identification of 5.3.5
    of damaged or destroyed structures 5.3.5.4.9
    of earthworks 5.3.5.1.6
    of furnishings 5.3.5.5.5
    of landscapes 5.3.5.2.3
    of museum objects 5.3.5.5.3
    of structures 5.3.5.4.4
    ruins 5.3.5.4.10
Recreation vehicles
    Also see Off-road vehicle use
    campgrounds 9.3.2.1
Recreational activities 6.4.3; 8.2.2
    management of 8.2.2.1
Recycling 9.1.4.2; 9.1.5.2; 9.1.6.1; 9.1.7
Reenactments 7.5.9
Regional directors
    and research permits 5.1.2
    authorities related to policy *Introduction*
Regional planning.
    See Planning
Regulations *Introduction*
Religion
    American Indian religious traditions 5.3.5.3.2
    religious activities in parks 5.3.5.3.2

Rescue
    See Search and rescue
Research
    activities in park 8.10
    anthropological studies 5.1.1; 5.3.5.3.7; 8.11.1
    archeological studies 5.3.5.1
    by others 4.2.2; 5.1.2; 8.11.3
    by NPS 4.2.1; 5.1.1; 8.11.2
    criteria for 4.2.2
    cultural studies 5.1
    ethnographic studies 5.3.5.3; 5.3.5.3.3
    for commercial purposes 4.2.4
    in interpretive and educational programs 7.5.4
    in wilderness 6.3.6
    paleontological studies 4.8.2.1
    permits for 4.2.2; 5.1.2; 8.10
    publication of data 4.1.2; 5.1.1; 8.11.2; 8.11.3
    removal of animals for 4.2; 4.4.2.1
    scientific and scholarly 2.3.1.4
    social science 8.11
    sociological studies 8.11
    specimen collecting 4.2.3; 4.2.4
Research natural areas 4.3.1
Reservation systems 8.2.6.2
Reservoirs 9.5
    fisheries management 4.4.3
Resource Damage 4.1.6; 5.3.1.3
Resources and values
    definition of 1.4.6
Restoration
    of cultural landscapes 5.3.5.2.3
    of degraded areas 9.1.3.2
    of historic structures 5.3.5.4.3
    of museum objects 5.3.5.5.2
    of native plants 4.4.2.2
    resource conditions 1.4.7.2
Revegetation 9.1.3.2
Rights-of-way 8.6.4
    in wilderness 6.4.6.1
    telecommunications antennas 8.6.4.3
    roads and highways 8.6.4.4
    utilities 8.6.4.2
    private property 8.6.5
Riparian Lands 4.6.6, 8.2.2.3, 8.6.8.2, 9.3.4.2
River use 8.2.2.3
Rivers
    Also see Water resources
Wild and scenic rivers 2.3.1.9
Roads
    Also see Transportation
    commercial use of park roads 9.2.1.2.1
    criteria for new roads 9.2
    design features 9.2.1.1
    facility siting 9.1.1.5
    in wilderness 6.3.5; 6.3.10.1; 6.4.3.3
    non-NPS roads 9.2.1.2
    purpose of park roads 9.2.1.1
    systems 9.2.1
Ruins 5.3.5.4.10

S

Sacred sites 5.3.5.3.2; 6.3.8
Safety 1.9.1.4; 8.2.5;
Sales
    of concessioner merchandise 8.6.2.4; 10.2.4.5
    of handcrafted items by demonstrators 7.5.7
    of interpretive items by cooperating
        associations 7.6.2; 8.6.2.4
Sanitary facilities.
    See Comfort stations, Toilets
Science
    Also see Research
    in decision making 1.4.7; 2.3.1.4 8.2.1
    in wilderness 6.3.6
Scuba diving 8.2.2
Sculpture
    indoor see Collections 5.3.5.5
    outdoor see Historic structures 5.3.5.4

Search and rescue 8.2.5.3
Secretary of the Interior
    authorities related to policy *Introduction*
Sewage treatment facilities
    use of NPS plants by others 9.1.6.1
Shell collecting 8.8
Shipwrecks
    management of 5.3.5.1.7
Shorelines
    management of 4.8.1.1
Shower facilities 9.3.2.1
Signs
    in wilderness 6.3.10.4
    informational signs 9.3.1.1
    navigation aids 9.2.5
    traffic signs 9.2.3
Skiing 8.2.2
    ski area development 9.3.4.3
Smoking
    in concession facilities 10.2.4.13
    in historic structures and museums 5.3.1.2
Snowmobiles 8.2.3.2
Soil resources
    management of 4.8.2.4
    protection of, during construction 9.1.3.1
Solid waste
    Also see Waste management
    addressed in river management plans 8.2.2.3
    backcountry use 8.2.2.4
Soundscape management 4.9
    in association with cultural resources 5.3.1.7
    in association with recreational activities 8.2.2
Special directives
    See Directives system
Special events 8.6.2
    in wilderness 6.4.4
Special park uses 8.6
Specimen collecting 4.2.3
Specimen trees 4.4.2.5
State historic preservation officers
    consultation with 5.2.1; 7.5.6
Statues 9.6.1
Stewardship
    cultural Resources 5.3
    human remains and burials 5.3.4
Structural fires 5.3.1.2; 9.1.8
Studies
    See Research
Submerged cultural resources
    management of 5.3.5.1.7
Subsistence 7.5.7
Superintendents
    authorities related to policy *Introduction*
    authorities related to visitor use 8.2
    responsibilities related to policy *Introduction*
Sustainability 1.8; 8.2; 9.1
Swimming 8.2.2

T

Telecommunications antennas 8.6.4.3
Threatened or endangered species
    management of 4.4.2.3
Through-traffic 9.2.1.2.1
Toilets
    in the backcountry 8.2.2.4
    in wilderness 6.3.10.3
    portable 9.3.3
    waterless 9.3.3
Tourism 8.2.7
    consultation with industry 7.5.6
    partnerships with commissions 7.6
    role in providing appropriate use 8.2
    commercial air tours 8.4.6
Toxic substances
    control to prevent water pollution see 4.6.3
    disposal of 9.1.6.1
Traditionally associated peoples
    partnerships 4.1.4

research 5.1
consultation 5.2.1
stewardship of human remains and burials 5.3.4
cultural landscapes 5.3.5.2
ethnographic resources 5.3.5.3
consultation 7.5.6
American Indian uses 8.5
Traffic signs 9.2.3
Trail stock
   See Domestic and feral livestock, Grazing
Trailheads 9.2.2.8
Trails and walks
   backcountry trails 9.2.2.2
   bicycle trails 9.2.2.4
   bridges 9.2.2.9
   equestrian trails 9.2.2.3
   hiking trails 9.2.2.2
   interpretive trails 9.2.2.6
   in wilderness 6.3.10.2
   national trails 1.2; 9.2.2.7
   surfacing of 9.2.2
   water trails 9.2.2.5
Tramways 9.2
Transportation
   accessibility 9.1.2
   aircraft 8.4
   alternative systems 9.1.7; 9.2
   construction 9.2.1.2.2
   design 9.2
   facilities 9.2
   off-road vehicles 8.2.3.1
   planning 9.2
   public transportation systems 9.2
   roads 9.2.1
   snowmobiles 8.2.3.2
   trails 9.2.2
Trapping 4.4.3; 8.2.2.6
Trash disposal
   See Waste management
Treaty rights
   authorization of consumptive use 8.9
   authorization of fishing 8.2.2.5
   authorization of mineral or rock collection 8.8
   authorization of American Indian activities 5.3.5.3.1
   authorization of subsistence 5.3.5.3.1
Trust resources 1.11.3

U

Unacceptable impacts 1.4.7.1; 8.2, Glossary
Universal design 9.1.1, 9.2, 9.2.2, 10.2.6.1
U.S. Constitution
   as source of policy *Introduction*
Utilities
   cost-sharing with municipalities and others 9.1.5
   criteria 9.1.5
   for concessions 10.2.6.4
   historic utilities 9.1.5.4
   in campgrounds 9.3.2.1
   in wilderness 6.2.1.2
   rights-of-way 8.6.4; 8.6.4.2
   use of municipal systems 9.1.5
   utility lines 9.1.5.3

V

Viewing devices 9.3.1.6
Visitor centers 9.3.1.3
   media in 7.3.2
Visitor experience and resource protection framework
   See Carrying capacity
Visitor facilities
   See Development
Visitor safety
   See Human health and safety
Visitor use
   See Public use
Volunteers in Parks 1.9.1.6; 7.6.1

W

Waivers of policy.
   See *Introduction*
Waste management 9.1.6.1
   Also see Solid waste
Wastewater treatment 9.1.5.2
Watershed and Streams 4.6.6
Water quality 4.6.3
Water resources 4.6
   conservation of 4.6.2; 9.1.5.1
   withdrawal for consumptive use 4.6.2
   sale of water to others 4.6.2
Water rights 4.6.2
Water systems 9.1.5.1
Wayside exhibits 7.3.2
Weather and climate 4.7.2
Weather monitors 9.4.5
Wetlands 4.6.5
Wild and scenic rivers 4.3.4
Wilderness
   accessibility in 6.4.6
   administrative facilities in 6.3.10.1
   airstrips in 6.3.10.1
   assessment process 6.2.13
   boundaries in 6.3.11
   campsites in 6.3.10.3
   commercial services in 6.4.3
   conditions and status of 6.3.4.2
   criteria for 6.2.11
   cultural resources in 6.3.8
   definition of 6.2.11
   designated wilderness 6.2.4
   education 6.3.12
   eligibility for 6.2.1
   environmental impacts 6.3.4.3
   ethics of 6.4.2.2
   facilities 6.3.10; 6.3.10.1
   fire management in 6.3.9
   grazing in 6.4.5.3
   management of 6.4
   mineral development in 6.4.5.2
   minimum requirement 6.3.5
   minimum tool management concept 6.3.6.1
   motorized equipment and vehicles in 6.4.2.3
   national wilderness preservation system 6.2
   planning 6.3.4
   potential wilderness 6.2.2.1
   private rights in 6.4.5
   proposed wilderness 6.2.2.2
   public use shelters in 6.3.10.3
   recommended wilderness 6.2.3
   recreational use in 6.4.2
   resource management 6.3.7
   resource and use monitoring 6.3.6.2
   review process 6.2
   rights-of-way in 6.4.5.1
   scientific activities/research 6.3.6
   signs in 6.3.10.4
   special events in 6.4.4
   special provisions of ANILCA 6.4.3.3; 6.4.4
   structures in 6.2.1.2
   toilets in 6.3.10.3
   trails and roads in 6.3.10.2
   wilderness study process 6.2
   zoning for 6.3.4.1
Wildfires
   See fire management
Wildlife
   See Animals
World heritage sites 4.3.7; 5.1.3.2.3

Z

Zones and zoning
   See Management zoning